In recent years a number of scholars of international relations have developed an interest in neo-Weberian historical sociology, but *The wealth of states* is the first sustained analysis of the overlap between historical sociology and international relations. John Hobson develops a new theory of international change using a sociological approach, through a detailed examination of nineteenth-century trade regimes, and the efforts of the Great Powers to increase their military capabilities before the First World War through tariff protectionism. His analysis reveals the importance of the state as an autonomous, 'adaptive' actor in domestic and international politics and economics, which is not dependent upon dominant classes, economic interest groups, the world economy or the geopolitical system of states. The book thus represents a distinctive approach which goes beyond the existing paradigms of Marxism, liberalism and realism.

D0645489

The wealth of states

CAMBRIDGE STUDIES IN INTERNATIONAL RELATIONS

Series list continues after index

The wealth of states

A comparative sociology of international economic and political change

John M. Hobson

Department of Government, University of Sydney

CAMBRIDGE
UNIVERSITY PRESS

Published by the Press Syndicate of the University of Cambridge
The Pitt Building, Trumpington Street, Cambridge CB2 1RP
40 West 20th Street, New York, NY 10011–4211, USA
10 Stamford Road, Oakleigh, Melbourne 3166, Australia

First published 1997

Printed in Great Britain at the University Press, Cambridge

A catalogue record for this book is available from the British Library

Library of Congress cataloguing in publication data
Hobson, John M.
The wealth of states : a comparative sociology of international economic and
political change / John M. Hobson.
    p.   cm. – (Cambridge studies in international relations: 52)
Includes bibliographical references and index.
ISBN 0 521 58149 4 (hardcover). – ISBN 0 521 58862 6 (pbk.)
1. International economic relations.
2. International trade – History – 19th century.
3. Protectionism – History – 19th century.
4. Economics – Sociological aspects.
I. Title.   II. Series.
HF1359.H63   1997
337–dc20   96–26315   CIP

ISBN 0 521 58149 4 hardback
ISBN 0 521 58862 6 paperback

For Sushila

Contents

ix

Contents

Figures

Tables

Acknowledgements

This book was written in two stages. From 1987 to 1991, it began as a piece of sociological research at the London School of Economics. Then from 1991 to 1995, I relocated to Melbourne to teach international politics at La Trobe University, where this work was transformed into one that has relevance for historical sociology and international relations. Through the course of this book, I have encountered many personal influences which I am pleased to acknowledge.

In the first stage I thank above all each of my supervisors, notably Professors Michael Mann and Ian Roxborough, as well as my third supervisor Professor Percy Cohen who oversaw the final nine months of work. Professor Alan Milward also very kindly gave time to read and comment on several of the early chapters. I also thank a host of people who read and commented on various chapters, notably Professors Giovanni Arrighi, Stephen Krasner, Mancur Olson and Peter-Christian Witt (for chapter 2). Professor Witt, in particular, very generously gave over a whole weekend to discussing this chapter in Hamburg, as well as providing me with masses of extremely useful information. Professors Patrick K. O'Brien and Olga Crisp pointed out some of the historical pitfalls of my earlier approach on tsarist economic history (chapter 3). I am especially grateful to Professor Crisp, who gave over many long but always enjoyable afternoons in the Institute of Historical Research in London, answering my simplistic sociological questions, none of which received simple answers.

Some of the data assembled here first appeared in an article I wrote which appeared in the *Journal of European Economic History* (1993), which produced a critique of the Davis and Huttenback enterprise, otherwise known as *Mammon and the Pursuit of Empire*. I received help from many sources for this (most of whom have been thanked in the article). However, I remain grateful to Professor John A. Hall, who managed to obtain two grants (from Harvard and McGill Universities) for me to carry out this research, and Professors Michael Mann, Olga Crisp, Avner Offer, Peter-Christian Witt and Jean-Claude Toutain, as well as Ruggero Ranieri, Kaoru Sugihara, Ben Tipton and David Stevenson, all of whom helped out with various aspects of the data.

I would also like to thank Dr Alan Hooper, as well as Derek Dale, Monika Beutel, Andrew Nicholas and Sally Abbott, who taught a superb political economy course at the University of Hertfordshire (a course that was genuinely multi-disciplinary, and which inspired me to go on to post-graduate research and, above all, to pursue a multi-disciplinary approach).

The generous personal support given me by Professor Tom Nossiter in my Master's year at the LSE is warmly acknowledged. I am also particularly grateful to Professor David Held, not only for his constructive comments on the thesis (all of which I have tried to incorporate in this finished version), but above all for his warm support and encouragement in the last four years.

Professors Michael Mann and John A. Hall, as well as Anthony Howe, all very kindly undertook the thankless task of reading the whole of the original manuscript. The former two actually read every word I wrote and made countless suggestions. I remain grateful to them for the considerable personal interest they have taken in my work. And as the following pages testify, their own work has very much informed my own interests and research projects.

In the second (Australian) stage of this book, I have had the good fortune to spend much time discussing and learning about IR with various friends and colleagues, most notably Joe Camilleri, Peter Lawler, Andrew Linklater, Albert Paolini, Chris Reus-Smit and especially my good friend Tony Jarvis. I am particularly grateful to the School of Politics at La Trobe University for providing a conducive environment for much of the writing of this book.

Special thanks go to Professor Linda Weiss, with whom I have had the great pleasure and good fortune of writing a book, *States and Economic Development* (1995). She has been there 'on the ground' through the last four years and has been a constant source of support and encouragement.

I am very grateful to John Haslam at Cambridge University Press for steering the book so efficiently through all stages of the production process. And I am particularly indebted to Karen Anderson Howes whose copy-editing has been outstanding. Finally I thank the two anonymous readers at Cambridge for their constructive comments.

Whether I have satisfied the many suggestions and criticisms that have come my way from the various people noted above is at best debatable and in all probability highly unlikely. Of course, I accept full culpability for the arguments and especially any mistakes made in this book.

A big thank you to David Farrow and my research assistant Michael O'Keefe, whose heroic computing efforts saved me more times than I care to remember.

Special thanks go to my parents, Tim and Nora, whose support and encouragement throughout my life have played an important part in the making of this book. At this point, I wish to acknowledge Milly and Yves, whose entry into my life has enriched it.

'Last', and as usual at this point in the acknowledgements, 'but not least', special thanks go to my partner Sushila Das. I am deeply grateful to her for enduring with me the not inconsiderable financial sacrifice that a modern-day Ph.D in Britain entails, not to mention the time we lost while I was researching. As anyone in this position will know, these words remain inadequate both in conveying her sacrifices, or in thanking her for enduring them.

1   A sociology of international relations and an international relations of sociology

A neo-Weberian sociology of international change

One of the principal limitations of international relations (IR from henceforth) has been an omission of the study of political and economic *change* (Cox 1986; Scholte 1993a, 1993b; Buzan, Jones and Little 1993: 26–7). Undoubtedly one major reason for this has been the dominant position held within the discipline by realism/neorealism, which emphasises stasis and continuity over structural change. In typical neorealist vein, Waltz argued that 'the texture of international relations remains highly constant, patterns recur and events repeat themselves endlessly. The relations that prevail internationally seldom shift rapidly in type or in quality. They are marked by a dismaying persistence' (Waltz 1979: 66; cf. Morgenthau 1964: ch. 1; Howard 1985: ch. 1; Gilpin 1981: 7, 230).

My primary purpose is to produce a sociological theory of structural international economic change, principally by 'bringing the state back in'. In addition I seek to develop a sociological framework which can both explain economic and political developments within the inter-state system, and develop a theory of the state which can enhance the study of IR (as well as historical sociology).

My sociological theory differs principally from the major alternative paradigms, in particular Marxism and realism, but also late develop-ment theory, statism and liberalism. The alternative theory seeks to reintroduce the state as an important conceptual variable. My major critique of the existing frameworks in IR is that they *all* fail to take the state seriously. This criticism applies particularly to neorealism. More-over, my theory of the state is one that is very different to traditional statist conceptions.

1

While a growing number of theorists are calling for a closer dialogue between IR and sociology, we need to remind ourselves that there is, of course, more than one sociological approach. I favour a 'neo-Weberian' perspective, which develops upon the works not only of Max Weber, but also Norbert Elias (1939/1994, 1970/1978) and, not least, Michael Mann (1986, 1993), Gary Runciman (1989) and Anthony Giddens (1985). At the highest level of abstraction, this approach is differentiated from Marxism and realism in several key ways. Firstly, the state (which is downplayed in neorealism and Marxism) constitutes an important (unit-force) variable in my account. Paradoxically, while many in IR are calling for the abolition of the state (or at least a reduction in its importance), I argue that the state has been under-examined within the discipline, and that the state should be 'brought back in'. In this account – following Weber – state capacity is based not simply on institutional factors but also on social power residing within society. It is important to note that many within IR mistakenly assume that Max Weber produced a theory of the state that emphasised only institutional factors. But Weber very much emphasised the social origins of states (see Beetham 1985: 152–7, 177–9; Michael Mann 1993: ch. 9). As we shall see, the major paradox of my Weberian position is that in 'bringing the state back in' to the process of economic change, we also need to 'bring society back in'.

Secondly, I reject single-factor explanatory models in favour of a multi-causal approach (i.e., a multi-factor argument). Max Weber's approach is very much a reaction to Marx's mono-causal economism, and unequivocally emphasises multi-causality (Randall Collins 1986; Michael Mann 1993; Kalberg 1994: 50–78), as even a cursory reading of his magnum opus, *Economy and Society* (1922/1978), makes amply clear. In my account, classes, states and external military and economic factors all combine to effect economic and political change (as emphasised in chapters 6 and 7). Thirdly, I argue that the international and national realms are not discrete (*pace* neorealism), nor is there a one-way linkage between the two, with the latter primary (*pace* Marxism). Rather, the international shapes the national quite as much as the national shapes the international (what I call 'dual reflexivity').

Finally, the prevailing assumption within IR is that Max Weber was a political realist (typified by Michael Smith's (1986) summary of the founding fathers of realism which includes, and indeed gives prominence to, Weber). While it is the case that Weber's political writings – especially on Germany – clearly tend towards realism, nevertheless his sociological works (for which he is best known) could not be sum-marised as realist. While elements of realist analysis seep into his sociological work (e.g., his theories of nationalism and imperialism), for the most part there is a non-realist basis to his work. Moreover, it is these non-realist strands that I extract and develop in this book.

Reconceptualising the state–economy relationship

Within the disciplines of sociology and economic history, the common explanation of economic change and government economic policy focuses on the importance of economic interest groups (an emphasis found typically in Marxist and liberal theory). So pervasive is this approach that it can be labelled the 'economistic consensus'. This book is fundamentally interested in reconceptualising the relationship between the political and the economic, from which a theoretical approach for international relations and sociology is developed. The central claim is that the national and international economy are embedded not only in the inter-state political system, but also in the domestic political realm (i.e., the state). As Edward Carr put it, 'the science of economics presupposes a given political order and cannot be profitably studied in isolation from politics' (1939: 117; see also Hintze 1975: 452; Elias 1970/1978: 140–2; Polanyi 1957).

However, to many if not most scholars within IR, this claim will appear not as a 'reconceptualisation', but merely a return to realist orthodoxy. Indeed, the 'recent discovery' of the international political realm by historical sociologists (mostly neo-Weberians such as Skocpol, Michael Mann, Giddens, Collins and John A. Hall) may seem like a revelation within the discipline of sociology, but to many IR scholars it will appear as little more than a step backwards towards an obsolete paradigm. While this book is highly critical of realism, it should be noted that the paradigm has something to offer. Indeed, the key realist insight – the emphasis on the importance of the interna-tional political system – is one that no theory of social, economic or political change can do without (cf. Linklater 1991). However (and this is a point that Linklater also makes), realism – especially in its neorealist guise – tends towards 'reductionism' by focusing excessively on the inter-state system and the distribution of political power (within anarchy) to the exclusion of state–society forces. As Critical and Marxist theorists have argued, an adequate theory cannot make do without an appreciation of domestic forces and the 'state–society complex' (e.g., Cox 1983, 1986, 1987; Linklater 1991; Justin Rosenberg 1994; cf. Shaw 1993; Halliday 1994).

Nevertheless we need to tread cautiously here, because, in Marxist and Critical theory, the 'state–society complex' is almost always little more than a synonym for 'class forces' (despite the not inconsiderable rhetoric to the contrary). This book reconceptualises the relationship between the state and economy. I agree with realists that the economy is affected by the action and exigencies of the inter-state system. But I also recognise that states are variously embedded in their own societies and domestic social structures, as Critical and Marxist theorists argue. However, my key insight is one that neither realists nor Marxists recognise: namely that states shape the economy and society for domestic (as well as international) reasons and that state action can be reduced neither to the inter-state system nor to the domestic social structure. The economy is therefore embedded in the political (and vice versa), but in a highly complex way. In short, the state–economy relationship is subject to the interweaving of complex 'multi-power' and 'multi-spatial' forces (cf. Michael Mann 1986: ch. 1; Elias 1970/1978; Runciman 1989).

This book develops this approach by exploring the causes of the shift from an international free trading regime to a protectionist one in the late nineteenth century (mainly in the European context). The usual explanation given focuses on the requirements of economic interests or classes, who, in the face of economic recession and increased imports, sought tariff protectionism from their national state (as in Marxist and liberal theory). Neorealism differs by focusing on the importance of the international distribution of political power, where states resort to protection as British hegemony declines. However, the argument made in this book suggests that the state raised tariffs partly as a response to developments within the inter-state system, partly as a response to the needs of various economic interest groups, and partly (and most importantly) as a response to the specific political, social and fiscal interests of the state (which cannot be reduced to geopolitical or class requirements). In sum, government economic policy-making is the outcome of the complex interaction of partially independent power forces, where the national and international economy is shaped by class, geopolitical, fiscal and political power variables emanating from inside and outside national boundaries. This 'reconceptualisation' of the state–economy relationship goes hand in hand with three further key objectives, which can be listed as follows:

(1) to develop a fiscal-sociological approach to international and societal, economic and political structural change from which I derive

(2) a non-realist theory of the state, state power and capacity, and the international system of states, in order to understand economic and political change, as well as

(3) to integrate IR and sociology (along with economic history), primarily through a sociologically redefined state, which resides within the vortex of the international and national realms.

A fiscal-sociological approach to IPE/IR

Known as *Finanzwissenschaft* in Germany (where it originated), under the auspices of Fritz Karl Mann (1943), Rudolf Goldscheid (1958), Joseph Schumpeter (1918/1954) and Norbert Elias (1939/1994) to name but a few, fiscal sociology has more recently attracted considerable attention among historical sociologists. Indeed, the sociology of taxation has become a growth area for neo-Weberian sociologists, being employed to explain some of the most important structural developments in the last five hundred years. Fiscal requirements emanating from developments in the inter-state system (geopolitics) informed the processes of state-formation (Weber 1922/1978; Elias 1939/1994; Hintze 1975; Ardant 1975; Poggi 1978; Giddens 1985; Kiser 1986/7; Levi 1988; Tilly 1990; Downing 1991; Weiss and Hobson 1995); the rise of capitalism and industrialisation (McNeill 1982; Giddens 1985; Michael Mann 1986, 1993; John Hall 1986; Weiss and Hobson 1995); social revolutions (Skocpol 1979; Randall Collins 1986; Goldstone 1991; Michael Mann 1993); social revolts (Ardant 1975; Tilly 1981; Goldstone 1991); and last, but by no means least, modern class relations (Vogler 1985; Weiss 1993). I add to this list the rise of protectionism in the late nineteenth century (although this could be extended back to the emergence of mercantilism in the eighteenth century).

Rudolf Goldscheid classically argued that 'the budget is the skeleton of the state stripped of all misleading ideologies' (cited in Schumpeter 1918/1954: 6), or as Edmund Burke put it, 'the revenue of the state is the state' (cited in Levi 1988). Because the state and the economy are fundamentally embedded in each other partly through taxation, it is therefore the case that the budget provides an important insight into

5

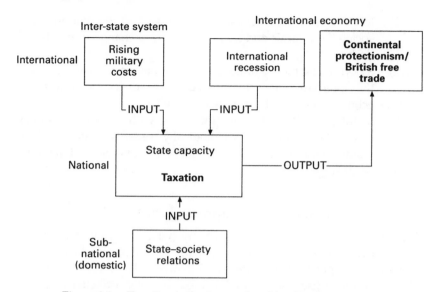

Figure 1.1:   Taxation in the international/national vortex

the state–economy relationship (cf. Schumpeter 1918/1954: 6–7). Equally as important, the sociology of taxation provides crucial insight into the relationship between the international, national and subnational dimensions. The fiscal-sociological works mentioned suggest above all that changes at the national level are not solely derived from processes that occur within national boundaries, as has been traditionally thought, but are significantly informed by external geopolitical developments. Thus these authors draw these connections by examining the impact of military developments in the inter-state system upon state economic and political policy. In this book, fiscal sociology is employed to explain changes in international trade regimes as well as domestic social change and state capacity. This is because states employed tariffs in large part as a fiscal accumulation strategy. The structural linkages between the international and national dimensions provided by taxation in the study of trade regime changes are illustrated in figure 1.1.

The lesson to emerge from this book is not so much that taxation has shaped the national and international dimensions. Taxation is important here in so far as it is something which is enacted or (in a stronger sense) imposed by states. Thus, states shape the national and international dimensions through taxation, as indeed states are shaped by international and sub-national processes. Put simply, the study of taxation provides particular insight into how states shape economies at the national and international 'levels', as well as insight into how states relate to societies, and the inter-state system and world economy.

Fiscal sociology and 'the wealth of states'

There are two basic reasons why I have labelled this book 'the wealth of states'. Adam Smith (1776/1961) famously examined the strategies and policies that enabled capital accumulation, upon which the 'wealth of nations' (or more accurately, the wealth of national economies) was founded. This book, however, examines the fiscal strategies and policies that enabled fiscal accumulation, upon which the 'wealth of states' is founded. Just as profits and capital accumulation comprise the nerve centre of capitalism, so tax revenues and fiscal accumulation constitute the sinews of the state. To paraphrase the subtitle of Adam Smith's book, a study of taxation is inherently an 'inquiry into the nature and causes of the wealth of states'. Chapters 2 through 7 of this volume examine the fiscal accumulation strategies undertaken by various states, which in turn affected their foreign trade policies.

Secondly, in the latter part of chapter 7, I examine the basis of a state's capacity to wage war (while simultaneously maintaining consent). The popular view held by Marxists and realists is that a state's military capacity is based on the strength and size of a state's national economy (best measured through GNP) – a view that finds its greatest expression in Paul Kennedy's *The Rise and Fall of the Great Powers* (1988). However, I argue that military capacity is based on a state's ability to extract taxation, which involves a fiscal-sociological analysis of a state's 'relative political capacity' (cf. Kugler and Domke 1986; Organski and Kugler 1980; Snider 1987). In short, we can understand 'the wealth of states' only by engaging in fiscal-sociological analysis.

A non-realist theory of state power: the social and institutional bases of state capacity

Fred Halliday (1987, 1994) has recently laid down some important linkages between sociology and IR. Halliday argues that the central linkage between historical sociology and IR revolves around the Weberian theory of the state. This will at first sight seem contradictory to many within the discipline, since IR has long been dominated by a 'statist' paradigm, known as realism. As Faruk Yalvaç put it,

> following a very interesting theoretical development, current socio-logical theories of the state are increasingly approaching a more traditional view of the state-as-actor model (i.e., realism) precisely at a time when the theory of international relations is getting away from this idea and taking a more sociological form. (1991: 94)

It would indeed be paradoxical for sociology to move into the theoretically defunct world of realist IR while IR moves simultaneously into the equally defunct world of Marxist and liberal sociology. I fundamentally reject the criticism made by many in IR (e.g., Yalvaç 1991: 94; Justin Rosenberg 1990a: 249) that the neo-Weberian historical sociology project is simply a realist wolf dressed up in sociological sheep's clothing, despite the fact that some authors in this tradition have mistakenly described themselves as realist – most notably, Theda Skocpol (1979: 31) and Randall Collins (1986). Indeed, one of the central tasks of this book will be to differentiate my sociological theory of state power from that espoused by neorealism. For, as Halliday rightly points out, the Weberian/sociological theory of the state is very different to the realist (see also the constructive comments in Shaw 1993: 62–5).

The central problem with realism stems from its inadequate theory and conception of the state. The most famous neorealist, Kenneth Waltz (1979), argued that the state is a national territorial actor, which is fundamentally constrained and embedded within an anarchical system of states. He specifically argues that we do not need a theory of the state. States are like firms in a competitive market system whose behaviour is determined by the system within which they exist (1979: 71–2, 76–8, 89–91, 93–4, 98–9, 105–6, 133–7). The units of the system are, therefore, irrelevant as conceptual variables.

This neorealist problematic gives rise to two key problems. Firstly, causal primacy is accorded the logic of the state system (characterised as international anarchy), such that states are viewed as little more than passive receptors (*Träger*) of external inter-state pressures. Ironi-cally, therefore, the state is denigrated as a conceptual variable, relegated in Waltz's terms to the irrelevant and reductionist 'second' level of analysis – or what Waltz termed the 'second image' (Waltz 1979: 40–60; see also 1959). This *passive* definition of the state is enshrined in the concept of 'sovereignty'. Secondly, neorealism sets up a problematical separation of the international and national realms.

Dealing with the second problem first, Waltz unashamedly argues that national developments are wholly irrelevant to international politics. By studying only the inter-state system and ignoring state–society variables (ontologically denigrated as 'process' as opposed to the superior 'deep structure'), he wholly separates the two spatial dimensions. A fundamental aspect of my sociological approach is the assertion that the national shapes the international quite as much as the international shapes the national – or what I refer to as the 'dual reflexivity' of the two realms.[1] The critical point to note is that because neither dimension is self-constituting, we cannot accord primacy to the inter-state system (nor for that matter to internal factors such as the mode of production or even the state), because both realms are *mutually constituted*. Moreover, by separating the international from the national, the state is 'squeezed' out of the neorealist explanatory schema.

As regards the problem of state power, neorealism makes two fundamental errors. Firstly, its emphasis on 'sovereignty' as the central defining aspect of the modern state leads to a paradoxical problem. On the one hand it reifies the state's domestic position in that it becomes a supreme actor wholly autonomous within society, which in turn ignores the crucial relationship between state and society (the state–society complex); and, on the other, it denigrates the state as a conceptual variable externally, reducing it to the primacy of the logic of international anarchy. Secondly, although it does recognise strength and weakness in states, its definition of state strength is inadequate. Neorealism argues that a strong state is one that can project its power externally and thereby change the policies and behaviour of other states in the state system. Or as Waltz puts it, 'an agent is powerful to the extent that he affects others more than they affect him' (1979: 192). A weak state conversely follows the lead taken by the strong state(s), and at best, as in hegemonic stability theory, enjoys a 'free ride'.

My alternative sociological definition attempts to overcome these two major faultlines in neorealism's depiction of the state. At a general level, my sociological theory views the state as variously imbued with power and autonomy, which cannot be simply reduced to the external realm of the state system. In Nettl's (1968) terms, *the state is a conceptual variable*. This enables me to reject neorealism's emphasis on 'passive' sovereignty, so that I can produce a more activist notion of the state.

More specifically, I replace the notion of 'sovereignty' with two variables: *state power* and *state capacity*. Sovereignty is problematic not just because it downplays the conceptual importance of the state, but because it is unable to differentiate adequately between states. States become 'like-units' because of the homogenising effects of the anarchical inter-state system. In my account, I place great emphasis on the 'uneven development of state power accumulation'. There are in fact several forms of state power, which in turn, depending on their configuration, go to make up a state's particular political capacity. These powers are derived from institutional assets as well as social factors. In turn, states can achieve differing degrees of 'relative political capacity', ranging from strong (Britain) to weak (tsarist Russia), with imperial Germany (as well as the United States, Canada, Switzerland and Australia) positioned between the two. As I point out below, the different degrees of state capacity lead to different economic and political policy outcomes, not least vis-à-vis trade policy and war capability.

Secondly, I define state strength/capacity quite differently from neorealism and traditional statism. A strong state is *not* one that can project its power externally in order to force others to bend to its will. Rather, a strong state is one that is able to successfully adapt to internal and external pressures, especially through cooperation with society. Conversely, maladaptability is the sign of state weakness. This begs the question: what is the source of state strength or capacity? A central focus of this study involves embedding the state not only in its international context, but above all in its social/domestic context. In particular, I argue that state capacity is enabled by state–society relations quite as much as by international processes. Most importantly, states enhance their internal and external political capacity by forming a close relationship with society. Fundamental to my formulation of strong states is the notion of *embedded autonomy* (Evans 1995; Weiss and Hobson 1995), or *bounded autonomy* (Zhao and Hall 1994). Strong states have a close embedded relationship with society (e.g., Britain), while, conversely, weak states seek to gain despotic power over society through repression (e.g., tsarist Russia). In other words, strong states seek power through cooperation (i.e., A and B), while weak states seek power through repression (i.e., A over B). Thus states should not be separated from societies, but should be recognised as mutually sustainable and interactive. I therefore place great emphasis on the state–society complex as a crucial determining variable not just with regard to state power, but also for international politics/economics – a position which is, ironically, perhaps closer to Marxist and Critical theorists (e.g., Cox 1986, 1987; Linklater 1991; Chase-Dunn 1989) than statists and realists. In short, state power and capacity are not something accorded simply through external military pressures, but perhaps more importantly, through *social* power.

This emphasis on the social basis of state capacity is one of the main aspects of my analysis which differentiates my neo-Weberian theory from realism. Speaking of the neo-Weberian theory of the state, Martin Shaw (1993: 65) correctly suggests that: '[this] sociological account may offer more than a supporting argument for a view of inter-state relations: it may see the system of states as existing in complex interaction with state–society relations'. However, while classes provide an input into state capacity, it is important to note that the state–society complex cannot be understood as something that is shaped solely by the needs of the dominant economic class, as Marxism suggests, or any particular interest group (as in liberalism and pluralism). The state has interests just as key economic actors within society have. The state is not simply a mirror of the requirements of key economic actors within society, nor are such societal actors simply passive receptors of state interests. Rather, state policy is the outcome of a bargaining process between two partially autonomous agencies: the state and key economic actors. Moreover, while state interests sometimes complement those of key economic actors, they can also abrade or diverge. I therefore employ the term 'competitive-cooperation' to capture this delicate *interdependent* relationship between state and societal actors (most notably the dominant economic class). The exact mixture of the 'competitive-cooperative' relationship between the state and dominant class varies not only within states, but also, comparatively, across states (linked to the 'uneven development/ accumulation of state power'). This is traced throughout this book, but developed through a comparative analysis in chapter 7.

Moreover, state capacity is not reducible to social power. States have various powers derived from *institutional* factors, which include the degree of concentration (high in unitary states, low in federal states) and penetrative/infrastructural power (a bureaucratic capacity to reach into society). In short, state capacity rests on institutional as well as social powers.

The key to my theory of state power is the notion that states are both domestic and international actors (cf. Halliday 1994: 84–6; see also

Hintze 1975: 183; Skocpol 1979: 32; Michael Mann 1988; Ikenberry 1988c; Linklater 1991; Jarvis 1993; Rosenau 1981). They are situated centrally within national society, but are also embedded within an external decentralised inter-state system and a global capitalist economy. Having this 'dual anchorage' enables the state to play off both the international and national realms through which it is able to enhance its power position both domestically and internationally. It is the state's unique spatial location, accompanied with the notion that states have power and autonomy, that provides the key to my analysis not only of social change and state capacity, but also of IR and IPE.

Because the state is both an international and a national actor, an examination of state power enables me to reveal the fundamental linkages between the national and international arenas. I depict states as residing within an international/national vortex. Indeed, there are actually no such things as the international and national systems understood in pure terms. Although they can be separated for analytical purposes (though not without considerable care), nevertheless they are embedded in each other. Neither is self-constituting, but each 'dimension' is constantly structured by interaction with the other. Although the state does not preside over all these trans-spatial interactions, it nevertheless plays a considerable role in promoting and enhancing the interpenetration of space.

Most importantly, the immediate ramification of this argument suggests that in order to understand economic change and government economic policy, we need to 'bring the state back in' as a unit-force power actor: that is, an 'actor' which has multiple interests and seeks to implement them. These interests are fiscal, military, economic and social. In strong contrast to Marxism, I argue that these interests cannot be reduced to the interests of the dominant class, even if they inadvertently or intentionally complement them. A crucial objective of this book is not only to show how and why the state shapes economic policy for its own interests, but also to derive a non-realist theory of state power and capacity. It is worth pointing out that the term 'bringing the state back in' emerged within sociology as a means to redress the economism of Marxism and liberalism (Evans, Rueschemeyer and Skocpol 1985). I also use it here as an antidote to neorealism, which has reified the inter-state system at the expense of the state. In short, my sociological theory of the state enables me to move beyond realism and statism in developing a theory of both IR and social change.

Moreover, this alternative non-realist theory of state power questions neorealism's central structuring principle: international anarchy. In this book, the inter-state system is not granted absolute power that constrains all states and forces them to bend to its demands. Rather the international system is also a crucial source of power and autonomy which states draw on in order to boost their domestic position. Moreover, the way in which states conduct their relations with society has crucial implications for their success in the inter-state system. If we accept that states have power and can make a difference in the international system, then the logic of anarchy must at the very least be downgraded. This is a major ramification of 'bringing the state back in'. As Hendrik Spruyt has recently argued, paraphrasing Wendt, 'anarchy is made by states' (1994: 264). But at the same time, states are partially constrained by the inter-state system: states make the inter-state system (and world economy), and the inter-state system (and world economy) makes states. States are simultaneously constrained by internal and external forces quite as much as they are empowered by factors emanating 'above and below' them.

In general, this book seeks to produce case studies and a general theory of the interrelationship between the international, national and sub-national realms on the one hand, and of societies, states and international political/economic systems on the other. This can be achieved through a redefined conception of the state, which enables a 'multi-factor' and 'multi-spatial' analysis. It follows that, because the international and national realms are embedded in each other, there can be no absolutely autonomous preserve of the disciplines of IR and sociology.

IR and sociology as mutually constituting: 'dual reflexivity'

A further consequence of my work is that IR could be enriched by incorporating a sociological approach. Focusing on the state's fiscal requirements provides an insight into shifts in international trade regimes. And as I shall argue in chapter 7, a study of taxation can enable an understanding of war in the inter-state system. It is interesting to note that various authors have been calling for the development of a sociology of IR, most notably Fred Halliday (1987, 1994; see also Linklater 1991; Jarvis 1989, 1993; Scholte 1993a, 1993b; Shaw 1993; Justin Rosenberg 1994). I develop their lead here.

At this point we can turn to the specific claim made by Fred Halliday (1987, 1994; cf. Shaw 1993: 64–5; Justin Rosenberg 1990b: 300), namely that the study of social revolutions can provide a bridge between historical sociology and IR. Drawing on Theda Skocpol's (1979) neo-Weberian analysis of social revolutions, he argues that revolutions are shaped by external changes emanating from within the inter-state system – namely defeat in war. This international pressure then leads to domestic revolution at the national level. At this point, Skocpol does not consider the implications of this for IR. This is Halliday's point for departure. He points out that in the aftermath of the revolution, a stronger, more centralised revolutionary state emerges (as Skocpol, following Weber, argued), but then goes on to initiate war in the inter-state system (Halliday 1994: 139–46). The core of this approach is what I shall refer to as the 'spatial trinity', based on an *international–national–international* causal chain, where defeat in war (external) leads to revolution (internal) which then leads back to war in the state system (external).

This conception of the 'spatial trinity' – so fundamental to a sociology of IR – is central to my approach. In fact, I employ two entwined spatial trinities in this book, which have implications not only for the study of the world economy (IPE) (as discussed in parts I and II), but also the study of war (IP) (see chapter 7). Firstly, I note that changes in the inter-state system, primarily the rise in fiscal costs associated with the 'second military revolution' and the growing international tension after 1870, pressurised states to find new sources of taxation at the national level to meet their increased military budgets. In the case studies examined here, most states chose to increase indirect taxes and hence raised tariffs (because tariffs are a principal form of indirect taxation). In the process, this fundamentally affected the international trade regime, which shifted from free trade (1860 to 1877, or 1879) to protectionism (post-1879) as a result of states raising taxes to meet higher military budgets. The international–national–international trinity is therefore fundamental to my IPE approach.

However, I reject the notion that the internal or domestic realm is simply determined by the external (a notion that reaches its apogee with world systems theory). Perhaps the most important part of my argument is that each state examined here – principally Britain, Germany and Russia, although also the United States, Canada, Switzerland and Australia – was endowed with a different degree of state capacity and different state–society relations. Where state capacity was highest – in Britain – the state was able to avoid resorting to regressive indirect taxes, and hence tariffs, and instead chose to increase progressive income taxation. As a result the state was able to avoid returning to protectionism, and maintained free trade instead. Where state capacity was low or moderate – especially in Germany and Russia – the state resorted to increasing regressive indirect taxes and hence tariffs, thereby shifting back to protectionism. There were also various state–society factors that impacted on tax and trade policies, in addition to the external impact of rising military costs. Thus national responses varied in line with differentials in state capacity and state–society relations. This then places emphasis on the state and the state–society complex at the national level as a partially autonomous conceptual variable. In particular, I emphasise the 'uneven development of state power accumulation' which not only shapes and mediates the impact of the international at the national level, but also goes on to fundamentally affect the international.

This spatial trinity, which I employ to explain tariff protectionism and free trade, also allows me to develop a theory of international politics and war. The 'strong' state response (Britain) of raising the income tax to meet higher state expenditures and societal pressures was a crucial factor in delivering Britain through the First World War and its turbulent aftermath. The 'weak' state response (Russia) of raising regressive tariffs and indirect taxes not only undermined the country's war capacity which led to defeat, but also alienated the lower orders, which in turn sought to topple the state from below. Germany was close to the Russian pole in this continuum.

If a sociological approach can enrich IR, I argue that IR can also enrich sociology, largely because the international realm has played such a fundamental role in shaping society and social development. A vital part of my argument is that the international and national dimensions are inherently related (what I call the 'dual reflexivity' of the international and national). It is perhaps ironic that sociologists have been slow to recognise the relevance of the international for studying society, given that it was the classical sociologists who first recognised that international forces have been crucial in shaping the development of societies (e.g., Sombart 1913; Weber 1922/1978, 1923/1981; Hintze 1975; Elias 1939/1994, 1970/1978). Moreover, the irony is reinforced by the fact that this observation has been made by IR theorists at least as often as sociologists (e.g., Burton 1972; Gourevitch

1978; Halliday 1994; Scholte 1993a, 1993b; Linklater 1991; Jarvis 1989, 1993; Almond 1989).

More recently, however, various sociology writers (mainly though not exclusively neo-Weberians), such as Norbert Elias (1970/1978), Theda Skocpol (1979), Michael Mann (1986, 1993), Anthony Giddens (1981, 1985), Bob Holton (1985), Randall Collins (1986), John A. Hall (1986), Gary Runciman (1989), Jack Goldstone (1991) and David Held (1995), as well as my own work (Weiss and Hobson 1995), have focused closely on the importance of international forces (mainly war in the inter-state system) in shaping social developments. And from within the Marxian tradition, Immanuel Wallerstein has famously argued that societies have been shaped fundamentally by external factors, notably the world capitalist economy (Wallerstein 1974, 1984, 1989).

However, while the intimate relationship between the international and national has been recognised by sociologists, there is on the whole in the sociological literature little understanding of the origins of these international pressures (see also Jarvis 1993: 208, 212–18). Indeed what has been missing from the sociological literature is the notion that national societies can shape the international realm (an insight that is perfectly congruent with a neo-Weberian approach, but has been underexamined only because it has traditionally fallen outside the limited disciplinary boundary of sociological inquiry). The main purpose of this book is to redress this imbalance and show how a neo-Weberian sociological perspective can enrich the study of IPE and IR. In the process, I seek to demonstrate how IR can enrich the study of sociology. Moreover, in chapter 7 I suggest a research agenda for what Jan Aart Scholte has called 'world-historical-sociological' studies, which is relevant for a broad range of social science disciplines, including IR, sociology, history, economic history, political science and political geography.

The issue of trade regimes and economic growth

Within IR a specific debate has raged between liberals and nationalist writers as to the relationship between trade regimes and economic growth/national welfare. As should be fairly obvious by now, it is not the focus of this book. However, chapter 6 provides some insight into this debate, and it is worth discussing this briefly.

Following the classical political economists, notably Adam Smith (1776/1961) and David Ricardo (1817/1971), liberals claim that free trade maximises not only trade, but above all *collective* economic growth and national welfare, as well as promoting interdependence and peaceful international relations. Nationalist/mercantilist writers, however, deny that free trade will *always* maximise collective economic growth, most notably when the international playing field is not level. As Friedrich List famously argued, against liberal political economy (or 'cosmopolitical' economy, as he called it), free trade maximises not international welfare, but merely the strongest economies over the weak (1841/1885: 132). Accordingly, he argues that 'infant-industry' or 'educative' protectionism promotes economic growth in the backward states, in turn an essential prerequisite for creating a level playing field (List 1841/1885; cf. Hamilton 1791/1985).

Nationalist writers tend to emphasise the importance of relative (zero-sum) gain as opposed to collective gain, heralding the importance of 'beggar-thy-neighbour tactics'. In this way, individual states gain only at the expense of others, thus implying overall a static or even a declining amount of collective international trade and economic growth. Conversely, as noted, liberals argue that free trade and specialisation through comparative advantage maximise trade and collective economic growth. Nevertheless, this dichotomy between liberals and many nationalists such as List should not be taken too far. Friedrich List was a great admirer of Britain's liberal political system, and strongly believed in a future world dominated by free trade and peaceful intercourse between states. Protectionism served merely as a short-term vehicle to create a level playing field, a necessary prerequisite before free trade could play a universal role (1841/1885: 127, 131, 175, 266). As List put it,

> The system of protection ... forms the only means of placing those nations [sic] which are far behind in civilisation on equal terms with the one predominating nation [sic] ... the system of protection regarded from this point of view appears to be the most efficient means of furthering the final union of nations [sic] and hence also of promoting true freedom of trade. (1841/1885: 127)

Unlike the nationalist writers, liberals embrace a highly ideological/normative position on this issue. The claim is that, at any point in time, free trade will always optimise collective economic growth and national welfare, while conversely protectionism will always reduce growth and welfare. But, as the historical record discussed in chapter 6 shows, this is highly problematic. In 1913 at the height of the mercantilist phase, real intra-European exports (measured as a proportion of total European income) were some 149 per cent that of the equivalent figure for 1860, and a not inconsiderable 128 per cent that of the 1870 figure (the latter date representing the height of the free trade era, the former representing its inception).[2] In short, the growth of European trade in the mercantilist era far outstripped that of the previous free trade era. Moreover, the economic development and export strength of each national economy was stronger in the mercantilist phase, especially for those which adopted protectionism in comparison to free trading Britain (although British export strength improved radically after 1900: see table 4.2).

Undoubtedly one exogenous explanation for this lies in the rapid economic growth brought on by the development of the second industrial revolution and the rapid industrialisation of various national economies, as well as the turn-of-the-century industrial boom. Thus liberals would claim that under such conditions of rapid economic growth, the increase in exports would have been even greater had free trade prevailed (implying that the export increase was merely a function of pronounced economic growth). But this raises two problems. Firstly, the fact is that there was a strong correlation between economic growth and protection. Secondly, this is made problematic by the fact that the increase in trade *outstripped* economic growth. Indeed the trade increase was not a simple function of economic growth. Rather, the increase in foreign trade among the developed countries exceeded economic growth, and by a considerable margin. In the 1877–92 mercantilist phase, annual export growth outstripped economic growth by as much as 242 per cent and as much as 146 per cent in the 1892–1913 phase. This compares to a figure of 224 per cent for the free trade era (1860–79). In short, not only did protectionism promote international trade, but in the 1877–92 period, real trade growth (factoring out the effects of economic growth) was higher than in the free trade period, although admittedly the 1860–79 period saw real export growth surpass that in the 1892–1913 period. Nevertheless, even in the 1892–1913 period, there was a clear correlation between export growth and protectionism.

In sum, the conclusions of chapter 6 suggest that the liberal claim, that protectionism undermines economic growth and can never secure growth comparable to free trade, fails to stand up against the historical record.

The advantages of a historical approach

It is worth pointing out that a historical perspective can provide some important insights into the study of trade policy. It would not be unfair to state that IR all too often suffers from adopting an *ahistorical* approach. Or to borrow the phrase coined by John Powelson (1994), IR is 'chronocentric': that is, it places undue emphasis on the present. Such a criticism is usually supported with a cliché: 'we can only understand the present by examining its roots in the past'. More importantly, though, failing to examine the historical roots of the present produces the illusion that what goes on today is somehow 'natural'; and that it can be adequately explained simply by examining the contemporary situation. However, one of the lessons of this book is that there is nothing natural about the free trade regime that emerged after 1945 (despite appearances to the contrary).[3] 'Freer' trade (though certainly not free trade) has comprised only approximately 15 per cent of the years between 1600 and 1995. In particular, we can gain considerable insight into freer trade since 1945 by examining protectionism historically.

My findings inform the study of international trade regimes in a number of ways. The freer trade regime found in the 'first world' since 1945 is usually explained in economistic terms: free trade suited the needs not only of American hegemony, but also of the industrial and financial classes of the advanced first world states, on account of their relative economic strength. As pointed out in chapter 6, a historical approach would show – from my sociological perspective at least – that free trade was only possible with the rise of the income tax. My basic argument is that tariff protectionism and trade regimes rest on a fiscal and political base. My specific argument for the prevalence of protectionism in the eighteenth and nineteenth centuries focuses on the weakness of state power and the need for governments to rely on indirect trade taxes (i.e., tariffs). However, as state power strengthened through the twentieth century, so states were able to shift away from trade taxes to income taxation, and hence towards free trade. This is reinforced by the fact that weak states – found mainly in the third world today – rely on trade taxes (i.e., tariff protectionism) for much of their revenue.

This fiscal analysis also helps explain why the rise of first world protectionism (usually termed 'the new protectionism') in the late twentieth century has taken the form of non-tariff barriers (NTBs), rather than the traditional 'tariff'. Freed from the constraint of fiscal revenue-raising through indirect trade taxes (i.e., tariffs) because of the income tax, states have resorted to NTBs as an alternative means of protecting their economies. Conversely, third world states, having to rely on customs revenue, tend to use tariffs in their protectionist policies. This raises a simple theoretical point: that free trade and protectionism are not simply *economic* phenomena; they rest on a political and *fiscal* base.

The structure of the book

This book sets out not only to produce a fiscal-sociological approach to trade regime changes from which a general approach to IR and sociology is developed, but also differentiates my product from all major rival theories: Marxism, liberalism, late development theory, statism and neorealism. This is important not just for 'product differentiation'. A theory is convincing only if it can be shown to improve on the rival paradigms. This in turn requires a detailed critical evaluation of the rival paradigms. Sections 1 and 2 of chapter 6 produce a detailed critique of 'economism'; the critique of Marxism is made in all chapters; of liberalism in chapters 2 and 6; of late development theory in chapters 3 and 6; and of neorealism in general and hegemonic stability theory in particular in chapters 6 and 7.

Part I examines a series of case studies, from which is drawn a comparative theory of national and international economic and political change in Part II. Part I examines the cases where states shifted to protectionism, notably those of imperial Germany (chapter 2), tsarist Russia (chapter 3) and the United States, Canada, Switzerland and Australia (chapter 5). In addition to the argument that these states increased tariff rates to provide fiscal revenues, I also emphasise the importance of state capacity in this process. Thus the weakness of state capacity in Russia and the only moderate degree of capacity in Germany help explain why tariff protectionism was chosen as the means to shore up the state's fiscal accumulation requirements. Chapter 4 considers the null hypothesis in which a state avoids protectionism and maintains free trade (i.e., Britain). The British state's high degree of capacity enabled a strong income tax rather than tariff revenue base (hence avoiding a return to protectionism) to meet its fiscal accumulation requirements. Chapter 5 resolves a theoretical conundrum that emerges from the previous three chapters by examining protectionism in the federal states of the United States, Canada, Australia and Switzerland. Here it is argued that a state's *degree of concentration* (low in federal states, high in unitary states) is more important than the *form* of state (parliamentarism/authoritarianism/ autocracy) in understanding taxation and trade policy.

For the general reader who is less interested in following through the detailed fiscal empirical case studies, it might be advisable to skip to Part II which incorporates the theory chapters (6 and 7), and then dip into the empirical chapters where necessary. Chapter 6 produces a general neo-Weberian fiscal-sociological theory of tariff protectionism and free trade, as a case study in structural economic change. This fleshes out the findings of earlier chapters to give a more complete multi-dimensional theory of economic change. It is important to note that the empirical case studies (chapters 2 through 5) do not seek to give a *complete* theoretical picture, which is produced in chapter 6. Chapter 7 seeks to achieve two core objectives: first and foremost, to develop a theory of states and state power/capacity which has implications not only for IR/IPE, but also historical sociology and economic history. Secondly, the chapter extends the fiscal analysis of state capacity to produce a framework which has direct ramifications for the international politics of war, as well as the sociological study of social change. The chapter closes with a proposed research agenda for what Jan Aart Scholte (1993b) calls 'world-historical-sociological' studies.

Part I

Case studies in structural economic change: states and trade regime changes, 1870–1913

2 Protectionism in imperial Germany: moderate state capacity and indirect taxation

The limits of economism: a critique of Marxism and liberalism

The traditional 'economistic' argument

The traditional economistic analysis of the rise and development of German tariff protectionism focuses on two main arguments. Firstly, it emphasises the impact of cheap foreign grain imports into Germany, mainly from the United States and Russia. Secondly, it focuses on the 'response', emphasising the importance of domestic socio-economic groups in the determination of government economic (tariff) policy. The account can be summarised as follows.

From 1862 (the year of the Franco-Prussian commercial treaty) to 1871, Prussia had become almost free trading. However, by the late 1870s, this trend was reversed (the change occurring in a period of no more than two or three years), with a 'switch to protection' completed by 1879. The change was allegedly prompted by the flood of grain from Russia and the United States,[1] which exerted serious pressure on the unprotected German grain markets. The tripling of cheap American wheat exports in the 1870s coupled with strong Russian and Austro-Hungarian grain exports, and the concomitant plummeting price of grain, forced Germany for the first time into grain import dependence (Lambi 1963: 132–3).[2]

In 1879, as a 'response', Germany reintroduced tariffs to protect the trading position of the Junker class (the powerful East Elbian/Prussian landowners). This analysis is made by liberals (e.g., Gerschenkron 1943: 26–7, 72–6; Rogowski 1989: 38–40; Calleo 1978: 13–15) as well as Marxists (Böhme 1967: 231–6; Wehler 1985; Berghahn 1987: 5; Puhle

1986: 86–7), and indeed by most authors (Gourevitch 1977: 285–91; 1986; Lambi 1963: 134–47; Senghaas 1985: ch. 1; Gallarotti 1985: 182; Snyder 1991: ch. 3).[3] According to Alexander Gerschenkron, the troubled Junkers were able to gain protectionist concessions from the state owing to their dominant political power base within the bureaucracy – an analysis that is also made by neo-Marxists. Both liberalism and neo-Marxism also emphasise that Junker gains were made at the expense of the 'duped' peasantry (Gerschenkron 1943: 16, 26–7, 57–8, 74–6, 85, 87; Berghahn 1973: 12; Fischer 1975: 6; Wehler 1985: 36–9).

This argument often comprises part of a broader economistic comparative picture. Thus for many Marxists as well as non-Marxists, what separated Germany from Britain is the importance of feudalism in the former – hence tariffs to protect declining dominant-class interests – and a strong bourgeoisie in the latter – hence free trade to protect their world dominance (e.g., Kindleberger 1978b: 19–30; Barkin 1987: 231; Pollard 1981: 257–60; Rostow 1978: 165–6; Calleo 1978: 67–9; Gourevitch 1986; Senghaas 1985; Simon Clarke 1988: 183–4).

The most immediate problem with this general theory, however, lies with one main fact: the Junkers were against tariffs on wheat and rye in 1879.

Reappraising the economistic account

In January 1879, the German Council on Agriculture (Der Deutsche Landwirtschaftsrat) voted for fiscal *against* protectionist tariffs; that is, it explicitly rejected grain tariffs, and continued to do so until 1885.[4] A similar stance was adopted by the Association for the Reform of Taxation and Economy (Vereinigung der Steuer- und Wirtschaftsreformer), which comprised 500 members, 450 of whom owned *Rittergüter* (privileged large estates). Moreover, in 1879, the provincial diets of East and West Prussia, Oldenburg and Lippe rejected protectionism; so too did the Farmers' Associations of Brandenburg, Königsberg and Silesia (Pflanze 1990a: 474; Lambi 1963: 147–8). Not only did the Junker-dominated Deutsche Landwirtschaftsrat oppose protection, but the provincial agricultural councils of East Prussia, Mecklenburg and other Junker-dominated areas remained staunchly opposed until the mid-1880s, when the depression in agriculture had continued without respite (grain prices did not collapse until *after* 1881). The tariff manifesto in the Reichstag received the signature of 87 per cent of Centre Party members (predominantly peasant-based), whereas it received only 60 per cent of sitting Conservatives (Barkin 1987: 227) – which suggests some hesitancy on the part of the Prussian agricultural community, particularly compared to the 'peasant party'. Given this overwhelming resistance to protectionism within the various Junker agricultural bodies in 1879, how can we explain the continuing desire for free trade?

There was still a strong commitment to free trade among many Prussian landowners. Above all, as Karl Hardach (1967) classically argued, many continued to benefit from grain exports – selling as much as half of their produce abroad.[5] Moreover, the Junkers were dependent on cheap (hard) wheat imports from Russia. This was because German wheat was too soft for making bread, and had to be mixed with imported hard Russian wheat before it could be exported (Broomhall 1904: 75; Jasny 1936: 75–6, 81; Pflanze 1990a: 283).[6] This was known as the Danzig or Stettin mix. Indeed, partly because German wheat was weak, it made sense to export it, especially to Scandinavia (Jasny 1936: 81). The lower prices of 1878/9, though not particularly significant, would have aided rather than hindered much of Prussian agriculture, enabling higher export earnings by cheapening the input price, and would therefore have been welcomed. This point is reinforced by the fact that German wheat producers (particularly in Prussia) were dependent on cheap imported Russian (rather than American) wheat (Tribe 1989: 124n.). Thus, a tariff on such wheat would merely increase the cost of the German export product, and would therefore only harm the trading interests of the Prussian landlords.

However, it is true that the law of 1879 stipulated a refund of the import duty paid on foreign grain if it was to be re-exported. Would this therefore have persuaded the exporting agrarians to favour protection? The problem with the 1879 law in this respect was that for the German exporter to obtain the refund, it was necessary for him to prove by means of a certificate of origin that he was exporting the very same imported wheat. As a result, it became extremely difficult to export the Russian wheat, because it had been mixed with German. This affected the producers of East Prussia – specifically Danzig, Königsberg, Memel and Stettin. Because these areas were dependent on exporting the Danzig/Stettin mix, they therefore lost a vital means of disposing of their grain in large quantities (Tirrell 1968: 270–1). This feature of the tariff adversely affected Prussian agricultural exporters such that in the 1880s much effort was made to have the certificates abolished (even on the part of shipowners, grain dealers and brokers), though it would not be until 1894 that the much-needed relief (that is, the abolition of the certificates) was granted to agriculture (Jasny 1936: 81; Farnsworth 1934: 320; Tirrell 1968: 271–2). The 1894 concession to agriculture embodied a recognition on the part of the chancellor that hitherto German wheat producers had lost out as a result of the 1879 Tariff Statute which had introduced the certificates.

In addition, as table 2.1 shows, German wheat exports increased after 1877, in turn necessitating an increase of cheap wheat imports, particularly from Russia. Table 2.1 tells an important story. Compared to the 1870s decadal average, wheat exports in the so-called 'calamitous' years of 1878 and 1879 were surprisingly good. Taking the decadal average as base 100, wheat exports for the years 1878 and 1879 were as much as 140 and 149 respectively. Moreover, if we take the 1877 figure as base 100 (the critical year as identified by the economistic consensus), then we find even bigger increases: 189 for 1878, and 202 for 1879. These were clearly substantial export increases and were significant enough to warrant anti-protectionist sentiment (not least for fear of retaliation) in large areas of German agriculture, especially in Prussia. It is important to note, therefore, *that 1878 and 1879 were not 'crisis' but 'boom' years for wheat exporters.*

Moreover, although imports were higher than exports, nevertheless *export increases* after 1877 dwarfed the import increases. Because imports were an essential ingredient in the German export product, wheat farmers would have benefited from the lower import prices (under conditions of free trade). Moreover, the higher wheat exports would themselves have prompted higher imports (especially from Russia), and would therefore, to a certain extent, have been a function of the export boom itself. More significantly, wheat exports dried up only after 1880 (Hoffmann 1965: 522), thus making free trade an attractive proposition in 1879. And given that prices did not collapse until *after* 1881, it would not be unreasonable to conclude that the Junkers would have been unaware of an agrarian crisis in 1879.

But it would be wrong to place price reductions in the late 1870s at the forefront of the analysis, as does the economistic argument. Indeed, perhaps the most significant problem with the economistic argument is its assumption that low grain prices in the late 1870s were determined solely by cheap imports. In fact, an important determinant of grain prices was the harvest.[7] The low prices in 1878 were determined by an excellent harvest (see the data in Hoffmann 1965: 292; see also Pflanze

Table 2.1: *German wheat imports and exports in the late 1870s (in millions of kg)*

Years	Imports	Imports (1870–9 = 100)	Imports (1877 = 100)	Exports	Exports (1870–9 = 100)	Exports (1877 = 100)
1875	499			393		
1876	685			570		
1877	940			388		
1878	886	156	94	735	140	189
1879	917	162	97	785	149	202
AVG 1875–9	785			574		

Source: Calculated from Broomhall (1904: 78), whose figures were taken from *Statistisches Jahrbuch für das Deutsche Reich.*

1990a: 284), while the high 1877 price was a function of a poor harvest. This means that farmers' incomes in 1878 and 1879 would have been no better or worse than in 1877. Put simply, the lower prices of grain commanded in the market place for the years 1878–9 would not have harmed farmers' incomes to anything like the extent that the economistic argument suggests. Moreover, as was noted above, the more cheaply priced wheat imports would have helped rather than hurt the Prussian Junker farmers.

A further problem with the economistic argument is its assumption that all grain producers were particularly sensitive to price changes. But rye production was relatively unresponsive to changes in price, because rye producers were not as market-orientated as their wheat-producing counterparts. This was because only 20 per cent of total rye production was destined for domestic human consumption; the remaining 80 per cent supplied animal fodder.[8] Thus, given the low market-orientation of rye producers, the lower 1878 price would not have been sufficient to inaugurate a shift away from free trade. It would take considerably more than just one or even two years of low prices to stimulate such a shift. In any case, the low 1878 price was largely a function of the excellent rye harvest that year.

But what of those rye producers who were market-orientated? Would they have favoured protection? The most important agrarian faction involved in rye production was the non-Junker large landowners.[9] In particular, those who owned a *Rittergut*, tended to have many of their estates abroad – particularly in Russia – and exported their produce into Germany. Not surprisingly, the largest and most powerful landowners unequivocally favoured free trade in rye even as late as the mid-1880s.

The economistic argument to a large extent bases its claim on the 'shock' factor of the flood of grain imports into Germany in the late 1870s. Major emphasis is laid upon the 'fact' that Germany had become a net importer of rye and wheat as well as barley in the 1870s, rendering the economy for the first time dependent on foreign imports. However, this omits two crucial points. Firstly, Germany had become a net importer of rye not in the 1870s, but as long ago as 1852, and intermittently since 1843, and had become a net importer of barley in 1866/7 (Pollard 1981: 268; Tribe 1989: 124n). And, secondly, while it is the case that Germany had become a net importer of wheat in the 1870s, this was largely because domestic demand had increased, mainly because of the growing unpopularity of rye as a bread grain (Teuteberg and Wiegelmann 1972: 133–45; Tribe 1989: 125). Therefore, Germany would have needed higher wheat imports, especially from Russia (as indeed occurred) in order to meet the growing domestic demand for wheat bread. In sum, grain imports into Germany were not a shock, and were certainly nothing new; rather, they were to an important extent planned and required. Therefore, the economistic picture of a Germany thoroughly penetrated by cheap foreign imports, imposed rather than wanted, is wide of the mark.

Finally, much of the economistic argument assumes that the Junkers were the dominant protectionist force in the 'alliance between Iron and Rye'. But this is incorrect. The Junkers displayed ambivalence to unite with industry for tariffs in 1879. David Calleo typically asks the question, 'how were the Junkers strong enough to impose agricultural protection upon the German bourgeois commercial and industrial interests?' The short answer is that they weren't. It was the industrialists who had approached the Junkers for protectionist support, and not vice-versa. Indeed, the industrialists had been marshalling their protectionist campaign even before 1875 (see Lambi 1963: ch. 8), although this point is acknowledged by Calleo (1978: 68). The deep suspicion of the industrialists on the part of a minority of feudal Junkers was not determined by any fear of being let down should they form an alliance. How could it have been when the agrarians held the upper hand politically? In fact, the agrarians' power was the reason why the industrialists had approached the agrarians to support protectionist tariffs in the first place. Their 'suspicion' was entirely rational since, firstly, they valued cheap agricultural machinery, which would only be jeopardised by an iron tariff; secondly, an iron tariff could lead only to foreign retaliation against German grain exports, thereby directly undermining their export potential; and thirdly, most importantly, they were against tariffs on grain imports.

If the Junkers had really desired tariffs for protection, why was the process of uniting with the industrialists (who were clearly committed to tariffs) in order to call for protection so half-hearted? Ironically, the fact of substantial bourgeois interests within both the Junkers and particularly high agriculture provided some basis for a reconciliation of agriculture with industry (see pp. 60–1). Nevertheless, such an alliance could be completed only with the help of an external coordinating body. Such a body was at hand in the shape of the Bismarckian state. For the fact is that, had it not been for Bismarck's gathering of these two groups under the protectionist umbrella, the tariff of 1879 might never have been legislated, certainly not in the form that it actually took, nor would the 'marriage of Iron and Rye' have taken place. Indeed as Erich Eyck points out, Bismarck's push for agricultural protection from 1878, and in particular his speech in December 1878, was a startling innovation, for 'until then [December 1878] nobody had thought that protection for agriculture was possible or even desirable. The majority of the farmers and landowners themselves had not asked for it' (Eyck 1968: 253).

This refutation of the traditional argument begs two questions: firstly – a complex question that I shall return to below – how do we explain the fact that the Junkers eventually came to support tariffs on grain in 1879? At this point, however, we can begin with a more immediate question: if Bismarck played such an important role in pressing for protectionism, what then were his motives? The answer lies principally in the realm of taxation and state power, to which I now turn.

Divergence of state and 'Junker' interests: 1879

The reform of imperial taxation was perhaps the most significant underlying motive impelling the tariff. This reform of taxation was primarily undertaken with the object of providing the empire (Reich) with a sufficient independent source of revenue, so that it need no longer rely on the *Länder* (state governments) and their legislatures for passing on tax revenues (known as matricular contributions,

Matrikularbeiträge). It was this internal fiscal requirement that was central to the German 'switch to protection' (with the geofiscal push coming later, in the 1880s). Bismarck placed such fiscal reform at the centre of his domestic agenda from 1872 onwards.

The pursuit of 'fiscal sovereignty'

Supplying finance and achieving fiscal sovereignty is the first prerogative of states. However, establishing fiscal sovereignty in the Second Reich proved to be a source of political controversy. There developed a specifically political/fiscal struggle between the federal Reich and *Länder* governments: a specific function of the federal nature of the political system. Most fundamentally, each level of government sought to achieve a monopoly of a specific source of taxation, with the *Länder* relying on direct taxation, and the Reich relying on indirect taxes.[10]

Article 70 of the German constitution adopted in 1871 stated that imperial (Reich) expenditures not covered by federal tax revenues would be supplied by matricular contributions from the *Länder*. These contributions were based on population size in each state. The central problem for Bismarck was the *Matrikularbeiträge*, because these contributions made by the *Länder* allowed them a political hold over the executive at the centre (since these sums were voted annually by the Reichstag). Bismarck's central political strategy involved abolishing the matricular contributions, which would in turn free the executive from parliamentary control, as well as the political constraints imposed by the *Länder* (Eyck 1968: 254; Lambi 1963: 168). At the same time, Bismarck sought to effect tax relief for the Junkers, by shifting to regressive indirect taxes.

In the run-up to 1879, Bismarck's hostility to the state governments was most visible in his attacks on the *Matrikularbeiträge*. In 1872, Bismarck stated in the Reichstag:

> An Empire that is dependent on the contributions of individual states lacks the bonds of a strong and common financial situation. The uneven burden of the *Matrikularbeiträge* is a question of equity, but their abolition is in my opinion part of well-formulated Imperial unity. (cited in Lambi 1963: 169)[11]

In 1875 he stated:

> To give the German Reich a powerful, unshakeable financial foundation, which provides it with a dominating position and brings it into

an organic union with every public interest in state, province, district and commune – that would be a great and worthy task, which could tempt me to devote to it the last scrap of my failing strength.

(cited in Taylor 1955: 157)

In November 1875 he told the Reichstag:

Speaking entirely from the standpoint of the Empire I seek as great a reduction as possible if not the complete abolition of the matricular contributions. (cited in Dawson 1904: 50)[12]

By the mid-1870s, the struggle between the Reich and the *Länder* took on a new potency. The problem as it emerged after 1875 was that general government revenues were diminishing. Customs revenues declined from RM 123m in 1873 to RM 100m in 1877. An important factor in the emerging fiscal crisis was the international economic recession (*Statistisches Jahrbuch für das Deutsche Reich* 1882: 157; Pflanze 1990a: 446; Kitchen 1978: 167; McKeown 1983: 89). It is often argued that the problem emerged as a result of the drying up of the French war indemnity payment. But the indemnity payment did not go into current federal expenditures. Of the total money passed over (RM 4,207m), 35 per cent went into the North German sinking fund and 21 per cent went straight to the *Länder* (see the note to table 2.8). More-over, the majority of the RM 1,826m which went to the Reich went towards paying off the sinking fund, with the remainder allocated to future spending (Witt 1970).

By 1878 the recession had led to the rise of fiscal crisis at all levels of government. In particular, without a new, independent and healthy source of revenue, Bismarck believed that the Reich would become fiscally paralysed. As a result of the revenue shortfall, the chancellor – in accordance with Article 70 – resorted to increasing the matricular contributions of the federal states. Paradoxically, this hurt both the *Länder* and the Reich, fiscally penalising the former, and exacerbating the Reich's dependence on the *Länder*. The conflict between the Reich and the *Länder* was forged through a chronic fiscal dependency of the former in relation to the latter in the mid-1870s (see table 2.2).

As table 2.2, column 3 reveals, the Reich was fiscally dependent on the state governments in the 1870s, relying on as much as 20 per cent of its income from matricular contributions, which contrasted strik-ingly with the post-1880 position. In addition to Bismarck's not inconsiderable resentment, these high contributions imposed enor-mous strain in the *Länder*. The matricular contributions were a major

Table 2.2: *The changing balance of fiscal power of the Reich and the* Länder, *1872–1913*

Period	(1) Net matricular contributions from *Länder* to the Reich (RMm)	(2) Net total Reich income (RMm)	(3) Net surplus matricular contributions as % of Reich income
1872–4	78	345	23
1875–9	78	461	17
1880–4	17	491	3
1885–9	−33	663	—
1890–4	−20	930	—
1895–9	−6	980	—
1900–4	21	1281	2
1905–9	31	1769	2
1910–13	50	2045	2

Sources and notes: (1) Matricular contributions: 1872–1911: Gerloff (1913: 522); 1912–13: Newcomer (1937: 23), taken from the *Statistisches Jahrbuch für das Deutsche Reich*. Note that these are 'net', that is, only those amounts that the Reich received in excess of the tariff revenues passed on to the *Länder* by the Reich.
(2) Calculated from Gerloff (1929: 16) and Witt (1970: 56, 378–9).
(3) Column 1 divided by column 2 × 100.

source of discontent for many taxpayers – especially farmers. It was this fiscal strain that pushed many farmers down the road to tariff protectionism.

In Prussia, matricular contributions increased by as much as 38 per cent between 1875 and 1879. Expressed in constant 1913 prices to eradicate the distorting effects of price changes, the real increase stands at a considerable 69 per cent. At a time when income was declining, such increases in expenditure caused considerable problems. The increase in the matricular contributions led to an increase in the direct tax burden, which in the 1870s was an important means of *Länder* and local government (*Gemeinde*) finance, while indirect taxes were reduced. Between 1871 and 1879, Prussian indirect taxes dropped by 28 per cent, while direct taxes increased by 20 per cent (Prochnow 1977: 40–1). Moreover, a Prussian budget surplus of RM 73.9 million in 1873 had turned into a treasury deficit of 30.1m by 1878/9 and 73.2m in 1879/80 (Gerloff 1913: 524).[13] Thus the healthy Prussian surplus of 11 per cent (of total expenditures) in 1872 had turned into an unhealthy deficit of just under 10 per cent by 1879.

Table 2.3: *German* Länder *matricular contributions expressed in current and constant 1913 prices (in RMm)*

Years	Total Länder matricular contributions Current	Constant	Prussia Current	Constant	Bavaria Current	Constant
1873	59	49	33	28	17	14
1874	51	46	33	29	15	13
1875	52	52	32	32	15	15
1876	56	59	32	33	20	21
1877/8	64	71	37	41	20	22
1878/9	70	85	42	51	20	24
1879/80	72	89	44	54	19	23

Sources and notes: Matricular contributions: Gerloff (1913: 40, 98–9, 106, 522, 526, 531). Price deflator: Mitchell (1992: 840). To 1876, the fiscal year (FY) went from 1 January to 31 December; in 1877, the budget year went from 1 January 1877 to 31 March 1878 (15 months); thereafter the budget year went from 1 April to 31 March. The effect of this is to exaggerate the amounts for FY 1877/8, though not for FY 1878/9 or thereafter.

Prussian matricular contributions represented as much as 7 per cent of total net Prussian income. This contrasted with the 1880–98 situation where Prussia paid only 1 per cent of its net income to the Reich, and 2 per cent in the post-1898 period (see appendix A, table A1). Nevertheless, total *Länder* contributions between 1875 and 1879 were some RM 90 million less than that requested (27.5 per cent of the total contributions actually paid). One cause of this problem was the depression after 1873, which led to lower tax and non-tax revenue yields (Hans Rosenberg 1943: 67–8; von Kreudener 1987: 115), as noted above. This sustained burden ratcheted up considerable social hostility in all the *Länder*, especially in Prussia. It was the fiscal strain rather than economic conditions that pushed many German farmers down the road to protectionism.

Fiscal crisis: redefining the 1870s agricultural recession

The economistic argument assumes that the agricultural recession of the late 1870s was brought on by the flood of cheap imports. However, the main problem most farmers faced was fiscal. Through the 1870s many states, especially Prussia, had rearranged their fiscal structures, devolving tax responsibility downwards to the city and village governments. In turn, these governments imposed surtaxes on the class and classified income tax, as well as on the land and building tax. These adjustments disproportionately increased the tax burden on urban property owners and village landowners, which not surprisingly proved to be a major cause of agrarian resentment in the face of developing fiscal crisis (although it is important to note that many Junkers were absolved of part of this increased fiscal burden because they came outside the jurisdiction of the village government) (Witt 1985: 137–54). Most Prussian property owners were burdened further by the increases in direct tax imposed by the Prussian government.[14] Tax discontent was felt particularly in the lower-middle income brackets, which in practice often paid higher rates than the middle to upper income brackets. Of central interest here is how these fiscal adjustments and increases in taxation specifically affected agriculture.

Beginning in the 1870s, the situation in agriculture worsened as mortgage indebtedness rose sharply, in turn a function of the rapid rise in land prices after 1860 (Tirrell 1968: 28–9; Pflanze 1990a: 284; 1990b: 11; Dawson 1904: 205). What was particularly resented was that the vast mortgages taken out were subject to surtaxes, which had increased through the 1870s. Owing to the lack of any mortgage tax relief, increased tax payments and surtaxes merely fuelled further agrarian resentment. Tax relief was becoming for many farmers (particularly of middle- and small-sized estates) not just a luxury, but rather a matter of survival (Daniel White 1976: 65). After 1876, many farmers were blaming the increased matricular contributions for their problems (in addition to the surtaxes at local level). The Heidelberg Convention of 5–8 August 1878 is usually portrayed by the economistic consensus as evidence of a protectionist will in agriculture. However, the convention's main objective was to solve the fiscal crisis. Indeed, the imperial government invited the finance ministers of the *Länder* to this convention specifically to enable a possible

> relief of the budgets of the individual states over the course of time, so that it would be feasible for them to eliminate or reduce oppressive taxes, or, if they considered it advisable, to give up certain appropriate taxes wholly or in part to the provinces, counties and municipalities.
>
> (cited in Daniel White 1976: 66)

It was the issue of tax relief that led many German farmers down the path of tariff protectionism. Many farmers preferred an increase in indirect taxes – e.g., tariffs – on 'non-essential' items, rather than on grain, to provide the required fiscal relief. This is crucial, because it demonstrates the point that German farmers did not favour grain protectionism for economic trading purposes (contrary to the economistic position). In Hessen, for example, few farmers favoured tariffs for protection until mid-1878 when it became clear that it was the only method by which their desired tax reform could be implemented – owing to the fact that Bismarck was unable to bring the tobacco industry under government control (Daniel White 1976: 65). Bavaria, while favouring tax relief from the matricular contributions, also preferred free trade in grain (Lambi 1963: 177; Daniel White 1976). Likewise, Prussian Minister of Agriculture Friedenthal opposed agrarian protection (Lambi 1963: 181).

Only the need for tax relief prompted much of agriculture to support grain protection in late 1878, because this was the only item that Bismarck was prepared to consider (Daniel White 1976: 67). Thus, on 26 February 1879, the central board of the Hessian Agricultural Association decided to support the chancellor, 'as a result of (financial) necessity'. They argued that the proposed tariffs would not aid agriculture directly, but that:

> The indirect advantage ... consist[s] in the fact that as a result of increases in the Reich's own revenues, the states will be put in a position to lower their direct taxes ... [This] would be achieved in a far more productive manner if a certain number of articles not considered everyday necessities of life but as superfluous luxuries [i.e., not grain tariffs] would be subjected to substantial increases of the tariffs levied upon them ... and even the [tobacco] monopoly would be preferable to the introduction of a general tariff on all imported articles.   (cited in Daniel White 1976: 67)

Fiscal resentment was felt particularly within Prussian agriculture. Prussian Junker farmers were resentful of increased direct taxes (even though they paid less tax as a proportion of their total income than middle-sized farms). Indeed, the Prussian Conservatives in 1876 formed the Association for the Reform of Taxation (a body that is commonly heralded as an embryonic manifestation of the growing protectionist identity of the Junkers). While this body aimed to strengthen the political position of the Conservatives and the empire, it was above all concerned with the fiscal issue. Adolf Niendorf argued that because the imperial constitution stipulated that indirect taxes and tariffs were to be the main source of Reich revenue, absolute free trade was impracticable (Lambi 1963: 140). During their courting of

Bismarck, their own materialistic aims were clearly apparent. An increase in indirect taxes would enable a reduction in matricular contributions (and hence direct taxes).

After 1876, when the Reich began rapidly to increase state assessments (especially for Prussia), Conservatives began to talk about tax relief. Agrarian resentment was often focused on or aimed at the rising urban capitalist/entrepreneurial class, which was perceived by the farmers to shirk its fiscal responsibility (Daniel White 1976: 63; Pflanze 1990a: 448). Even as early as 1873, Johannes Möllinger argued in the Landtag that farmers in the Grand Duchy paid three times more direct tax than the urban entrepreneurs.

All over Germany, landowners could unite on the issue of tax relief, with initial differences expressed only over the source of the fiscal bounty. Thus, while tax relief through tariffs (that is, 'revenue' as opposed to specifically 'protectionist' tariffs – thereby precluding grain tariffs) was desirable to the Junkers, tariffs for *protection* from foreign grain imports were far less attractive. Still dependent on exports and on foreign (hard) grain and cheap industrial (machinery) imports, the Prussian landlords had to weigh the advantages and disadvantages of tariffs. Fiscal interests – the factor of potential tax relief – pushed them down the tariff road, while their trading interests pulled them back towards free trade.

On 5 April 1878, Bismarck raised the question of the restoration of the iron tariffs (which had been abolished only in 1877) in the Prussian ministerial council – his first practical move towards protection. He had also decided to include agricultural tariffs in his protectionist plans. This is significant because through 1877 grain prices had been very high. Therefore, grain prices could not have been an important consideration in Bismarck's shift towards tariff reform. He told Kardorff:

> My plan is to present a bill to the Bundesrat before the end of this session of the Reichstag which would be known in the country before its dissolution ... I want tariffs on tobacco, spirits, sugar, if possible coffee, and shall not flinch from imposing duties on grain.
> (cited in Lambi 1963: 166; Pflanze 1990a: 454–5)

On 29 March 1878, Bismarck told the South German protectionist Professor von Mayr to work out a memorandum connecting the protectionist system with the fiscal plan. Bismarck's fiscal strategy revolved around two interwoven themes: first and foremost, to supply the Reich with revenues independent of the states' matricular contributions; and, secondly, to provide tax relief for the agrarians, especially the Junkers.

State autonomy: co-opting the dominant Junker class

The main reason why tariffs on grain imports were so desirable for Bismarck was their very considerable fiscal yield. Because of grain's high demand inelasticity (everyone eats bread and it cannot be substituted), and given the vast quantity of grain imports in the late 1870s, even a low tariff would be fiscally lucrative. However, the immediate problem that Bismarck faced was that the Junkers still supported free trade in 1879. Bismarck valued their support and thereby sought to bring them round to grain protectionism.

Before discussing the strategies employed by Bismarck to co-opt the Junkers into supporting grain tariffs, it is worth pausing to consider why Bismarck valued their support. Marxists point out that the state was dependent on the political support of the Prussian Junkers, who held on to political power even though their economic power had been eclipsed. There is clearly some truth in this. The Junkers managed to hold disproportionate power in the Bundesrat, which had substantial powers – it considered all government bills first, it could dissolve the Reichstag, and it could even declare war. It was crucial for Bismarck that he get the Bundesrat on side, for the simple reason that tariffs could be increased only with the consent of both the Reichstag and the Bundesrat (Article 5 of the constitution). Article 5 of the German constitution stated that:

> In the case of bills concerning the military establishment, the navy, or the revenues specified in Article 35 (tariffs, salt and tobacco tax, etc.), whenever a difference of opinion arises in the Bundesrat the vote of the presidency (i.e., of Prussia) is decisive, if it is cast in favour of a continuation of the existing arrangements.
>
> (cited in D'Lugo and Rogowski 1993: 75)

The Bundesrat comprised representatives from all the *Länder*. The Junkers held considerable political sway in the Bundesrat for two reasons. Firstly, Prussia held an overall majority of seats. In particular, fourteen negative votes could block any constitutional amendment, and Prussia held seventeen (D'Lugo and Rogowski 1993: 75). Secondly, the Junkers had a significant say in choosing Prussia's representatives. Furthermore, Bismarck valued the support of the Conservatives in the Reichstag (which largely represented the Prussian Junkers), who of course supported the right-wing strategies that Bismarck sought to employ. Moreover, Bismarck was partial to the cause of the Prussian landowners, not least because he happened to be one.

There were two principal strategies that Bismarck would employ to bring the Junkers round to supporting grain protectionism: firstly, the 'fiscal carrot', where an increase in indirect taxes would enable future direct tax relief for the agrarians, and, secondly, the 'political carrot', where through the tariff Bismarck would promote a more right-wing government *Kartell*, which would promote the Reich's executive autonomy as well as Junker interests.

The fiscal carrot

This Bismarckian strategy sought to persuade the Junkers to support protectionism through emphasising upper-class tax relief that would be achieved with a return to protectionism. In turn, this could be achieved firstly by reducing the states' matricular contributions and, secondly, by accumulating sufficiently large indirect tax revenues at the central Reich level, which could then be reallocated to the *Länder* and *Gemeinde*, thereby enabling eventual direct tax relief for upper-income earners. Indeed, in preparation for the 1878 Heidelberg Conference, Bismarck stated that fiscal policy

> should provide the Reich with such an amount of own income derived from indirect taxation that the pressure on the federal states' budgets would be lowered to such an extent that the states would be put into a position to abolish or reduce taxes, which they regarded to be oppressive, and to transfer such taxes in part or totally to the local authorities which the states regarded appropriate for that purpose.
>
> (cited in Daniel White 1976: 66)

Bismarck's twofold strategy of upper-income tax relief struck a chord particularly at the agrarian level. In the period to 1879, state government dissent over taxes was evidenced by the increasing calls to the Bundesrat for a decrease in the tax burden. Ironically this opened the way for Bismarck to attack the *Matrikularbeiträge* (which represented the political preserve of the *Länder* in their fight to maintain their autonomy vis-à-vis the Reich).

In attempting to persuade the Junkers to support agricultural protection, Bismarck made much of the tax relief that the tariff would provide. Thus, on 21 May 1879, he stated,

> If cheap corn is the goal at which we have to aim, we ought long ago to have abolished the land tax, since it burdens the corn-growing industry at home, which produces 400 million cwts., against the 27 or 30 millions which we import. But no one has ever thought of such a thing: on the contrary the tax has been gradually increased throughout all Germany, so far as I know, and in Prussia it has increased 30 per cent since 1861, viz., from 30 to 40 millions.
>
> (cited in Henderson 1967: 49–50)

Bismarck reinforced the agrarian complaints, claiming that estate owners paid excessive taxation (though, in the case of the Junkers, there is plenty of evidence to show that this was not the case, since the Junkers in particular were able to hide much of their gross income from the taxing authorities). Capitalists, Bismarck argued, were subject only to the personal income tax, and he reckoned that they paid approximately 3 per cent of their incomes in taxation. In contrast, he argued, the estate owner paid an extra 6–7.5 per cent through real estate taxes, while the surtaxes added a further 10–20 per cent to their total tax bill (Pflanze 1990b: 47). Furthermore, there was much resentment over the taxation of mortgaged estates, where the whole amount borrowed was subject to land tax as well as surtax.

On 5 May 1878, Bismarck instructed Hoffman and Hobrecht to work out a programme that combined the establishment of fiscal tariffs with the restoration of the iron duties. Detailing the 'first stage' of his fiscal package 'to shift from the false track of direct taxes', Bismarck wished to raise enough revenue to abolish *Matrikularbeiträge* completely, while also being able to distribute revenues to the states in order to provide further tax relief. He wished to abolish direct taxes on individual incomes up to RM 6,000, which would benefit the upper-income groups (Dawson 1904: 63–4; Pflanze 1990a: 463–4), given that a mere 3 per cent of the tax-paying population in Prussia earned as much as RM 7,200 per annum (Hoffmann and Müller 1959: 68–72).[15]

As I noted earlier, the majority of German farmers came to support protectionism so as to enjoy tax relief. Protectionism received strong backing from each federal state at the Heidelberg Conference. The final outcome was that all states agreed that the reform (i.e., drastic reduction, though not abolition) of the *Matrikularbeiträge* should be implemented by an increase in imperial indirect taxes (Lambi 1963: 176).

However, indirect protectionist taxes would be more beneficial to the average farmer than to the Junker, who managed to avoid much of his tax bill. Thus tax relief might have seduced much of German agriculture into supporting protectionism, but alone it could not have appeased the Junkers. The linchpin of Bismarck's co-optation strategy involved the construction of a right-wing government *Kartell*, which would appeal specifically to the Junkers.

The political carrot

The tariff proved to be both a carrot that would enable Bismarck to entice the Junkers into supporting tariff protection in general, and a stick that would be used against the National Liberals and the Social Democrats (SPD) in order to shore up the Reich's executive power. In short, forging a right-wing government *Kartell* would not only lure the Conservatives into supporting tariff protection, it would also enhance the autonomy of the executive in parliament.

Until the mid-1870s Bismarck was close to the National Liberals, who had provided him with essential support in consolidating the empire. However, this relationship became strained towards the end of the decade, due firstly to the refusal of the left wing of the party under Lasker to support protectionism and, secondly, above all, the party's desire for parliamentary scrutiny of the executive. Bismarck's tax proposals were aimed in part to bypass the checks of the federal states and the Reichstag. Not surprisingly, the National Liberals rejected these proposals. Clearly, if Bismarck was to secure these objectives, he would have to marginalise the National Liberal Party. In 1877 the elections offered him some hope in doing precisely this, with the left wing's position in the Reichstag diminished and the more moderate faction under Bennigsen strengthened.

By February 1878, the National Liberal Party made ministerial responsibility the *sine qua non* for their approval of the Bismarckian tax project (Lambi 1963: 171). In February, Bismarck decided to split the National Liberals once and for all. His aim was to eliminate the threat of ministerial responsibility which would continue to stand over him as long as the National Liberals continued to exist. Fortunately for Bismarck, the 'irreconcilable' Pius IX died and Cardinal Pecci was elected as Leo XIII. Just before his election, Pecci had expressed hope for the improvement of relations between Berlin and the Vatican. Bismarck's opportunity to build a new government majority by drawing in the Catholic Centre Party (the Centrum) was thereby handed to him (Henderson 1975: 219). He moved immediately towards the Centrum, for if he formed a new government coalition with the Conservatives and Free Conservatives, the Centre Party would hold the balance of power in the Reichstag. This would allow him to push through the tariff proposals and, of course, free him from his hated dependence on the National Liberals.

The issue of protection was the one important tie between Bismarck and those parties he was drawing closer to. In October, a coalition of 204 deputies (forming a majority of the chamber) declared their over-whelming support for protectionism. This body, known as the Free Economic Association of the Reichstag, brought together mainly Cen-trists, Conservatives and Free Conservatives. In this was the nucleus of a right-wing government *Kartell*. The Progressives and the left wing of the National Liberals, however, were the only forces in the Reichstag that were solidly against protection. Hence, through the tariff, Bis-marck could crystallise the political alignments that would give him a new right-wing majority.

Determined to split the National Liberals and at the same time to marginalise the Progressives, Bismarck put through an anti-socialist bill in the Reichstag following an assassination attempt against the emperor in May 1878 (although the bill was rejected). Then on 2 June there was a second attempt on the life of the emperor, this time by Karl Nobiling. When the news of the attempted assassination reached Bismarck, he exclaimed, 'Now I have got them.' 'The Social Demo-crats?', he was asked. 'No, the National Liberals!' (cited in Sheehan 1982: 183). Bismarck saw in this a perfect 'opportunity to destroy the only powerful party of the time' (Weber 1922/1978: 1390). He promptly dissolved the Reichstag and another election was held on 30 June. During the campaign the Conservatives attacked the National Liberals and the Progressives for voting against the anti-socialist bill. Bismarck's plan was entirely successful. The elections saw a clear swing to the right, with National Liberal seats declining by 23 per cent, Progressive seats declining by 26 per cent and Social Democrat seats by 25 per cent. In contrast, the Free Conservatives increased their seats by some 50 per cent, as did the Conservatives, while the Centrum remained about the same (calculated from Sheehan 1978: 184).

On 5 May 1879, the Reichstag debates revealed the rift in the National Liberal Party and the final estrangement of the left wing under Lasker from the right under Bennigsen, as had been intended by

Bismarck. On 8 May, Eduard Lasker on the left publicly denounced Bennigsen and the majority of the party. With the split of the National Liberals, the way was clearly open for the construction of a right-wing *Kartell*. Seizing this opportunity, the Junkers came round to grain tariffs. Having prepared the way for protectionism, Bismarck's only remaining task was the final negotiation with the Centre Party.

The final compromise

Although the Centre Party was prepared to side with Bismarck's tax plan, nevertheless, the party suggested that a certain amount of revenue from the tariff should be set aside to cover the needs of the empire, and that the rest should be turned over to the individual states (in order to maintain the federal principle). This led to the Clausula Franckenstein,[16] which eventually allowed for RM 130 million (approximately £6.5m) of tariff revenues to be kept by the Reich, with the surplus going to the *Länder*. However, as we shall see shortly, this problem was easily circumvented by Bismarck, who, having passed on most of the customs revenues to the *Länder*, simply increased the matricular contributions and thereby clawed these revenues back. Initially the Centrum also insisted upon the annual approval of the tariff by the Reichstag, but the Conservatives and Free Conservatives rejected this, and the party thereby dropped this requirement. With the announcement of the Franckenstein amendment, the right-wing National Liberals immediately attempted to do a final deal with Bismarck. But the parliamentary rights that were desired by the party were vehemently rejected by the chancellor, who clearly preferred the lesser evil, namely the maintenance of the *Matrikularbeiträge* (Gall 1986: 109; Weber 1922/1978: 1390, 1464). With the formation of this new right-wing coalition, the stage was thereby set for an increase in executive power. Furthermore, the tariff had not only allowed Bismarck to form a new, politically desirable coalition, but had also split the National Liberal Party. Finally, with free trade still important in the eyes of many farmers, especially the Junkers, Bismarck agreed to the figure of RM 10 per ton – the minimum rate he was prepared to accept (Lambi 1963: 181–8).

The tariff bill received imperial assent by a vote of 217 to 117 on 9 July 1879, part of it coming into operation on 15 July, part of it on 1 October and the remainder on 1 January 1880. All the duties were intended to be revenue producing, though some articles were selected for special taxation on account of their proven fiscal productiveness, such as colonial goods and coffee, tea, petrol, tobacco, and wines and spirits (Dawson 1904: ch. 5).

Convergence of state and 'Junker' interests: the 1880s

Initial evaluation of the 1879 tariff

The 1879 German tariff met with only limited economic success in offsetting the decreased prices, and virtually no success in preventing the further deterioration of grain prices through the 1880s. Indeed this factor suggests the lack of a clear *protectionist will* on the part of both the agrarians and the government in 1879. In gauging the economic effectiveness of the tariff, we need to examine the extent to which it increased domestic grain prices.

The grain tariffs were well below 10 per cent, general estimates suggesting 5 per cent for wheat and 7.5 per cent ad valorem[17] for rye (Lambi 1963: 226; Pollard 1981: 258). Even if we assume that the price of grain would increase by the whole amount of the tariff, then the 5 per cent tariff on wheat would not make good the 13 per cent dip in price after 1877, nor fully restore the 9 per cent drop viz. the decadal average price. Similarly, the 7.5 per cent rye tariff could not make good the 16 per cent reduction in the 1877 price, nor the 13 per cent drop on the decadal average.

As explained earlier, much of agriculture had been dependent on low-tariff industrial iron and steel imports, which had supplied it with cheap machinery. The fact that industry received moderately high rates of between 15 per cent and 25 per cent (Webb 1980: 310) had contributed to various sections of agriculture's ambivalence over the tariff. Accordingly, agricultural producers would have felt the pinch of higher industrial prices on machinery, leading to the claim that agriculture had been sacrificed on an industrial altar. Moreover, the 1879 tariff hurt the German wheat exporter because he received no refund for the higher-priced Russian wheat. (I noted earlier that German wheat exports were dependent on the Stettin or Danzig mix, whereby soft German wheat had to be mixed with Russian hard wheat before it could be exported.) This was *a* factor in the radical drop in wheat exports after 1880, although the major factor was the shift in consumer preference for wheat bread instead of rye (Teuteberg and Wiegelmann 1972: 133–45).[18] Indeed, average wheat exports dropped by approximately 80 per cent after 1880 (Broomhall 1904: 77).

Thus, the German wheat producer was less competitive (by very approximately 5 per cent of the price per ton) in the foreign arena than before the tariff was implemented. And certainly the problem was exacerbated by the foreign retaliation that was stimulated by Germany's switch to protection. Thus one of the traditional sources of income for Prussian agriculture had dried up as a result of the 1879 tariff. In sum, the economic gains of the 1879 tariff were so slight as to bring into question its economic rationale. In conclusion, as will be discussed later, the fiscal rationale for protection in 1879 was much greater than the economic (cf. Karl Hardach 1967).

The agrarian shift to protection after 1881

I noted above that the tariff failed to halt the long-term decline in grain prices. Many authors argue that the 1879 tariff was responsible for the price increases in 1880 and 1881. In fact, the tariff was responsible for no more than 50 per cent of the increased price on wheat and no more than 20 per cent of the increased rye price. The main reason for the upturn in prices in 1881 was a very poor harvest (see Hoffmann 1965: 292–3; Pflanze 1990b: 43, 179). After 1881, grain (especially wheat) prices plummeted. This was partly due to a series of good harvests, with wheat harvests averaging 2.32 million tons and rye 4.01m tons (1882–7), which compared to 1.77m tons for wheat and 3.55m tons for rye (1870–7).[19] This means that, although farmers were indeed becoming concerned with lower grain prices, the final grain price was not solely determined by cheap imports, but also by good harvests. This meant that farmers' incomes would have held up to a greater extent than assumed by the economistic consensus. The key point to note here is that lower grain prices would not have prompted calls for protectionism *to the extent* that economistic theory has traditionally assumed.

Moreover, in strict contrast to the picture painted by the economistic consensus (most notably Lambi), agricultural prices dropped significantly only in the years after 1881, rather than after 1877 (see figure 2.1). By 1886, the price of wheat had fallen by 21 per cent on the 1879 figure, a 28 per cent reduction on the 1870s decadal average, and no less than 31 per cent on the 1877 price. Such major decreases in the early 1880s began to impact on agriculture.

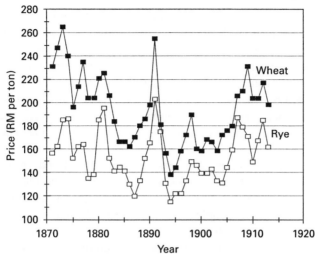

Figure 2.1: German grain prices, 1870–1913

These price reductions overlapped with a series of other problems within agriculture, especially rising mortgage indebtedness, which peaked in the mid-1880s (Heß 1990: 262–79; Tirrell 1968: 28).[20] These mortgage problems, in turn exacerbated by land taxes and surtaxes, and coupled with the sustained reductions in grain prices, prompted an agrarian shift towards protectionism (Daniel White 1976: 67). Not surprisingly, mass-based agricultural calls for protection were heard only *after* 1882 (rather than 1877 as the economistic consensus assumes). By 1885, tariffs were requested at most levels of agriculture. Bismarck raised the duties from RM 10 per ton in 1879 to RM 30 per ton in 1885. However, these increased duties were still not high enough to offset falling prices, with agricultural interests throughout Germany demanding further increases. This economic factor was a crucial variable in the further raising of the duties two years later in 1887 to a substantial RM 50 per ton.[21] Also by 1885, the Junkers had finally come round to the economic cause of tariff protectionism, and joined the general call for agricultural tariffs. However, this questions the economistic argument that the 1885 and 1887 grain tariffs were enacted specifically at the behest of the Junkers.

In his analysis of German protectionism, Gerschenkron, as does neo-Marxism, made two fundamental mistakes. Firstly, he argued that agricultural tariffs were enacted by the state purely for the selfish interests of the Junker class (1943: 47). Indeed, in general, the economistic argument assumes that the Junkers were the most vociferous in demanding protection. Secondly, Gerschenkron assumed that the peasants had been duped (through 'false consciousness') by the Junkers into supporting protectionism. The peasantry were said to receive *negative* protection because tariffs raised the cost of fodder (the main input to hog-raising). In addition, higher grain tariffs lowered the demand for meat, especially among the working class, therefore further undermining the peasantry's economic position (Gerschenkron 1943: 26–7, 72–6).

Taking the second point first, peasants were not duped: rather, they received major benefits from the state. Firstly, they benefited particularly by non-tariff measures, especially health regulations which were particularly efficient at keeping out foreign meat imports (Hunt 1974; Webb 1982: 318). As Webb points out, by the 1890s, the levels of protection on beef and pork had come to match that of arable products (1982: 322–6). More importantly, the peasantry were not economically backward or irrational, as Gerschenkron assumed. Rather, as Robert Moeller points out, they pursued rational agricultural practices – especially mixed farming. While animal production took precedence, nevertheless grain production was not unimportant. The minimum grain production undertaken by peasants would have comprised at least 10–20 per cent of total farm income (Moeller 1981: 375; Hunt 1974). And in those years when grain prices were high, the peasants would sell their arable produce. Not surprisingly, grain tariffs were wholly welcomed by peasant farmers (Moeller 1981: 372–82; Barkin 1987: 227). Moreover, it was for rational economic reasons that the peasant party – the Centrum – favoured tariffs, and had done so consistently since the 1870s.

In sum, the coming together of the dominant and lower classes – that is, the Junkers and peasantry – in support of agricultural protection was not the product of false consciousness on the part of the peasantry. Indeed, 'the alliance of pork and rye [i.e., peasant and Junker] actually reflected economic reality' (Webb 1982: 324). Therefore, Gerschenkron's assumption that peasant and Junker interests were diametrically opposed is incorrect. But more importantly, it also brings into question the central economistic assumption that protectionism was the outcome of Junker requirements. Rather, it was the Junkers who at the last moment jumped on the *already rolling protectionist bandwagon*. And much of the highest echelons of agriculture even as late as 1885 rejected tariffs. In short, as regards the economic input into tariff protection (as opposed to the fiscal aspect), the requirements of *agriculture in general* were primary, of which Junker interests were a part.

Fiscal politics and the deepening of agricultural protection

Kenneth Barkin aptly summarises the neo-Marxist position of Hans Rosenberg, who sees the tariff as unleashing selfish interest-group politics in contrast to the more 'elevated constitutional and political issues that prevailed in the 1860s and 1870s' (paraphrased by Barkin 1987: 226). I have dealt with the critique of the interest-group argument above. Here we note that it was precisely these 'elevated constitutional and [fiscal] political issues' that were so fundamental to the creation of the tariff increases in 1879, 1885 and 1887.

Although it accumulated new revenues from the 1879 tariff for the Reich, Bismarck's secondary dream of providing tax relief to the states remained largely unfulfilled. This was because the Reich remained dependent on net matricular contributions from the *Länder*. Prussia's net contribution effectively wiped out the surplus earmarked for the tax cut (Pflanze 1990b: 46). Bismarck feared that unless tax relief was forthcoming, rural voters would desert the government in the approaching 1881 imperial elections (Daniel White 1976: 74–5). Thus, in October 1880, he introduced two new tax bills in the Prussian Landtag to reduce direct taxation, though they were rejected, not least by the National Liberals, who feared such taxation's anti-parliamentary nature. A whole series of tax bills was then introduced including a bill for stamp duties, a national defence tax, a beer tax and an imperial tobacco monopoly, none of which became law. However, Bismarck achieved moderate success in 1883 when a statute which suspended the lowest two brackets of the class tax was passed. Nevertheless, the statute had little political or fiscal importance.

Thus by 1883 Bismarck had achieved little success in his desire to liquidate direct taxes at the *Länder* level. In desperate need for new revenues, and having completely failed to instigate some kind of imperial monopoly, once again he would turn to increasing indirect taxes (Pflanze 1990a: 522). A further factor had by now come into play. By 1883, most of agriculture was calling for protection (as noted above). As in the late 1870s, an important reason for the growing protectionist sentiment was the fiscal issue (Daniel White 1976: 101). According to Gustav Schmoller, foreign imports comprised only half the problem faced by farmers; taxes were particularly onerous (cf.

Daniel White 1976: 113), and an increase in indirect customs revenue was urgently required. As tables 2.5 and 2.6 show (see pp. 63–4), the new tariff enhanced the fiscal position of the government. In 1886 tariff revenues were RM 238 million compared to RM 139m in 1879 (Witt 1970: 56; *Statistisches Jahrbuch für das Deutsche Reich* 1882: 157). However, this still did not enable significant tax reductions for the *Länder*. The hindrance was of a somewhat complex nature. In short, the problem was that although tax revenues had indeed been passed on down to the rural communities via the Lex Huene after 1885,[22] as Bismarck had intended, nevertheless these communities embarked on a major increase in expenditures. 'Thus any gains which may have accrued to the owners of agricultural land came in the form of increased governmental services rather than in tax reductions' (Newcomer 1937: 38; see also von Kreudener 1987: 119).

Thus, by 1886, Bismarck was doubly frustrated in his long-term fiscal project. Having failed to inaugurate the desired tax relief to the agrarians, he was additionally faced with an increase in Reich expenditures which was leading to annual deficits. The taking out of loans, up to a massive RM 410m (approximately £20m) annually in peacetime to cover the deficits, merely intensified the fiscal problem, since it led to higher interest and amortisation payments. Bismarck's attempt at initiating yet another government monopoly in the Reichstag, this time on liquor, was rejected. With agriculture calling for protectionism, and fiscal crisis staring him in the face, Bismarck raised tariff rates again in 1887.

Owing to these various reforms in taxation always (though not exclusively) for the purpose of higher revenue, the empire enjoyed a short period of financial prosperity after 1888. Customs revenues in the 1880s were 97 per cent higher than in the 1872–80 period, enabling Bismarck to bypass the *Länder* fiscally. After 1885, and in particular after 1887, the increase in customs duties led to a growth spurt in Reich revenues. This enabled Bismarck to pass revenues on to the *Länder* and *Gemeinde*, as well as retain larger sums for the Reich.

In sum, the 1880s protectionist policy was inspired by a different set of factors than the earlier 1879 tariff. Whilst in 1879 the state had gone against the Junkers' trading interests in order to enhance Reich fiscal autonomy, nevertheless Junker consensus was obtained through Bismarck's creation of a right-wing *Kartell*, as well as his promise to grant the Prussian landowners tax relief. In the 1880s Bismarck no longer had to manipulate the Junkers to enhance the state's fiscal autonomy, because by then the Prussian landowners – as well as the German agricultural community – came to support protectionism for trading as well as for fiscal reasons. Thus, in sociological terms, whilst *state fiscal* and *dominant class trading* interests diverged in 1879 over the tariff, they harmonised around the grain tariffs in the 1880s. This coming together in the 1880s changed again in the 1890s, as the two once again diverged.

Qualified divergence of state and 'Junker' interests: the 1890s

Beginning in 1892, the new Reich chancellor, Count Leo von Caprivi, reduced Germany's grain tariffs by instigating a series of commercial treaties. The economistic argument claims that Caprivi effectively sacrificed agriculture on an industrial altar. As a result, the economistic argument focuses on the agrarian backlash that this prompted, which supposedly led to Caprivi's dismissal, in an effort to show that where governments ignore the needs of the dominant class, they are eventually punished and brought to heel.

Perhaps the most glaring problem with the economistic claim is the lack of explanation for Caprivi's 'New Course' in the first place. Indeed, it is one thing to argue that a chancellor will be dismissed should he fail to satisfy the dominant Junker class, but it is another thing entirely to explain the divergence in the first place. It is surprisingly easy to suggest that the various Reich chancellors (post-Bismarck) did not have the Junkers' interests at the very forefront of their minds. The 1892–4 trade treaties in particular would suggest that the much-heralded link between the Reich and the Junker class was less organic than portrayed by the economistic consensus.

Accounting for the 'New Course'

The 1890s witnessed a drastic drop in grain prices. The 1894 price was approximately one-third the 1873 price (if 1900 = 100, then 1873 = 244 and 1894 = 84). The world price averaged a mere RM 106.5 per ton in the 1890s (Pollard 1981: 266; Rostow 1978: 164–5; Broomhall 1904: 78). However, as with earlier periods, grain prices were *not* a simple function of world prices or cheap imports, but were affected by the harvest. In particular, the high 1891 price was a freak, owing to a very poor harvest, while the very low prices after 1891 were partly a function of a series of good harvests. This means, therefore, that farmers' incomes would not have been so badly affected as a prima facie examination would suggest.

Nevertheless, economic conditions were a concern for agriculture. After 1892, the economic rationale for tariff protection remained strong given the reduction in prices. And, by the 1890s, the linkage between world and domestic German grain prices had grown strong. If the Junker class was so powerful and could supposedly dictate government policy, as much of the economistic consensus claims, then this would have been the time for tariff rates to be increased radically.

But in 1892–4, through a series of trade treaties, Reich chancellor Caprivi reduced grain tariffs on wheat and rye from RM 50 to 35 and on oats from RM 40 to 28 per ton. Even so, it is important not to exaggerate these reductions, which at first sight appear to have been substantial. The real effect of these reductions was only minimal for the first part of the decade, because although the *specific* rate was substantially reduced by 30 per cent (over the 1887 rate), the *actual* reduction calculated as a percentage of the value of the produce was only minimal. This was because although the fixed rate came down, so too did grain prices, thus nullifying the tariff reduction. Thus, between 1889 and 1890, the ad valorem rate for rye was between 46 and 49 per cent and for wheat between 33 and 34 per cent. After the trade treaties had come into effect, by 1894–6 rye tariffs stood at 42–6 per cent, and for wheat 32–3 per cent (i.e., virtually no different to the 1889–90 rates). But as prices recovered after 1895, by 1900–2, ad valorem rates for rye declined to 33–7 per cent and 27–8 per cent for wheat (Webb 1982: 314), because grain prices had increased.

Even so, at a time when German agriculture was facing up to the lowest prices witnessed for over half a century in the face of substantial mortgage indebtedness, the government was actually reducing tariffs, when we would expect a so-called 'pre-capitalist state' to be *increasing* protectionist rates. From the Junkers' point of view, Lambi's words do not seem overly dramatic: 'Caprivi's commercial policy ... sacrificed the interests of agriculture to the conclusion of commercial treaties advantageous to industry' (1963: 231). Or as Tipton put it: 'By 1894 ... declining world grain prices and increasing indebtedness made the reduction of duties on Russian grain seem the culmination of an unspeakable betrayal' (1974: 965). The Conservative *Kreuzzeitung* thundered that 'from now on we must devote our energies to a war of annihilation against capitalist liberalism and everything that supports it [read Caprivi]' (cited in Kitchen 1978: 212).

The Caprivi treaties affected the agrarians not only economically, but also politically. According to Ploetz (of the Farmers' League), the German farmer no longer viewed the Radical but rather the kaiser as his enemy. In particular the Junkers blamed the emperor, whose absolute power had been used against them. Thus according to Ploetz, the Junkers favoured constitutional monarchy, but considered the growth of absolutism to be a serious danger to the state. As he put it: 'An absolute Empire we do not have and we do not want' (Ploetz, in *Korrespondenz des Bundes der Landwirte*, cited in Tirrell 1968: 313). Although this claim is undoubtedly rhetorical, it clearly reflected considerable tension between the Junkers and the state. Indeed, at the political level, the Conservatives seemed to invoke a spirit of independence from the government which had hitherto been unthinkable (Dawson 1904: 138–9). The Junkers immediately formed the organisation known as the Bund der Landwirte (BdL) in order to fight the government.

The BdL proposed the Kanitz Motion, which sought an increase in tariff rates on grain by approximately 60 per cent (Dawson 1904: 136–7; Tribe 1989: 93). The motion was an attempt to guarantee a minimum price for grain: RM 215 for wheat and RM 165 for rye (Tirrell 1968: 302). Note that the projected price for wheat was only 5 per cent higher than the 1878–80 price (which was according to the economistic consensus supposedly at crisis point at that time), although the projected rye price constituted a 19 per cent increase on the 1879 figure. Despite having the full support of the Farmers' League, the motion was convincingly defeated in the Reichstag by 159 votes to 46 (Tirrell 1968: 302). The rejection of the Kanitz Motion led one commentator to point out that 'National government policy was not therefore a simple reflection of Junker interests' (Tribe 1989: 93).

Furthermore, the treaties had been passed in the face of vehement opposition on the part of the agrarians in general, and the Conservatives in particular. On aggregate, of the three major treaties – Romanian, Russian and Austrian – 13 per cent of Conservatives voted for, 75 per cent voted against, whilst the difference – some 12 per cent – either abstained or were absent. In short, approximately 87 per cent of Conservatives did *not* support the treaties. The Conservative Party's voting patterns for each of the major treaties are shown in table 2.4.

Table 2.4:   *The German Conservative Party's rejection of the Caprivi trade treaties*

	Austrian treaty	Russian treaty	Romanian treaty
Total number of deputies	68	67	67
For	18	6	2
Against	36	54	62
For as % of total	26.5	9.0	3.0
Against as % of total	52.9	80.6	92.5
Abstained or absent	20.6	10.4	4.5
Total 'non-supporters'	73.5	91.0	97.0

Source: Tirrell (1968: 136, 243, 294).

Even when the treaties had been ratified, the agrarians intensified their agitation: 'We must tear up the treaties with Austria and Italy', announced the Conservative *Kreuzzeitung*. Later on, when the Russian treaty came into operation, the *Kreuzzeitung* stated: 'the German farmer will now be inclined to regard the emperor as his political enemy' (both quoted in Dawson 1904: 131). In this formulation, the link between authoritarianism and *Junkertum* was somewhat looser than suggested by economistic theory.

Thus, throughout the 1890s, agrarian opposition against both the government and the emperor continued. Thus, for example, in 1899 the BdL pressurised Conservative members in the Prussian Landtag to vote against the construction of a canal connecting eastern with western Germany, since the East Elbian landowners recognised the subsidising effect that this waterway would have for western land-owners (owing to its cheapening of transport costs of grain to eastern markets). However, this violated the emperor's wishes. As a result, Wilhelm resorted to punishing the dominant agricultural class, and expelled twenty of them from government administrative posts.

In addition, the trading privilege that the East Prussian landowners had enjoyed through the graduated freight rate schema was finally done away with (despite considerable Prussian resistance) in order to appease farmers throughout the empire – especially in the south (Tirrell 1968: 272–8). Nevertheless, overall, most landowners, large and small, felt aggrieved by the Caprivi treaties. While it would be wrong to conclude from this treatment of agriculture that the state could dispense with the agrarians simply as it pleased, it would be equally as incorrect to argue that the state acted simply as the political embodiment of the Junkers.

It would, however, be wrong to exaggerate the rift between the Reich and Junker class. For the fact is that farmers did receive some benefits. In particular, in 1894 the problem with the old import certificate scheme (introduced in 1879) was finally resolved, such that a subsidy was automatically granted to grain exports which was equal to the level of the import tariff (Tirrell 1968: 271–2; Webb 1982: 314). Secondly and most importantly, the most substantial benefit that accrued to the large landowners as a result of government policy was the subsidy paid from the alcohol tax (alcohol was distilled from potatoes produced by the large landowners). Moreover, as a result of the sugar excise, some 3,900 large landholders received large subsidies from the state (see Witt 1970: 47–8).

State 'fiscal' interests versus Junker 'trading' interests

What had caused this attack upon Junker privilege or, at least, the failure of the state fully to protect Junker privilege? The immediate problem was that the Reich's fiscal interests failed to harmonise with the trading interests of the Junkers. Politically, Caprivi had sought to conciliate opposing tendencies in the Reichstag (see Pflanze 1990b: 390–1). His more 'reformist' approach was applied to taxation, seeking a less regressive tax base. Thus he presided over a more progressive Prussian tax regime in 1891, with the higher rate raised to 4 per cent (although this ultimately failed to punish the Junkers, since they were able to avoid paying much of their direct tax bill, as noted earlier, and, moreover, the proceeds of this tax went to the agrarians in the villages, and were largely spent by them) (Kitchen 1978: 252). He also lowered the extremely high (regressive) indirect taxes, most notably the tariff on grain. Between 1888 and 1890, bread prices in Berlin had doubled (Nichols 1958: 141), causing popular unrest. In direct response to working-class agitation, Caprivi lowered the tariff on wheat, rye and oats, providing some relief for the consumer at the landowners' expense.

More important, however, was the Reich's desire for revenues. This might seem contradictory, as it could be argued that lowering tariffs would lower revenues. The lowering of the grain tariffs, however, did not hinder the fiscal needs of the Reich, firstly because the reduced rates were secured on a significant increase in grain imports, and secondly because the lower rates enabled an increase in imports. Between 1891 and 1902, total wheat and rye imports were some 179 per cent those of the 1880–90 period (calculated from Broomhall 1904: 78; Farnsworth 1934: 348; Jasny 1936: 140; Timoshenko 1928: 96). Between 1891 and 1902, customs revenue was 192 per cent that of the 1880–90 period (calculated from *Statistisches Jahrbuch für das Deutsche Reich* 1882: 157; 1892: 174–5; 1904: 220). Thus, although the rates had decreased, the vast increase in imports yielded substantial customs revenue. Added to this was the fact that, towards the latter part of the 1890s, the price of grain began to recover. Because tariffs were set according to *specific* rates, when the price of imports increased, so too did the revenue yield. Indeed, this had been anticipated by the Prussian finance minister, Miquel (Tirrell 1968: 220), as well as Caprivi (Kitchen 1978). Between 1885–9 and 1895–9, customs revenue increased by over 60 per cent.

A second reason for the trade treaties was that Caprivi sought to enhance the export position of the industrialists. If we look predominantly within the first world, German industrial exports had been hampered by the excessively high grain tariffs (which had stimulated foreign retaliation against German exports). Caprivi argued that some tariff concessions, mainly on agricultural goods, would have to be made to foreign countries in order to persuade them to lower their tariff barriers. Caprivi famously told the Reichstag: 'We must export. Either we export goods or we export men. The home market is no longer adequate' (cited in Henderson 1975: 221). It was this rationale that had of course led the Junkers to complain that agriculture had been sacrificed on an industrial altar.

Thus although the fiscal position of the Reich was enhanced by Caprivi's tariff programme, the lowering of the grain tariffs clearly flew in the face of the Junkers. It is not always possible for the interests of the state and the dominant class to coincide. This is because the state lies at the centre of several power networks or nexuses. States have a variety of interests, not least military, fiscal, political and economic. In pursuing these, states have to bargain with various groups in society. In the 1890s, the state leaned towards the industrialists, and in the process put the Junkers off-side. The constant bargaining process with the various groups in society sometimes leads to tensions with key groups. This relationship can be best characterised as one of 'competitive-cooperation'. The state sought to cooperate with the Junkers most of the time, mainly to enhance its own power. But it also competed with the Junkers, which occasionally led to tensions. In sum, therefore, the 1890s trade treaties can be understood only if we accept the notion that states have interests and partial autonomy (for a fuller discussion, see chapter 7).

Finally, the economistic argument states that Caprivi's downfall was sealed by the Junkers, who hated his commercial treaties (e.g., Berghahn 1973: 83–4). A similar fate, and for similar reasons, was said to befall successive chancellors, Prince Chlodwig von Hohenlohe and Bernhard von Bülow, the latter having tried to penalise the Junkers fiscally by bringing in a Reich inheritance tax. However, while the needs and power of the Junkers played a part in these events, this was only a small part of the causal chain. The main reason for the downfall of all three chancellors was ultimately their failure to keep the emperor on-side rather than their ability to put the Junkers off-side. Caprivi, as Reich chancellor (1890–4), alienated the emperor through a host of initiatives. In particular, he effectively limited the kaiser's power in decision-making, as well as upsetting many key political power groups within the government (Nichols 1958: 163–7; Röhl 1967: 64–84; Craig 1987: 245, 255, 260–1). His successor, Prince Chlodwig von Hohenlohe (1894–1900), was similarly dismissed, having lost the favour of the emperor, mainly because of his failure to enact a *Staatstreich* against the Reichstag, particularly against the growing power of the left (Craig 1964: 246; 1987: 265). Moreover, the dismissal of von Bülow had nothing to do with the inheritance tax. The economistic claim is flawed by the simple fact that the kaiser actually wanted to see the instigation of a Reich inheritance tax aimed specifically against the landed upper classes. Indeed, so determined was the kaiser in having the Conservatives accept the Reich inheritance tax that he stated: 'I am willing to impose the [inheritance] tax laws upon the country if the third reading results in an equally small or even smaller majority against the bill' (cited in Jarausch 1973: 63). Rather, as the kaiser told von Bülow's wife at the chancellor's farewell dinner: 'You must not believe that the inheritance tax or the [collapse of the] bloc felled Bernhard. You must seek the true reason in the events of November [i.e., the *Daily Telegraph* episode]' (Kaiser Wilhelm cited in Jarausch 1973: 64; see also Epstein 1959: 83–6; Craig 1987: 283–4). Alienating the kaiser rather than the Junkers was the common denominator in the downfall of each of the chancellors. Once again, the economistic argument errs by exaggerating the power and influence of the Junker class.

Qualified convergence of state and 'Junker' interests: 1902/1906

Tariffs and fiscal accumulation

By the very early years of the twentieth century, the Reich was facing the onset of fiscal crisis, both at the Reich and *Länder* levels. After 1898, the Reich turned to increasing the net contributions of the *Länder* (as it had done in the 1870s). But with the *Länder* struggling to make ends meet, the Reich was forced into borrowing (Percy Ashley 1909: 18, 20; Witt 1970: 386). Reich debt had risen from a tiny RM 16m in 1876 to a massive 4,844m by 1910 (Witt 1970: 386). In desperate need of new revenues, the Reich increased the tariff, anticipating over RM 100 million (approximately £5m) as a result of the increased corn duties alone.

However, the 1902/6 tariff hike was not instigated solely at the behest of the state's fiscal requirements. The state was also responding to the economic wishes of the Junkers, who as noted above had been actively pushing for a renewed round of agricultural tariff increases since 1894. However, the role of the Junkers in securing this tariff hike was not the most important factor. Moreover, although agriculture improved after 1900, the fact remains that German agriculture had suffered reduced protection throughout the 1890s and saw little relief until 1906 – a full fourteen years after the Caprivi trade treaties had been instigated. Once again, this reinforces my claim that the linkage between the Reich and Junker class was somewhat looser than portrayed by the economistic consensus.[23] Nevertheless, my argument in turn should not be exaggerated. It is necessary to note a few qualifications to this argument (already alluded to earlier).

Firstly, while tariff policy did not always go the way the Junkers wanted, there was in fact a range of other factors which weighed in their favour. Firstly, the Reich's excise tax policy was particularly beneficial. Excises on spirits, sugar and other commodities were highly beneficial to the Junkers (mainly the 3,900 who owned distilleries). The excises had provided constant relief throughout the late nineteenth century. Moreover, in 1908/9, approximately RM 69 million was passed on, giving each distillery on average some RM 17,700 in extra annual income, which was derived from the consumer but not channelled into the Reich's coffers (Witt 1970: 41–64).

Secondly, the fiscal federalism of Germany also conferred major benefits. I have noted that the Reich was dependent on indirect taxes while the *Länder* relied on direct taxes. This was particularly beneficial to the upper classes, because where direct taxes were levied – that is, at the state and local government levels – the Junkers had majority control owing to the distorting effects of the three-class voting system. In this system, voters were classified according to their wealth, measured through their tax contributions. The wealthiest third were taken first (known as voters of the first division – which of course included the Junkers), followed by the voters of the second division. The third division might well have comprised 90 per cent of the electorate. Each class or division then selected an equal number of representatives for an electoral college which in turn selected representatives for the Prussian house of representatives. As D'Lugo and Rogowski (1993: 75) put it, 'in terms of actual voting power, the wealthiest 10 per cent of the electorate sometimes held two-thirds of the votes'. Moreover, the diets of the local authorities had very narrow franchises; in many towns, a mere 10 per cent of the men eligible to vote in the Reichstag elections could actually vote. Accordingly, the upper-income groups could to a certain degree control the extent of direct taxation and welfare expenditures at the local level (because of their disproportionate representation), while not having to worry too much about the universal suffrage at the Reich level, because at that level there was no real alternative to regressive indirect taxes, which of course, benefited the wealthy (Witt 1986). Moreover, in Prussia, not only was the house of lords dominated by the aristocracy, but it also had full fiscal powers. Thirdly, as was noted earlier, the Junkers wielded influence through their privileged position within the Bundesrat (in which Prussia had considerable influence).

Not surprisingly, many commentators – Max Weber (1919/1970: 373) included – have been led to conclude that the political system was made for and on behalf of the Junkers (see also the discussion of Weber in Beetham 1985: 152–7). Paradoxically, this was undoubtedly a major source of the Reich's weakness (cf. Tipton 1976: 118–21). Nevertheless, the political set-up of the German Reich conferred many benefits on the Junkers, although there were clear limits to Junker class power vis-à-vis the Reich government.

The 'Junker' class and tariff protectionism, 1879–1913: a reappraisal

Before we examine the fiscal causes of tariff protectionism, it is important firstly to establish the place of the Junkers in my explanation. Throughout this chapter, I have sought to downgrade the importance of Junker class interests in tariff policy. This, however, should not be entirely surprising (even from an economistic perspective), not least because although tariffs clearly played a part in satisfying the economic interests of the Junkers (after 1885), it is in any case questionable how central protectionism was to their *overall* economic position. Moreover, the economistic literature has exaggerated the importance of the tariff to Junker economic interests as the principal means of overcoming the problem of low grain prices. Perhaps the main problem here is that the cheap agricultural imports were not the sole (nor at times even the main) cause of lower grain prices. To a certain extent the price of grain was determined by the exigencies of the harvest. High prices were partly determined by poor harvests, low prices by good harvests. Paradoxically, therefore, it was sometimes the case that the highest agrarian incomes were derived in those years when the price was lowest (because of a good harvest). Thus the price reductions in the 1870s would have been welcomed by the Junkers. Moreover, the steeper price reductions of the 1880s and 1890s were partly determined by good harvests, which would not have been as unwelcome as the economistic argument suggests. In addition, we have seen how the Junkers relied on other fillips, such as the excise tax. Moreover, the East Elbian landowners were particularly concerned over internal freight rates from west to east. These high transport rates were valued by the Junkers, since they were effectively a form of protection from domestic competitors. However, Junker interests played a part in the formation of German tariff policy, as has been explained above, but so too did much of German agriculture. To single out the Prussian landowners as the driving force behind tariff policy is incorrect.

But there is a deeper level at which the importance of the Junkers needs to be questioned. In contrast to the economistic picture of the Junkers as a wholly unified and highly powerful class, the Junker class was in fact a highly fractionated body with an array of interests. Indeed, these various interests were sometimes internally contradictory. Thus, in 1879, the state played off the 'fiscal' from the 'trading' interests of the Junkers in pursuit of Reich 'fiscal sovereignty'.

However, the Junkers were divided internally not only over trade and taxation in 1879: throughout the 1871–1913 period there was a further line of cleavage, notably between agrarian and bourgeois Junkers. In the 1879–85 period, over 65 per cent of the East Prussian Junker estates were bourgeois in origin (Heβ 1990: 56–97), and reliant on industrial sources of income (Pflanze 1990b: 17–18; Weber 1919/1970: chs. 14–15). To complicate matters further, the economistic argument portrays the Junker class as lying at the pinnacle of the agrarian and indeed social scale. But the Junkers were in fact a lowly group compared to the high agrarians, the latter of whom comprised barons (*Barone*), counts (*Grafen*), princes (*Fürsten*) and dukes (*Herzöge-Mark*).[24] They owned a minimum of 1,000–2,000 hectares and a maximum of about 10,000, compared to a maximum of 1,000 hectares for the Junkers, and enjoyed a much higher status. Interestingly, as with the Junkers, there was a close affiliation with the industrialists (Heβ 1990: 56–97).

The upshot of this discussion is essentially twofold. Firstly, the economistic claim that the Junkers were wholly rational, homogeneous and internally unified is incorrect. They were not simply a 'feudal dominant class par excellence'. They were closely related to the so-called 'bourgeois enemy' (as, ironically, Eckart Kehr (1977) pointed out through the notion of the 'feudalisation' of the bourgeoisie). These lines of cleavage enabled the state to play off the different interests of the Junkers against each other, in order to get its own way with respect to tariff policy. But the main ramification of this analysis is that class analysis cannot provide a sufficient explanation of German government economic policy. This does not mean that the Junkers were irrelevant to the government's tariff and taxation policies, or to German politics more generally – far from it. It simply means that we have to downgrade the importance of the agrarian dominant class as *the* independent variable in explaining these phenomena. As Geoff Eley aptly puts it,

> A convincing case could be made ... that recent German historiography has reduced the character of the political process to an institutional structure of ... interest [class] representation within the economy, and has neglected the party political and parliamentary arenas to the point now of distortion.
>
> (Eley 1986: 37–8; cf. Tribe 1989: 89; Mooers 1991: ch. 3)

It is to these political factors that we must now turn.

Moderate state capacity and the fiscal origins of tariff protectionism, 1870–1913

Why then did Germany make the 'switch to protection' in 1879, and indeed deepen its commitment to protectionism in the decades to 1913? If Junker economic interests were not central, we need to begin by looking at the state and its fiscal needs.

Federalism and the problem of 'low concentration'

The central reason for Germany's shift to protectionism lay in the state's weak capacity, which in turn led it to rely on indirect taxes and tariffs. Most importantly, the Reich was a federal state, institutionally suffering from what I term 'low concentration'. This refers to the fact that central federal states had only a limited range of options when extracting taxation. In particular, they had to rely on indirect taxes as the main source of their revenues (because the state governments were dependent on direct taxes). This essentially forced central federal states to rely on tariff protectionism as an important source of revenue (as discussed in chapters 5 and 6). Interestingly, the post-1878 fiscal function of tariffs followed a historical trend in Germany, since prior to 1871 the majority of German states had used tariffs in order to accumulate government revenues (Dumke 1991).[25]

As tables 2.5 and 2.6 demonstrate, the tariff (and indirect taxes) provided the mainstay of central government finance from 1879 to 1913, and indeed until 1918/19 (see especially figure 6.8, p. 208). Customs revenues provided some 43 per cent of all taxes, while indirect taxes comprised some 74 per cent (1872–1913). In particular, customs revenue as a proportion of total net income (table 2.6) stood at 29 per cent (1875–9), but jumped to 42 per cent after the 1879 tariff act, and rose to 52 per cent after the 1885 and 1887 tariff acts, dropping off only gradually after 1900 as net state property revenues increased relatively. Moreover, the single most important tariff revenue-yielding item was grain (Witt 1970: 56) – comprising some 30 per cent of total customs revenue from 1890 to 1911 (calculated from *Statistisches Jahrbuch für das Deutsche Reich* (1882: 157; 1892: 172–5, 185–6; 1896: 159, 165; 1900: 180; 1904: 220; 1908: 277, 284; 1912: 335, 348)).

The primary objective of Reich tariff and taxation policy was to achieve 'fiscal sovereignty': that is, fiscal independence from the *Länder* governments. However, because of the Franckenstein clause, the Reich

Table 2.5: *Reich (net) income, ordinary and extraordinary, 1872–1913 (in RMm)*

Period	(1) Total (net)	(2) Total indirect taxes	(3) Of which, customs	(4) Of which, excise	(5) Direct taxes	(6) Net state property revenues	(7) Extra-ordinary revenue	(8) Net matricular contributions
1872–4	345	224	110	114	—	43	—	78
1875–9	461	263	121	141	—	93	44	78
1880–4	491	335	191	144	—	101	38	17
1885–9	663	431	270	161	—	123	142	(33)
1890–4	930	623	360	263	—	128	193	(20)
1895–9	980	741	439	302	—	204	44	(6)
1900–4	1281	819	488	331	—	275	165	21
1905–9	1769	1007	607	400	20	377	336	31
1910–13	2045	1311	701	610	44	598	40	50

Sources and notes: Calculated from Witt (1970: 56, 378–9) and Gerloff (1929: 26). Totalling cols. 3–8 does not equal col. 1. This is because the total (col. 1) was taken from Witt, though he did not provide a figure for net state property (which is important for the discussion in this book). I therefore made a rough calculation of net state property by deducting state property expenditures from state property revenues. This will inevitably be crude because of the problem of operating expenditures and deficits, which have not been accounted for in these calculations. Nevertheless, the data are close enough for the requirements of this book.
(1) This includes ordinary and extraordinary loans. This figure is *net* of state property (i.e., SP expenditures have been deducted).
(2) Total indirect taxes comprising customs and excise revenue (cols. 3 and 4).
(5) This comprises inheritance tax.
(6) SP expenditures have been deducted. These include railways, banking, post and telegraph, stamps, playing cards, fees, administrative income, disability fund, growth tax and remittances from south German states for reserved rights to levy indirect taxes.
(7) Loans.
(8) Comprising those amounts returned to the Reich *in excess* of the amounts passed from the Reich to the *Länder* (from the tariff revenues). Note that the figures in parentheses are deficits, and have been deducted from total income (col. 1) accordingly.

was forced to hand over all tariff revenues to the *Länder* (keeping only RM 130m). To circumvent this problem, the Reich simply increased the state assessments, thereby clawing back the passed-on customs revenues (Newcomer 1937: 21–2; von Kreudener 1987). Moreover, from 1883 to 1898, the Reich, because of the increased tariff revenues and matricular contributions, was able to recoup much of the passed-on

Table 2.6: *Major revenue categories as a proportion of total net ordinary Reich income, 1872–1913*

Period	(1) Total indirect taxes	(2) Of which, customs	(3) Of which, excise	(4) Direct taxes	(5) Net state property	(6) Net matricular contributions
1872–4	65	32	33	—	12	23
1875–9	63	29	34	—	22	19
1880–4	74	42	32	—	22	4
1885–9	83	52	31	—	24	(6)
1890–4	85	49	36	—	17	(3)
1895–9	79	47	32	—	22	(1)
1900–4	73	44	30	—	25	2
1905–9	70	42	28	1	26	2
1910–13	65	35	30	2	30	3

Notes: Calculated from table 2.5. Note that figures in parentheses in col. 6 are deficits, and that extraordinary income from table 2.5 is not included in the total.

revenue, but was also able to pass over significant sums of money to the *Länder* for their own expenditure programmes. This was congruent with Bismarck's desire to achieve Reich fiscal sovereignty, since it enabled the executive to become effectively independent of the *Länder* for revenues (thereby reversing the direction of fiscal dependency). This is illustrated in table 2.7, which shows that the Reich achieved fiscal independence between 1883 and 1898 (a considerable achievement, given that the Reich had depended on as much as 23 per cent of its revenues from the *Länder* in 1872–5 – see especially table 2.2). In sum, therefore, the tariff had a solid political-fiscal core, derived from the federal nature of the state (i.e., the 'low concentration' of the federal state).

'Partially embedded state autonomy' and tariff protectionism

As will be discussed in detail in chapter 7, perhaps the most important aspect of a state's capacity is its linkages with society. Where these are dense and cooperative throughout society, then states derive considerable strength both internally and externally. While tsarist Russia had only limited linkages, which were in any case highly abrasive, and Britain had strong cooperative linkages with both the dominant and the subordinate classes, Germany was situated partway along this

Table 2.7: *The fiscal balance of payments between the Reich and the* Länder, *1875–1914 (in RMm)*

Year	(1) Levies on Länder[a]	(2) Distrib- utions to Länder	(3) Balance viz. Länder	Year	(4) Levies on Länder[a]	(5) Distrib- utions to Länder	(6) Balance viz. Länder
1875	52	—	−52	1895	383	400	+17
1876	56	—	−56	1896	399	414	+15
1877	64	—	−64	1897	420	433	+13
1878	70	—	−70	1898	455	468	+13
1879	72	—	−72	1899	490	477	−13
1880	64	38	−26	1900	528	509	−19
1881	85	68[b]	−17	1901	571	556	−15
1882	85	84	−1	1902	580	556	−24
1883	74	85	+11	1903	566	542	−24
1884	64	105	+41	1904	220	196[d]	−24
1885	103	116	+13	1905	213	189	−24
1886	119	137	+18	1906	230	206	−24
1887	171	176[c]	+5	1907	227	195	−32
1888	208	278	+70	1908	220	195	−25
1889	215	355	+140	1909	169	121	−48
1890	301	379	+78	1910	228	180	−48
1891	316	383	+67	1911	212	164[e]	−48
1892	316	353	+37	1912	247	195	−52
1893	369	339	−30	1913	255	203	−52
1894	385	382	−3	1914	246	194[f]	−52

Sources and notes: 1875–1911: Gerloff (1913: 522); 1912–14; *Statistisches Jahrbuch für das Deutsche Reich,* cited in Newcomer (1937: 23). State government levies also presented in Cohn (1972: 206–7).
[a] The figures in this column do not include the special payments by the southern states for the privilege of retaining beer and spirits taxes and the postal and telegraph service.
[b] Stamp taxes added.
[c] Spirits tax added.
[d] Distribution of customs and tobacco tax discontinued.
[e] Distribution of stamp taxes discontinued.
[f] Spirits tax distribution fixed.

continuum. The Reich had cooperative relations with the dominant agrarian class, but abrasive relations with the lower classes (mainly the proletariat). There were two main ramifications of this as far as tariff and tax policy was concerned.

Firstly, the Reich government had no real will to instigate a strong progressive tax base, which could best be achieved by the income tax. This was because the state lacked the ability to go fundamentally against the wishes of the landed class. Secondly, the state was keen to maintain highly regressive taxation which punished the poor and lower classes. Indeed, the tariff regime adopted achieved precisely this (Gerloff 1908: 164; Witt 1970: 52; Hentschel 1978: 203). The tariff rate on wheat in 1913 was 38 per cent and on wheat flour 45 per cent (Liepmann 1938: 64), while on rye it stood as high as 48 per cent (Webb 1982: 314). This directly inflated the price of bread, such that in 1913 the Berlin price was some 26 per cent higher than the world market price (Liepmann 1938: 62). For the majority of the population (that is, those earning less than RM 800 per annum) in 1895, grain tariffs consumed no less than 69 per cent of their total tax burden. The equivalent figure for those earning over RM 10,000 per annum was 1 per cent (calculated from Neumann, cited in Lotz 1931: 780; cf. Hentschel 1978: 202). Not surprisingly, the Reich's reliance on regressive taxation was an important factor in alienating the working classes and all parties left of centre (Paul Kennedy 1987: 327–31; Berghahn 1987: 35),[26] which was reflected in the victory of the Social Democrats in the 1912 election (Sheehan 1978: ch. 12; Kaiser 1983: 461; Berghahn 1987: 34–6).[27] But the fiscal basis of the tariff was not simply connected with taxation pressures; it was also linked to Reich expenditure pressures. What then were these?

The military origins of tariff protectionism, 1880–1913

Reich tariff policy was also aimed at meeting higher central government expenditures (see tables 2.8 and 2.9). Nevertheless it is important to note that the 'switch to protectionism' in 1879 was *not* expenditure-led. Total government expenditures remained remarkably stable throughout the 1870s (see col. 4, table 2.8). They could not, therefore, have had a direct impact on tax (and hence tariff) policy at that time. This reinforces my claim that the switch was based on *taxation* arguments (connected to the pursuit of Reich fiscal sovereignty). But, equally, it is clear that expenditures increased by as much as 50 per cent in the mid-1880s, which had a direct impact on raising tariffs in 1885 and 1887.

What did these expenditures comprise? In one of the major historical surveys of Reich government expenditure, Andic and Veverka (1964: 189, 203, 205–9) argue that social rather than defence expenditures

Table 2.8: *Reich expenditures (ordinary and extraordinary) and expenditure burden, 1872–1913 (in RMm)*

	(1)	(2) Defence	(3) Civil	(4)	(5)	(6)
Period	Total	expenditures	expenditures	t/NNP	d/NNP	c/NNP
1872–5	1095[a]	418	41	6.1	3.0	0.3
1876–80	718	583	126	5.1	4.1	0.9
1881–5	776	461	312	5.1	3.0	2.0
1886–90	1373	818	555	7.5	4.5	3.0
1891–5	1553	883	670	7.3	4.2	3.2
1896–1900	1878	841	1037	7.2	3.2	4.0
1901–5	2253	1155	1098	7.3	3.7	3.6
1906–10	2872	1564	1308	7.4	4.0	3.4
1911–13	3104	1965	1139	6.6	4.2	2.4

Sources and notes: Expenditures: 1872–5: calculated from *Statistisches Jahrbuch für das Deutsche Reich* (1880: 152–9); 1876–1913: calculated from Gerloff (1929: 18) and Witt (1970: 380–1). Both authors used the same primary source, *Statistisches Jahrbuch für das Deutsche Reich*.
[a] 1872–5 includes in the total those amounts received from France in reparations following the Prussian victory in the Franco-Prussian War. The allocation of these funds is not included in the *Jahrbuch*. A breakdown is given in Witt (1970). The total indemnity was some RM 4,207m. Of this, 1,480m went straight into paying off the north German sinking fund; 560m went to paying for the war pension fund set up just after the First World War and was spent to 1904; 216m was put aside for fortress building, spent to 1891; 129m went to building fortresses in Alsace-Lorraine; and 109m went to railway building, also in Alsace-Lorraine.
(1) Ordinary and extraordinary expenditures. Note that this figure is *gross* – that is, state property revenues have *not* been deducted. This figure is taken from Gerloff. (Witt presents only expenditures *net* of state property income.)
(2) Army and navy expenditures plus all hidden military expenditures. The figures for 1872–5 are taken from the *Statistisches Jahrbuch für das Deutsche Reich* (1880: 152–63). From 1876 on, the figures are from Witt. These are higher than those supplied by Gerloff because Witt uncovered various military items (from the Bundesarchiv rather than the *Jahrbuch*) that were 'hidden' in the civil budget (so as to give the appearance to the international community of a less militaristic Reich). Included here are the following items: military pensions, (purely) strategic railways, military expeditions to east and south-west Africa, the widening of the north-east canals, monies devoted to colonial troops, and all interest paid on loans taken out specifically for military purposes. These are all legitimate items for inclusion, with the possible exception of the interest on military loans, only because it is not standard practice in most national accounts to include this item (although ideally it should be). Nevertheless, because these interest payments would not make a significant difference to the overall defence figure, the data produced here would not overly exaggerate the actual Reich defence expenditures. The exception to this is with the 1872–5 figures, which Witt gives as RM 822 million (per annum). Witt included the

amount of money apportioned to the north German sinking fund, which constitutes approximately two-thirds of this sum. This considerably distorts the military expenditure figure. Therefore, we have used the *Statistisches Jahrbuch* figure instead for this four-year period only (and omitted the interest payments for 1872–5).

(3) These expenditures are *gross* (i.e., state property revenues have not been deducted). These were calculated by subtracting those civil expenditures presented in Gerloff that were included in Witt's military expenditure figure (which were originally presented in the civil budget in Gerloff). These are, therefore, lower than those presented by Gerloff. Civil expenditures are discussed below in more detail.

(4) Total expenditures expressed as a proportion of national income (i.e., net national product at factor cost). See appendix B for national income sources.

(5) Defence expenditures expressed as a proportion of NNP. It is worth noting that these figures differ from an earlier set produced by the author (John M. Hobson 1993). This is because the earlier estimates used the defence expenditures provided by Andic and Veverka (1964). These are clearly lower than those produced by Witt. Justification of Witt's data is provided above.

(6) Civil expenditures as a proportion of NNP.

Table 2.9: *Major expenditure categories as a proportion of Reich expenditures, 1872–1913*

Period	(1) Defence (gross)	(2) Civil (gross)	(3) Defence (net)	(4) Civil (net)
1872–5	38[a]	4[a]	98	2
1876–80	81	18	94	6
1881–5	59	40	95	5
1886–90	60	40	95	5
1891–5	57	43	94	6
1896–1900	45	55	91	9
1901–5	51	49	88	11
1906–10	54	46	89	11
1911–13	63	37	89	11

Sources and notes: [a] 1872–5: Gross figures do not add to 100 because the French indemnity payments have not been included in the individual categories, though they have been included in the total.

(1 and 2) Expenditures expressed as a percentage of *gross* total expenditures. Calculated from table 2.8.

(3 and 4) Expenditures expressed as a proportion of *net* total expenditures. Calculated from Witt (1970: 380).

account for the secular growth of government expenditures in this period. Given that the expenditure push in the 1880s played an important part in the tariff hikes in 1885 and 1887, it is therefore important to establish its composition.

Table 2.10 shows clearly that the administration of state property – government enterprises – was the main civil expenditure item, followed by general administration. Social welfare expenditures were a marginal item, comprising a mere 4.4 per cent of total gross expenditures from 1872 to 1913 (calculated from *Statistisches Jahrbuch für das Deutsche Reich* (1882: 154–7; 1892: 170–3; 1896: 157–9; 1900: 178–9; 1904: 218–9; 1908: 276–7; 1912: 339–41)), or 3 per cent, if we deduct military pensions, which Witt (1970: 380–1) correctly includes in the defence category. Equally as important is the fact that *net* civil expenditures comprised only a very minimal component of total expenditures (Gerloff 1929: 20). This is because the main civil expenditure item – state property – was offset by considerable state property revenues (as is made clear in the *Statistisches Jahrbücher*). Since state property expenditure increases paid for themselves, this item could not have stimulated new tax increases and therefore tariff rises. Indeed, Reich military expenditures comprise some 93 per cent of total net Reich expenditures in the 1872–1913 period, while civil expenditures comprise no more than 11 per cent (1901–13) (see table 2.9). In sum, taxation increases, and therefore the tariff, had a *military rather than civil core*.

Conclusion: moderate state capacity and protectionism

The traditional economistic argument assumes that the state responded to the *trading* needs of the agricultural Junker class when it raised grain tariffs in 1879, 1885, 1887 and 1902–6. However, this account exaggerates the power and centrality of class factors to the detriment of state–society, institutional, fiscal and geopolitical factors. In particular, the federal nature of the Reich ensured a reliance on indirect taxes and hence tariff protectionism. In addition, the Reich government was primarily interested in gaining 'fiscal sovereignty'; that is, fiscal autonomy from the *Länder*, which was achieved through tariff protectionism. This was complemented by geofiscal requirements after 1880, with the increase in the military budget. In addition, the state's

Table 2.10:   *Reich civil expenditures, 1901–1912*

Period	(1) Administrative (RMm)	(2) Administrative as % of total	(3) Social welfare (RMm)	(4) Social welfare as % of total	(5) State property (RMm)	(6) State property as % of total
1901–5	513	23	124	6	502	22
1906–10	393	14	142	5	687	24
1911–12	338	11	149	5	792	26

Source and notes: Statistisches Jahrbuch für das Deutsche Reich (1904: 218–19; 1908: 276–7; 1912: 339–41). Note that debt is not included. Although much of this went into paying off extraordinary military expenditures, some of it had a civil function. It is not possible to make the necessary breakdown. Nonetheless, the civil figure would be only very small. Note also that Gerloff does not provide a breakdown of the civil expenditures, and Witt understates civil expenditures because he uses only net expenditures. These figures differ marginally from those produced by Schremmer (1988: 476).
(1 and 2) This comprises: Bundesrat, Reichstag, Reich chancellery, treasury, foreign affairs and ministry of interior, as well as colonial and justice ministries.
(3 and 4) Invalid funds and pensions.
(5 and 6) Post, railways and telegraph.

partially embedded autonomy ensured that the state would rely on indirect taxes at the expense of a progressive tax regime. Fiscally privileging the dominant classes while undermining the working class was undoubtedly a factor in the state's shift to protectionism and indirect taxation.

In short, the weakness of the Reich government in terms of its institutional make-up and its specific relations with society, coupled with military expenditure requirements, led to the switch to protection and its subsequent deepening. The Second Reich was forged not simply through blood and iron, but perhaps more importantly on the backs of the poor on a more mundane fiscal diet of bread. It would tragically take the experience of defeat in the First World War and a subsequent revolution to prove that states cannot fiscally live by bread alone. This aspect of German Reich fiscal policy was not only reflective of a certain degree of weakness, but was a factor in undermining the state during and after the First World War (as discussed in chapter 7).

Protectionism and industrialisation in tsarist Russia: weak state capacity and indirect taxation

In the last chapter, the focus was specifically on tariffs and their linkages with the fiscal-military, political and economic objectives of the Reich government. In this chapter, the focus is broadened; we examine the development of not only tariff policy, but also industrialisation. As will become clear, this broadening is unavoidable, because tariffs were intimately connected with tsarist industrialisation. In the last chapter, the focus of my critique was on liberalism, and especially Marxism. In this chapter, my critique shifts to the theory of 'late development', espoused classically by Alexander Gerschenkron in his book, *Economic Backwardness in Historical Perspective* (1962). On first sight, this might seem surprising, given that Gerschenkron is widely perceived as one of the founding fathers of so-called 'statist' theory. However, as will become clear, my approach is almost as critical of Gerschenkron's 'statism' as it is of Marxism, neorealism and liberalism. My central critique of late development theory is that not only does it underestimate the state, but it also tends towards economism. I begin with a summary of late development theory, focusing not only on Gerschenkron, but also on the argument developed specifically for Russia by Theodore von Laue (1963), before developing a critique in subsequent sections.

The limits of economism: a critique of 'late development theory'

The 'Witte system' as economic

To understand late development theory's explanation of tariff protectionism, we need to begin by explaining the theory of late industrialisation, because tariff policy was conceptualised as a function of this process. It makes sense to begin with the Witte period (1892–1903), which was when Russian industrialisation supposedly received the critical boost through the specific policies of the Finance Ministry. In his classic conception of Finance Minister Sergei Witte's policies, von Laue assumes a perfect long-term economic rationality; so much so that he has defined these policies as the 'Witte system' (1963: 71). This 'system' was based upon Friedrich List's national system of political economy, which sought to found political power upon a broad industrialised base, the ultimate purpose of which was to 'catch up' with the first developers, particularly Britain.

The theory of 'late development' begins with the assumption that Russia (as well as Germany, Austria-Hungary and Italy) was backward in 1850, mainly because of a lack of an indigenous bourgeoisie (Russia being at the top of the 'backward' league table). Accordingly, the only way development could be achieved was for the state to intervene and 'substitute' for the lack of such a bourgeoisie, thereby acting as a 'surrogate entrepreneur' (Gerschenkron 1962: 119–42; 1970: 122–4). In short, the state would act as a substitute for a non-emergent bourgeoisie, and implement a long-term economic programme of full industrialisation. According to Gerschenkron, the tsarist state did this so successfully that after 1907 Russia was said to have entered an autonomous and self-sustaining period of development (cf. Rostow 1971: 87–8, 117; 1978: 427–8).[1] What did this 'forced industrialisation' comprise?

The 'Witte system' revolved around the immediate creation of a vast railway network. The railways would extend backwards promoting the growth of an indigenous iron and steel industry, as well as forwards, enabling the exploitation of the vast but idle resources of Russia which had lain dormant for so long (von Laue 1963: 76–9). Heavy industry would be enabled also through high protectionist tariffs, subsidies and guaranteed government contracts. Thus the first years of the 'Witte system' were summarised by von Laue (1963: 99) as:

(1) *Railroad construction + capitalism = industrialisation*

Furthermore, because of the paucity of domestic capital, foreign capital would be sought. This would be achieved through the stabilisation of the rouble, in turn enabled by going on to the gold standard. According to von Laue (1963: 113–14), conversion to gold revised the formula of the Witte system to read:

(2) *Railroad construction + capitalism + gold standard = rapid industrialisation*

This project would lead to an overall prosperity, for railway construction would provide the 'fly-wheel' by promoting heavy industry, which in turn would help the growth of light industry, finally leading to the stimulation of rural production and prosperity (von Laue 1963: 77). In particular, the whole project would be cemented in place through high regressive taxes (indirect taxes, including tariffs), known as the policy of 'forced savings'. This involved fiscally punishing rates of taxation levied on the peasantry and working class, the revenues of which would be channelled into industrialisation (Gerschenkron 1962: 17, 20, 124–7). In short, high indirect taxes would produce revenues for industrialisation.

Perhaps the central argument in Gerschenkron's model is his notion of the 'great spurt'. The great spurt in industrial growth rates that occurred in the 1890s was, he argues, the result of an intended industrial strategy enacted by Sergei Witte. And, as noted above, Gerschenkron claimed that this growth spurt laid the foundations for a second growth phase (1907–14), which was based on an autonomous consumer-based demand rather than state interventionism (1962: 44–6, 119–42, 353; 1970: 122–4). For late development theory, once the economy was up and running, the state's interventionist role would simply wither away.

In sum, the 'Witte system' as envisaged by late development theory embodies the central notion that the state consciously intervened in the economy in order to industrialise on a broad basis. Tariff protectionism was envisaged as a function of this specific economic project. A similar set of arguments is used to explain earlier bouts of protectionism, notably from 1877 to 1892. Thus successive finance ministers raised tariffs in order to protect domestic industry, especially heavy industry; and to generate a balance of payments surplus, in order to accumulate gold, which was required for converting the currency on to the gold standard, which was in turn a vital prerequisite for attracting foreign capital so as to achieve rapid industrialisation. In this account, therefore, protectionism (as well as state policy in general) has a fundamental *economic core*, designed specifically to promote long-term industrialisation.

There are five major critical points aimed at late development theory, all of which will provide the foundation for the alternative approach developed in this chapter. In general, late development theory:

(1) exaggerates the 'economic rationality' of the tsarist state, in so far as tsarism was influenced by fiscal and geopolitical objectives, which often cut across 'pure economic' imperatives – thus industrialisation was to an important extent the unintended consequence of the state's activities, as opposed to the rationally intended strategy assumed by Gerschenkron;

(2) exaggerates the far-sightedness of tsarist economic policy, since autocracy was preoccupied with short-term objectives;

(3) exaggerates the coherence of tsarist bureaucracy, where in fact the fragmented nature of the bureaucracy was fundamental to the construction of both protectionist and industrialisation policies (what I call 'centralised bureaucratic struggle'); in particular, Gerschenkron and von Laue assume that the Finance Ministry and the state were synonymous;

(4) misunderstands the nature of the tsarist state and its despotic desire for a 'partial' rather than a 'full' industrialisation; and

(5) underplays the importance of the inter-state military system and its impact on domestic state policy.

Perhaps the central irony is that Gerschenkron relies essentially on an *economistic* approach, to the detriment of specifically political, fiscal and geopolitical analysis. It might be objected that the late development model does actually recognise the importance of war and international politics.[2] I argue, however, that the state was motivated mainly, though by no means exclusively, by short-term fiscal-military objectives, the realisation of which unintentionally led to a 'partial industrialisation'. Seen from this angle, late development theory can be seen to ascribe too much economic rationality to state policy. The state was less inclined towards economic development per se than to shoring up its short-term fiscal-military requirements. In this sense, I perceive – popular appearances to the contrary – Gerschenkron's late development theory to have much in common with the liberal and Marxist perspectives, in that it exaggerates the economic rationality of the state. Indeed, there is, not surprisingly, a clear affinity between late development theory and Marxism. For example, Bob Jessop claims in characteristic Marxist fashion that strong capitalism as witnessed in the early developers will have weak minimalist states, while conversely weak capitalism as witnessed in late developers (e.g., Bismarckian Germany and autocratic Russia) will have strong interventionist states (Jessop 1978: 22; see also Wehler 1985; Berghahn 1973). Moreover, such an argument is found throughout much of the general social science literature, forming a remarkable point of agreement across different perspectives.

Through an ongoing critique, I shall provide an alternative socio-logical perspective to explain protectionism in particular and industria-lisation in general. I begin my analysis with an examination of the military developments that were so important in stimulating tsarist economic and tariff policies. There were principally two military factors that informed the post-1860 Russian industrialisation and protectionist era: the defeat in the Crimean War (1854–6) and the 'second military revolution'.

War and the drift to industrialisation and protectionism

The impact of the Crimean War

The crucial period to be discussed, 1860–1913, is immediately preceded by Russia's defeat in the Crimean War (1854–6). According to Gerschenkron, the Crimean defeat imparted a severe blow to the Russian state (1965: 708). It was the severity of this defeat that prompted the state to attempt to 'catch up' economically with the first industrialisers. The central question here is how severe was this defeat? More specifically, was this defeat severe enough to lead the state into a 'long-term forced development strategy'?

Most commentators agree that this defeat was not costly to Russia. Indeed the war's 'immediate effects upon Russia were slight, for it had to give up only the mouth of the Danube and a small strip of Bessarabia. It lost no additional land and did not have to pay an indemnity' (Curtiss 1979: 530). The small-scale nature of the war neither threatened the sovereignty nor presaged the collapse of the regime (Seton-Watson 1988: 330–1). The Russian state was bolstered by its geopolitical situation. It was still a huge power with a massive army, although there had been substantial losses. Crucially, its economic backwardness was not seen as a major obstacle to the military base of the state. Russia's large population obscured the real poverty of the economy. In general, Russia's overall size in both the economic and the geopolitical dimensions obscured the empire's underlying weakness.

It is interesting to compare this to the situation in Japan, whose sovereignty was threatened by Commodore Perry in 1853. Japan's reaction to this lay in stark contrast to Russia's Crimean defeat. Most authors concur that this was a moment of profound crisis for the Japanese, affecting the very sovereignty and legitimacy of the Tokugawa state. It led on to the Meiji Restoration in 1868, in which the Shogunate was finally toppled in a 'revolution from above'. The national crisis brought on by Perry's landing was exacerbated by the fact that Japan was a small island country. It was widely accepted in Japan that it would have to abandon its hitherto 'splendid isolation' from the world and develop rapidly if it was to remain a viable entity within the inter-state system. Thus, one of the main developments relevant to my discussion is that the Meiji state set about rapidly to implement a relatively broad-based industrialisation. The state underwent a radical transformation (the aforementioned Meiji Restoration in 1868), and sought to develop the economy (Trimberger 1978; Bendix 1978: 483). This was derived from the new popular axiom: *fukoku kyohei*, or 'rich country, strong army' (Weiss 1993: 333–7; Trimberger 1978: ch. 4; Weiss and Hobson 1995: 84–5).[3]

The irony was that, far from the Crimean defeat posing a threat to tsarism, the state was paradoxically able to use it to enhance its own political power base at the expense of the nobility. Unlike the Japanese state, tsarism did not turn to the 'rich country, strong army' strategy, largely because it felt that it did not have to. Instead tsarism enacted a minimalist economic response, preferring a 'partial' to a 'full' industrialisation. A partial industrialisation merely shored up the immediate military weaknesses of Russia that had become apparent in the Crimean War. In general, the main difference between a partial and a full industrialisation in this context was that the former was more the outcome of specific short-term military policies (i.e., economically unintended), while the latter was the result of an intended, long-term rational development plan (viz. Gerschenkron). However, to argue that the Russian state sought a partial industrialisation for military reasons only would be facile. In my analysis, the economic objectives of the Finance Ministry play *a* role but are, however, substantially downgraded in importance.

At this point it makes sense to differentiate between 'market-promoting strategies', where the state intentionally stimulates the development of the economy, and 'unplanned market influence', where the state follows its own autonomous fiscal-military and state-building activities, which unintentionally promote capitalism. In the latter situation, the economy 'drifts' forward (Michael Mann 1993: 298–9). Therefore, I argue that industrialisation and protectionism in Russia were stimulated mainly for short-term military purposes (i.e., unplanned market influence), but were also, though to a much lesser extent, informed by the long-term economically rational activities (i.e., market-promoting strategies) of the Finance Ministry. Overall, industrialisation and protectionism 'drifted' forward after 1860.

It is worth noting that this takes us to one of the central aspects of tsarist industrialisation: the tension and conflict between on the one hand the Finance Ministry, which was partly motivated by long-term economically rational policies, and on the other hand the Ministry of Interior, the War Ministry and, above all, tsarist autocracy, which favoured short-term military and political policies. Ultimately these political contradictions within the state structure were resolved in favour of autocracy, which restrained the economic reformism of the Finance Ministry. This 'centralised bureaucratic struggle' informed not only industrialisation, but also tariff protectionism (as we shall see shortly).

Why did tsarism not stimulate a full industrialisation? My answer is essentially threefold. Firstly, the state was not strong enough to do so. Secondly, above all, autocracy believed that it did not have to. Thirdly, autocracy (as opposed to the Finance Ministry) did not want to. The limited nature of the defeat enabled the state to maintain its despotic preferences. This meant that autocracy would seek to constrain industrialisation. Limiting industrialisation meant that no strong bourgeoisie or proletariat would emerge to challenge the despotism of the state. In addition, the peasantry was to be held back through the emancipation settlement (although, as we shall see, the state only partially succeeded in this respect). In one sense, therefore, it might be wrong to accredit the Russian state complete failure, since it never intended a full industrialisation in the first place.

If industrialisation was to an important extent the unintended consequence of the state's short-term fiscal-military policies enacted as a response to the Crimean War, what were the lessons of the defeat? They were fourfold:

(1) The state had only a very weak fiscal base.
(2) The state had only a very weak (and almost non-existent) communications/supply infrastructure in operation.

    (3)   The weapons used by the military were ineffective against those produced by the 'industrialised-war' economies of Britain and France.

    (4)   The rouble suffered war-induced bouts of depression.

After 1860, each of these four deficiencies would be resolved (though not entirely successfully) through a partial industrialisation, of which tariff protectionism formed an important component. Before we deal with each of these problems and its attempted resolution, we need to examine the second military factor that prompted a 'partial' industrialisation: the 'second military revolution'.

The second military revolution

The immediate origins of this phenomenon[4] were found with the Prussian military revolution of the 1860s, which soon produced what Disraeli termed 'the German revolution in European affairs' (cited in Paul Kennedy 1988: 184). Part of this revolution was founded upon the level of industrial attainment from which accrued certain military advantages. Prussia's strong iron and steel industries enabled it to supply an increasingly important set of armaments industries, naval shipyards and a network of strategic railways (McNeill 1982: 242–56). Superior supply capacity through railways, as well as more advanced weaponry, all founded on a strong administrative base, enabled Prussia's victory over France in 1871 (Howard 1976: 98–102; McNeill 1982: 262–306; Stone 1984: 72; Sen 1984; Michael Mann 1993: 495–9; Fuller 1985: 53–5). The Prussian way of war became the standard which all other great powers had to emulate. These revolutionary military developments had two specific effects upon the various national-economic policies of the great powers. Firstly, they led to a rapid increase in government expenditures (see figure 6.4 and appendix B, table B1); and, secondly, they had specific consequences for the industrial policies of these states. States sought to improve their military-industrial base, through what McNeill (1982) has aptly called the 'industrialisation of war'.

    This combined with the already acute problem of supply-logistics in Russia to provide a vital impetus for railway building and basic industrial development in order to satisfy the military exigencies of the Russian autocracy. It is in this context that we need to relate Russia's industrial policy from the 1860s onwards. Indeed, the impact of this revolution was exacerbated in Russia owing to the Crimean War legacy. Thus, the need for a military infrastructure together with the costs that this entailed had, certainly by the 1870s, led tsarism to shift its policies.

Late development theory assumes that tsarist government expenditures increased in the late nineteenth century, although these were said to be *economic* in origin. We need to begin, therefore, with an analysis of the origins of tsarist expenditures after 1860.

The military origins of tariff protectionism and industrialisation: the expenditure push

Why did tsarist government expenditures increase after 1860? As noted above, late development theory argues that Russian fiscal policy had a strong *economic* bias. As von Laue put it:

> How much the government spent for its various economic activities in these years may come as a surprise. Roughly totalled the appropriations for all economic ministries (finance, agriculture, communications) and the service of the government debt (contracted largely for railroad construction) amounted to over 52 per cent of the combined ordinary and extraordinary budgets in 1894 and 55 per cent in the following year. The army and navy combined claimed about half as much, nearly 29 per cent in 1894 but only 22.5 per cent in 1895. What was left went to the administrative agencies, the Ministry of Interior with its extensive organisation and its police, diplomatic service, schools and universities, the church, the courts of law, the Ministry of Justice and the Imperial household. Obviously the economy rather than defence was the beneficiary of Witte's financial management. (1963: 100–1; cf. Gerschenkron 1970: 102)

A subsequent revisionist swing has countered this by arguing that charges for debt repayments cannot be simply labelled as 'economically productive expenditure', because they were derived to a significant extent from extraordinary military expenditures. And though railways contributed to the growth of government debt, much of this was military-inspired. Thus Peter Gatrell has claimed that it 'would be idle to maintain that tsarist expenditure had a productive purpose' (Gatrell 1986: 221; cf. Kahan 1967: 461–6; Gregory 1982: 256; 1991: 73; Rogger 1983: 119; Seton-Watson 1952: 122; Feis 1930: 210; Crisp 1976: 97).

Table 3.1: *Russian gross central government expenditures, 1870–1913 (in Rb m)*

Period	(1) Gross total	(2) Gross civil	(3) Of which, gross economic	(4) Gross defence	(5) Debt
1870–4	583	307	194	187	89
1875–9	864	317	174	418	129
1880–4	808	316	153	257	236
1885–9	936	356	186	255	325
1890–4	1103	501	271	310	292
1895–9	1611	881	645	391	338
1900–4	2154	1273	825	584	298
1905–9	2854	1441	862	933	479
1910–13	2999	1768	1074	775	456

Source and notes: Calculated from Khromov (1950: 514–29).
(1) State property revenues have not been deducted.
(2) Includes: (a) *administration* – state council and higher government authorities, clergy/church, Ministry of Imperial Court, Ministry of Foreign Affairs, Ministry of Justice, Ministry of State Control, Administration of State Horses, Administration of Transcaucasia, Ministry of State Properties; (b) *civil* – Ministry of Education and Ministry of the Interior, as well as extraordinary expenditures on the harvest, food reserves and expenditures in China; and (c) the items in col. 3.
(3) This includes Ministry of Communications, Finance Ministry, State Credit, Administration of Ship and Port, Ministry of Trade and Industry, and Administration for Land and Agriculture. Note that after 1900 some 50 per cent of total Finance Ministry expenditures went on the liquor monopoly. These have not been included in this sub-total.
(4) Army and navy, plus all extraordinary expenditures.
(5) This has been included with its own heading, as is normal practice. For the origins of the debt, see discussion on p. 81.

However, there are two main problems here: firstly, both sides of the argument have variously interpreted what is actually to be included in the 'economic' and 'military' categories; and, secondly, confusion is exacerbated by von Laue's usage of *gross* economic expenditures as opposed to Kahan's use of *net* economic expenditures. In order to achieve closure in this debate, let us begin by analysing gross economic expenditures (which take in all economic expenditures and do not deduct state property revenues).

Tables 3.1 and 3.2 show that *gross economic* expenditures were not as significant as von Laue claimed, nor were they as low as various revisionists have argued. But more importantly, two further major sets

Table 3.2: *Major categories of Russian expenditures as a proportion of the total, 1870–1913*

Period	(1) Total civil	(2) Of which, economic	(3) Defence	(4) Debt	(5) Net civil	(6) Net defence
1870–4	53	33	32	15	29	48
1875–9	37	20	48	15	17	64
1880–4	39	19	32	29	12	46
1885–9	38	20	27	35	5	42
1890–4	45	25	28	26	12	45
1895–9	55	40	24	21	15	45
1900–4	59	38	27	14	9	59
1905–9	50	30	33	17	0	73
1910–13	59	36	26	15	0	86
Average (1870–1913)	51	32	30	19	9	59

Notes: Calculated from table 3.1. Note that *net civil* expenditures were calculated by deducting state property revenues. After 1905, these were so large that they outstripped all economic expenditures.

of revisions to these crude data are needed. Firstly, we need to take into account the fact that some of the debt interest payments should be apportioned to the 'military' rather than the 'economic' category, because a certain proportion of loans was taken out for defence spending. In addition, we need to take into account the fact that a proportion of railway expenditure went on defence (for strategic lines). The second major revision requires the calculation of *'net' rather than 'gross'* economic expenditures (as will be explained below).

My calculations suggest that in the 1870–1913 period, military loans comprised some 42 per cent of total extraordinary expenditures, while economic loans comprised some 35 per cent. Amending table 3.2, average *military* expenditures as a proportion of total expenditures would rise from 30 per cent to just over 38 per cent, while *economic* expenditures would rise from 32 per cent to 39 per cent of total expenditures, narrowing the gap only very marginally (although it should be noted that this significantly understates the military component of debt interest repayment, because most of the loans taken out prior to this period were military in origin).

The treatment of railways is extremely difficult because the identification of a railway line as either military or economic in origin is highly interpretative. It is, however, undoubtedly the case that a sizeable proportion of the Russian railway network was constructed with military motivations in mind. Indeed, Witte (1921) complained in his memoirs that a large proportion of railway expenditure was 'diverted' into the construction of (unproductive) military-strategic lines. It is unfortunately not possible to come to a reliable estimate of the proportion of lines that were military. However, guesstimating that 30 per cent of railways were strategic would swing the balance firmly in favour of military over economic expenditures as a proportion of all government expenditures (particularly if the debt interest repayments incurred through extraordinary railway expenditures were reapportioned along similar lines). This is because such a calculation would require subtracting 30 per cent of railway expenditures (a very considerable amount) from the 'economic category' and adding it to the 'military category'. It would be reasonable to conclude that defence-based expenditures (taken on a broad basis) comprised the major proportion of the tsarist budget, but that economic services, although less significant than von Laue claims, would still be more important than the revisionist argument assumes.

The second major revision requires an estimation of net rather than gross expenditures. This is because what primarily concerns us is ascertaining the actual nature (military or economic) of the *expenditure push* in the late nineteenth century, in order to derive the specific source (economic or military) which led to the increased taxes. This can be done only by estimating *net* civil and defence expenditures as a proportion of total net expenditures. This is because (as I noted in chapter 2) state property (SP) expenditures – which are included only in the 'economic' category – were funded not through taxes but through SP revenues (i.e., they financed themselves and therefore did not require the raising of new taxes). When deducting the revenues that the state properties brought in from the expenditures that they received, we are left with only a very modest sum. In short, SP expenditures – and therefore 'economic' expenditures (because they provide the vast majority of all economic expenditures) – could not have been responsible for taxation increases. On the basis of the revised calculations made in table 3.2 (cols. 5 and 6), it is clear once again that defence as a proportion of total expenditures clearly outweighs 'civil' spending. Thus, as Arcadius Kahan (1967) originally argued, the expenditure push in the 1870s was clearly based on military requirements, which intensified in the decades to 1913.

Table 3.3: *Real Russian central government expenditures (cge/NNP expressed in %), 1860–1913*

Period	(1) cge/NNP	(2) d2/NNP	(3) Gross eco2/NNP	(4) Net eco2/NNP
1860–4	(12.5)	(5.7)		
1865–9	(12.5)	(5.3)		
1870–4	(13.7)	(5.5)	(4.8)	2.7
1875–9	(17.8)	(9.9)	(3.9)	2.3
1880–4	(14.7)	(7.1)	(3.2)	1.2
1885–9	14.8	6.9	3.5	0.5
1890–4	15.9	7.2	4.2	1.2
1895–9	18.5	7.8	7.6	1.5
1900–4	18.8	7.7	7.2	0.8
1905–9	21.7	10.2	6.8	0
1910–13	17.5	7.0	6.4	0

Source and notes: National income data: See appendix B. Note that figures in parentheses are only extremely approximate, because of the crude estimates of national income for this period only.
(1) Central government expenditures as a proportion of national income.
(2) Represents ordinary plus extraordinary military expenditures plus debt interest and extraordinary debt payments apportioned on the basis that 42 per cent of all extraordinary expenditures were military in origin; ordinary and extraordinary expenditures on so-called 'strategic' railways, guesstimated to be about 30 per cent of all railway expenditures.
(3) Represents ordinary plus extraordinary economic expenditures (described in table 3.2). Also included are 20 per cent of all debt interest and extraordinary debt expenditures. The amounts on so-called 'strategic' railways have been deducted.
(4) As for col. 3, but with state property revenues deducted.

This argument is reinforced by a final set of calculations (see table 3.3, cols. 2 and 4). Ascertaining the increase and actual burden of government expenditures cannot be done by simply taking raw figures expressed in current or constant roubles (the basis of which all previous discussions on tsarist expenditures have been made), but must be done by calculating the 'real' burden (i.e., expenditures measured as a proportion of national income, or the cge/NNP ratio). Although this is not without its problems (discussed fully in appendix B), it is undoubtedly the least inferior method (Gavin Kennedy 1983: 36).

Table 3.3 (col. 1) shows that in real terms total tsarist government expenditures increased considerably after 1860, especially after 1875. On the basis of the discussion above, I have recalculated economic and military expenditures (hence 'd2' and 'eco2'). Although these figures are undoûbtedly crude, nevertheless they provide a clearer picture than previous discussions.[5] It is interesting to note that these military expenditures are extremely high – easily the highest in Europe.[6] Column 4 demonstrates that net economic expenditures were not responsible for the fiscal spurt, thereby reinforcing once again my conclusion that defence provided the foundation for the shift to indirect taxes and tariff protectionism.

Table 3.3 also makes clear that tsarist central government expenditures increased dramatically in real terms. This means that economic growth cannot explain such an increase (as I have factored out the effects of such growth by dividing these expenditures by national income). The question now becomes: what form did these new taxes take?

Weak state capacity in the shift to indirect taxation

After 1870, the mainstay of Russian central government revenues lay with indirect taxes and, though to a lesser extent, state property revenues.

I note in tables 3.4 and 3.5 that there is a certain arbitrariness in the treatment of these revenue categories, especially with regard to state property and indirect taxes. I have included the state liquor monopoly under excises, although others – following the Russian archival sources procedure – have included it in the SP category (e.g., Bogolepoff 1918: 333–9; Miller 1926: 129; Gorlin 1977: 249; Gatrell 1994: 150). Its inclusion under state property would have significantly increased its importance, and simultaneously have reduced the proportion of indirect taxes. This raises an important issue, because it has been argued in a major recent study of European finances in the late nineteenth century that states shifted over to state property revenues away from taxation, partly in order to conceal the fiscal burden to wary taxpayers, and partly to avoid the constraints of parliamentarism (Michael Mann 1993: 358–402). Certainly in Russia and Germany, there is a clear shift towards gross state property revenues, as the various tables in this book reveal. However, this argument is somewhat overstated for one main reason. To make the claim that states moved away from taxes and towards non-tax revenues (i.e., SP revenues), it must be shown that *net* SP revenues increased, because much of the SP revenues went simply to maintaining state property rather than substituting for

Table 3.4: *Russian central government revenue, ordinary and extraordinary, 1870–1913 (in Rb m)*

Period	(1) Net total	(2) Gross total	(3) Total indirect taxes	(4) Of which, customs	(5) Of which, excise	(6) Direct taxes	(7) Net state property	(8) Extra-ordin-ary
1870–4	452	592	256	52	204	74	51	71
1875–9	689	816	306	73	233	80	82	221
1880–4	652	796	360	94	266	72	107	114
1885–9	779	942	419	119	300	97	160	103
1890–4	899	1119	497	150	347	87	197	119
1895–9	1099	1564	674	199	475	94	226	104
1900–4	1274	2083	746	222	524	224	114	191
1905–9	1812	2793	983	254	730	193	159	477
1910–13	1983	3075	1261	327	934	243	468	11

Source and notes: Calculated from Khromov (1950: 494–529). Figures do not always add to the figures given in the total columns due to rounding.
(1 and 2) The table presents two totals, the gross total (col. 2) and the net total (col. 1) – that is, net of state property expenditures.
(3) Comprises cols. 4 and 5.
(4) Levied on foodstuffs, as well as semi-manufactures and finished manufactured goods (see table 3.6 for details).
(5) It is important to note that this includes the state spirit monopoly after 1894/5 (see pp. 84–5 for further discussion). These are levied principally on spirits, tobacco, cigarettes, sugar, petrol, salt (to 1886) and matches.
(6) This includes poll tax (to 1886), redemption payments, land and immovables, state industry (i.e., corporation tax) and tax from money capital.
(7) This includes mining, mint, post, telegraph and telephone, stamp duties, court dues, property transfer, goods and boats in port, passenger and cargo duties, fire insurance and state properties. To obtain net revenues, the following expenditures have been deducted: Ministry of Communications, Ministry of Finance, Ministry of State Properties and Ministry of State Control.
(8) This comprises mainly loans, but also includes interest from deposits in state banks, revenues from railway companies and repayment of loans, as well as treasury income.

taxation in the other areas of finance. In other words, only *net* SP revenues (i.e., those amounts available after meeting the running costs of government property) can substitute for taxes. The net revenues as shown above are not as significant as indirect taxes.

Nevertheless, especially given the arbitrary treatment of SP revenues undertaken in this study of Russian finances (because I apportion the liquor monopoly under excises), we can conclude that the mainstay of Russian central government finance in the late nineteenth and early

Table 3.5: *Major revenue categories as a proportion of Russian central government (net) ordinary income*

Period	Total indirect taxes (%)	Of which, customs (%)	Of which, excise (%)	Total direct taxes (%)	Net state property (%)
1870–4	67	14	54	19	13
1875–9	65	16	50	17	18
1880–4	67	17	49	13	20
1885–9	62	18	44	14	24
1890–4	64	19	44	11	25
1895–9	68	20	48	9	23
1900–4	69	20	48	21	11
1905–9	74	19	55	14	12
1910–13	64	17	47	12	24

Source and notes: Calculated from table 3.4; figures may not add to totals because of rounding. As with table 3.4, there is a certain arbitrariness in the construction of these categories. This is most problematic with the treatment of the liquor monopoly. This could be included in state property rather than under excise which would alter the balance in favour of SP.

twentieth centuries lies principally with indirect taxes (i.e., customs and excise), but also, though to a lesser extent, with state property revenues (see also figure 6.8). And rather than emphasise the difference in these categories, it is worth noting one main similarity: both forms of revenue constitute fiscal income *derived from regressive transactions*, as opposed to revenue derived progressively from income. The increasing importance of indirect taxes is matched by the rise in customs revenue – the direct outcome of the shift to tariff protectionism after 1877. Tables 3.4 and 3.5 demonstrate this clearly. According to table 3.5, therefore, calculated as a proportion of total net ordinary income, customs revenue began in 1870–4 at a low point of 14 per cent, rose steadily, peaking at 20 per cent (1895–1904), before dropping back to 17 per cent in the final years before the First World War. In contrast, direct taxes came down from 19 per cent (1870–4) to 9 per cent (1895–9), jumped up to 21 per cent (1900–4) as the corporation tax kicked in, but shrank back to 12 per cent of net revenues prior to the war. Nevertheless, in the main, direct taxes in Russia were regressive, particularly given the absence of an income tax. The other significant item is the use of loans, which varied from 32 per cent (1875–9) covering the Turkish war, to a low of 1 per cent (1910–13).

In sum, tsarism not only moved away from direct taxes (in contrast to Britain), but also, more significantly, failed to introduce an income tax, and relied heavily on regressive indirect taxes and tariffs as well as non-tax revenues (state property and loans). Many authors have observed this shift (e.g., Crisp 1976: 27; 1991: 257–8; Gerschenkron 1965: 781; Gatrell 1986: 218; Yaney 1973: 288–90; Robinson 1973), though few have proffered an explanation. It is important to examine the causes of the shift to indirect taxes, since this will help explain why tsarism shifted to tariff protectionism after 1877. It will be argued here that there was a network of overlapping multiple power logics involved in the shift to an indirect tax regime.

The various ingredients of tsarist state power added up to a profoundly weak state capacity, which had a particular impact on taxation policy. As discussed in chapters 6 and 7, a weak state capacity comprises the following ingredients:

(a)   high state autonomy,
(b)   low-moderate penetrative (infrastructural) power,
(c)   low degree of 'concentration', and
(d)   high degree of 'centralised bureaucratic struggle'.

Overall, tsarism suffered from a weak state capacity, though it enjoyed a high degree of concentration. This fundamentally affected tariff and taxation policy, as well as industrialisation more generally. I shall take each in turn.

High (isolated) state autonomy

An important aspect of tsarism's weakness, which in turn had ramifications for tariff and taxation policy, was its high level of state autonomy, accrued through the state's distance from society. Ironically, in pursuing high autonomy and despotic power, tsarism was fundamentally weakened, having no real base in society, cut adrift to wander aimlessly, seeking for the most part merely to repress society. This strategy of repression occurred in all areas of government policy. Consistent with this gamut of repressive policies, tsarism chose to punish the lower income orders through highly regressive taxation – hence indirect taxes and tariffs. After the 1861 emancipation of the serfs, successive finance ministers increased the rate of fiscal extraction from the lower classes. In the 1890s, Witte intensified this trend, increasing the tax rate by over 40 per cent above the already high 1885 level (Kahan 1967: 462–4). The Russian tax regime was by far the most regressive of any in Europe. Indirect taxes averaged over 7.1 per cent of national income (two and three times the rate of its authoritarian and liberal counterparts, respectively Germany, Britain and the United States).

In terms of the incidence of taxation, it is likely that the peasantry were to some extent able to substitute non-taxed goods for those which were subject to high tariffs and excises (Crisp 1991: 257–8; see also 1976: 31). The peasantry could minimise their indirect tax payments by substituting non-taxed goods (for example, honey was used to avoid the sugar tax, and consumers often brewed their own alcohol to avoid the vodka tax). This means that much of the very high tax burden must have fallen on the shoulders of the proletariat in the cities.[7]

Thus, just as the state had enacted repressive labour policies, so it similarly levied highly regressive taxes, penalising the peasantry and above all the urban proletariat. No progressive income tax was forthcoming in such a political climate. Nevertheless, it would be incorrect to explain the regressive indirect mode of taxation simply through emphasising the *form* of state (i.e., autocracy) and its will to repress the lower orders. At this point we need to broaden the discussion and analyse the 'capacity' of the Russian state, which was based on a number of modes of state power.

Low-moderate state penetrative power

The second aspect of Russia's weak state capacity is its low-moderate penetrative power. It is essential to have a relatively high degree of infrastructural penetrative power in order to be able to collect a personal income tax (Levi 1988; Ardant 1975; Michael Mann 1993; Snider 1987). In Russia, the state's penetrative power was not sufficient to allow the collection of an income tax (unlike in Britain), thus making indirect taxes and non-tax revenues somewhat inevitable. Nevertheless, the introduction of an income tax was discussed after 1900. Its passage was, however, blocked by the interventions of various ministries, especially agriculture, and trade and industry (Gorlin 1977: 253–65). In short, 'centralised bureaucratic struggle' was an important factor not only in the shift to indirect taxes (as noted below, pp. 89–91), but also in the blocking of the income tax. Even so, when an income tax was finally introduced in 1916 under the extreme pressures of war, its yield was pitifully low (see chapter 7).

High degree of concentration

The degree of state concentration is highly significant in the development of protectionist policies. In general, states with low concentration – federalism – tended in the nineteenth century to rely overwhelmingly on indirect taxes, and hence tariffs (see chapters 5 and 6). States that have a high concentration have the luxury of being able to choose any fiscal mix, whether this be based on direct or indirect taxes, or even non-tax revenues. The Russian state, although it had a high concentration, chose to rely on indirect rather than direct taxes (and hence protectionism) because of its overall incapacity. That is, its high or isolated autonomy, its low-moderate penetrative power and (as we shall see below) its high degree of 'centralised political struggle, led it to rely on indirect taxation.

High degree of 'centralised bureaucratic struggle'

'Centralised bureaucratic struggle', which had major ramifications not only for tariff policy but for industrialisation in general, was a function of Russia's patrimonial state (to be examined in more detail below, pp. 107–12). This was also a major source of the state's weakness and incoherence. Of specific interest here was the administrative struggle between the Ministry of Interior (MVD) and the Finance Ministry (FM), which informed not only the industrialisation process, but in particular the shift to an indirect mode of taxation.

From a historical perspective, it was perhaps inevitable that the FM would attempt to take over many of the economic functions of the MVD (as the MVD had enjoyed hold over various economic functions in the first half of the nineteenth century since its inception in 1802). As the industrialisation process advanced, the FM's challenge intensified. Conflict became overt between these two ministries, occurring in a number of areas, most notably labour policy (McDaniel 1988), and also in the area of taxation. To an important extent, the administrative prestige of the MVD in the bureaucracy was founded upon its role vis-à-vis the *obshchina* (the village commune or *mir*). Indeed, the *obshchina* was initially created to a large degree by the MVD (Emmons 1968: 209–318; Yaney 1973; Field 1976: 173–232; Orlovsky 1981: 61–2), largely for fiscal reasons (Gerschenkron 1965; Gregory 1991; Rieber 1966, 1982). The MVD would be responsible for both policing and directly collecting the communes' taxes. This hold over the affairs of the communes enhanced the prestige and power of the MVD within the bureaucracy. It is worth pointing out, too, that the manner in which the noble dominant class was stripped by the state of its economic power through the emancipation considerably enhanced the prestige of the MVD.[8]

It was clear, therefore, that if the Finance Ministry wished to increase its power over the MVD, its main rival, it would need to undermine the latter's source of power – that is, its role as tax collector in the *obshchina*.[9] This could be accomplished by reducing the redemption payments to such a level that the MVD's fiscal role would be reduced. What better way to ensure this than by replacing direct with indirect taxes? As Gerschenkron pointed out 'the shift to indirect taxes that was taking place inevitably reduced the role of the police [MVD] in matters of tax collection' (1965: 781). Not only did this directly undermine the administrative role of the MVD, but it was also forced to concede to the FM's desire to be involved in rural tax collection. Thus the FM used specific increases in excise taxes and tariffs as a political power tool with which to force concessions from the MVD.

This political strategy was begun by Finance Minister N. Kh. Bunge, with the increase in tariffs in 1885 at a time when redemption arrears were beginning to spiral upwards. Having forced the MVD's hand, the FM was able to create an institution of tax inspectors in 1885. From 1885 onwards, there was a tax inspector from the FM in each *uezd* (tax district) to check up on financial operations, much to the disgust of the MVD (Gerschenkron 1965: 781; Yaney 1973: 364). Then in 1891, Vyshnegradsky's New Mendeleyev tariff increased the size of the indirect tax base, again forcing the MVD to cooperate further with the FM in rural tax collection. In 1903, an increase in the tariff and indirect taxes enabled the FM's inspectors to assume additional responsibilities in tax collection. Finally by 1905 the elected village tax-collector, formerly subordinated to the MVD, came under the effective jurisdiction of the FM (von Laue 1963: 176; Yaney 1973: 364). In sum, the specifically political struggle between the FM and MVD played an important part in the shift to an indirect mode of taxation.

Finally, it is important to note that the weakness of the economy and low personal income levels ensured the continuance of indirect taxes as opposed to progressive income taxation. It is an important part of this chapter's argument that Russia's weak economy was inextricably entwined with the despotic nature and weakness of state power (see also Weiss and Hobson 1995: 93–112, 127–9). The high degree of isolated (weak) state autonomy meant not only regressive taxes, which punished the majority of the population, but also the stifling of *widespread and strong* economic development (see chapter 7).

In conclusion, the weakness of the economy, the limited yield of current direct taxes, the moderate level of state infrastructural/penetrative power, the high degree of centralised bureaucratic struggle and the state's patrimonial/autocratic nature ensured Russia's move to an indirect tax regime. Because tariffs were a principal form of indirect tax, I have in this section traced the political causes of the 'switch to protection'.

The fiscal-military origins of tariff protectionism, 1877–1913

In previous sections, we have examined the fiscal and expenditure causes of the state's shift to indirect taxes. In this section I seek to develop the linkage between state–society relations, geopolitics, indirect taxes and tariff protectionism. I argue that tariff protectionism served four main objectives (listed in order of their importance):

(1) to provide revenues for the state to meet its higher expenditures (which were mainly military in origin);
(2) to shore up the financial base of the economy, in order to attract not just foreign investors, but also foreign lenders in times of war and for peacetime military spending;
(3) to enable the state to divide and rule the capitalist class; and
(4) to provide protection for the defence industry.

The following sections take each of these in turn.

Geofiscal requirements and tariff protectionism

As in Germany, Italy, Austria and Canada, fiscal crisis emerged in Russia by the end of the 1870s. I noted in previous sections that this was due firstly to the sudden rise in military expenditures associated with the Turkish war (1877–8), as well as various fiscal problems, most notably the drying up of direct tax revenues. According to the data produced in table 3.3, government expenditures in the late 1870s had risen by no less than 142 per cent over the 1860s, all of which was derived from military expenditures. I also noted the state's response – notably the shift to indirect taxation. This was manifested in Finance Minister Reutern's decision to increase tariffs in 1877. This was achieved principally through changing the method of payment of customs at the ports, from paper roubles (whose value had diminished) to gold specie, in order to maximise customs revenue. Its actual effect was to raise the real tariff rate by between 30 and 50 per cent (Hoffding 1912: 76–7; Sobolev 1918: 307). Thus, as in Germany, Italy, Canada and Austria, tariff rates were effectively increased in the late 1870s to meet taxation requirements, in order to stave off fiscal crisis (though prompted by the war with Turkey in the Russian case). And although expenditures were stable in the 1880s, they remained consistently higher than in the prewar period. All this required higher tariffs.

Accordingly, to boost revenue, tariffs on manufactured goods were raised in 1881 (by 10 per cent), in 1884 (by 10 per cent) and again in 1885 when duties were raised on 168 items, involving a further 20 per cent increase. In 1887, the duty was raised again on many important goods (such as pig iron, steel, coal and coke), with a further hike of some 20 per cent in 1890, followed by the 1891 'New Mendeleyev' tariff. After 1900, government expenditures reached a peak due to the Chinese and Japanese conflicts. Thus, in 1901, tariffs were increased further. These were known as the 'Chinese duties' because they were introduced in order to meet the expenses specifically arising from the Chinese conflict (Hoffding 1912: 80). This was followed by the next major revision of the tariff upwards in 1903, by which time average tariff rates were just below 40 per cent (Hoffding 1912: 76–8).

I noted above that military expenditures and defence-associated expenditures provided the base of the government expenditure spurt in the late nineteenth century (see especially tables 3.2 and 3.3). Indeed, throughout the post-1877 period, this geofiscal rationale remained an important aspect of tsarist tariff policy (Hoffding 1912; Seton-Watson 1952: 119–21; Kahan 1967: 470–7; Crisp 1976: 27, 29–31; Gatrell 1986: 166–7; Gregory 1991: 74). This was reflected in the growing share of customs revenue in total tax revenue (see tables 3.4 and 3.5). Perhaps the most lucrative targets (or victims) of customs taxation were raw materials and semi-manufactures (as well as food). As table 3.6 shows, the reason for this was not hard to find. Raw materials and semi-manufactured imports comprised between 50 per cent and 67 per cent of total imports after 1900 (Miller 1926: 76; Khromov 1950: 476–9), and proved to be fiscally lucrative.

Table 3.6: *The significant tariff revenue-yielding items in Russia, c. 1900*

Item	% of total	Yield (Rb m)
Tea	15.0	44.4
Raw cotton	12.0	35.4
Machines and parts	10.6	31.5
Herring	3.9	11.4
Unworked metals	3.7	11.0
Wool and down	2.2	6.3
Woollen manufactures	2.0	5.9
Coke and coal	2.0	5.8
Chemicals	2.0	5.8
Oranges and lemons	1.9	5.6
Iron and steel manufactures	1.8	5.3
Combed wool	1.8	5.3

Source: Miller (1926: 71).

The importance of industrial inputs (raw materials and semi-manufactures) in the customs revenue is revealed particularly in table 3.6, while their rates are charted in table 3.7. While German Reich customs revenues were substantially based on a fiscal diet of bread, in Russia, food and industrial inputs were selected.

Standard trade theory assumes an economic rationale to tariff policy. States are assumed to levy high tariffs on finished products and levy much lower rates on raw materials and semi-manufactures, so as not to raise the costs of production for the domestic producers. Table 3.7 demonstrates this assumption to be problematic in the Russian case. While an important reason for this lay with the fiscal requirements of the state, there was a further political rationale: namely the autocracy's desire to divide and rule the capitalist class (to be discussed in detail in subsequent sections).

It may be objected, however, that surely it is a well-established principle of public finance that the way of extracting the largest possible proceeds from tariff duties is to tax at a moderate rate a few articles of general consumption (as happened in Switzerland, as well as in Britain after 1846). Why Russia did not follow this 'Swiss' path is shown by the following characteristic quotation from a memorandum presented in 1882 to the Imperial Council, by Finance Minister Bunge:

> the revision of certain clauses of the tariff arises from the need of strengthening the resources of the Imperial treasury. A higher

93

Table 3.7: *Russian customs duties, 1855–1912 (in %)*

Period	Food-stuffs	Raw materials, semi-manufactures	Manufactured goods	All items
1855–9	36.8	7.5	23.2	20.9
1860–4	31.9	7.0	18.2	18.4
1865–9	33.1	8.2	9.9	14.6
1870–4	28.1	8.3	11.6	10.1
1875–9	32.5	9.7	14.9	14.6
1880–4	32.4	11.7	18.6	18.0
1885–9	56.7	16.5	28.4	28.2
1890	59.6	18.3	26.0	28.7
1891	64.5	20.5	30.1	31.9
1892	68.8	22.4	27.7	33.1
1893	62.3	20.6	28.1	31.9
1894	63.2	23.2	24.6	30.4
1895	63.9	24.5	24.1	31.9
1896	65.0	25.8	24.7	32.1
1897	67.8	29.5	26.5	35.2
1898	69.4	31.8	25.8	36.2
1899	68.8	28.8	25.6	34.1
1900	81.0	25.0	25.0	33.0
1901	92.0	32.0	27.0	36.9
1902	96.0	31.0	28.0	40.0
1903	89.0	30.0	26.0	38.0
1904	91.0	28.0	26.0	37.0
1905	95.0	27.0	26.0	38.0
1906	91.0	25.0	29.0	38.0
1907	76.0	25.0	30.0	35.0
1908	69.0	27.0	29.0	35.0
1909	75.0	24.0	26.0	33.0
1910	77.0	22.0	26.0	30.0
1911	69.0	23.0	26.0	30.0
1912	67.0	22.0	27.0	30.0

Sources: 1855–99: Khromov (1950: 484–5), 1900–9: Hoffding (1912: 86); 1909–12: Miller (1926: 71); Gatrell (1986: 167); 1901 (all items): derived by calculating customs revenue as a percentage of total imports; data taken from Khromov (1950).

customs revenue can in some cases be secured by a lowering of the tariff rates, if an increase in consumption can be expected; whereas in other cases it may be secured by a moderate rise in the duties if an increase in consumption is not to be expected, but it can yet be assumed that the trade can bear the higher duty.

(cited in Hoffding 1912: 83)

Clearly Bunge preferred the second method since, as he went on to argue,

> a lowering of the tariff rate promises an increase of the customs revenue only in the more or less distant future and on the condition of a sufficiently high standard of material well-being in the population. But the present condition of the Treasury cannot be improved by an increase of revenue which is only to be expected some years hence, and the great mass of our people are not so well off that the increase of consumption could make up for the lowering of duties. It appears, therefore, necessary to have recourse to the increase of duties only providing that this increase should not make the duty of all articles inaccessible to the people and diminish the consumption.
>
> (cited in Hoffding 1912: 84)

This reasoning was endorsed by many European finance ministers. This was because states operate fiscally with regard to short- or very short-run calculations. Moreover, since Europe had undergone a period of free trade from 1860 to the late 1870s, it was fiscally profitable for these states to raise tariffs even to a considerable degree (since the tariff rates began from a very low base). The application of tariffs on the flood of imports proved to be fiscally lucrative. Thus, in sum, the first objective of tariffs was their fiscal yield, which, as we have seen in earlier sections, was destined mainly to fund the military ambitions of the tsarist state.

Exhaustion of current forms of taxation

In addition to the weakness of the state, indirect taxes were promoted in part because current sources of (regressive) direct tax revenue were drying up. After 1861, part of the fiscal obligation that the peasants incurred in the *obshchina* was the payment (known as the 'redemption payment') of the state for the land passed on in the 1861 emancipation. This 49-year 'mortgage' proved to be a thorn in the side of the authorities, since large arrears rapidly developed. From 1876 to 1880, tax arrears for the country as a whole amounted to 22 per cent of the budgeted revenue from direct taxes (Gerschenkron 1965: 768; Rogger 1983: 77; cf. Robinson 1973: 95), though this figure obscures the massive regional disparities (Gatrell 1986: 197, 267; Robinson 1973: 95–6). The government's response was to write off much of the arrears at various intervals (e.g., Tsar Alexander III in 1881 reduced the redemption debt by about 10 per cent of the arrears – 27 per cent of average annual payments – as a sign of goodwill) (Gatrell 1986: 196), with a further reduction in 1884 (Gerschenkron 1965: 769; Rogger 1983: 77). Despite various write-offs and reductions, by 1900 the accumulation of arrears stood at a massive 119 per cent of the average annual assessment for 1896–1900, and rose to 138 per cent by 1903 (Robinson 1973: 96). This led to the formal abolition of the debt in 1905.

Russian, and indeed general, historians have traditionally assumed that these problems were a function of high taxes and peasant poverty (Gerschenkron 1962: 125–7, 130; 1968: 230; Robinson 1973: ch. 6; Volin 1970; Kochan 1966; von Laue 1963). But as Simms (1977) points out, Russian general taxes were rising, which was a reflection of higher peasant income, and peasants were managing to retain a surplus *after* paying their taxes (see also Crisp 1976: 27–8; 1991: 257; Gregory 1991: 71). If the peasants were so impoverished, how can we explain the fact that by 1916 the peasantry possessed 80 per cent of the land, including half of what the gentry had retained in 1861? The real reason for the redemption payment arrears lies not with peasant poverty, but rather with peasant resentment at having to pay for something which they believed was rightfully theirs (Crisp 1991: 257). This finding is important to my argument, not least because it means that the state was able to substitute indirect taxes for redemption payments and 'direct taxes', and in the process increase tax receipts (otherwise there would be no point in shifting to indirect taxes). In short, a rising peasant and proletarian income (however small) provided an important base for the switch to indirect taxes.

In sum, the capacity of the redemption payments to produce arrears was greater than that of any other 'tax', and in addition, it cost about five times more to collect than any other tax, though it produced only 6.4 per cent of the total net tax revenue (Gerschenkron 1965: 780). As direct taxation was proving to be ineffective, the Finance Ministry's first prerogative was to find a more lucrative source of revenue. The vast increase in imports meant that tariffs could provide an efficient and effective source of revenue since they were far less expensive to administer. The second major reason for the move to indirect taxation was its superior fiscal yield to current sources of taxation.

The financial-military origins of tariff protectionism, 1877–1913

The second major function of tariff protectionism was financial: to stabilise and convert the rouble on to the gold standard. In fact, to a large extent these two aspects – the fiscal and the financial – cannot be treated in isolation from each other, given also that they were linked by military considerations.

As noted above, one of the major reasons for the Crimean defeat was the financial weakness of the Russian state. This merely reinforced what had become a historical precedent in Russia: the excessive reliance on borrowing and printing paper money in times of war (Crisp 1953: 156; Pintner 1959: 85; 1967: 184; Miller 1926: 117). Printing paper money led to inflation and the undermining of the rouble. This not only contributed to the Crimean defeat (Paul Kennedy 1988: 176; Seton-Watson 1988: 248; Pintner 1959: 85–7), but also repelled potential foreign investors, and above all foreign creditors who might buy up tsarist treasury bonds, all of whom would naturally fear a vulnerable rouble. The lesson of the Crimean War was clear: 'the extension of tsarist international commitments thus seemed to emphasise the vulnerable and unstable financial health of the country' (Gatrell 1986: 209, see also 215; cf. Crisp 1953: 156–7; 1976: 155; Kipp 1975: 442–4). Thus, the state was faced with a dual problem. Firstly, the devaluation of the rouble through wars jeopardised the potential of the state to maintain itself in future conflicts. Secondly, in the Russian case, warfare had various negative linkages with the economy, by undermining the currency and reducing the pool (potential and actual) of credit available for economic development either from abroad or at home.

The problems of monetary devaluation engendered by tsarist military adventures informed the monetary policy agendas for all post-1860 finance ministers. Thus Reutern set about restoring the currency by building up a gold reserve, enabled through tariff protectionism.[10] But just as he was winning his battle vis-à-vis the currency, his work was undone by the war with Turkey. Unfortunately for Reutern, 'power politics took precedence over financial [economic] soundness' (von Laue 1963: 17), and in the space of just three months at the end of 1876, the value of the rouble fell by almost 10 per cent. As a result of the massive increase in the circulation of notes (Crisp 1953: 156; von Laue 1963: 80), the rouble's value had fallen by a third by 1879 (Gatrell 1986: 215; Miller 1926: 117). In 1877, Reutern had decreed that all payments of customs duties be collected in gold. This would increase the revenue collected at the ports of entry (as already discussed), as well as enable the treasury to increase its gold reserve. In this, Reutern set a precedent, in that all subsequent finance ministers would use the tariff as the prime weapon in their fight for monetary stability. Nevertheless, it was too little too late to save Reutern's economic policies.

Reutern's successor, N. Kh. Bunge, enjoyed initial success in stabilising the rouble, also using tariff increases as a central weapon in monetary policy. However, his monetary policy was also undone by the military activities of the state with his last year ending little short of disaster. The government's financial condition, already strained by annual deficits, was further weakened by tension over Afghanistan, thereby endangering Russian bonds on the London stock market, and then exacerbated by the formidable Bulgarian crisis. In addition, the danger of war with Austria-Hungary called for an increase in Russian armaments which Bunge's budgets simply could not sustain. With the subsequent military campaigns in central Asia (1882–4) and the Bulgarian crisis of 1886, the paper rouble sank to an all-time low; Bunge's 'broader policies of economic development could not be satisfied in the face of rampant military costs and inadequate revenues' (Trebilcock 1981: 226). In short, Bunge's hands were tied by the autocracy's geopolitical ambition both to maintain an army and to compete in the international military arena in the manner worthy of a great power. 'No straining at the bootstraps could raise Russia above her backwardness, particularly if her government became involved in costly military expenditures' (von Laue 1963: 23).

Bunge's successor, Vyshnegradsky, was even more single-minded in his pursuit of fiscal and monetary stability, of which the tariff was again a central component. Indeed, the tariff, through creating a positive balance of payments, brought gold into the country (Lyashchenko 1970: 561). Vyshnegradsky instigated the Mendeleyev tariff of 1891, which secured a general level of protection of 32 per cent ad valorem. In addition, Vyshnegradsky set about the collection of tax arrears from peasants, which had the effect of forcing them to market their grain (Crisp 1953: 160). The tariff was successful in achieving surpluses on the balance of trade, which averaged 311.2 million gold roubles annually between 1887 and 1891, compared to a mere 68m between 1882 and 1886 (Crisp 1953: 161; see also Gregory 1982: 314). Vyshnegradsky managed to increase revenues considerably, mainly from indirect taxation, state-owned railways and crown lands and forests (Crisp 1953: 161; Trebilcock 1981: 228; Lyashchenko 1970: 561; see table 3.4), which also improved his ability to purchase gold bills from abroad. However, he did little for the economy in other spheres. Hardly any state funds were ploughed back into the national economy for a future increased yield. In general, 'it was a policy concerned with budgetary indicators rather than productive power, maximising the extraction of current resources rather than the creation of new ones' (Trebilcock 1981: 228; cf. von Laue 1963: 25).

Vyshnegradsky was succeeded in 1892 by Sergei Iu. Witte, on whose ministry the late development account places so much emphasis. Contrary to the late development analysis, however, Witte's industrialisation programme was subject to the same fiscal-military constraints and imperatives that his predecessors had faced. The move to convert the currency on to gold was no different. Von Laue and Gerschenkron have argued that Witte adopted the gold standard to stabilise the currency in order to attract foreign capital, in turn to promote rapid industrialisation. However, this was only a part of Witte's intention. As we have seen, the principal problem for finance ministers throughout the nineteenth century was the acquisition of foreign loans required to wage war.

Witte, perhaps more than his predecessors, was only too aware of the destructive effects that war had placed upon the economy, having witnessed the demise of Reutern's and Bunge's policies before him. In his memoirs, Witte wrote:

> As we had lived under the regime of paper currency since the Crimean War the very notion of metallic currency had become obscured in the press and in the minds of educated people generally. We had grown accustomed to paper currency as one gets used to chronic disease in spite of the fact that gradually it ruins the economy ... The economic wealth and consequently the political strength of a country depends upon three factors: natural resources, capital and labour, physical and intellectual. In capital ... [Russia] is poor for the reason that the history of the country is a continuous chain of wars. (1921: 59; see also p. 72)

So clear were the deleterious effects of war upon the economy to Witte that he was led to put aside approximately Rb 400 million in free cash reserves in case of emergency, which 'was prompted by the feeling that never left me after the ascension of Emperor Nicholas to the throne that sooner or later a bloody drama would be staged in this or that part of the country' (Witte 1921: 78). Stabilising the rouble and going on to the gold standard was vital for security reasons. Indeed,

> the major advantage of the possession of a gold reserve is an element of power within a country. It is a guarantee of solvency in arranging

> for loans and affords the possibility of reverting to a paper currency
> during a time of financial pressure, for example in war.
>
> (Drage, cited in Miller 1926: 107)

The importance of foreign loans in funding government expenditures is revealed by the fact that, between 1885 and 1900, the proportion of public debt held by foreigners was a considerable 58 per cent, and a still significant 52 per cent in the 1901–13 period. There was also a further budgetary factor involved leading to the need for foreign loans. Witte had carefully manipulated the budget so that he could ostensibly present a fiscal surplus (important to maintain business confidence). This was done by simply switching major expenditures from the ordinary to the extraordinary account. Because the extraordinary account was funded mainly by foreign loans, it was vital to appease foreign lenders.

That military requisites played an important role in Witte's move to gold is reflected in his memoirs, in which he stated that

> the establishment of the gold standard definitely established Russia's
> credit and put her financially on an equal footing with the other
> European powers. Owing to it we weathered the Japanese war and
> the subsequent revolutionary movement. Without it, economic and
> financial collapse would have occurred at the beginning of the war
> and all the economic achievements of recent decades would have
> been annihilated.   (1921: 59; see also p. 78)

The establishment of the gold standard was clearly appreciated by Tsar Nicholas II. He praised Witte for 'strengthening the country's power and defence, and the prosperity of the state'. Addressing Witte directly, the tsar stated, 'You solidified the independence and stability of the currency, increased the resources of the Treasury [and] the demands of the growing [military] budget' (1 January 1903, cited in Witte 1921: 78).

This fiscal-military function of the gold standard complemented the additional need to attract foreign capital (as indeed late development theory contends). The fluctuations in the rouble prior to conversion in 1897 had undoubtedly hindered commercial transactions with foreign companies. On the attainment of the gold standard and with the arrest of monetary fluctuations, 226 foreign companies immediately set up in Russia, although this was in part premised on a range of other factors.[11]

In sum, the gold standard was adopted for a variety of reasons: commercial viability, the desire for foreign capital and, perhaps most importantly, for the politico-military reason of securing loans for both peacetime and wartime military expenditures. This was the end to which tariff protectionist policies were aimed. From Bunge's term in office through to Witte, exports were increased and imports curtailed. Indeed, tariff policy was successful in achieving a positive balance of trade, in turn increasing Russia's gold reserve, enabling gold conversion in 1897.

Dividing and ruling the bourgeoisie through protectionism

In standard trade theory, from Marxism to liberalism through to late development theory, the assumption is that states raise tariffs primarily to protect the profits and market share of domestic national producers. In the context of tsarist Russia, this argument is highly problematic. This is because the tariff was used as a weapon of autocratic 'divide and rule' policy, which was wielded specifically against the capitalist class (Rieber 1982: 105, 106–11). Peter Gatrell has recently described tsarist tariff policy as 'highly selective' (1994: 167). Another description might be 'schizophrenic'. Parts of industry did well out of protectionism, while others fared badly. As I noted above, the problem was that in many instances tariffs were levied on raw materials and semi-manufactured goods (i.e., manufacturing inputs) partly in order to enhance government revenue. As a result, Russian producers of finished manufactures often found that their products were becoming uncompetitive internationally and domestically, because they were having to pay such high input prices on raw materials and semi-manufactures due to the high tariffs applied by the state (Hoffding 1912: 81; Sobolev 1918: 308–9; Kahan 1967: 470–1; Crisp 1976: 29–30; Gatrell 1986: 167). On many occasions, Russian producers actually suffered *negative* protection. In particular, from 1895 onwards, there were many occasions where raw materials and semi-manufactured goods actually incurred a higher duty than the finished product. Between 1895 and 1912, Russian inputs – raw materials and semi-manufactures – were tariffed at an average 26.7 per cent, compared in 1912 to 3 per cent in Germany and 0.1 per cent in Britain (Sobolev 1918: 309). This was particularly onerous for Russian industry, because the cost of raw materials was far and away the major cost input. For example, raw materials comprised 65 per cent of the cost of production for the textile industry, 43 per cent for the metal industry and 62 per cent for the food industry (Varzar 1918: 123).

Tariff policy significantly increased the costs of manufacturing, particularly in the Baltic and Polish regions (Crisp 1976: 30). The higher raw materials prices certainly hit the native *Kustar* industry.[12] Fiscal duties were also placed on complex machinery, an industry which would not develop for the foreseeable future (Crisp 1976: 30). Much of the revenue from customs was derived from cotton imports (yielding 20 per cent of revenue in 1912). The tariffs on raw cotton and machinery increased the price of Russian cotton fabrics, despite productivity improvements (Crisp 1976: 30). The capital goods industry was similarly adversely affected (Savin 1918: 207–10; Kahan 1967: 470; Gatrell 1994: 52, 167). The tariff was a major factor in the increase in iron and steel prices – the major manufacturing input. Prior to 1914, the iron and steel tariff raised the cost of inputs per *pud*[13] in southern Russia to between Rb 0.95 and 1.20 (but Rb 1.45 in St Petersburg). In free trading Britain, however, the cost was substantially lower – between Rb 0.75 and 0.90 (Gatrell 1994: 287).

The Russian merchant shipbuilding industry suffered in particular from the high costs of raw materials imports (due specifically to the 1891 tariff), exacerbated further after 1898 when the government abolished the tariff on finished vessels. While the larger firms switched to other products, those remaining 'in this unsympathetic environment ... barely maintained their share of the market' (Gatrell 1994: 52). As a result, Russia developed only a small merchant shipbuilding industry.

Other manufacturers, who received a tariff on their finished product, found that the tariff on the basic raw material on which they relied was raised often without a compensatory increase in the finished item. Hoffding (1912: 81) cites the example of the chocolate manufacturers. The duty on chocolate manufactures stood at Rb 12.2 in 1900 (but could not be increased because it was fixed by the treaty with France). However, in 1900, in order to increase the customs revenue, the duty on cocoa – the basic raw material for the industry – was raised from Rb 4.5 to 6.8 per *pud* with no increase in the tariff on the finished item. This was supposed to be a 'temporary' ('Chinese') duty increase to meet the extraordinary expenses in the Far East. However, the duty was not subsequently repealed.

Against this background of rising manufacturing input prices, many producers were highly disappointed to receive no protection whatsoever. As well as the Russian machine tool industry, various producers of agricultural machinery felt particularly aggrieved. This prompted the 1896 Third All Russian Congress on Trade and Industry, which constituted a rebellion against Witte's policies in general, and his tariff policies in particular. Agricultural industrialists were particularly aggressive, attacking the high price of iron and steel, which made machinery very expensive (von Laue 1963: 134–6). Von Laue concedes that, by the late 1890s, 'even the industrialists were fed up with Witte, especially over tariffs' (1963: 129). A more important conference was held in 1908, where much of heavy industry complained that the government had not done enough for them. Their pleas for help similarly went unheeded (Gatrell 1994: 163–6).

Moreover, even in those cases where the government granted high tariffs on finished goods, this did not always provide the anticipated fillip to domestic producers. As Kirchner (1981) points out, the tariff was only one problem that foreign exporters faced when trying to penetrate the Russian market. Domestic Russian producers would often buy foreign products over domestic goods for a variety of reasons, even when such a good was heavily protected. Thus Russian producers sometimes bought from abroad because, although the tariff would inflate the price of the foreign good, it might cost more to buy domestically because of high internal Russian freight rates. Or foreign goods might be more attractive because they had superior delivery times, or because they were marketed more effectively, or simply because they were better made. In addition, Russian business practices demanded that firms extend credit to customers. While this frequently constituted a problem for domestic Russian firms, many foreign firms were often able to extend the necessary credit, providing a compelling incentive to buy foreign goods.

Equally as important, Kirchner points out that foreign exporters (e.g., German ones) were less concerned about the level of Russian tariff rates than other factors, such as the decline of the Russian rouble to 1897, which increased the cost of foreign products exported into Russia. Indeed, the assumption that tariffs were a vital impediment to foreign export penetration into Russia has been exaggerated. It seems that foreign firms were well aware that the Russian government used tariffs to augment its treasury. Certainly, based on the archival work undertaken by Kirchner, it seems that foreign producers exporting into Russia treated tariffs as an occupational hazard, and simply learned to circumvent the problem.

In sum, tsarist tariff policies, which were significantly informed by autocratic as well as fiscal rationality, cut across any pure notion of economic rationality, in the process hindering the development of much of Russian industry. However, it would be wrong to exaggerate the negative impact of tsarist tariff policy, since various parts of industry did well out of protectionism. These industries were for the most part connected to the defence industry.

The state and geopolitics: protecting the defence industry

Before examining the convergence of the state's military requirements with the tariff requirements of the defence industry, it is necessary to examine the military-industrial environment. I noted at the beginning of this chapter that the impact of the second military revolution and the Crimean War defeat placed the development of a defence industry high on the government agenda. Both these events taught the government that, above all, a strategic railway network was vital to the defence of Russia (see John M. Hobson 1991: 132–7). In addition, Russia's navy had been proved hopelessly inadequate, while the weaponry was found wanting against the superior technology of the French and British industrialised arsenals (Paul Kennedy 1988: 173; Skocpol 1979: 84; Gerschenkron 1965: 708). In sum, Russia's military inadequacies exposed in the Crimean War prompted a shift in policy within the state bureaucracy. Indeed a

> substantial connection grew up between the experience of defeat and the delineation of new objectives. For it was precisely the superior armaments and transportation of the western allies which demonstrated to the tsar that Russia's deficiencies in railways, steam-engines, iron foundries and machine shops could impose costs in a currency which the empire respected.
>
> (Miliutin, cited in Trebilcock 1981: 220)

As a result, from the 1860s onwards, 'the government made a conscious effort to develop home production of military essentials wherever possible' (Edward Goldstein 1980: 561). Thus, in the government discussions over railway building, the supporters of a network were motivated by either fiscal or military concerns. 'While neither group ignored the long-term [economic] effects, neither considered them primary' (Rieber 1966: 38; 1982: 80; cf. Kipp 1975: 446; Ellison 1965: 535; Miller 1926: 183). Accordingly, the state set about building railways, especially with strategic requirements in mind. These had increased by a colossal 2,000 per cent between 1855 and 1875 (see

Gatrell 1986: 150–4; Miller 1926: 182–201; Seton-Watson 1988: 405–6); and between 1886 and 1901, the network doubled again.

The railways, though having an important military function, had vital knock-on or multiplier effects for economic development, linking forwards and backwards. Between 1895 and 1899 (at the height of the second railway boom), the average yearly percentage of domestically produced iron and steel supplied to the railways was a substantial 58 per cent (Gatrell 1986: 153), though Crisp (1976: 31) gives the figure of 73 per cent for 1890–1900. Crisp and Gatrell argue that the railways provided an important base for the development of Russian industrialisation in general (Crisp 1976; 1991: 263–4; Gatrell 1994: 14), as of course did Gerschenkron. According to Gatrell, between 1895 and 1900, railway investments represented 25 per cent of total net investment; he goes on to point out that if investment in transport equipment was included, the figure would be nearer 30 per cent (Gatrell 1986: 152–3). This clearly exceeded Fremdling's 25 per cent estimate that was crucial in stimulating Germany's industrialisation (Fremdling 1977). The state also set about enabling the arms industries and naval shipyards, which simultaneously promoted the capital goods and coal, iron and steel industries (Sen 1984: 106–9). Not only did specific military policies have a direct impact under Witte, but they continued to do so in the 1907–14 period. Peter Gatrell has disaggregated various industrial output data in order to establish the specific linkages between the state's military policies and economic growth. He shows that the state's military policies primarily underlay the substantial industrial growth rates of the economic boom years, 1908–14 (Gatrell 1982; 1994: 176–96; see also Falkus 1968: 52; Trebilcock 1981: 281–4).

Late development theory conceptualises Witte's emphasis on heavy industry within a broad economistic framework, arguing that these industries are economically strategic to industrialisation (Gerschenkron 1962: 20, 126, 360–1). These industries include coal, iron, steel, machinery, transport and general engineering. However, as Gautam Sen points out and as discussed above, this set of industries is also 'strategic' in a military sense (Sen 1984: 7). At this point, it is worth pausing and considering the common objection to my argument: that military expenditures were not sufficiently large enough to be able to spur on industrialisation, since a large proportion went on paying and feeding the troops (e.g., Pintner 1984; Gregory 1982, 1991). My argument is that industrialisation (albeit 'partial') was prompted not so much through the military budget, but through institutional supports that militarism gave rise to. Fiscal-militarism was an important and, on some occasions, a key determinant in many of the major 'economic' reforms: the 1861 emancipation of peasants; the decision to go on to the gold standard in 1897; the decision to develop the railway network after 1860; the decision to support various Russian heavy industries through a host of measures; and, last but not least, the basis for the switch to protectionism after 1877 and its subsequent deepening.[14] Moreover, the military-motivated expenditures after 1860 (detailed in table 3.3) were sufficiently large to have a significant multiplier effect on economic development. And only a small part of the figures derived in table 3.3 (col. 2) would have been spent on feeding the Russian conscripts.

To return to the specific subject matter of this section, tariff policy was aimed to a significant degree at securing a military-strategic base of heavy industries. Thus, in 1877, the state imposed higher tariffs on locomotives and wagons, and restricted the importation of rails. Prior to that time, as much as 50 per cent of rails were furnished by foreign suppliers of iron. In 1870 only two factories in the Urals produced rails (though not without difficulty). Table 3.8 presents those articles which incurred such prohibitive tariff duties.

These industries were in fact the core of Russia's heavy industrial base, and constituted the vital inputs to military production, namely the railway, armaments factories and shipbuilding industries. In addition to these highly protectionist tariffs, the government guaranteed the sale of their products by the direct placing of supply contracts. The state injected nearly Rb 70m between 1868 and 1878 into rolling stock factories (representing orders for 900 locomotives and 32,000 wagons). This was an essential part of the government's programme which sought to achieve a self-sufficient military-industrial base (Gatrell 1986: 151). As Feis points out, in particular, 'the metallurgical works were dependent upon the Russian government for armament and railroad equipment orders' (1930: 222). Indeed, government orders were vital to the success not only of engineering firms, but also of the iron and steel industry. In the mid-1890s, government contracts accounted for as much as 66 per cent of all southern Russian metal firms' business (Gatrell 1994: 58–9; see also Kirchner 1981: 372). In addition, a hidden subsidy was often involved, with domestic industry often charging much higher prices than foreign competitors (Gatrell 1994: 59; Lyashchenko 1970: 560). A further fillip to be noted here was the state's approval of the iron and steel syndicate (known as Prodamet). On the

Table 3.8: *Russian tariff rates on heavy industry, 1868–1891 (duties in copecks per* pud*)*

Product	1868	1891
Pig iron	5	25–53
Iron	20–50	90–150
Rails	20	90
Machines	30	250
Locomotive engines	75	300

Sources: Hoffding (1912: 78); Lyashchenko (1970: 558).

whole (though not in all cases), the creation of this iron and steel cartel, comprising some twelve firms (mainly south Russian), led to a higher-priced end product (Gatrell 1994: 56–9). Of course, it might well be objected that the high tariffs on industrial inputs would have been just as prejudicial to the profit-making activities of the Russian defence industries as it would have been for their civilian counterparts. But the key point here is that the Russian state was prepared to absorb the additional costs of armaments, railways, shipbuilding etc.

Thus with a combination of high protective tariffs, favourable supply contracts and various institutional arrangements, the Russian state created a military-industrial base, the achievement of which was sought by most European states in the late nineteenth century. This was the final objective of tsarist tariff policy as it emerged after 1877.

Autocratic versus capitalist rationalities: the state versus the capitalist class

In the sections above, I noted that the state did much to constrain the development of the capitalist class as well as capitalism more generally. One method through which this was achieved was the divide-and-rule strategy of tsarist patrimonialism, of which the tariff was a part. In this final section I set out to examine and explain this general process.

Patrimonial arbitrariness versus capitalist legal predictability

By the end of his term in office, Witte began to pressurise the tsar to remove some of the existing barriers to full-scale industrialisation. In particular, Witte complained to Tsar Nicholas II about the lack of such a legal system in an 1899 memorandum, combining it with a plea for a greater influx of foreign capital (also important to his industrialisation programme). He argued that there was an excess of red tape at many different levels, which impeded the setting up of companies (including the need for a special decree permitted by the tsar), a lack of effective company law and a general lack of a conducive business climate (see von Laue 1963: 180–1).

Indeed, it is widely recognised that the lack of an effective legal system was a major obstacle to the development of capitalism (Raeff 1966; Pipes 1974: 183, 193–7; Szamuely 1988: 50–1; Bendix 1978: 106–23, 504–8; Weber 1922/1978: 1095; Owen 1982: 77). In addition to the almost prohibitive reams of bureaucratic red tape, entrepreneurs had to face a hostile climate in terms of business trust and confidence. Indeed 'trust' simply did not exist (Stone 1984: 210; McDaniel 1988: 21–3). More importantly, the bureaucracy had imposed strict limitations on small businesses. Where there were partnerships (full or trust), the 1807 Imperial Manifesto decreed that such partnerships could hold only for one company and could not extend beyond this bare minimum. Most importantly, company liability was 'unlimited'. Consequently only a small amount of entrepreneurs dared to set up in business. Moreover, Russian businesses often remained small. There was, as a result, a dearth of middle-sized companies. Even the large industries operated under the terms of the restrictive law of 6 December 1836, which gave the bureaucracy immense authority over the establishment of such corporations, which lasted until 1917 (Owen 1982: 64–70). In addition, as von Laue conceded, 'the advocation of the Western type of corporate law could not prevail against the Russian system of administrative reviews of each separate case' (1963: 97).

Predictability and property rights were consistently rejected in favour of *patrimonial* (autocratic) *arbitrariness*. Similarly the 'distinction between law and administration so crucial in a liberal political system remained vague in practice and the autocracy refused to recognise the judicial norms that it had enacted itself' (McDaniel 1988: 20). Hence no 'rule of law', deemed to be so important for capitalist development in the west, was forthcoming (McDaniel 1988: ch. 1; Orlovsky 1981: 10). Why then was there a lack of conducive property and company law (and indeed rule of law), and why above all, was the political system set up in such a way as to constrain the full development of capitalism?

The problem was that such a legal reform would involve a compromise of autocracy's political power. During the nineteenth century, autocratic power became decentralised within the central bureaucracy. As the bureaucracy expanded, so too did the number and complexity of the tasks to be performed. As a result, the tsar lost his monopoly of policy-making power in part because he simply could not read each piece of legislation, and in part because bureaucratic elements sought to implement their own political objectives. To prevent the dilution of their power, successive tsars in the nineteenth century turned to specific defensive monarchical strategies. These were numerous. The first weapon of patrimonial defence was to prevent the formation of a rational-legal mode of calculation within the state bureaucracy. Historically, patrimonialism works *arbitrarily* and is not limited by formal abstract rules. The emperors of the nineteenth century managed to maintain this element of arbitrariness within the bureaucracy. As part of this process, high-ranking officials in the nineteenth century lacked the rational-legal separation of the all-important private and public spheres. Political administration was treated as a purely personal affair of the ruler (Yaney 1973: 199–200, 221, 228–9; Raeff 1957: 90–1; Weber 1922/1978: 1028–31, 1088–90). Decisions were made on an ad hoc basis and in strict contrast to 'ideal type' rational bureaucracy.

The second patrimonial defensive strategy was the traditional practice of 'divide and rule'. Thus 'although in some measure limited by the high bureaucracy, Alexander II successfully played factions off and never permitted individual ministers or groups of officials to institutionalise and therefore possibly perpetuate their fleeting victories' (Orlovsky 1981: 18). As the nineteenth century progressed and the ministries took on more roles, so the tsars increasingly resorted to an ever stricter policy of 'divide and rule', favouring one ministry and then another. In particular, the tsar constantly played off the Finance Ministry with the Ministry of Interior:

> The tsar would support one of them against the other, so as to prevent their unification in to one massive political organisation, and it was this fact that led to the tsar's personal favour continuing to play such a vital role in government [during the] 1880–1905 [period]. (Yaney 1973: 307; cf. Orlovsky 1981: 12)

Indeed, most of the tsar's ministers readily sought the support of the emperor against their colleagues if they felt they had any hope of getting it (Yaney 1973: 293). Given the highly unpredictable nature of the tsar's whims, the high-ranking officials became very insecure both in their tenure of office and in the support they could expect for their policies. Accordingly, 'each ministry followed its own narrow interests regardless as to whether these complemented or contradicted the policies of the other branches of government' (Fuller 1985: xxii). Not surprisingly, the government swung from one direction to another and failed to achieve a unified and coherent policy direction. As the central bureaucracy split into numerous competing ministries and factions or satrapies, each vying for the tsar's favour, so this centralised bureaucratic struggle became institutionalised into the policy-making arena leading to incoherence and ultimately to an *institutionalised paralysis of government* (cf. Yaney 1973: 307–11; McDaniel 1988: 29–31; Anan'ich 1982: 125, 134–5). Indeed, throughout his tenure at the Finance Ministry, Witte had spent much of his time in conflict with other ministries such as the War Ministry and especially the MVD, which he claimed often undermined his 'economic project'. As he put it in his memoirs, 'All my efforts to facilitate the formation of joint stock companies were systematically thwarted by the Ministry of the Interior' (1921: 76). Perhaps most fundamentally, viewing tsarist state policy as a constant function of the Finance Ministry, as Gerschenkron does, is inadequate because governmental policy was in constant flux, switching between ministries at the behest of autocracy.

Thirdly, the state employed the patrimonial strategy of constraining the development of social groups within civil society (Weber 1922/ 1978: 1006–69; Pipes 1974: ch. 4; Blum 1968: ch. 11; Raeff 1966; McDaniel 1988). By limiting the power of social groups, tsarism aimed to maintain and indeed enhance its despotic power. With its historical disdain for rival sources of power, tsarism did much to inhibit the organisation of the industrialists as an interest group, fearing that they might overstep their state-designated mark by becoming independent of government control (McDaniel 1988: 24; Gatrell 1994: 325–9). They had the further disadvantage of tending to bring in their wake a proletariat, which the autocracy feared for its revolutionary potential.

Above all, patrimonialism was content to allow the development of capitalism, but only so far as to promote the military base of the state. Thus, while the phenomenon of 'patrimonialism' helps explain why Russia underwent only a partial industrialisation, it also provides a key explanation of tariff policy. The all-important patrimonial divide-and-rule strategy informed tariff policy, with much of industry receiving negative protection, while others fared quite well. This divide-and-rule strategy was also central to the fostering of state industries so as to provide a counterweight to private industry (Pipes 1974: 193–203), which was particularly evident in the area of defence (Gatrell 1994: 62–4, 112–14, 166–72, 194–6, 215–16, 257–9, 277–82, 289–90, 323–9). Moreover, autocracy was successful in inhibiting the growth of a strong domestic bourgeoisie (both politically and economically):

> Indeed if Western experience had given rise to the assumption that the capitalist bourgeoisie would fight for representative government and political liberty, then the conduct of Russia's business class belied that assumption. (Rogger 1983: 122)

It was not just that this class remained extremely small until 1914, but even Plekhanov, the great Russian revisionist, was forced to note the bourgeoisie's political inertness even though, quite contradictorily, he continued to believe in its progressive role. Indeed, the bourgeoisie's essential conservatism and narrow social base kept them, as a group, small and ineffective. Members of this class who actually sat in the Duma never made up more than 9 per cent of its total membership (cf. Pipes 1974: 219–20). Furthermore, they often collaborated with the conservatives and rightists who now wished to strengthen the state and resist the democratisation of political institutions. Thus, as Michael Mann has argued, constitutionalism reinforced the developments of an autonomous organic capitalist class, whereas autocracy tended to block it or cross-cut it with other political divisions (1986: 479). The bourgeoisie remained weak and divided (Gatrell 1994: 113, 323–9).

These patrimonial regime strategies cut across capitalist rationality, thereby undermining the full development of the capitalist class as well as capitalism itself. Tsarism's refusal to renege on its despotic power principle ultimately undermined Witte's long-term industrialisation project. Witte's insistence on expanding the process of industrialisation clashed with autocracy's desire to remain autonomous of indigenous economic groupings. Autocracy was only interested in bourgeois elements in so far as they could satisfy its own military impulses. Beyond this sphere autocracy was not prepared to go, and capitalism remained constrained. When Witte challenged this, he was not surprisingly dismissed (cf. Anan'ich 1982: 134).

Tsarism fundamentally viewed state power as something which could not exist alongside capitalist power (unlike in Germany and especially Britain), because it placed a premium on despotic autonomy *over* society, rather than 'organic' power *through* society (see chapter 7). Tragically, and indeed ironically, this led to a weak state and economy (McDaniel 1988: 31–2). But surely it might be argued that the Russian economy developed rapidly after 1861 and had become a country approaching a modern advanced industrial stage of development. If this is the case, then clearly autocracy had allowed and enabled greater development than has been assumed by my analysis. How developed then was Russia on the eve of the First World War?

Conclusion: partial industrialisation, state incapacity and tariff protectionism

My question posed above can be rephrased: what evidence is there that the economy had failed to 'take off' after 1907 into a modern form of sustained and autonomous development? In 1914 the economy suffered from a chronic dualism with a relatively modern industrial sector and a large (and still relatively) backward agrarian sector, even though the latter had developed considerably after 1860 (Gregory 1972: 432). Moreover, the proletariat comprised between 2 and 8 per cent of the total population (depending on which set of workforce estimates are used). Dualism existed not only between sectors but, perhaps more importantly, within the industrial sphere itself. Businesses were divided between cartel and *Kustar*. Entrepreneurship was split between a modern sector of trained technologists opposed to a traditional sector of corruption and incompetence; finance was divided between a new set of industrial banks and the older Russian state banks (Trebilcock 1981: 275; Rogger 1983: 127).

Most importantly, according to Paul Gregory, by 1914 the autonomous preconditions for modern forms of growth had *not* emerged:

> One can say that Russia was obviously backward relative to its major European competitors both at the beginning of the 'modern period' (1861) and at the end of the tsarist era. This conclusion emerges unambiguously from the per capita figures and from social indicators.
> (Gregory 1982: 159; see also Gregory 1972: 422–3, 432; Falkus 1968: 62; Pollard 1981: 243)

To add to these problems, Russia was severely in debt, to the tune of Rb 8,800m in 1914 (Bogolepoff 1918: 344; Crisp 1976: 202), or 47 per cent of national income.

However, this is *not* to preclude the fact that there was strong economic growth after 1870, which accelerated after 1885. As Gatrell argues: 'any characterisation of the Russian economy which implies that the population in general was caught in a poverty trap fails to do justice to the record of economic growth, particularly in the period after 1885' (1986: 46). Nevertheless, Gerschenkron's view of 1907 as constituting the first year of an industrial take-off into autonomous growth is wide of the mark. We need, therefore, to revise downward Gerschenkron's central claim, that the growth spurt associated with the Witte period 'was truly a great one' (1962: 129).

In sum, tsarism was relatively successful in constraining capitalist development, even though it had allowed and to a certain extent enabled development (although much of this had been unintended). In short, the economy was based upon the more immediate needs of tsarism, as it went about its patrimonial and fiscal-military objectives. In particular, the state created in effect a 'patrimonial economy'. The tradition of bringing the economy into the *service* of the state, while at the same time preventing its full development, is one of the main political strategies of patrimonialism (Weber 1922/1978: chs. 12–13). This contrasts clearly with the embedded/organic states, such as Britain, where the state enabled the development of the economy, from which it ultimately derived strong fiscal-military benefits. Tsarism, however, cared little for the development of the economy, but merely used it to extract immediate fiscal-military benefits, even if this undermined strong long-term economic development.

This patrimonial logic also applied to tariff protectionism. Thus tariff protectionism was not planned according to a rational economic goal, but was subsumed within the political logic of a partial industrialisation undertaken by a patrimonial state. Tariff policy provided the state with much-needed revenues, but it simultaneously enabled it to punish the poor and lower classes (because of the regressive nature of this tax), as well as divide and rule Russian industrial producers. This state repression is the basis of the state's incapacity.

A second aspect of the state's weakness that specifically affected tariff policy was its limited reach (penetrative/infrastructural power) into society, which effectively ruled out an income tax, and ensured a reliance on indirect taxes and tariffs because of their ease of collection. Thirdly, the state was severely divided into competing political factions (within the bureaucracy). The specific conflict between the Finance Ministry and the Ministry of the Interior also promoted a shift to indirect taxes and tariffs. Finally, as in Germany, increased military expenditures provided the 'expenditure foundation' for the resort to indirect taxes and tariffs.

The Russian case offers least support for the Marxist argument that states act either in the short- or long-term interests of the capitalist class. The state was engaged in an active strategy of undermining the power of the capitalist class and constraining industrialisation within narrow patrimonial confines. But this hurt not only the short-term interests of the bourgeoisie; more importantly, it undermined the long-term interests of the capitalist class (as discussed in chapter 7), because patrimonialism ultimately undermined the state's internal and external capacity, leading to the death of tsarism in 1917. Lenin's apt words of irony uttered in 1905 would apply equally well to the situation confronting the state in 1917:

> the military might of autocratic Russia has proved to be a sham. Tsarism has proved to be a hindrance to the organisation of up-to-date efficient warfare, that very business to which tsarism dedicated itself wholeheartedly, of which it was so proud, and for which it offered such colossal sacrifices in defiance of all opposition on the part of the people. (Lenin, cited in Fuller 1985: xix)

4 Free trade versus protectionism in liberal Britain: strong state capacity and the conflict over taxation

Even in Britain in the late nineteenth century, and particularly after 1900, protectionism became an important issue in domestic politics. Nevertheless, Britain maintained a unilateral free trading posture. This chapter seeks to establish, firstly, why free trade was maintained especially after 1900 and, secondly, what caused the Conservative Party's shift to protectionism by 1910. Before we examine the fiscal basis of British trade politics, it is important to begin by critically reappraising the economistic arguments found in the general social science literature (which purport to explain not only the causes of the Conservative move to protectionism, but also the Liberal Party's desire to maintain free trade).

The limits of economism

The common explanations of Conservative protectionism and Liberal free trade found throughout the social sciences are typically economistic. The common economistic explanations for the Conservative Party's shift to protectionism after 1900 usually offered are as follows:

- Protectionism was a means to offset the economy's decline, which was premised on Britain's poor export performance; or
- protectionism was a means to reduce unemployment so as to attract working-class support.

The common economistic explanations for the defeat of tariff reform and Britain's maintenance of free trade are as follows:

- Free trade was retained because of the government's deference

to the City of London (which was supposedly free trading)
over the so-called protectionist interests of industry; or

- free trade was retained because British liberal philosophy
  favoured a weak non-interventionist state through which
  economic development could be maximised.

We shall take each of these in turn.

The drying up of Britain's export capacity and the interrelated 'decline of the British economy'

In short, this argument claims that tariff protection – initially through
'imperial preference' – would strengthen Britain's exports, thereby
restoring Britain to its 'former greatness' (see discussions in Friedberg
1988: ch. 2; Lake 1988: 149–51). There are several major problems with
this argument. Firstly, although Britain had clearly suffered a relative
decline in economic performance some time after the middle of the
nineteenth century, national growth rates at the time of the Conservative Party's embrace of tariff reform (by 1910) had significantly
improved.

Table 4.1 shows that although economic growth rates (GDP) were
low in the 1901–7 years (and had dipped slightly in the 1874–1901
period), nevertheless after 1907 they returned to the levels achieved in
the *boom* years of the middle of the nineteenth century. However, it is
important to note that not all economic historians see the post-1900
(and especially post-1907) situation in a positive light. Aldcroft and
Richardson (1969: 4, 11) cite growth rates of 2.1 per cent per annum for
1890–1900, but only 1.1 per cent per annum for 1900–13. Similarly,
François Crouzet (1982: 51), borrowing from Deane (1968), cites
growth rates of 2.4 per cent per annum for 1890–1900 but only 1.2 per
cent for 1900–10. Moreover, Feinstein (1972: 11) breaks down the post-
1900 period, citing 1.5 per cent per annum for 1900–7 and 1.6 per cent
for 1907–13. However, though it is not true in every case, nevertheless
most data sets fail to break down the 1900–13 period, thereby
providing an overly pessimistic picture because of the downturn in the
early years of the decade. There is no doubt that growth rates picked
up after 1907. This is not necessarily to suggest that all was well with
the British economy, but merely to point out that at the time that the
Conservatives embraced protectionism, the economy had picked up.

It is also important to establish the condition of heavy industry, the

Table 4.1: *Annual growth rates (%) of key economic indicators (by cycles) in Britain, 1856–1913*

Period	(1) National income (GDP; from Lewis)	(2) National income (GDP; from Feinstein)	(3) Manufac- turing production	(4) Manufac- turing and mining	(5) Industrial production
1856–65	2.0	2.0		2.6	3.2
1865–74	2.1	2.1		2.9	2.5
1874–83	1.7	1.7	1.7	2.4	2.1
1883–90	1.8	1.9	1.7	1.8	1.9
1890–1901	1.8	1.8	1.3	1.9	2.2
1901–7	1.4	1.5	1.4	2.0	0.0
1907–13	2.2	2.1	3.1	2.6	3.6

Sources and notes: In the case of GDP growth rates, two of the most authoritative sources are presented (since economists' estimates vary). The following sources have been cited in a series of useful charts in Pollard (1989: 2):
(1) W. Arthur Lewis (1978: 260–4);
(2) Feinstein (1972: 19);
(3) Hilgerdt, cited in Pollard (1989);
(4) W. Arthur Lewis (1978: 148–50);
(5) Feinstein (1972: 24–5).

supposed decline of which was said to be the spur for Chamberlain's protectionist schema. Table 4.1 also shows that although industry was in poor shape in the early years of the twentieth century (as it was in the rest of Europe as world recession bit), nevertheless industry did particularly well in the 1907–13 years, at the time when the Conservatives embraced protectionism.

But more importantly, the contemporary case for Britain's decline was even less certain for several reasons. Firstly, even as late as the early twentieth century, techniques for calculating national income had not emerged. It is true that there had been contemporary individual attempts conducted in order to establish national income, but they were sporadic, unsustained for any reasonable time period and, most of all, inaccurate. As Julian Amery put it:

> it is difficult in this over-documented age to realise how little statistical information was available even to government departments at the turn of the century. Export and import figures were known from the Customs returns. There was no statistical information at all, however, about production, investment, capital movements or even employment. (Amery, cited in Friedberg 1988: 44)

Thus contemporary assessments of the condition of the British economy were based on a wholly different set of figures. Contemporaries focused instead on the Customs Department's records of imports and exports, which 'were used to assess the nation's condition as the indicator of Britain's economic performance' (Friedberg 1988: 44; Pollard 1989: 3). It was these figures that Joseph Chamberlain used to 'prove' that the economy was declining. Therefore, we need to examine the condition of Britain's exports.

Table 4.2 shows that Chamberlain's argument, set out in a series of speeches, that British exports were declining after 1870, and in particular, were stagnant from 1890 to 1900, was empirically correct (speech at the Albert Hall, 7 July 1905, in Tariff Reform League 1910: 267; and speech at Glasgow, 6 October 1903, cited in Friedberg 1988: 70). This was supported at the time by a Customs Department memo (Friedberg 1988: 79). Thus, 'export growth rates, even when corrected for prices, show a clear dip in the 1880s and 1890s, calling forth the understandable concern for protectionism . . . of those periods' (Pollard 1989: 4).

However, the most striking aspect of the British export story in the 1870–1913 period was that, after 1901, export growth rates increased dramatically. Clearly, this is a very different scenario to the one depicted by Chamberlain. Aldcroft and Richardson estimate the increase of exports (especially manufactures) at the staggering rate of 4.2 per cent for the period 1900–13, compared to 0.4 per cent from 1890–1900 (1969: 4; also Imlah 1958; Kirby 1981: 140). Furthermore, these increases were striking even on an international basis, with British export growth rates at the top of the European league table (Pollard 1989: 7). In addition, export growth considerably outstripped import growth (Semmel 1960: 88). Thus, if the case for decline was based on trade returns (as was the case), it was clear that if Britain had 'declined' until 1900, it was positively booming thereafter. More fundamentally, the basic argument that protectionism could *restore* stagnant export growth rates is problematic because export growth rates rapidly increased after 1901. Even Aaron Friedberg, who details a more pessimistic picture of the overall position of the economy to 1914 than presented here, concedes that emphasis on the trade returns would have lulled people into complacency (1988: 80).

The use of the trade figures by Chamberlain upon which to base his arguments for protectionism had, certainly after 1906, when the Conservative Party really shifted to tariff reform (and therefore when it mattered most) backfired. And this was clearly recognised at the time.

Table 4.2: *Annual growth rates of British exports (by cycles and decades), 1860–1913*

Period	(1) Domestic exports	(2) Exports (Aldcroft)	(3) Exports (Schlote)	(4) Export volume
1865–74	3.1			4.5
1874–83	0.6			3.3
1883–90	0.9			2.1
1890–1901	1.1			1.3
1901–7	5.5			4.8
1907–13	5.0			3.8
1860–9	4.6	3.2	4.4	3.9
1870–9	0.6	2.8	2.1	2.6
1880–9	1.6	2.9	2.1	2.8
1890–9	1.0	0.4	0.7	0.8
1900–9	4.2			3.8
1900–13	5.0	5.4	3.3	4.1

Sources and notes: (1) Calculated from current price data. Pollard (1989: 4).
(2) Aldcroft (1968). These differ from domestic exports in that they include re-exports.
(3) Schlote (1952).
(4) By cycles, Schlote (1952). By decades, Pollard (1989: 4).

Thus Winston Churchill was not wrong when he claimed as early as 1903 that from the point of view of the trade returns, there was no (economic) case for tariff reform (Churchill to Balfour, 25 May 1903, cited in McCord 1970: 136–7). If the *economic* arguments for protectionism were problematic in 1906, by 1909 they would be virtually obsolete. Churchill's comment would be vindicated in the 1910 elections. As he put it in 1908:

> It is one of Nature's revenges upon those who seek to violate economic harmonies that the very period which had been predicted for our downfall and disaster should have witnessed the most surprising manifestation of our industrial productivity.
>
> (cited in Paul Kennedy 1987: 301)

And in 1909 the research office of the Conservative Party, speaking of the campaign for the forthcoming election, stated that: 'it was difficult to respond to the argument "vote for what the foreign 'dumper' dreads" ... when exports (and indeed total trade), had just reached a new record' (cited in Paul Kennedy 1987: 301).

Thus far we have dealt with the issue of decline and the rise of protectionism in the Conservative Party. But there was a further set of problems with Chamberlain's scheme, as envisaged in *economic* terms. In particular, as a means of actually improving Britain's export capacity, imperial preference was highly problematic and suffered from a variety of problems (see John M. Hobson 1991: 185–94). These can be briefly summarised as follows.

Firstly, the majority of Britain's export markets resided *within* the first world (approximately 66 per cent, according to John A. Hobson 1902: 30–9; cf. Cain 1979: 50; Crouzet 1975: 215, 219, 223; Lance Davis and Huttenback 1988: 160), as was well understood at the time (Sykes 1979: 34). Preference would not only have undermined these lucrative first world markets (Kirby 1981: 19; Aldcroft and Richardson 1969: 82; Cain 1979: 50; Crouzet 1975: 226; Saul 1960: 45, 63–4), but was also damaging because the empire was unable to absorb an increasing share of Britain's exports (Ritchie, cited in Sykes 1979: 34; see also Fraser 1966: 229; Saul 1960: 135; Cain 1979: 40). However, the main obstacle to preference came principally from the colonies.

Firstly, the colonies valued protection for their infant industries (Zebel 1967: 140; Rempel 1972: 17; Cain 1979; Friedberg 1988: 84–5). More importantly, protectionism was valued for the government revenues that it produced (since the colonial governments were heavily dependent on customs revenues). As the Canadian prime minister, Sir Wilfrid Laurier, explained at the Imperial Conference of 1907, free trade within the empire was ruled out for government revenue reasons (see Tariff Reform League 1910: xv). Secondly, imperial preference required the British government to apply tariffs to raw materials. But this was politically impossible, since it would make the British export product less competitive (Marrison 1977). In short, 'there is good reason to believe that plans for an "imperial zollverein" would have foundered on colonial resistance. Hence it was nonsensical' (Friedberg 1988: 84, 63; cf. Giffen 1971: 387–404; Saul 1960: 228).

Tory protectionism and employment?

Many 'Whole Hoggers'[1] at the time had focused their ideological campaign for tariff reform on its supposed 'employment function'. But in the Edwardian era, unemployment, though a problem, was not understood by the electorate as something which could be abolished, or even reduced, by tariff reform (Harris 1972: 366). Significantly,

Balfour in 1909 argued that 'neither now nor on any other occasion, in private or in public, tell any of my countrymen that the whole difficulty in unemployment is going to be solved by tariff reform' (*The Times*, 31 December 1909, cited in Murray 1980: 251). Hewins had noticed this as early as 1903, reporting that Balfour had been irritated by the Tariff Reform League slogan, 'Tariff Reform means work for all.' And even Garvin's passionate calls for protectionism to be linked with providing employment were to go unheeded (see Garvin, *Observer*, 3 October 1909, reprinted in Garvin 1910). Indeed, as José Harris points out, in the 1910 elections Unionist leaders had to restrain their party members from making rash promises about the abolition of unemployment under a system of protection (1972: 319). So adamant was Balfour on this point that he deliberately toned down the Conservative manifesto to read that tariff reform would only 'lessen unemployment'.

Clearly, the shift to protectionism within the Conservative Party was premised on factors other than 'eliminating' unemployment, or 'restoring' the economy, or 'boosting' exports. Before providing an alternative explanation, it remains for us to examine briefly some of the major economistic arguments for Britain's maintenance of free trade.

The City of London and free trade?

The most common argument found in the literature which purports to explain Britain's rejection of protectionism and subsequent maintenance of free trade is the claim that the British state was dependent on the City of London, which in turn was the great promoter of free trade (Glyn and Sutcliffe 1972: 41; Kirby 1981: 21; Semmel 1960: 142; Fielden 1969: 98; Longstreth 1979: 163; Cain and Hopkins 1986).

Indeed, much of the literature argues that the British state consistently favoured the interests of the City over those of industry. As Sidney Pollard has recently put it: 'Manufacturing lost its bid for protection ... commercial policy, in so far as it existed, was meant to safeguard "trade" and the City investor and banker' (1989: 244). While it is fair to say that the state has broadly favoured the City over industry (Ingham 1984; Michael Mann 1988; Weiss and Hobson 1995: ch. 7), this statement must not be taken too literally. That is, it cannot be assumed simply that the state always acted in the interests of the City over industry. In particular, the problem with this general formulation is that in the Edwardian era, the City was overwhelmingly supportive of the Conservative Party – the party of protectionism.

Why was this so? The whole basis of the maintenance of free trade as it emerged in 1909 was its principal link with the income tax, which the City was vehemently ranged against. In 1910, the City interests unequivocally declared their preference for indirect taxation over income taxes (and hence protectionism over free trade) by voting for the Conservative over the Liberal Party.

Free trade as a function of weak state interventionism?

It is a major part of my overall argument that what differentiated Britain from Russia and Germany was its strong state capacity. As discussed in the conclusion to this chapter (and chapters 6 and 7), Britain's strong state capacity rested on a particular configuration of state powers. The ability to levy high direct taxation, which penalised the upper income groups, revealed a degree of social interventionism that was unparalleled in Britain's authoritarian Continental counterparts. Moreover, the income tax required a high level of penetrative power, which was lacking in the central governments of Germany and Russia. The so-called 'minimalist' policy of free trade rested on strong social interventionism – namely the reliance on the income tax. To a certain extent, in this period at least, protectionism rather than free trade was a function of weak state capacity.

Taxation and trade politics, 1870–1900

It was only too apparent that the Unionist calls for protection had little or no grounding in the sphere which they claimed to represent, namely the economy, and that the 'major reason for the failure of Chamberlain's campaign was that, apart from iron and steel, the major industries ... still prospered under free trade' (Rempel 1972: 97). Having surveyed each of the major economistic arguments, it seems clear that economism can explain neither the Conservative Party's conversion to protectionism nor the Liberal government's maintenance of free trade. The debate over protection versus free trade was really a conflict over partially autonomous electoral and fiscal strategies. Trade policy was subordinated to tax strategies. The radical, Philip Snowden, gave testimony to this in 1910, when he stated that 'the real inwardness of the Tariff Reform programme was not a question of protecting British industries, but was the alternative to a democratic budget' (Snowden, *Northern Daily Telegraph*, 30 November 1910, cited in Peter

Clarke 1969: 327). For the most part, therefore, particularly after 1906, the economic reasons given in terms of protecting British industries provided a smokescreen behind which lay the Conservative tax strategy of maintaining fiscal privileges to the upper income groups. The remainder of this chapter develops an alternative fiscal-sociological explanation.

My claim is that the politics of free trade and the Tory desire for tariffs were intimately connected to the politics of taxation. As regards the maintenance of free trade after 1870, I posit three null hypotheses:

(1) A state maintains free trade because state expenditures do not significantly increase in the 1870s or 1880s (i.e., fiscal stability).

(2) A state maintains free trade because it can obtain taxes from non-indirect sources (i.e., direct taxation).

(3) A state maintains free trade because it has a relatively high degree of state capacity.

Fiscal stability and free trade, 1870–1900

If economic factors did not play a *central* role in either the Conservative shift to protectionism or the Liberals' maintenance of free trade, we need to look at the impact of political and fiscal factors – in particular, government expenditures and revenues. So far we have established that both Germany and Russia shifted to protectionism after 1877, due in part to the need for increased revenues to meet higher government expenditures. This leads to my first null hypothesis:

> A country remains free trading after 1870 if government expenditures do not increase.

As table 4.3 (col. 1) shows, central government expenditures expressed in real terms came down on trend from 1860 (though with a low point in 1870–4), and in contrast to Germany and Russia remained remarkably stable from 1875 to 1899 (see also figure 6.4 and appendix B, table B1). The remarkable stability of British central government expenditures is reflected through a comparative analysis: in real terms, between 1870–4 and 1895–9, the British real government burden (expenditures as a proportion of national income) increased by a mere 6 per cent, compared to 18 per cent in Germany, 32 per cent in Austria, 35 per cent in Russia and 54 per cent in Italy. Thus, according to the first null hypothesis, we would not expect to see significant moves

Table 4.3:   *British central government expenditures expressed as a proportion of national income, 1860–1913*

Period	(1) cge/NNP	(2) d1/NNP	(3) d2/NNP	(4) c/NNP
1860–4	9.9			
1865–9	8.6			
1870–4	6.9	2.3	4.9	1.6
1875–9	7.5	2.6	5.2	1.9
1880–4	7.7	2.6	5.3	2.2
1885–9	7.7	2.8	5.1	2.3
1890–4	7.3	2.5	4.4	2.1
1895–9	7.3	2.6	4.2	2.2
1900–4	10.7	5.8	7.2	2.6
1905–9	8.0	3.3	4.6	2.6
1910–13	8.2	3.3	4.3	4.1

Sources and notes: National income is (as explained in appendix B) net national product at factor cost, and taken from Feinstein (1972).
(1) Central government expenditures as a proportion of national income: Mitchell and Deane (1962: 397–9). This source is the same for defence and civil expenditures.
(2) This aggregates ordinary and extraordinary army and navy expenditures.
(3) This adds debt interest expenditures to d1, given that loans were taken out for military purposes.
(4) Civil expenditures.

towards protectionism in Britain prior to 1900 owing to the lack of a government expenditure spurt. For fiscal reasons, then, Britain, unlike many Continental states, could maintain free trade to 1900.

However, as table 4.3 also shows, there was an increase in real terms of the government expenditure burden *after* the turn of the century, largely due to the Boer War. If the fiscal hypothesis is correct – that a government expenditure spurt can promote a shift to protectionism – we would expect to see a movement towards tariffs and indirect taxes immediately after the turn of the century, coinciding with the expenditure push. As we shall see shortly, such a protectionist movement emerged under the leadership of Joseph Chamberlain.[2]

The revenue pull: reaching the limits of the old mode of taxation

It would be incorrect, however, to argue that what brought on moves towards protectionism in the Conservative Party, especially after 1906,

Table 4.4: *British central government revenues, ordinary and extraordinary, 1870–1913 (in £m)*

Period	(1) Gross total	(2) Net total	(3) Indirect taxes	(4) Of which, customs	(5) Of which, excise	(6) Direct taxes	(7) Net state property	(8) Loans
1870–4	73	69	45	21	24	16	5	—
1875–9	77	72	47	20	28	14	6	—
1880–4	83	77	46	19	26	20	7	—
1885–9	90	82	46	20	26	25	7	—
1890–4	97	88	49	20	29	26	9	—
1895–9	112	100	54	21	32	33	11	—
1900–4	178	164	68	30	37	50	12	31
1905–9	154	137	68	33	35	53	13	—
1910–13	177	157	69	33	37	66	14	—

Sources and notes: Calculated primarily from Mitchell and Deane (1962: 393–4, 397–8); also Mallet (1913). Figures may not add to totals because of rounding.
(1) Includes not only ordinary and extraordinary revenues but also gross state property revenues (i.e., SP expenditures have not been deducted).
(2) SP expenditures have been deducted. Although gross total income is presented, the preferred figure is *net* total (which is used to derive table 4.5).
(3) Includes cols. 4 and 5.
(4) These were principally revenue tariffs (i.e., non-protectionist).
(6) This aggregates land and assessed taxes, property and income taxes, and death duties.
(7) This represents net revenues from post, telephone and telegraph.
(8) These are not itemised in Mitchell and Deane (1962). They are calculated by subtracting total income from total expenditures. This is significant only for the Boer War years at the turn of the century. Aggregating cols. 3–8 does not match col. 2. The data in Mallet (1913: 475) taken with the Mitchell and Deane (1962) data seem to indicate that the difference between the two figures is made up of 'revenue paid to local taxation accounts'.

was solely a government expenditure push. More important was the impact of the mode of taxation. The Conservatives were particularly concerned with the current social relations of taxation, whereby the tax burden was shifting away from the lower classes towards the upper income groups.

Tables 4.4 and 4.5 demonstrate that from the 1870s onwards, direct taxes substituted for indirect taxes. From a high point of around 66 per cent of total income (in the 1870s), indirect taxes had dropped to 54 per cent by the end of the century, before dropping to 45 per cent in the final years before the First World War. In contrast, direct taxes

Table 4.5: *Major revenue categories as a proportion of ordinary and extraordinary total net central government income in Britain, 1870–1913*

Period	Total indirect taxes	Of which, customs	Of which, excise	Direct taxes	Net state property	Loans
1870–4	65	30	35	23	8	—
1875–9	66	28	38	19	9	—
1880–4	60	25	34	26	9	—
1885–9	56	24	31	30	9	—
1890–4	56	23	33	30	10	—
1895–9	54	21	32	33	11	—
1900–4	42	18	23	31	7	18
1905–9	50	24	26	39	9	—
1910–13	45	21	23	41	9	—

Source and notes: Derived from table 4.4. Note that gross state property revenues averaged approximately 15 per cent of total net income in the 1870s and rose to an average of 20 per cent (1900–13). Totals do not reach 100 per cent because of the discrepancy discussed in the notes to table 4.4.

progressively rose from a low point of 19 per cent at the end of the 1870s to 33 per cent by the end of the century, rising to 38 per cent in the Boer War years, peaking at 41 per cent in the final years of peace, with net state property revenues remaining constant (see especially figure 6.8). The increasing rate of direct taxation through this period is illustrated in table 4.6. Table 4.6 shows that the rate of income tax bottomed out at 3d in the pound (1875–9), having been as high as 10d in the pound twenty years earlier (1855–9). From 1875–9 onwards, the standard rate of income tax rose rapidly, almost tripling by 1895–9 and quadrupling in the Boer War years. Not surprisingly, after 1895, the Conservatives were becoming increasingly alarmed at this 'creeping rate' of income tax which directly hurt the party's electoral base. As they would later argue, the basis of 'socialism' was precisely this creeping rate of 'fiscal' collectivism.

This gradual change in the social relations of taxation (away from the poor and increasingly towards the rich) impacted profoundly on the politics of the Edwardian era, and came to differentiate the two main parties. As the Conservative Edward Hamilton put it: 'An income tax at 8d in the pound seemed already to be too high a rate for times of peace' (cited in Friedberg 1988: 102). In 1903, when the government was forced to raise the income tax to 15d in the pound for one year during the Boer War, many Conservative supporters openly

Table 4.6:   *Income tax rates in Britain, 1843–1913*

Period	Standard rate (d in the £)	Index (1875–9 = 100)
1843–4	7	233
1845–9	7	233
1850–4	7	233
1855–9	10	333
1860–4	$7\frac{1}{2}$	250
1865–9	5	167
1870–4	$4\frac{1}{2}$	150
1875–9	3	100
1880–4	$5\frac{1}{2}$	183
1885–9	7	233
1890–4	6	200
1895–9	8	267
1900–4	12	400
1905–9	12	400
1910–13	14	467

Source and note: Mitchell and Deane (1962: 427–9). Note that the rate often varied significantly within the quinquennial periods (especially in a war period such as 1900–4).

withdrew support. As a result the government lowered the rate by 4d to 11d the following year. As Charles Ritchie recalled in an address to the City on 17 July 1903, 'years ago ... the principle of taxation in this country was that direct taxation should only be half of indirect taxation, but as years had gone on that proportion had been reversed' (cited in Emy 1972: 113). As the emerging fiscal crisis developed, both parties chose their fiscal weapon: the Tories would wield the defensive 'shield' of 'old regime' indirect taxes and protectionism, while the Liberals opted for the 'lance' of 'new regime' income taxation and free trade.

Fiscal crisis and the rise of Tory protectionism, 1900–1906

The fiscal origins of Tory protectionism

The Boer War contributed to the mounting fiscal crisis of the British state. To meet these rising expenditures, the ruling Conservatives resorted to raising indirect taxes since further increases in the income tax were out of the question. As well as raising tea and tobacco duties, new customs duties were brought in – particularly a tariff on corn (this by a free trade chancellor, Michael Hicks-Beach). This was in addition to an import duty on sugar and an export duty on coal (levied in 1901–2). But it was agreed that further levies on wine and beer would yield little, and any additional increases on tea and tobacco were deemed politically unwise. A general tariff on all imports had been discounted mainly because free trade forces were still dominant in the party. Chamberlain's alternative formulation – that of a moderate tariff to be levied on finished manufactured imports – would emerge only after 1906 as the preferred option to resolve the fiscal situation.

Nevertheless, the need for higher indirect taxes and tariffs (because excises were deemed to have reached a peak) was presenting a tough dilemma for the Conservative free traders. This was posed as early as 1901 by the free trading chancellor, Michael Hicks-Beach, who, in searching for a solution to the fiscal problem, noted that:

> Heavier direct tax would not be borne; any attempt to increase the existing indirect taxes would be useless on a falling revenue, and the only possible new indirect taxes which would produce any important amount, without a complete return to protectionist policy, would be small duties on corn, or meat or petroleum, on the political objections to which I need not dwell ... For these reasons it seems to me absolutely essential that a real check should be imposed on the continued increase of ordinary expenditure for which we have been responsible since 1895–6.
>
> (Hicks-Beach to Salisbury, May 1901, cited in Sykes 1979: 26)

The choice then was between retrenchment (i.e., cutting expenditures) or tariff protectionism. For the moment, the former won out. Thus, with the Tory cause of free trade still dominant, Charles Ritchie revoked the 1902 corn tariff a year later (in Chamberlain's absence). Importantly, the withdrawal of the corn duty in 1903 had stimulated a full-blown row over the issue of protectionism within the Conservative government. In the wake of this political crisis, several leading members of the cabinet – both free traders and protectionists – resigned in protest, including Joseph Chamberlain (who immediately went on the offensive through his own personal campaign). But the situation was looking bleak for the Tory free traders, because retrenchment could provide only a stop-gap measure for the continuing fiscal plight of the government. In the light of this, by 1903, Edward Hamilton's 1901 statement was compelling: 'The conclusion to which I have with great reluctance come is that it is necessary seriously to consider the question of enlarging our sources of revenue and of broadening the basis of our taxation system' (cited in Friedberg 1988: 108).

It was felt within government circles that excise taxes had for the most part reached the limits of both fiscal productivity and political acceptability. And increases on already high rates of existing indirect taxes would lead only to a net reduction in revenue owing to the subsequent decrease in consumption. The old mode of taxation was reaching its limits. For the Conservatives, free trade had become a fetter to the development of fiscal accumulation. Increasing income tax rates was out of the question, and increases in excises were rejected as their yield would be inadequate. Increasingly after 1900, it was becoming clear that Tory expenditures could be met only through customs revenue – that is, tariff protectionism. This fiscal scenario was pre-empted by Chamberlain, whose (protectionist) preference scheme rested in part upon raising indirect taxes through tariffs. In 1903 Joseph Chamberlain planted the fiscal 'seed', which would grow rapidly after the Tory election defeat in 1906.

Joseph Chamberlain, protectionism and the push for indirect taxes

An important and explicit strand of Chamberlain's imperial preference scheme was the role that tariffs would play as a fiscal instrument. While it would be incorrect to assume that taxation was central to his project, the fiscal aspect of his scheme was important in so far as it laid the foundation for the Conservative Party's future conversion to protectionism.[3] Chamberlain brought the issue of old age pensions and welfare reformism on to the Conservative agenda (although his final scheme in late 1903 did not involve old age pensions, essentially for fiscal reasons, as discussed below, pp. 130–1).

For Chamberlain, there were essentially two possible fiscal schemes for raising indirect taxation: a *minimum* and a *maximum* revenue scenario. Thus:

> (1) *tariff on wheat + tariff on manufactures + maintaining existing food duties = maximum revenue scenario (hence social reform)*

> (2) *tariff on wheat + tariff on manufactures − compensatory food duties = minimum revenue scenario (hence no social reform)*

Initially Chamberlain favoured the maximum revenue scenario which would enable him to fund an old age pensions scheme. That is, the tariff revenues from wheat and manufactures, combined with the existing tariff duties, would provide the necessary funds for working-class pensions. In this scheme, tariffs on manufactures were mainly fiscal (although they would undoubtedly provide a fillip to heavy industrialists – especially the Birmingham producers). In May 1903, Chamberlain proposed his maximum revenue scenario: 'in tariff reform lay the solution to the revenue problem which has hitherto held up social reform' (cited in Sykes 1979: 37).

However, the opposition immediately raised the spectre of the 'dear loaf', since wheat tariffs would naturally raise the price of bread, thus hurting the pockets of the working class. In the end, Chamberlain climbed down after considerable pressure, abandoning the maximum revenue scenario and with it the old age pensions scheme. As he put it, 'I am not asking you to impose further burdens upon the people of this country. I am not asking you to raise the amount of taxation in this country. I am asking you to transfer taxation from one article to another' (speech at Newcastle, 20 October 1903, cited in Tariff Reform League 1910: 266). In other words, the revenues that would be collected from grain tariffs would be compensated for by simultaneously reducing the current tariff on other foodstuffs so as to maintain the existing indirect tax burden (formula 2, minimum revenue scenario).

The fiscal rationale for tariffs on manufactured goods was central even to his minimum revenue option. The problem with the tariff on wheat – the essence of his imperial preference scheme – was that a 5 per cent tariff on such foodstuffs would raise between £5.8m and £7.5m. However, the real cost to the consumer would be between £14m and £15m because of the increase in the cost of bread (see Marrison 1977: 219–20). Therefore, according to the *Free Trader* (as well as the estimate made by an anonymous revenue official reported in *The Times*), if the family food budget was to remain approximately the same, £14m would have to be cut from the already existing food duties as well as £1m on the tobacco duty. This was close to a 100 per cent reduction in the food duties. Chamberlain finally proposed instead a 75 per cent reduction on tea and 50 per cent on cocoa and coffee. This would have reduced the exchequer revenue by some £8m (rather than the £15m recommended by the *Free Trader* and the revenue official). This meant that the consumer was still worse off by approximately £7m. In the end, the estimated government revenue deficit was reckoned to be approximately £3m (Marrison 1977: 225). The crucial point here is that this deficit was to be made good by a tariff on finished industrial goods. Chamberlain reckoned that a 10 per cent tariff on finished goods would raise between £9m and £15m. Actually, this was highly optimistic (John M. Hobson 1991: 213–23; Marrison 1977). It was more likely that the final exchequer surplus would be in the region of some £5m, rather than Chamberlain's estimated £6m to £12m. While this amount was inadequate to support an old age pensions scheme, it would, however, enable a basic imperial preference scheme.

In sum, this discussion raises two points: firstly, preference required tariffs on manufactured goods so as to raise government revenues; secondly, Chamberlain's maximum revenue scenario would later provide the foundations of the Tory conversion to protectionism after 1906. What brought this conversion was the 1906 election defeat and the rise of 'socialist taxation'.

'Protectionism or socialism': direct versus indirect taxation

'Socialist' finance and the emergence of Labour

Although the Conservatives actually increased their vote to 2.46 million votes in 1906 (over 1.67m in 1900), the radical vote (Liberal and Labour) more than doubled from 1.52m in 1900 to 3.11m. Probably no one had been so wrong in their predictions than Joseph Chamberlain, who predicted that:

> before the dissolution I reckoned the majority would be 140 with the Irish. After the dissolution, which improved our position, and up to now, I put the majority against us at 80. I am curious to see how far these guesses prove correct.   (cited in Fraser 1966: 273)

Sadly for Chamberlain, who had spent forty days and forty nights in the political wilderness, the majority against turned out to be 356. Not surprisingly, such a defeat proved a turning point for the party. And with it the party switched to protectionism.

The 1906 election results proved to be a massive shock for the Conservative Party. Comments such as that made by Leo Maxse that 'we may remain in opposition for half a generation' were common (Maxse to Bonar Law, 29 January 1906, cited in Green 1985: 669). 'What is going on is a faint echo of the same movement which has produced massacres in St Petersburg, riots in Vienna and Socialist processions in Berlin', said the Conservative leader (Balfour, cited in Sykes 1979: 115). The election was perceived by the Conservatives not so much as a great Liberal victory as the expression of the 'solidarity of labour ... the conviction for the first time born in the working classes, that their social salvation is in their own hands' (Balfour to Joseph Chamberlain, 24 January 1906, cited in Amery 1969: 791). It was not so much the Liberal as the Socialist threat that worried the party. As Chamberlain put it to Bonar Law on his election defeat, 'You have gone down in the Labour wave' (19 January 1906, cited in Green 1985: 682). As the Conservatives saw it, the political atmosphere was becoming increasingly saturated with 'socialist' ideology.

However, thus far, the Conservatives had little or nothing with which to fight the increasing 'socialist menace'. Indeed current Conservatism suddenly appeared redundant. The party needed rejuvenation and, in particular, it needed to court the working class. It sought to achieve this by embracing the cause of welfare reformism through working-class pensions. But this of course had fiscal implications: where would the money come from to pay for them? The party came to accept Chamberlain's maximum revenue protectionist scheme as the means to pay for the proposed pensions. As Parker Smith, who lamented the loss of the working-class vote to Labour in Scotland put it, tariff reform was now vital not for imperialist or preferentialist reasons, but as the

> only effective argument against the spoliatory schemes of taxation which will be put forward. Fresh sources of revenue are required by men of all parties for social schemes. In opposing confiscatory proposals, we must have an alternative policy of taxation.
> (Smith to Balfour, 28 January 1907, cited in Sykes 1979: 119)

The alternative method of revenue extraction to the income tax, therefore, was an all-round moderate tariff. For many Conservatives, this meant sacrificing the good of the economy (as they saw it) to protectionism, if only because the alternative – socialist taxation – was unthinkable.

The constant depiction of the Liberal programme as 'socialist' by the Conservatives was not an ideological smear campaign. The growing 'socialist menace' must have been quite terrifying for much of the Conservative Party. The rise of egalitarianism, coupled with what must have looked increasingly like the arrival of Robin Hood in the guise not of outlaw but state, would have seemed like an unspeakable betrayal, which in their eyes could have led only down the road to serfdom. Indeed to paraphrase Marx's discussion of the French bourgeoisie in *The Eighteenth Brumaire of Louis Bonaparte*, 'picture to yourself the English "bourgeois", how in the throes of "socialist" panic his "trade-crazy" brain is tortured, set in a whirl and stunned by rumours of a socialist fiscal coup d'état, by the seeming "communist" conspiracies of the radicals. Think of all this and you will comprehend why in this unspeakable, deafening chaos of confusion, conspiration, usurpation and fiscal revolution, the bourgeois madly snorts at his parliamentary constituency, "Rather an end with protectionism than socialist taxation without end."' Arthur James Balfour understood this cry.

Balfour's switch to protectionism

In the pre-1906 period, Balfour had managed to avoid coming to a decision over free trade or protectionism. He had certainly never been convinced of the economic case for tariffs, and had at best ventured only so far as endorsing a moderate retaliatory tariff. Beyond half-heartedness Balfour would not tread, much to the anger of both the Chamberlainite faction and Unionist free fooders (see John M. Hobson 1991: 223–5; Fraser 1966).

Yet the striking fact to emerge was that, by 1907, Balfour had been fully converted to tariff reform. In addition, while he had earlier stated that retaliatory tariffs would have to be levied on a selective basis, after 1907 he was calling for an all-round general tariff. What then had led to this U-turn? The election defeat and the rise of 'socialist taxation' provided the major impetus. The appearance of Philip Snowden's *Socialist Budget* was especially confrontational:

> The existence of a rich class whose riches are the cause of the poverty of the masses is the justification for the socialist demand that the cost of bettering the conditions of the people must be met by the taxation of the rich. (cited in Fraser 1966: 287)

He went on to argue that the poor should pay no taxes; all indirect taxes should be abolished. To make good the lost revenue (and to provide surplus funds), he proposed to more than double the income tax, which would add £72m at the Exchequer.

But it was not so much the fear of the Labour Party's calling for progressive and high income tax rates that concerned the Tories as the fact that the Liberal Party had embraced a similar tax programme. While the Liberal Party had clearly been moving that way ever since the introduction of Harcourt's death duties in 1894, it was certainly prompted by the rise of the Labour Party. As Engels aptly put it, 'The Liberals know full well that for them it is a question of catching the Labour vote if they intend to continue their existence as a party' (Engels to Bebel, 5 July 1892, cited in Peter Clarke 1971). The fact that the Liberals had now come to embrace a radical 'socialist' tax strategy set the alarm bells ringing in Tory ranks. As they saw it, socialist insurrection would come not at the barricades but through the 'insidious' use of taxation 'in instalments': 'For the purposes of our time, what we shall have to grapple with is not the utopian creed but the budgetary method. Practical Socialism ... is a system of finance' (Maxse, cited in Fraser 1966: 287). Compared to Snowden's 'revolutionary' fiscal prescriptions, tariff reform appeared – even to the staunchest of free traders – to be infinitely preferable.[4]

In addition, the Chamberlainites had already put the revenue arguments at the forefront of their case. This case was built upon a twofold political infrastructure. Firstly, it was argued that for the Conservatives to attract the working class, they would need to offer significant social reforms. With their defeat at the 1906 election and the simultaneous rise of Labour, reformism, it was argued, was essential if the Conservatives were to regain electoral support. Secondly, tariff reform would provide a more acceptable alternative to income taxation for most, if not all, Unionists. As Chamberlain had put it in the House of Commons in May 1906, the only alternative to revenue from tariffs was 'confiscation'. Only tariff reform could provide 'without robbery or jobbery' the necessary financial basis for further social reform (Chamberlain in *Outlook*, January 1907, cited in Murray 1980: 88).

All this impacted upon the Tory leadership. In the early months of 1907, Balfour entered into discussions with W. A. S. Hewins. Hewins pointed out that the system of taxation was rapidly reaching crisis point. With the increasing levels of government expenditure incurred after 1890 (and especially after 1900), revenues would need to rise similarly. A large war or an economic crisis, Hewins argued, would 'smash the present system' (cited in Fraser 1966: 284). In particular, he correctly showed that, since 1842, British governments had come to increasingly rely on direct taxes – a trend which had accelerated under the Unionist governments after 1895 (see tables 4.5 and 4.6). With the government's plans to raise direct taxes further, it had become imperative for the Conservatives to find an alternative revenue base. Almost inevitably this meant an increase in indirect taxes, and hence tariff reform, since existing excises were perceived to be at a peak. Indeed, the issues of Britain's relative decline, the problem of dumping and unemployment were for Hewins (and Balfour) of secondary importance. His primary objective, which was to become Balfour's, was the necessity of extracting revenues from non-direct sources (see Sykes 1979: 130). In particular, Balfour favoured indirect taxes to meet the increased costs of the Edwardian era. A memo on food taxes was sent to Balfour on 11 February in which Hewins proposed food tariffs, not because they were essential for preference and imperial unity, but rather because they provided increased revenues which would allow a reduction in the income tax.

Tariff reform, as an alternative to socialist taxation, was Balfour's primary concern. Thus, there had been a change in emphasis over the original protectionist project of Joseph Chamberlain. Although Chamberlain had favoured a shift towards indirect taxes away from direct sources, this objective had comprised only a part of his overall scheme. In his Savoy hotel speech in 1907, Balfour focused primarily upon the revenue aspect of tariff reform, whilst the preferential aspect was at best only secondary. As he stated, 'Some revision of our fiscal system and some broadening of the basis of taxation would be absolutely inevitable if we were the only commercial nation in the world, and if we had not got a single colony' (speech at a Central Conservative Association Meeting, Hull, 1 February 1907, cited in Tariff Reform League 1910: v).

The Savoy speech marked a turning point for both the Conservative Party and the tariff reform campaign. Indeed, after this 'realigning' speech, Balfour – like Bismarck almost thirty years before him – emerged as a tariff reform leader. With Balfour at the helm, the Conservative Party could – and would – unite upon the cause of protectionism. Issues of economic decline, unemployment, imperial unity had failed to impress Balfour. In the end, the electoral defeat, the rise of Labour and progressive socialist taxation jolted Balfour out of his complacency. At the annual conference of the National Union in Birmingham on 14 November 1907, he boldly stated that a broadening of the basis of taxation through a general tariff would finance social reform. After all, he argued without even a hint of irony, 'social reform has long been the work of the Unionist Party' (Balfour, *The Times*, 15 November 1907; see Sykes 1979: 129–44).

The Unionist conversion to tariff protectionism

It was clear by now that the conflict of 'free trade versus protection' had been superseded by the fiscal issue of 'direct versus indirect' taxation. This was neatly summarised by Cromer:

> the more I see of the political situation, the more I am inclined to think that free trade versus protection is falling into the background and that the real fight before long will be socialist versus anti-socialist.
>
> (Cromer to Lord Robert Cecil, 28 May 1909; cited in Sykes 1979: 183)

Around this fiscal issue, and under the decisive leadership of Balfour, the party came rapidly to unite. This was most clearly reflected in the radical development of the Unionist Free Traders. After 1906 they were confronted with the dilemma of maintaining free trade and accepting 'socialist' income taxation, or choosing protectionism and rejecting progressive 'socialist' income taxation. As Balfour classically put it:

> We are between the Devil and the Deep Sea. Shall we go to the Devil of protection with our friends or the deep sea of socialism with our political adversaries?
>
> (Balfour to Cromer, 9 January 1909, cited in Sykes 1979: 183)

Whilst both options were problematic for the free trading Unionist faction, the choice as to whether to favour the 'good' of the national economy as they and many others saw it or the fiscal privileges of the upper income groups was quickly resolved. According to Cromer, it was

> almost certain that a very large number of shaky even perhaps some rather strong free traders will practically combine with the tariff reformers rather than bear any very heavy fresh burthens in the shape of direct taxation.   (Cromer 1908, cited in Murray 1980: 88)

Cromer was not wrong. In 1908, Lord Lansdowne announced to the annual meeting of the Liberal Unionist Council that, 'we shall be driven to it [tariff reform] by the exigencies of the financial situation' (Lansdowne, 20 November 1908, cited in Murray 1973: 557). The Duke of Northumberland, who had previously resisted Tory protectionism, now turned to support Balfour. Thus he wrote J. St Loe Strachey, the 'only chance we have of success is to find a different way of raising the money to that proposed by the government, and as far as I know Tariff Reform is the only alternative'. And again: 'Protection cannot be worse than Socialism ... And as ... Tariff Reform or Socialism are the only possible alternatives at the moment, I am quite prepared to swallow the former' (Northumberland to Strachey, 7, 13 and 21 September 1909, cited in Blewett 1968: 121). Perhaps more striking still was the conversion of Lord Hugh Cecil (the leading 'free fooder'), who only two years earlier had argued in a letter to Balfour, 'we are passionately afraid of protection, we think that it will lead to corruption and class division, to a general Americanism of our politics … Protection seems to us an evil of the same class as Home Rule' (4 May 1907, cited in Blewett 1968: 95; see also the passionate statement made by Ripon, cited in Sykes 1979: 64). Two years later, the very same Cecil wrote the Earl of Bessborough: 'Mr Lloyd George and Mr Winston Churchill seem to me to desire to plunge the country into Socialism, and if I have to choose between socialism and tariff reform I unhesitatingly choose the latter' (Cecil to Earl of Bessborough, 29 September 1909, cited in Peter Clarke 1969: 327).

The Unionist free traders made it clear that the days when they would support the opposition in order to satisfy their free trade strategies were over. From 1907 onwards, they would unite with the party and embrace the 'devil' of protection in order to avoid the deep sea of socialist taxation. When the 1909 budget was announced, the remaining Unionist free traders turned to protectionism. St Aldwyn wrote Robert Cecil:

> This budget seems to me to have given the final shove to the movement of the Unionist party to tariff reform. A man may be a free trader by [economic] conviction and reason … but if he has anything to lose … he will certainly prefer an indefinite tariff reform policy to the fiscal policy which is initiated by the present budget.
> (St Aldwyn to Cecil, 28 May 1909, cited in Rempel 1972: 193)

By 1910, these once fervent free traders were now denouncing free trade as 'evil' and a policy that had to be defeated at all costs. What had led to this radical U-turn? Certainly economic conditions played no part whatsoever. If anything, economic conditions in 1910 were even more conducive to free trade than they had been in 1903 (at least according to the theory that had led the Unionists to embrace free trade passionately in the first place).

By late 1907, the real issue around which the two parties fought was the raising of tax revenue. Certainly on the Conservative side, it was not trade but tax strategies which informed the conflict. Put simply, the political conflict was only incidentally about the economic basis of tariff reform versus free trade; the real issue was that of progressive (Liberal) income taxation versus (Conservative) customs taxation. As it turned out, the Liberal government successfully launched its fiscal attack upon the forces of privilege.

The state in conflict with the dominant classes

The budget attack presented

On 29 April 1909, Lloyd George presented his budget to the House of Commons, proclaiming that:

> This, Mr Emmott, is a war budget. It is for raising money to wage implacable warfare against poverty and squalidness. I cannot help believing that before this generation has passed away, we shall have advanced a great step towards that good time when poverty, wretchedness and the human degradation which always followed in its camp will be as remote to the people of this country as the wolves which once infested its forests. (cited in Cross 1966: 102–3)

For the Conservatives, their nightmare scenario had been realised. The budget sought a sharp increase in the death duties by a third, bringing the top rate on estates worth over £1m to 15 per cent; the introduction of new land taxes which went up to a 20 per cent tax on the unearned increment in value when the land was sold; the introduction of a super-tax of 2d in the pound on incomes over £5,000; and an increase in the income tax from 12d to 14d in the pound. In addition, the budget aimed to sweeten the middle classes by inaugurating child tax allowances, as well as introducing a lower rate of tax for earned than unearned income (Cross 1966: 103; Rempel 1972: 192; Rowland 1968: 217).

Table 4.7 reveals the social impact of the budget on the different income groups. While the new tax regime remained onerous upon the poorest income group (those on £50 per annum), nevertheless the budget clearly hit the upper income groups (between £5,000–£50,000 per annum). Table 4.7 (cols. 4 and 6) shows that those earning £5,000 paid at least 20 per cent more after the budget, those on £10,000 paid about 60 per cent more, while those on £50,000 paid over 75 per cent more. Only those below £2,000 (especially the lower middle classes) were better off. As figure 4.1 shows, the radical social impact of the budget created an entirely new and increasingly progressive profile to Britain's tax regime.

Table 4.7: *Personal tax rates in Britain, 1903/4 and 1913/14*

The radical social impact of the 1909/10 Liberal budget

Income £ per annum	(1) 1903/4 earned income (% tax)	(2) 1903/4 unearned income (% tax)	(3) 1913/14 earned income (% tax)	(4) 1913/14 earned income 1903/4=100	(5) 1913/14 unearned income (% tax)	(6) 1913/14 unearned income 1903/4=100
50	9.1	9.1	8.7	96	8.7	96
100	6.2	6.2	6.0	97	6.0	97
150	5.0	5.0	4.9	98	4.9	98
200	5.6	7.8	4.8	86	7.0	90
500	6.6	8.8	5.8	88	9.9	113
1,000	7.4	10.3	6.6	89	12.2	118
2,000	6.6	9.8	5.8	88	12.0	122
5,000	5.6	9.6	6.8	121	12.4	129
10,000	5.1	9.5	8.1	159	15.1	159
20,000	4.9	10.0	8.3	169	16.0	160
50,000	4.8	10.2	8.4	175	18.1	177

Source and notes: Herbert Samuel, originally printed in the *Statistical Society of London Journal* (1920: 176–7), reproduced in Murray (1980: 294).
(1 and 3) Overall rate of personal taxation paid as % of earned income.
(2 and 5) Overall rate of personal taxation paid as % of unearned income.
(4 and 6) Comparison of pre- and post-budget tax regimes (where 1903/4 tax rates = 100).

But most intimidating of all for the Conservatives was the fact that the provisions for the income tax were designed to meet the *future* needs of 'inevitable fiscal expansion for national defence and social reform' (Murray 1980: 172). Indeed, Lloyd George told the House of Commons that the budget was not a mere 'temporary shift'. Rather these new taxes were of 'such an expansive character' that they would grow as the country's demands increased (cited in Murray 1973: 566). This conjured up frightening images for the Conservatives. *The Times* summarised the Conservative sentiment: 'the doctrine of social ransom has never been carried quite so far', and 'the fundamental right of ownership was at stake' (30 April 1909, cited in Emy 1972: 122). The budget grew into 'the most prolonged struggle over a single measure in the history of the House of Commons', involving no less than seventy days of parliamentary debate and 554 divisions (Cross 1966: 104). Nevertheless, the new budget remained in place despite various attempts made, particularly by the House of Lords, to undermine its base.

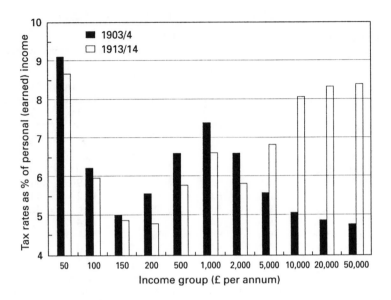

Figure 4.1:   The radical social impact of the Liberal budget (1909/10)

The state against the landed upper class

It was said that Lloyd George had organised a 'thanksgiving service' at the Treasury. In similar fashion, just before the budget, Churchill had said of the upper classes, 'We shall send them up such a budget in June as shall terrify them, they have started the class war, they had better be careful' (cited in Murray 1980: 108). Indeed, in private, Lloyd George even alarmed Churchill with his talk about setting up a guillotine in Trafalgar Square. The conflict with the House of Lords that followed the budget was grist to the mill of the Liberals' radical project of attacking the forces of privilege.

The issue of the House of Lords formed a vital strand to the whole Liberal strategy of securing the party's electoral hegemony. Thus Lloyd George's acclaimed joy on finding the Lords to be ranged against his finance bills was not surprising, for it enabled him rhetorically to reduce the whole fiscal controversy to a simple conflict of 'Landlords versus the People': would old age pensions be funded by the taxation of the 'parasitic' landlords (through land taxes) or through the taxation of the stomachs of 'the People'? Indeed, on hearing that the Lords had rejected his budget, Lloyd George might well have said (to paraphrase

Bismarck), 'Now I have got them.' Who, the Conservatives? 'No, the Lords of course!' By combining the issues of the income/land tax proposals and the Lords, Lloyd George was able to considerably boost the popularity of the budget, given the rife hostility that was felt up and down the country against this class of 'unearned' privilege. However, it is also the case that in order effectively to smear the Lords with the income tax, he would need to arouse their hostility to the budget even prior to its hearing. In doing so, he could achieve a further political aim: to break the political power of the House of Lords. This all rested on their rejecting the budget. These two aims – to smear the Lords with the budget, and to challenge their constitutional power – became effectively one strategy.

Thus, in 1908 Lloyd George began his attack on the Lords, almost willing them to reject his tax proposals, which he intended to place before Parliament the following year: 'They [the Conservatives] are going to tax your bread, they are going to tax meat [and] timber ... and other foreign commodities ... and if the Lords want to stake their privileges upon it by all means let them do it' (*The Times*, 22 December 1908, cited in Murray 1973: 559–60). In July 1909, three months after the original budget speech, Lloyd George delivered his most damning attack. In his Limehouse speech (euphemistically dubbed by the Conservative F. E. Hirst the 'slimehouse speech'), he declared that the landlord was a gentleman who did not earn his own wealth: his income was produced by others, but squandered by him. Reiterating John A. Hobson's argument, he stated that the value of their land was determined by the growth of the community. In addition, he argued that even their mining royalties were derived on the backs of capitalists who had risked not only their own money, but also, more importantly, the lives of miners. He stated that,

> When the Prime Minister and I knock at the door of these great landlords and say to them, 'Here, you know these poor fellows have been digging up royalties at the risk of their lives, some of them are old, they have survived the perils of their trade, they are broken, they can earn no more ...', we ask, 'Won't you give them something towards keeping them out of the workhouse?' However they simply ... scowl at you and we say, 'You thieves!' And then they turn their dogs on to us and every day you can hear their bark ... If this is an indication of the view taken by these great landlords of their responsibility to the people who, at the risk of their life, create their wealth, then I say their day of reckoning is at hand.
>
> (*The Times*, 31 July 1909, cited in Murray 1980: 191)

This speech marked a watershed in the campaign. Lloyd George's attacks on the Lords continued unabated. He followed up the Limehouse speech with an equally vicious attack made in Newcastle:

> The Peers may decree a revolution but the people will direct it. If they begin, issues will be raised they little dream of ... It will be asked why five hundred ordinary men, chosen accidentally from among the unemployed, should override the judgement – the deliberate judgement – of millions of people. (cited in Cross 1966: 106)

The government and Lloyd George in particular were now 'deliberately challenging the Lords to do their worst' (Cross 1966: 106), and the Lords were forced to defend themselves. Not surprisingly, therefore, the Lords rejected the budget by 350 votes to 75 – the largest rejection ever of a House of Commons bill. On Friday, 3 December 1909, Parliament was prorogued. Lloyd George was delighted, for the Lords had fallen into his trap: 'We have got them at last and we do not mean to let them go until all the accounts in the ledger have been settled' (*The Times*, 4 December 1909, cited in Murray 1980: 235).

Was the attack on the Lords simply part of a government strategy to shore up the power of the new capitalist order at the behest of industry and above all the financial capitalists in the City of London? The budget was aimed just as much at the City of London (and to a lesser extent at industry) as it was at the Lords.

The state in competition with the City of London

As noted earlier, the traditional view is that the City of London was the epitome of free trade interest in Britain. This is made problematic, however, by the fact that the most powerful group to mobilise against the 'free trade budget' was the 'City of London'. Moreover, the financial interests in the 'City' were the most vociferous in their opposition to the budget. On 24 June 1909, Lord Rothschild chaired a meeting of 1,000 City traders and merchants. While the spokesmen accepted that they should bear a fair share of tax, they argued that the free trading budget would damage the nation's commerce and industry. The City unequivocally supported the protectionist Conservative Party.

Why then, it must be asked, did 'finance capital' favour the party of protection rather than that of free trade? There were two reasons for this: first and foremost, the City, the richest income group in the

142

country, resented higher income taxation (Cain 1979: 57–8). Thus it was said of the meeting of 24 June, chaired by Lord Rothschild and attended by many financiers, that it was 'really a meeting of the rich men who won't pay for the dreadnoughts they were clamouring for' (Lord Lansdowne, 25 June 1909, cited in Murray 1980: 129). Secondly, it seems that there was considerable ambivalence in the City over the economic case for free trade, with many favouring protectionism.

According to a memorandum written by H. A. Gwynne for Joseph Chamberlain in December 1903, there were four broad categories that comprised the 'City interests', all with varying trade preferences. The first category was the money dealers (bankers, finance houses and stock brokers). Of these, Gwynne reckoned that the stock brokers were 'almost to a man in favour of protection' (1903/1982: 393). The bankers who favoured free trade, he argued, did so more out of 'City' deference to the instincts of people such as Lord Goschen, Giffen and Harvey (of Barclays) rather than to a clearly defined set of preferences formulated from their own business experience. In addition, various governors of the Bank of England (notably Hambro and Gibbs) and several colonial bankers clearly favoured protection. Furthermore, the majority of those involved in banking and finance houses who favoured free trade did so only because they felt that Chamberlain's tariff reform campaign came at a singularly inopportune moment. In 1903 the money market in London was depleted due to the recent Boer War as well as the limited financial methods employed by the government (Gwynne 1903/1982: 394–5). By 1910, this particular problem would no longer exist. In addition, there were some bankers who had from the beginning been interested in protection, but had felt that Chamberlain's proposal was too vague to be convincing. Thus, they very much supported the establishment of a judicial and expert commission to inquire into the question more fully. Finally there were many who would have supported Chamberlain had he included a scheme for securing a sound national system of commercial and technical education.

The second faction in the City comprised the shipping interests. The majority of these representatives favoured protection (Gwynne 1903/ 1982: 396). Nevertheless, there was a vocal minority which favoured free trade. The main motive for this free trade sentiment was based on the fact that imperial preference taxed food and raw materials, which would make it harder for these interests to compete internationally as well as nationally. However, those who dealt with raw materials and colonial goods in neutral markets (such as China and Japan) clearly favoured protectionism. The third faction, composed of 'middlemen' and 'large importers', was largely opposed to tariff reform as it would increase the cost of raw materials, and hence undermine the competitiveness of the British product. The fourth category comprised colonial houses. They greatly favoured preference but felt that it would be impractical, not least because the colonies relied predominantly on tariffs for government revenue. But practical realities aside, this group favoured protectionism (Gwynne 1903/1982: 397).

The upshot is that, firstly, the traditional argument that the City of London was a free trading interest group *par excellence* might well be in need of revision. Moreover, Anthony Howe (1992) has recently argued that even in 1846, the City was against the shift to free trade. Secondly, the City was in favour of protectionism in 1909 as a means to avoid higher personal income tax bills. Support for the party of protection was unequivocal. In 1906, Sir Edward Clarke, the free trade MP who represented the City, was driven out of Parliament by London tariff reformers. In the subsequent by-election Sir Frederick Banbury, one of the most doctrinaire right-wing tariff reformers in British politics, won the constituency (Rempel 1972: 173–4). Indeed, many City people had changed their minds. Thus, Garvin gleefully reported that 'Sir Walter Gilbey, who spent thousands of pounds to put [the Liberals] in, says he would spend six times as much to put them out' (Garvin to Northcliffe, 10 May 1909, cited in Paul Kennedy 1987: 333). In the 1910 general elections, the City made its choice and gave its overwhelming support to the party of protection. As Cain put it: 'The Unionist heartland was that part of England dominated by commercial and financial power – much of it centred on overseas trade and foreign investment' (1979: 57). Indeed, City businessmen, together with country landowners and tariff crusaders, 'had common cause to oppose a budget which not only hit their pockets but also seemed to prove that money could be raised for social reform without tariffs' (Cross 1966: 105).

The dilemma that the free trade City factions faced was only too clear: vote Liberal to maintain free trade and 'die' with the income tax budget; or vote Conservative to inaugurate tariff reform and 'die' with protection. In the end, once again to paraphrase Marx, the free trade interests of the City madly snorted at their parliamentary constituency, 'Rather an end with Protection than "Socialist" (direct) taxation without end.' However, in contrast to the French bourgeoisie in 1850, this time there was no Bonaparte waiting to save them. As events turned out, of course, the City 'died' with the income tax budget. Thus,

144

had the City got its way, Britain would almost certainly have relinquished its hold on free trade in order to return to protectionism, albeit mainly for fiscal reasons.

It may be argued, however, that even if this is true, could it not be the case that the budget itself was 'designed' to maintain the 'business' rather than the personal fiscal interests of the City? There are several problems even with this softer formulation. Firstly, protectionism was favoured by much of the City interests in relation to its pure business activities, as already discussed. Secondly, as Rubinstein points out, it was not the City that defeated tariff reform but rather, 'it was its rejection by the liberals and non-conformists – based in industrial areas or reliant upon heavy industry – which did so' (1977: 123). In particular, it was the northern industrial areas which supported free trade and voted with the government. At a general level, free trade was favoured by a majority of industrialists (Peter Clarke 1971; Semmel 1960: 146; Halévy 1952: 14; Rempel 1972: 97). Thirdly, the real issue at stake in 1909/10 was not trade, but tax strategies. Thus the budget enabled the maintenance of free trade partially as an unintended consequence of the Liberals' desire to increase direct taxation in order to attract the working and lower middle classes.

Hence the view that the City dictated or had a monopolistic influence on government policy formulation has in this instance been exaggerated. The British state did not act *constantly* at the behest of the City; had it done so, Britain would have returned to protectionism prior to the First World War. Does this mean that the state ignored the needs of the dominant class in its pursuit of fiscal accumulation? We should not assume that the state was absolutely autonomous of the dominant class. The next section argues, however, that the state in fact entered into competitive-cooperative relations, shoring up not only state power, but also capitalism.

Conclusion: strong state capacity, free trade, the income tax and the 'compromise of embedded liberalism'

One of the foremost international relations theorists has argued that international politics in the post-1945 era was based on the 'compromise of *embedded liberalism*' (Ruggie 1983). Here he was referring to the dualism between an international liberal laissez-faire arena and a domestic *interventionist* Keynesian counterpart. That is, Britain and the other powers after the Second World War would accept international free trade only on condition that they could intervene domestically so as to minimise adjustment costs. In short, international laissez-faire rested on domestic interventionism. Ruggie developed this term from the work of Karl Polanyi, whose approach forms the basis of my perspective.[5] This Polanyian-inspired term has special relevance for one of the major arguments of this chapter, namely that British free trade from the outset (i.e., post-1846), but increasingly after 1900, could be characterised as a 'compromise of embedded liberalism'. External free trade, especially after 1900, was possible only on the back of a strong income tax base. That is, external free trade could be achieved only through radical fiscal domestic interventionism. The compromise occurred between the state and the dominant capitalist classes. The capitalist classes accepted (though grudgingly) the rise in the income tax in return for the maintenance of free trade. Put differently: free trade came at a domestic price – the increase in income tax rates. Thus the 'compromise of embedded liberalism' actually began (albeit in Britain as opposed to the whole of Europe) well before 1945.

Indeed, while this compromise occurred explicitly in 1909, it could be said to have begun, though more informally, in 1842, when Peel introduced the income tax so as to prepare the way for free trade (see chapter 6). The state anticipated a reduction in tax revenues with the end of protectionism and therefore reintroduced the income tax (which would provide a buffer or fall-back position). Throughout the subsequent 1842–1909 period, as we have seen above, income tax rates progressively crept up (with direct taxation displacing indirect taxes), so that by 1900 considerable concern was expressed within the Conservative Party. Of course, the Conservatives after 1906 favoured a return to protectionism as a means of countering the 'hated' income tax. But the Liberal government prohibited such a return (at least before the First World War), and pushed through an increase in the income tax – the price of the maintenance of free trade.

I noted earlier that the state under the Liberals had gone against the long-run fiscal interests of the dominant classes – the landed gentry, the City of London and the industrialists. However, as with the Prussian Junkers in 1879, the British dominant classes were internally divided between favouring free trade for trading purposes, but tariffs for fiscal reasons. Because of this crucial division, the state was able to play off one with the other. That is, the state gave the capitalists free trade, but in the process raised direct tax rates for the benefit of the working and lower middle classes. Thus the fiscal conflict with the dominant classes was accompanied by cooperation in trade concerns. The dominant class came to accept the 'compromise of embedded liberalism': that the price of free trade was higher direct taxation. To use the terminology of Margaret Levi (1988), the British state enhanced its relative bargaining power vis-à-vis the dominant classes by maintaining free trade. This enabled an accumulation of sufficient state capacity to increase the income tax against dominant class interests. In the process, this led to a substantial increase in the state's relative political capacity (discussed in chapter 7). Free trade strengthened the *terms of rule* (or what Norbert Elias (1939/1994) calls the 'balance of social power') in favour of the state, enabling it to instigate radical taxation strategies against the long-term fiscal interests of the capitalist class as a whole. Simultaneously, the state played off the dominant from the working and lower middle classes, giving the latter groups the income tax in order in part to gain their votes. Paradoxically, this Bonapartist balancing act between and within classes was perhaps superior to any political manoeuvre undertaken by any other European state.

The principal lesson here is that a broad and deep notion of 'embedded autonomy' leads to higher state capacity than 'abrasive' or 'isolated autonomy' (the latter representing the tsarist path). Indeed, it was the strong direct tax base that placed Britain above Germany and Russia in terms of political capacity (as will be examined in detail in chapter 7).

5 Tariff protectionism and indirect taxation in federal states: the United States, Canada, Australia and Switzerland

So far, we have seen that *authoritarian* Germany and *autocratic* Russia chose to enhance their tax base by resorting to indirect taxes and hence made the switch to protectionism after 1879 and 1877 respectively. In clear contrast, the liberal-parliamentary British state resorted to direct taxation to enhance its tax base, and therefore maintained its free trading stance. On the strength of this, it might be argued that the authoritarian/autocratic states, anxious to repress the working classes and enhance despotic power, increased indirect (regressive) taxes and tariffs, while the parliamentary state sought to gain the support of the working and lower middle classes and so increased the tax burden on the richer income groups. On this reading, the *form* of state (i.e., its proximity to the electorate) supplies the key to taxation and trade policies such that:

> *parliamentarism = free trade/direct taxation;*
> *authoritarianism = protectionism/indirect taxation.*

Closely linked to this is a more specific second argument: the importance of political parties. It could be argued that political parties and their tariff preferences comprised an important independent variable in the determination of trade regimes. In this vein, the fact that the Liberal Party was in power after 1906 (which favoured direct taxation and free trade), as opposed to the Conservative Party (which favoured indirect taxes and protectionism), was crucial to Britain's maintenance of free trade. In general, for most parliamentary states (including semi-parliamentary Germany), there is a clear divide between left parties, which favour free trade and direct taxation, and right parties favouring tariffs and indirect taxes.

But there is a further key state power variable to be examined here:

148

the degree of 'concentration'. That is, in federal states the central government exercises less power than in unitary states. Thus many of the tasks performed by the central government in a unitary context are undertaken by the provincial state governments in a federal system. The degree of concentration of the central state – high in unitary states, low in federal states – has specific ramifications for tax and trade policy. In particular, for political reasons, federal central states came to rely on indirect taxes (hence tariff protectionism) while unitary states had greater choice as to which tax regime they would adopt (hence the 'potential' of free trade). So there are three specific questions to be addressed in this chapter:

(1) Is there an inherent relationship between the 'form' of state and trade regimes: low proximity to electorates (authoritarianism/autocracy) and indirect taxes/tariff protectionism, and, conversely, high proximity to electorates (parliamentarism) and progressive taxes/free trade?

(2) Is there a clear relationship between party political preferences and the rise and fall of tariff rates, where left parties promote direct taxation/free trade, and right parties support indirect taxation/tariff protectionism?

(3) Is there a relationship between a state's concentration and trade policy? Specifically: high concentration (unitarism) = free trade; low concentration (federalism) = protectionism?

If the *form* of state is more important than its *concentration* (federal or unitary), then we would expect the four states under discussion in this chapter – the United States, Canada, Australia and Switzerland – to rely on a low tariff/free trade regime, preferring progressive income rather than indirect taxes, given their liberal/parliamentary nature. If party politics is the main variable, we would anticipate a general shift towards free trade, and at least considerably lower tariffs under left-wing parties than right-wing ones. However, if the low degree of *concentration* is more important, we would expect these governments to favour indirect taxes and tariffs. In the process, we will be able to gain a much fuller understanding of the political factors that shaped the trade and tax regimes of Britain, Germany and Russia (undertaken more fully in chapter 6).

I have already noted in chapter 2 that, in Germany, one of the key reasons for the Reich's tariff increases was to gain revenue independent from the *Länder* governments (i.e., the Reich–*Länder* struggle). By way of an initial conclusion, I shall argue that on the evidence of the federal states examined in this chapter, the *form* of state and the role of political parties play *a* role in the determination of tax and trade policy, but that the *federal* nature of the state (i.e., low concentration) should be accorded greater weighting. This is because in all the cases examined here, despite their liberal/parliamentary nature, protectionism and indirect taxes were favoured over free trade.

Indirect tax and protectionism in the United States, 1789–1913

Indirect taxes and the emergence of tariff protectionism

Tariff protectionism formed the mainstay of American foreign economic policy from the end of the eighteenth century to the first few decades of the twentieth century (and even to 1945). The notion that the American state was akin to a minimalist night-watchman is belied by the fact that it levied the highest tariff rates in the first world, bar Russia. Moreover, tariff policy was as much about taxation as it was about protection: 'Through most of the history of the republic, tariffs and taxes were virtual equivalents' (Hansen 1990: 529; see also John M. Hobson 1991: 279–300; Taussig 1964; Dewey 1968; Percy Ashley 1920; Tarbell 1911; Ratner 1967).[1] The tariff owed its predominance to the *federal* nature of the American state.

The problem of central provision in the United States began in the early years of the Continental Congress, which were marked by a profound political and fiscal struggle with the state governments. The Articles of Confederation (1781) included no financial provisions, thus putting the Congress at the mercy of the thirteen independent legislatures (Studenski and Kroos 1952: 25; Ratner 1967). The War of Independence changed all this, and swung the balance of power towards Congress. In order to overcome the resulting fiscal crisis, a convention was set up in 1787, in which Congress was granted an independent source of revenue (as well as the right to make expenditures). Article 1, Section 8 of the constitution states that:

> The Congress shall have power to lay and collect taxes, duties, imposts and excises to pay the debts and provide for the common defence and general welfare of the United States ... to regulate commerce with foreign nations, and among the several states, and with the Indian tribes ... [and] to make all laws which shall be

necessary and proper for carrying into execution the foregoing powers.

More specifically with regards to tariff policy, Article 1, Section 10 states that:

> No state shall, without the consent of the Congress, lay any imposts or duties on imports and exports, except what may be absolutely necessary for executing its inspection laws; and the net produce of all duties and imposts, laid by any state on imports or exports, shall be for the use of the Treasury of the United States; and all such laws shall be subject to the revision and controul [sic] of the Congress. No state shall, without the consent of Congress, lay any duty of tonnage.

The constitution ensured that central and local governments would be allowed their own unique and independent sources of taxation. Thus the fiscal 'instrumentalities of each were constitutionally immune from taxation by the other' (Studenski and Kroos 1952: 39–40). Until 1787, the states had presided over the use of direct and indirect taxes. Thereafter, the preserve of indirect taxes was granted to the central government, while the state governments would maintain a monopoly of direct taxes (as happened in Germany, Canada, Australia and Switzerland).

On 6 April 1789, the new Congress met with the initial purpose of providing a national revenue. Madison stated that:

> The deficiencies in our Treasury have been too notorious to make it necessary for me to animadvert upon that subject ... a national revenue must be obtained, but the system must be such a one that, while it secures the object of revenue, it shall not be oppressive to our constituents. Happy it is for us that such a system is within our power; for I apprehend that both these objects may be obtained from an impost on articles imported into the United States.
>
> (cited in Young 1872: v)

Thus the Tariff Act of 4 July 1789 was adopted to produce much-needed government revenue, since 'direct taxes could not be thought of; and even the excise would be unpopular' (House statement, 15 June 1789, cited in Young 1872: 13–14). At the same time, the preamble to the act made clear its intentions: 'it is necessary for the support of the government for the discharge of the debts of the United States, and the encouragement and protection of manufactures, that duties be laid' (cited in Young 1872: 15).

Table 5.1: *Major revenue categories as a proportion of US federal income, 1790–1913*

Period	(1) Total indirect taxes	(2) Of which, customs	(3) Of which, excise	(4) Direct taxes	(5) Net state property
1790–4	98	94	4	—	2
1795–9	94	87	7	—	6
1800–4	92	87	5	—	8
1805–9	95	95	—	—	5
1810–14	88	85	3	—	12
1815–19	85	75	10	—	15
1820–4	89	89	—	—	11
1825–9	91	91	—	—	9
1830–4	85	85	—	—	15
1835–9	55	55	—	—	45
1840–4	86	85	1	—	14
1845–9	90	90	—	—	10
1850–4	92	92	—	—	8
1855–9	88	88	—	—	12
1860–4	81	59	22	4	14
1865–9	73	36	36	13	14
1870–4	83	54	30	4	12
1875–9	89	50	39	—	11
1880–4	90	55	35	—	10
1885–9	91	58	34	—	9
1890–4	93	52	41	—	7
1895–9	87	44	43	—	13
1900–4	89	45	44	—	11
1905–9	91	49	41	—	9
1910–13	87	46	41	4	9

Source and notes: Calculated from US Department of Commerce (Bureau of the Census) (1949: 296–8, 302–3, 309–10 (Series P89–98, P109–19, P165–9); 1975).
(1) Comprises (2) and (3).
(2) Levied on most goods.
(3) Levied on spirits, wines, liquors, tobacco and manufactures.
(4) Comprises income and profits (corporation) taxes, and taxes on banks.
(5) State property revenues *net* of state property expenditures. The major items are sale of public lands and surplus postal receipts.

Protectionism and taxation, 1790–1913

Table 5.1 shows the importance of customs revenue in the US federal government budget. From 1790 to 1860, customs receipts constituted a staggering 85 per cent of total net tax revenue, while from 1861 to 1913 tariff revenues comprised a still considerable 48 per cent.

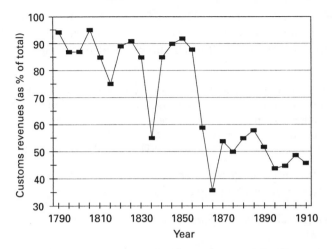

Source: US Department of Commerce (Bureau of the Census)
1949: 296–8, 302–3, 309–10 (Series P89–98, P109–19, P165–9);
and 1975.

Figure 5.1: The tariff as a proportion of US federal government
income, 1789–1913

The importance of the tariff in federal income from 1790 to 1913 is
illustrated in figure 5.1.

The first and foremost objective of tariff protectionism was to
provide the federal government with revenues. And the majority of
these expenditures were raised to meet military requirements. From
1861 to 1913, defence consumed some 53 per cent of federal expenditure (though the proportion rises to 65 per cent with debt interest
included), while civil expenditures comprised only 34 per cent (calculated from Department of Commerce (Bureau of the Census) 1949:
299–301, 309–10 (Series P99–108, P165–9)). American fiscal rationale
dictated the need for balanced budgets (at least until 1913). Thus when
the government revenue account was in surplus, tax rates were
lowered and when it was in deficit, tax rates were raised. Because of
the affinity between tax and tariff rates, the rise and decline of tax rates
was more or less mirrored by the rise and decline of tariff rates. Thus,
when the budget was in surplus, tariff rates were lowered. This
rationale specifically informed the tariff acts of 1832, 1833, 1846, 1857,
1872 and 1883. When budget deficits occurred, taxes were increased
and hence the tariff was raised. This rationale informed the tariff acts
of 1791–1801, 1841, 1842, 1861, 1862 and 1864. The main exceptions to

this were the tariff acts of 1828, 1875 and 1890, where rates were increased in the face of a treasury surplus, and had an unequivocal protectionist rationale. Ida Tarbell summarised this aspect of US tax policy:

> The nation [sic] intends to raise money to carry out our business by putting a duty on certain raw and manufactured goods brought from foreign countries. If we find we are getting too large a revenue we will cut down the duty, if too small we will raise it.
>
> (1911: 1; see also Hansen 1990: 529–33)

In short, the implicit government revenue formula for maintaining budget equilibrium as it affected tariffs was:

(1) *Fiscal deficit + higher tariffs = increased revenue and budget equilibrium;*
(2) *Fiscal surplus + lower tariffs = decreased revenue and budget equilibrium.*

However, even if we except the acts of 1828, 1875 and 1890, this revenue formula needs to be qualified. For example, in 1846, although tariffs were lowered to reduce the revenue in the face of budget surpluses, the effect was to create new increased and sustained government revenues. At this point we need to add a further variable: the trade cycle (see the general discussion in chapter 6, pp. 213–15). Thus, when the economy was booming and imports bountiful, tariff revenues would (*ceteris paribus*) naturally increase. Under such conditions, lower tariff rates could actually lead to higher revenues as in 1832, 1833, 1846–56 and 1883. When the economy was in recession and imports curtailed, tariff revenues decreased, and thus rates were increased, as in 1842, 1860 and 1875. However, this trade variable for the most part worked in harmony with the 'revenue formula' noted above.

If the role of the tariff was primarily to provide the federal government with revenues, it remains to be seen how important the two main parties were in the rise and decline of tariff protectionism. Mark Hansen has recently argued that the two major parties were split in their choice of trade regime throughout the nineteenth century. Thus he claims that tariffs went up under the Republicans and down under the Democrats (1990: 539, 543). He calculates that Democrat Presidents set tariff duties 9.51 percentage points lower than their Republican counterparts (1990: 544). Or as Gallarotti points out, four out of the five tariffs after 1880 support this idea: 'both increases occur under Republican presidents and two (1894 and 1913) of three reductions under Democrat presidents' (1985: 179). However, while party politics played a part, it is important not to exaggerate its role.

Firstly, while a 9.51 per cent differential in the tariff was not insignificant, it was hardly consequential. The minimum tariff rate on dutiable goods never once went below 16 per cent for all imports in the period 1820–1913. Mostly, rates were pitched between 30 per cent and 50 per cent. At this level, even a 10 per cent difference in rates between the two parties was not especially significant. Secondly, the Democrats, certainly until 1887, were never free trading, as their Liberal counterparts in Britain had been. Rather, they had accepted as part of political life that tariffs were the essential means through which the government accumulated its revenue. Indeed, the Democrats fully endorsed the statement of the Free Trade Convention at Philadelphia in 1831 where it was stated that:

> the people prefer, in times of peace, duties raised on the importation of foreign merchandise to any internal tax, direct or indirect ... Duties on imports amounting to an average 20 per cent of the value appear necessary to the support of the government.
> (cited in Percy Ashley 1920: 149)

And again in 1846, Secretary of the Treasury William Walker argued that

> No horizontal scale of duties is recommended because [this] ... would be a refusal to discriminate for revenue, and might sink that revenue below the wants of the government ... experience proves that as a general rule, a duty of 20 per cent ad valorem will yield the largest revenue.
> (cited in Young 1872: xciii)

By just about any criterion, an average 20 per cent ad valorem rate is protectionist!

It was only in 1913 that the difference between the two parties became evident in respect to tariff and tax policy, and even then it was not significant in practical terms. In that year, with the Democrats back in power, the scene was set for a move towards a more progressive tax regime (and free trade). On 22 April, Oscar Underwood put forward a House bill which envisaged a sweeping downward revision of the tariff, the central aim of which was to ease the cost of living for the masses (Ratner 1967: 323). In addition to the lowering of indirect taxation, Cordell Hull had drafted an income tax amendment, which would be ratified as the Sixteenth Amendment. The federal income tax would levy a flat 1 per cent rate on all incomes over $3,000 (for a single person), ranging to 6 per cent on very high incomes, with a maximum effective rate of 7 per cent. In the end, the Underwood tariff lowered average rates of duty on all imports to 17.7 per cent, though dutiable import rates were still as high as 40.1 per cent (Department of Commerce (Bureau of the Census) 1960: 888). This represented only an ambivalent move away from protectionism towards free trade. It is true that the Democrats had tried to effect a move towards free trade before 1913, but on each occasion, this came to little or nothing (John M. Hobson 1991: 286–90; Ratner 1967: 174–84; Terrill 1973: ch. 4; Kennan 1910: 262–9; Seligman 1908: 531–89).

The real divide between the two parties, though in evidence in 1913, effectively came to light at the policy level only *after 1917*, when the Republicans were responsible for various tariff hikes. Relieved of tariffs for their revenue function owing to the high fiscal yield of the income tax, Republican administrations (Harding and Hoover) sought to boost protectionist duties (i.e., where tariff rates were so high or prohibitive that imports would be so cut as to reduce government revenues), whilst the Democrats (Wilson and Roosevelt), sought to lower them. The presence of federal budget deficits or surpluses no longer affected or constrained their tariff calculations. Thus, 'despite surpluses, inter-war Republicans thrice sent duties higher. Despite deficits, inter-war Democrats thrice sent duties lower' (Hansen 1990: 547). Party politics did come to affect tariff policy, but only tentatively as late as 1913, and not significantly until after 1917. By then, the Republicans stood for tariffs and indirect taxes, while the Democrats represented free trade and the income tax. In sum, although the Democrats clearly favoured freer trade prior to 1913, such a policy was blocked by the constraints of the need for revenues. In short, the federal (low-concentration) aspect of the American state was more important in the shaping of tariff policy than the policy objectives of the two major parties in the long nineteenth century (1789–1913). This analysis can be concluded through a critique of the trade regime explanation provided by hegemonic stability theory, best represented in the work of David Lake (1988).

Hegemonic stability theory in the fiscal-sociological mirror

In attempting to derive US tariff policy from the international economic environment, David Lake (1988) downplays party differences (more so than I do). However, while Lake is correct to point to limitations in the 'party-based' argument, he is wrong to emphasise the importance of the United States's position within the international economy as the key to explaining trade policy.

Lake argues, in particular, that the nature of the international economic structure played an important (though not singular) role in the United States's shift towards freer trade in 1913, in clear contrast to the high protectionism of the 1909 Payne–Aldrich Act. Principally he refers to the growing protectionist sentiment emanating within the Conservative Party in Britain (in turn a function of the country's waning hegemonic power). He states that protectionist sentiment in the Conservative Party was still only weak in 1909 and had failed to gain the 'unequivocal' support of Arthur Balfour. This meant that the United States could continue to 'free ride' on British free trade which looked certain of being maintained for at least another few years (Lake 1988: 146–7), and thereby maintain protectionism. How then does he explain the lower tariff rates of the 1913 Underwood tariff compared to the 1909 Payne–Aldrich Act?

In 1912, he argues, Bonar Law replaced the 'hesitant' Balfour as leader of the Conservative Party, committing the latter to an unequivocal stance of protectionism (Lake 1988: 151). With the prospect of 'Britain's almost century-old [sic] commitment to free trade ... clearly in jeopardy ... [the] United States could no longer free ride on Britain's leadership' (1988: 151–2). Given the United States's position as the most productive nation-state, the need for export expansion meant that domestic protection would have to be reduced: hence the 1913 Underwood Tariff Act (Lake 1988: 152–63).

The problem with this formulation lies at the empirical level. Arthur Balfour became *fully* converted to protection by 1907. His hesitancy over the question of protectionism began in 1903 and ended four years later. By 1909, the Conservative Party was in favour of tariffs (though as a means to counter the direct tax policy of the Liberals – as detailed in chapter 4). In fact if anything, pre-war protectionist sentiment within the Conservative Party was *at its zenith* in 1909/10, waning thereafter (see Sykes 1979: ch. 13). Thus, exactly the international conditions that Lake exposed as underlying the Underwood tariff existed at the time of the Payne–Aldrich tariff. Therefore, if Lake was correct, we would expect a radical lowering of US tariffs in 1909. The fact remains that tariff rates remained high in 1909 (equivalent to the 1894 level). It would not, therefore, be unfair to conclude that the international economic structure (as defined by Lake) could not have led to the lower US tariff rates of the 1913 act. More significant was the popular desire for a more progressive tax regime, which entailed low regressive taxes (freer trade) and the adoption of an income tax. The logic of the rise of the income tax (and hence ultimately of free trade) was therefore premised in politics as well as the condition of the country's economy. This perspective can be extended to 1945.

After 1917, when revenue dependence on the tariff was significantly diminished, governments were able to adjust tariffs in a less constrained manner, as noted above. Paradoxically, the link between tariffs and revenue loosened after 1917 with the increase in the federal income tax. Advocates of high protection indeed argued that

> the income tax [acted] as a guarantor of sufficient revenue to maintain defence and other essential services, so that the loss of revenue due to the extremely high tariffs enacted in 1929 would not cripple the government.   (cited in Webber and Wildavsky 1986: 424)

Thus, with the predominance of the income tax, the Democrats were able to extend freer trade while simultaneously increasing progressive income taxes. As a result, the Republican Smoot–Hawley tariff was significantly revised downward in 1934. And the New Deal income tax provisions paved the way for the American policy of virtual free trade after the Second World War.

Indirect tax and protectionism in Canada, 1867–1913

Indirect taxes and the emergence of tariff protectionism

As in Germany in 1871, the United States in 1789, Switzerland in 1848 and Australia in 1901, federation in Canada in 1867 led to a strict fiscal demarcation between central and provincial governments. Explicitly, according to the British North American Act (passed on 1 July 1867), each province was limited to 'direct taxation within the Province', while the dominion (central federal government) was given unlimited power for 'the raising of money by any mode or system of taxation' (cited in Perry 1955: 46). But in practice, such was the level of popular revulsion to direct taxation in Canada that the dominion chose to rely on indirect taxes. Indeed, the provinces were given a virtual monopoly on the means of direct taxation, mainly as a way of limiting their revenue capacity – since high direct taxes were politically impossible (Perry 1955: 47). In contrast to the German situation, the dominion was to provide a large proportion of provincial revenues through grants. In 1874, 58 per cent of provincial revenues were derived from central government subsidies. Although this figure declined thereafter, the figure stood as high as 29 per cent even as late as 1913 (Perry 1955: 123) – a level that Bismarck could only have dreamed of. Interestingly, the fiscal base of the dominion in Canada was from the beginning stronger than that of the Reich government in Germany vis-à-vis its respective state governments in this period.

However, the major similarities between Germany and Canada were that both governments relied on not only indirect taxes but especially customs for their revenue. In addition, both governments were adversely affected by the international depression after 1873. As in Germany, lower imports in Canada led to a decreasing customs revenue after 1875.

As table 5.2 shows, from a peak in 1873, imports had dropped 37 per cent by 1879. This had an immediate impact on the customs revenue taken by the dominion, a phenomenon simultaneously experienced by the Reich.

However, the revenue problem was exacerbated by the government expenditure programme, largely associated with the task of national construction (Perry 1955: 53), as charted in table 5.2 (col. 4). The increases in government expenditure, coming at a time when revenues were drying up, pushed the government rapidly towards fiscal crisis. The rise in the real expenditure burden was striking, increasing by 49 per cent in the 1873–6 period relative to the previous three years. In the final years of the decade (1877–80), the increase in comparison to the 1870–2 years was still a considerable 23 per cent. Since expenditures could not be easily retrenched, a resort to higher taxation was becoming increasingly inevitable. Complementing the growing fiscal crisis was the reaction of the industrialists, who were facing considerable competition from their American counterparts. Following the abrogation of the Reciprocity Treaty by the United States in 1866, US manufacturers found themselves in the fortunate position of having easy access to the Canadian market. Conversely, Canadian manufacturers had to face mounting US imports, while having one of their major export markets simultaneously closed off (Perry 1955: 53–5).

Thus the mounting fiscal crisis at the dominion level complemented the difficult economic situation experienced by Canada's manufac-

Table 5.2: *Canadian imports, revenues and expenditures, 1868–1879 (in Can$m, current prices)*

Year	(1) Total imports	(2) Tariff revenues	(3) Dominion expenditures	(4) Dominion expenditure burden (cge/NNP)
1868	67	8.6		
1869	63	8.3		
1870	67	9.3	18.0	4.3
1871	84	11.8	19.3	4.4
1872	105	12.8	25.7	5.7
1873	125	13.0	39.0	8.5
1874	123	14.3	33.5	7.1
1875	117	15.4	32.9	6.7
1876	93	12.8	32.0	6.4
1877	94	12.5	32.5	6.3
1878	90	12.8	30.5	5.7
1879	79	12.9	30.8	5.6

Source: Imports: Dominion Bureau of Statistics (1925: 452). Government expenditures and revenues: Dominion Bureau of Statistics (1925: 455, 741–2). Expenditure burden: central government expenditure (CGE) as a proportion of national income (in per cent). National income: calculated from Firestone (1958). For a fuller discussion of Canadian national income data, see appendix B.

turers. The solution to both these problems lay with increasing tariffs (Easterbrook and Aitken 1958: 392–3). Accordingly, the Liberal government under Mackenzie hiked tariff rates to 17.5 per cent on finished manufactures as well as imposing a moderate tariff on semi-manufactured goods (McInnis 1960: 325). Even so, it was quickly realised that tariffs would have to be further increased in order to make good the rapidly diminishing government revenue. At this point the Liberals refused to make the necessary increases, which cost them the 1878 election (Finlay and Sprague 1979: 192–3).

The 'National Policy' and protectionism, 1879–1913

By 1878, fiscal crisis was bearing down upon the dominion government. Speaking of the fiscal problem, Finance Minister Cartwright stated in his 1878 budget speech:

> It is not often in the commercial history of any country we are called
> upon to chronicle so great a reduction, not merely in the total volume
> of our trade, but also in the revenue derived therefrom, as we have
> seen within the last two or three years ... The volume of our trade
> and commerce collectively had been reduced from $218m to $168m
> while the duties derived from customs alone had fallen off from
> $15.4m to $12.5m.   (cited in Perry 1955: 64)

As in Germany, the solution to the problem was at hand in the form
of the Conservative 'National Policy' (instigated in 1879), which raised
the general tariff rate on dutiable imports to 26 per cent in 1880,
peaking at 31.9 per cent in 1889 before coming back down to 26 per
cent in 1913 (Dominion Bureau of Statistics 1925: 458). The tariff rate
on total imports went from 14 per cent in 1878 to 20 per cent in 1880
(Dominion Bureau of Statistics 1925: 458; cf. Bairoch 1988: 148). The
rate imposed on various products was also increased: for example,
50 cents per ton on coal, cotton textiles from 17.5 per cent to 30 per
cent, pig-iron from zero-rated to $2 per ton, primary iron and steel
from 5 per cent and zero-rated to 12.5 per cent and 17.25 per cent
respectively, and machinery from 10 per cent to 25 per cent. Tariffs
were also levied on agricultural goods: wheat, corn and other bread-
stuffs (Perry 1955: 66–7).

As tables 5.3 and 5.4 show, tariff protectionism and the customs
revenue derived from it provided the mainstay of Canadian central
government finance in the period to 1913.

Throughout the 1870–1913 period, indirect taxes comprised 83 per
cent and customs 64 per cent of total net tax revenues. That the tariff
was a fiscal instrument is evidenced clearly in the various budget
speeches given by successive finance ministers of both major parties.
The Liberal finance minister W. S. Fielding characteristically stated in
his budget speech in 1904:

> (The) tariff ... has on the whole proved most satisfactory. It has
> proved a good revenue tariff ... It has included a considerable
> measure of *incidental protection*, and in that respect it will command
> the admiration perhaps of some Honourable gentlemen opposite,
> who are more anxious for protection than some of us on this side of
> the House.   (cited in Perry 1955: 102, Perry's emphasis)

To claim that protection for industrial and agricultural producers
occurred only as an unintended byproduct of the central state's
revenue requirements (hence the term 'incidental protection') would,
however, be to go too far. If this had been its original intent, after 1867

161

Table 5.3: *Canadian central government (dominion) revenues, 1870–1913 (in Can$m)*

Period	(1) Gross Total	(2) Net Total	(3) Total indirect	(4) Of which, customs	(5) Net state property
1870–4	20.1	19.1	16.8	12.2	0.2
1875–9	22.9	21.2	18.4	13.3	0.2
1880–4	30.8	28.8	24.9	19.4	0.4
1885–9	35.3	32.5	27.6	21.3	0.8
1890–4	38.0	34.7	29.4	21.5	0.5
1895–9	39.1	35.5	29.2	20.7	0.9
1900–4	59.7	55.6	44.4	33.1	1.8
1905–9	80.1	74.9	60.1	46.3	2.8
1910–13	131.0	122.2	100.4	82.1	2.9

Source and notes: Dominion Bureau of Statistics (1925: 739–42). Note that the columns do not add to the 'total' figure. This is because various income revenues were included in the total figure but were not apportioned to the individual categories in the *Year Book*.
(1) This is the total amount without state property deductions.
(2) Gross total minus state property expenditures.
(3) Includes excise and customs (col. 4).
(5) State property revenues minus SP expenditures. SP revenues include only post office and interest on investments.

Table 5.4: *Major revenue categories as a proportion of net Canadian dominion income, 1870–1913*

Period	(1) Total indirect	(2) Of which, customs	(3) Net state property
1870–4	88	64	1
1875–9	87	63	1
1880–4	86	68	2
1885–9	85	66	2
1890–4	85	62	1
1895–9	82	58	3
1900–4	80	60	3
1905–9	80	62	4
1910–13	82	67	2

Source and notes: Calculated from table 5.3. The figures in col. 1 do not add to 100 because certain incomes were included in the 'total' figure but were not apportioned to the individual categories.

Table 5.5: *Main sources of Canadian customs revenues, 1868–1913*

Import item or group	1868	1880	1890	1900	1910	1913
Coal	—	3.7	3.6	3.8	5.2	4.4
Cottons	12.4	12.5	4.7	4.8	4.5	5.8
Electric motors	—	—	—	0.6	1.5	1.9
Fruits and vegetables	0.6	1.6	2.1	2.2	2.5	2.4
Glass	—	1.1	1.4	1.1	1.1	2.9
Grain and grain products	1.1	1.5	1.8	0.4	0.4	0.4
Iron and steel	3.9	9.9	12.1	12.8	17.9	25.8
Spirits and wine	14.6	8.0	9.6	9.4	9.5	8.0
Sugar and molasses	14.4	15.6	12.8	6.9	5.1	3.6
Tea	10.7	4.7	0.1	—	—	—
Wood	—	1.0	1.6	0.5	0.8	1.1
Woollens	13.2	11.9	13.1	7.9	10.6	7.5

Source: Perry (1955: 71, 106).

the needs of industry and national economic construction also became an important influence.[2] Though they were perhaps not as central as the state's revenue requirements, nevertheless the needs of industry were an important factor in tariff policy.

Perhaps the most striking aspect of tariff policy was the degree to which the dominion had moved away from pure 'revenue' tariffs on sugar, spirits and tea as its major source of customs revenue towards more 'protectionist' tariffs, particularly on iron and steel. The importance of agricultural and industrial goods as revenue-raising instruments is shown in table 5.5.

In 1868, sugar, spirits and tea accounted for 40 per cent of all tariff revenue compared to a mere 4 per cent for iron and steel. By 1913, the ratio had reversed. Sugar, tea and spirits now accounted for 12 per cent, while iron and steel comprised 26 per cent of all tariff revenues. The linkage between protectionist tariffs and government revenue was closer than ever. Despite various similarities between Canadian and German trade and tax policies (described above, pp. 159, 161), there was one striking difference. While the German empire was forged on a staple fiscal diet of bread, Canada initially emerged on a fiscally liquid diet of spirits, wine, tea and sugar, increasingly exchanged for a more solid fiscal diet of iron and steel. Paradoxically, iron and steel taxes were easier to swallow than the massive bread taxes of the German empire, and this undoubtedly helps explain why fiscal friction was so much greater in the Kaiserreich than in Canada. The tariff as both a revenue producer and a protectionist buffer for agriculture and industry played a central role in forging a national state and economy (Easterbrook and Aitken 1958: 394, 504). In particular, the tariff revenues enabled the state to pay for national railway construction. Iron and steel thus paid their own way.

Finally, we come to the question of the role of political parties in the determination of tariff policy. As in the United States, there was a split between the Liberals and the Conservatives with the former favouring freer trade and the latter preferring protectionism. But as with the American Democrats, the Canadian Liberals' desire for free trade was substantially constrained by the revenue requirements of the federal state. So strong was this constraint that when they returned to government in 1896 after eighteen years in the political wilderness, they failed to reverse the Conservative shift to protection inaugurated in 1879 (McNaught 1975: 325; Bairoch 1988: 148). As one historian put it, having attacked the system of protection in the election campaign, on returning to office, the Liberal government's 'urge to destroy it [the system of protection] dwindled to the vanishing point ... the idea of moderate protection had triumphed over the old liberal doctrine of free trade' (McInnis 1960: 379). In its long subsequent period of government (1896–1911), the Liberal government did virtually nothing to reform the protectionist system. Moreover, as noted above, the Liberal government raised protectionist tariffs in 1874 in order to eradicate the revenue deficit (although it is true that the Liberal government refused to increase tariff rates further in 1876 to make good the budget problem). In sum, the Liberal desire for free trade was stifled by the practical need for federal revenues through protectionist tariffs.

Indirect tax and protectionism in Australia, 1901–1913

Indirect taxes and the emergence of tariff protectionism

In most major accounts of Australian tariff policy in the colonial period (until 1901), and in the subsequent federation period (1901–13), it is agreed that fiscal considerations played a central role. Particularly from the middle of the nineteenth century on, protectionism became important in the Australian colonies. Although protectionist sentiment was important, fiscal issues were vital. Only New South Wales bucked this trend, preferring free trade over protection in the pre-federation period. However, this was possible in New South Wales only because the state government was able to derive most of its revenue from land sales, while Victoria and Queensland in particular relied on customs tariffs (Butlin 1959: 42–4, 51–3; Howe 1994).

But the significant point to note is the central place of the tariff in federal government finance after 1901 (the year of federation). The constitution stipulated that the commonwealth would appropriate and monopolise the means of tariff revenue collection (Giblin 1980: 48). The famous Braddon clause, Clause 87 of the Constitution,[3] stipulated that the federal government would retain only 25 per cent of revenues raised by the tariff, the remaining 75 per cent being passed on to the state governments. The political rationale for this was identical to that found in Canada (though in clear contrast to Germany): namely the desire to keep the states dependent on the (central) commonwealth government (Deakin 1980: 17; Copland 1980: 35–6; Levi 1988: 148–9; Mills 1980: 64). It is worth noting that the Braddon clause, which gave the commonwealth considerable autonomy from the state governments, was due to expire in 1910. But in 1909 at the Premiers' Conference, Prime Minister Deakin persuaded the state premiers to support a further extension of the commonwealth's fiscal power. Not only did the commonwealth take over the states' debts, but it also paid the states a per capita payment of A$2.50 (or 5s). The net position was to make the commonwealth even more dominant, paying even more to the states than under the old Braddon clause (Alexander 1973: 34–5). Ironically, this was precisely the inverse situation to the one that Bismarck had faced in the 1870s and 1880s. Indeed, Bismarck might have had more success in his struggle with the state governments had he perhaps been born an Australian Democrat or Canadian Liberal rather than a mere Prussian landlord!

Although revenue requirements were central, protection was not incidental but actually intended. As the government stated at the time, a tariff 'must necessarily operate protectively [i.e., for industry] as well as for the production of revenue' (cited in Shann 1948: 397). Indirect taxes provided approximately 98 per cent and customs 80 per cent of net tax commonwealth income between 1902 and 1913 (cf. Groenewegen 1983: 173–4; Levi 1988: 148; Copland 1980: 37). The individual year breakdowns are provided in tables 5.6 and 5.7.

Table 5.6: *Australian commonwealth income, 1902–1913 (in £m)*

Year	(1) Gross total	(2) Net total	(3) Total indirect taxes	(4) Of which, customs	(5) Of which, excise	(6) Direct taxes	(7) Net state property
1902	11.3	8.8	8.9	7.7	1.2	—	—
1903	12.1	9.5	9.7	8.2	1.5	—	—
1904	11.6	8.9	9.1	7.6	1.5	—	—
1905	11.5	8.8	8.8	7.0	1.8	—	—
1906	11.9	9.1	9.0	7.1	1.9	—	0.1
1907	12.8	9.8	9.6	7.7	1.9	—	0.2
1908	15.0	11.7	11.6	9.3	2.3	—	0.1
1909	14.4	10.8	10.8	8.6	2.2	—	—
1910	15.5	11.7	11.6	9.5	2.1	—	0.5
1911	18.8	14.5	13.0	10.5	2.5	1.4	0.1
1912	20.5	15.5	14.7	12.1	2.6	1.4	—
1913	21.9	15.7	15.6	13.1	2.5	1.6	—

Sources and notes: Commonwealth Bureau of Census and Statistics (1909: 800; 1910: 789; 1915: 692). State property (SP) expenditures taken from Barnard (1986: 18). Note that 1901 was omitted because only a half-year figure is available; 1902 was the first full fiscal year of federation. The individual revenue categories do not equal the gross total because the *Official Year Book* includes various revenues in the gross total that it does not itemise. In addition, the table does not include a column for gross SP. Note also that the individual categories do not always equal the net total because of problems incurred with deriving net state property. In those years in which there was a significant SP deficit (i.e., where SP expenditures outweighed revenues), I have entered a dash in the net SP column, but deducted the whole amount from the gross total to derive the net total. (This does cause a problem that becomes apparent in table 5.7.)
(1) Total revenue including gross state property.
(2) Gross total, less gross state property expenditures.
(6) Comprises land tax, which only came into existence in 1911.
(7) Mainly postal revenues, but also, 'defence revenues', patents, trade marks, copyrights, quarantine, coinage and public service pensions funds.

The composition of the products yielding the majority of customs revenue comprises a significant number of manufacturing and agricultural inputs. Between 1903 and 1913, agricultural and textile products, together with metals and machinery, produced approximately 43 per cent of customs revenue (Commonwealth Bureau of Census and Statistics 1908: 802; 1910: 791; 1915: 693). Given that customs revenue provided Australia with no less than 80 per cent of its net income, the role of the *protectionist* tariff as a fiscal weapon is clear.

Table 5.7: *Major revenue categories as a proportion of Australian federal income, 1902–1913*

Year	(1) Total indirect taxes	(2) Of which, customs	(3) Of which, excise	(4) Direct taxes	(5) Net state property
1902	100	88	14	—	—
1903	100	86	16	—	—
1904	100	85	17	—	—
1905	100	80	20	—	—
1906	99	78	21	—	1
1907	98	79	19	—	2
1908	99	79	20	—	1
1909	100	80	20	—	—
1910	99	81	18	—	4
1911	90	72	17	10	1
1912	95	78	17	9	—
1913	99	83	16	10	—
Average for 1902–13	98	80	18	3	1

Note: As was noted in table 5.6, the individual revenue categories will not always add to 100 because of problems incurred with the treatment of net state property revenues. See the notes to table 5.6 for details. Nevertheless, this is highly problematic for one year only – 1913.

What of the role of political parties in the formation of Australian tariff policy? Was there the familiar left–right divide, with the left favouring free trade and the income tax, and the right leaning towards protection and indirect taxation? Although initially it appeared as though such a divide might have occurred, this turned out not to be. The Australian Labor Party (ALP) came to embrace protectionism, although the terms upon which it did so were unique to Australia (and therefore exceptional). The Parliamentary Commission, reporting in 1907, recommended that, 'where protective duties are substantially increased, provision should be made to secure payment of reasonable wages for persons engaged in the industries benefited' (cited in Shann 1948: 398). This followed the Harvester Judgement in 1907, which suggested imposing excise taxes on industry, which would be re-funded to those industries which paid a 'fair and reasonable wage'.[4] This was a means by which the federal government punished those industrialists who took advantage of the tariff and paid less than that declared by the act to be 'the fair thing'. In this way, it was believed that protectionism was no longer a piece of 'class legislation', and was thereby embraced by the ALP as a form of welfarism. Indeed, the ALP acquiesced to the extension of protection in 1908–11, 1914, 1921 and 1926, with the 1908–11 rates double those of 1902 (Shann 1948: 399–400). So, for this exceptional reason, the party variable has no application in the Australian case.

Indirect tax and protectionism in Switzerland, 1870–1913

Switzerland rarely features in the literature as a protectionist economy.[5] The usual assumption tends to be that, like Britain, Switzerland was free trading. But this is incorrect. Liepmann estimates that in 1913, the average tariff in Switzerland was 11 per cent (1938: 415). While these rates are fairly low, they are by no means representative of a free trading economy. The initial question that interests us is whether a fiscal rationale was evident. Again, as with the United States, Canada, Germany and Australia, there was a strict demarcation between revenue sources – indirect taxes and tariffs being the preserve of the federal state, direct taxes being monopolised by the state governments (cantons) (Bickel 1964). As table 5.8 shows, customs revenue was a central component of Swiss central government income (contributing over 80 per cent).

In fact, of all the countries examined in this book, Switzerland relied more on customs revenue than any other 'first world' state.

Swiss tariff rate increases followed the usual Continental pattern, with increases in 1884, 1887, 1891 and 1902 (the latter coming into force in January 1906). Described by Bairoch (1988: 68) as 'semi-protectionist', tariff rates were broad in scope, covering some 1,112 items. However, these tariff rates were too low to have any real economic effect, either in terms of keeping out imports or in terms of increasing the profit rate of Swiss producers. The state's desire for fiscal accumulation was primary (cf. Percy Ashley 1920: 334).

The Swiss case raises one crucial question that so far has not been addressed. The economistic argument would predict Switzerland to be free trading, because of the high trade dependence of the Swiss economy. Although the economy was rather more protectionist than anticipated by the economistic model, nevertheless it could be claimed that low tariffs in Switzerland question the validity of my fiscal

Table 5.8: *Swiss central government tariff income as a proportion of net income, 1885–1910*

Period	Customs income as % of net
1885–9	68
1890–4	80
1895–9	92
1900–4	62
1905–10	93

Source and notes: Statistisches Bureau des Eidgenossenschaft, Departments des Innern (1891: 210–11, 250–1; 1894: 310–11, 312–13; 1904: 206–7, 302–5; 1913: 288–9; 1914: 206–9). State property expenditures include post, telegraph, telephone and railways. These comprise well over 90 per cent of total state property expenditures. Net income was derived by subtracting state property expenditures from gross total income.

hypothesis. Thus it might be asked: would not my fiscal hypothesis predict moderate or even high protection in the Swiss case, given that it was a federal state? Put differently, would not Switzerland's high trade dependence ultimately constrain the level of protection sought by the state?

My argument will be that the nature of the economy and the need for revenue complemented each other. As Alfred Bürgin points out, the Swiss constitution of 1848 made it clear that the Swiss state could not directly intervene in the economy. However, the constitution also provided that tariffs were to be the sole concern of the federal government, since their revenue constituted the backbone of the federal budget (Bürgin 1959: 234–5). In particular, the importance of Switzerland's export trade was specifically recognised, such that the federal state was expected to adhere as closely as possible to free trade (Bürgin 1959: 230). However, given the revenue problem, it was accepted that mild protectionism was essential.

Undoubtedly, the export dependence of the Swiss economy constrained tariff policy, in that tariff rates could not be inflated significantly for revenue purposes, as the economistic argument would claim. However, given the importance of imports (a massive 40 per cent of national income between 1885 and 1913), high tariffs for revenue reasons were not required. A very low tariff (of less than 10 per cent) would still produce as much revenue as a 30 per cent tariff in Russia or the United States. Indeed, countries like Russia and the

Table 5.9: *Central government expenditure burdens of various states (cge/NNP), 1870–1913*

Period	Switz-erland	United States	Can-ada	Aust-ralia	Ger-many	Britain	Aust-ria	France	Italy	Russia	Japan
1870–1913			6.1		8.0	7.7		12.0			
1885–1913	3.5	3.3	5.3	6.1[a]	7.2	8.0	9.7	11.6	14.7	18.3	28.4
Switzerland as base 100	100	94	151	174	206	229	277	331	420	523	811

Sources and notes: See appendix B.
[a] The figure for Australia is for 1902–13.

United States, whose imports comprised a mere 6 per cent and 7 per cent of national income respectively, had no choice but to levy high average tariff rates in order to acquire sufficient central government revenues. But with imports which were six to seven times higher (in real terms) flooding in to Switzerland, a low across-the-board tariff would produce sufficient revenue.

At the same time, large amounts of revenue were not required by the federal government. There were three main reasons for this. Firstly, Switzerland had a particularly low level of concentration. Thus, in 1888/9, Swiss federal government expenditures comprised 26.8 per cent of central and canton expenditures, rising to a mere 32 per cent in 1913, but would be well under 20 per cent if we included in the total the local government expenditures. This political make-up of the Swiss state eased the pressure for high income and, therefore, high tariffs.

Secondly, and equally as important, Swiss central government expenditures were very low, as table 5.9 shows.

The Swiss central government expenditure burden compared to those of various other powers ranged from 66 per cent that of Canada, 57 per cent (Australia), 49 per cent (Germany), 44 per cent (Britain), 36 per cent (Austria), 30 per cent (France), 24 per cent (Italy), 19 per cent (Russia) and a mere 12 per cent (Japan). The only exception to this was the American case, where the Swiss central government burden was 106 per cent that of its American counterpart. What is particularly striking is that the Swiss central government burden was so much lower than the other central governments in *federal* states, bar of course the United States. Clearly, this eased the pressure on the Swiss central government to levy high tariffs and taxes.

170

Table 5.10: *Comparative military burdens (d/NNP), 1870–1913*

Period	Switzerland	United States	Britain	Austria	Italy	Germany	France	Russia	Japan
1870–1913		0.9	3.1	3.1	3.3	3.8	4.0		
1885–1913	1.0							5.1	8.2
Switzerland as base 100	100	90	310	310	330	380	400	510	820

Sources: John M. Hobson (1993), and appendix B.

Thirdly, Switzerland was a *neutral* state, incurring very low military expenditures, as revealed in table 5.10.

Again, with the exception of the United States, the Swiss military burden was extremely low. This was an important factor in Switzerland's low central governmental expenditure (CGE) burden. But equally as important, there was no expenditure-push in Switzerland based on higher military expenditures, unlike, of course, in Germany and particularly Russia. Swiss military expenditures remained remarkably stable throughout the 1885–1913 period, fluctuating within a narrow range of 0.9 and 1.0 per cent of national income.

All this added up to a federal government that was fiscally very weak. However, while the arguments so far help explain why there were no major pressures for the state to raise high taxes and tariffs, there is still one main anomaly remaining. As tables 5.9 and 5.10 show, although the Swiss government and military burdens were indeed considerably lower than most countries, nevertheless they were about equal to the American burdens. And yet of course, the United States had a high tariff regime. To explain why Switzerland's tariff regime was low requires additional variables: the import dependence of a country's economy and its export dependence. A country's level of import dependence has direct consequences for its tariff policy.

The main difference between the United States and Switzerland is that the latter was heavily dependent on imports, while the United States's virtual import independence was no less striking. This had direct ramifications for revenue extraction. Because the United States's imports were in real terms very low, high tariffs were required to extract sufficient customs revenue (as already noted). Conversely, Switzerland's massive flow of imports meant that it could levy low tariffs and yet accumulate sufficient income. In sum, to explain the Swiss case, as well as all others in this book, we need to integrate an economy's import dependence with the fiscal argument in order to fully understand tariff policy (to be discussed in chapter 6).

Conclusion: towards a sociological theory of states and trade policy

I began this chapter by asking two closely related questions: firstly, whether the *form* of state (i.e., regime type) is more important than its *concentration*, and, secondly, whether political parties have a significant impact on trade policy. If parliamentarism has an affinity with free trade and autocracy/authoritarianism with protectionism, then we would expect the United States, Canada, Switzerland and Australia to be free trading. Clearly, this is not the case, suggesting, as we saw in the authoritarian cases of Germany (in chapter 2) and Austria-Hungary (see note 7 in chapter 6), that the *low concentration* (i.e., federalism) of these states was the decisive variable. Nevertheless, the *form* of state is not irrelevant, and is an important variable that differentiates the unitary states of Britain and Russia (to be discussed in chapter 6).

We have also seen that political parties – in the cases of the United States, Canada and Australia – while certainly playing a role in trade regime changes, were not critical. In general, left-wing parties favoured free trade and the income tax, right-wing parties indirect taxes and protectionism. But we have seen that in Canada, the United States and Australia, left-wing parties were substantially constrained by the needs of raising tariffs in order to provide the central government with tax revenues (as is also the case in Germany). Indeed, as I noted in chapter 4, the Canadian Liberal prime minister, Sir Wilfrid Laurier, told the Imperial Conference of 1907 that free trade within the empire was ruled out for revenue reasons (see Tariff Reform League 1910: xv). In addition, the Canadian Liberals from 1896 to 1911 maintained the moderate to high protectionism which they helped set in motion back in 1874 precisely for revenue reasons, while in the United States, the Democrats favoured a general tariff also for revenue reasons. In Australia, the ALP, after some initial reticence, came to embrace the cause of protectionism (albeit under unique circumstances).

While I began the chapter with the questions concerning the role of political parties and the form of state, I finished with a discussion of an economic variable hitherto ignored: the degree of trade dependence. A full appraisal of this, together with a complete theory of trade regime changes, will be undertaken in the next chapter.

Part II

Theorising international and national structural economic and political change

6 A sociological theory of international economic change: the transition to tariff protectionism, 1870–1913

The limits of economism: a critique of Marxism, liberalism and late development theory

Traditional analysis of social and economic change (whether domestic or international), from economic history to historical sociology through to international relations and political science, has in general exaggerated the importance of economic factors as explanatory variables. This chapter will argue that economic variables are important, but that they *alone cannot* provide a sufficient explanation of trade regimes in the nineteenth century. Rather they need to be integrated into a fiscal, political and geopolitical analysis. The empirical chapters 2 through 5 have employed a fiscal-sociological approach to explain tariff protectionism. This chapter will broaden the discussion by spelling out not only the geofiscal and political sources of protectionism, but also integrating economic variables into the analysis. For while I argue that geofiscal, fiscal and political variables are extremely important, they in turn cannot fully explain the transformation in trade regimes in the late nineteenth century.

Before we critically examine the various economistic theories, we need to gauge how protectionist each national economy was between 1880 and 1913. There are two general measurements of how protectionist an economy is. Firstly, average tariffs can be calculated on *dutiable imports only* (expressed in each country's col. 1 in table 6.1), and secondly, average tariffs calculated on *all imports*, whether they are tariffed or not (expressed in each country's col. 2 in table 6.1). Perhaps the best method is the latter. A country might have prohibitive tariffs on a few items, but have low tariffs or none at all on the majority of goods. The first method might mistakenly describe the economy as protectionist. The second method involves calculating customs revenue as a percentage of total imports, thus taking into account the fact that not all imports are tariffed, thereby producing a more accurate reading.

However, it is important to note that even this estimation procedure has its problems. This is because very high (prohibitive) tariffs produce no revenue at all, and low tariffs might produce considerable revenue (assuming sufficiently large imports).[1] Suppose a country levies only prohibitive tariffs on a broad range of goods. Because the customs revenue produced will be zero, then the average tariff will be incorrectly estimated as zero. Nevertheless, despite its problems, it is probably the least unsatisfactory method available. The one exception to this is Britain, which derived revenues (see col. 2 for Britain in table 6.1) from pure revenue tariffs (i.e., tariffs which perform no protectionist function at all). In this one case, col. 1 will be more representative. Table 6.1 charts, where possible, both measurements of tariff rates. Having established the actual levels of protection in each country, we can now appraise the various economistic explanations provided in the social science literature, beginning with the trade dependence variable.

An economy's trade dependence

One of the most common economistic explanations for a country's trade regime found in the general literature revolves around the importance of an economy's trade dependence. Thus, it is often claimed that Britain was free trading because of the economy's high export dependence, where tariffs on imports would have been avoided for fear of potential foreign retaliation on Britain's all-important export trade. Conversely, Russia and the United States were able to levy high tariffs because of the economy's low export dependence, and therefore did *not* have to fear foreign retaliation. This argument suggests that there is an inverse relationship between trade dependence and tariff rates: the higher the trade dependence, the lower the tariff rates; conversely, the lower the trade dependence, the higher the tariff rates.

There are several problems with this formulation, though as we shall see later this argument is not without some merit. To appraise this argument, we need to correlate 'trade dependence' with the level of protection undertaken. The best way to calculate the extent of a country's dependence on trade is to measure its value against national

Table 6.1:   *Tariff rates of various states, 1880–1913*

Period	Britain (1)	(2)	Switzer-land (1)	(2)	Germany (1)	(2)	Canada (1)	(2)	Australia (1)	(2)	United States (1)	(2)	Russia (1)	(2)
1880–94	0	5	—	4	—	8	28	20	—	—	46	28	—	26
1895–1904	0	5	—	5	—	9	29	17	—	—	47	26	—	35
1905–13	0	5	—	4	—	7	27	17	31	18	42	22	—	33
1913	0	—	11	—	16	—	26	17	—	—	40	18	73	30
1880–1913	0	5	—	4	—	8	28	18	28	18	45	26	—	31
Rank[a]	7		6		5		4		3		2		1	
Tariff Level			Low		Low-moderate		Moderate		Moderate		High		High	
Code	FT		LP		L/MP		MP		MP		HP		HP	

Sources and notes: Australia: (1 and 2) Commonwealth Bureau of Census and Statistics (1909: 643; 1916: 592). Canada: (1 and 2) Dominion Bureau of Statistics (1925: 458); USA: (1 and 2) US Department of Commerce (Bureau of the Census) (1960: 888); Russia: (2) Khromov (1950: 484–5); Hoffding (1912: 86); Miller (1926: 71); see table 3.7.
FT = free trade; LP = low protection; MP = moderate protection; HP = high protection.
[a] This ranks each country, where the most protectionist economy (i.e., tsarist Russia) is ranked 1 and the least protectionist (i.e., Britain) is ranked 7.
(1) Average tariff rates on *dutiable* imports only; see above for sources. Note that for 1913, the figures were taken from Liepmann (1938: 383–98, 415). For Canada, Australia and the United States, see above. However, note that for all other countries prior to 1913 reliable data on tariff rates on dutiable items do not exist (and I have chosen not to use the sporadic data that do exist).
(2) Average tariff rates on *all* imports calculated by measuring customs revenue as a proportion of national income; see appendix B for sources.

income (Deane and Cole 1969: 28; see table 6.2). The levels of protection are derived from table 6.1; they are set against the levels of trade dependence (derived from table 6.2) and are displayed in figure 6.1. Figure 6.1 examines this inverse relationship between general trade dependence and tariff rates. While the model's predictive capacity is strong in the cases of Britain, Germany, the United States and Russia, in the cases of Australia, Canada and Switzerland, it is less reliable.

However, the model specifically correlates an inverse relationship between *export* dependence and tariff rates (i.e., high export dependence = free trade; low export dependence = protectionism). Figure 6.2

Table 6.2: *The trade dependence of various national economies, 1875–1913*

Period	Switzerland E	I	T	Britain E	I	T	Australia E	I	T	Germany E	I	T	Canada E	I	T	Russia E	I	T	United States E	I	T
1875–84	30	38	68	26	37	63							15	19	34	10	6	16	8	7	15
1885–94	30	40	70	24	32	56				16	19	35	13	16	29	8	6	14	7	7	14
1895–1904	29	42	71	21	31	52				16	19	35	16	15	31	9	6	15	8	6	13
1905–13				26	34	60	28	21	49	18	22	40	18	25	43				7	5	12
Average for:																					
1875–1913	30	40	70	24	34	58							16	20	36	9	6	15	8	7	13
1885–1913										17	20	37									
1905–13							28	21	49												
Level of trade dependence	High			High			Moderate-high			Moderate			Moderate			Low			Low		

Sources and notes: Trade data: Australia: Butlin (1962: 256–7); Britain: Imlah, cited in Mitchell (1992: 557, 562); Canada: Dominion Bureau of Statistics (1925: 458); Germany: Hoffmann (1965: 520, 524); Russia: Khromov, cited in Mitchell (1992: 556, 561); Switzerland: Mitchell (1992: 557, 562); United States: US Department of Commerce (Bureau of the Census) (1960: 537–8). E: exports; I: imports; T: total trade; all measured as a proportion of national income.

Appendix B provides a full discussion of national income, and its attendant methodological problems. It is worth noting that even with something as seemingly straightforward as exports and imports, there are considerable problems with constructing such data. Of the two methods of measuring trade, this table relies on 'special' rather than 'general' trade. The omission of re-exports in the 'special' trade calculation is only problematic in the British and Swiss cases, leading to an underestimation of export dependence by approximately 10 per cent (Kuznets 1967: 19–20, 96). Bosshardt and Nydegger (1964) produce a slightly higher figure for Switzerland. Nevertheless, my data compare favourably with other sets (e.g., Kuznets 1967).

One further problem emerges from how trade has been valued. The f.o.b. (free on board) method applied to exports and the c.i.f. (cost, insurance and freight) method applied to imports will lead to a distortion of the data. The basic effect will be to underestimate export dependence and exaggerate import dependence (Woytinsky and Woytinsky 1955: 37).

Figure 6.1: The 'general' linkage between trade dependence and trade regimes

Trade regime	Switzerland	Britain	Australia	Canada	Germany	United States	Russia
Actual trade dependence	High	High	Moderate-high	Moderate	Moderate	Low	Low
Model's prediction	Free trade	Free trade	Low protection	Low-moderate protection	Low-moderate protection	High protection	High protection
Actual regime	Low protection	Free trade	Moderate protection	Moderate protection	Low-moderate protection	High protection	High protection
Predictive capacity	Weak-moderate	Strong	Weak	Moderate	Strong	Strong	Strong

Notes: Rows 1 and 2 are derived from table 6.2; row 3 is derived from table 6.1.

Figure 6.2: The 'specific' linkage between export dependence and trade regimes

Trade regime	Switzerland	Britain	Australia	Germany	Canada	United States	Russia
Actual level of export dependence	High	Moderate-high	High	Moderate	Moderate	Low	Low
Model's prediction	Free trade	Free trade	Free trade	Moderate protection	Moderate protection	High protection	High protection
Actual regime	Low protection	Free trade	Moderate protection	Low-moderate protection	Moderate protection	High protection	High protection
Predictive capacity	Weak-moderate	Strong	Weak	Moderate	Strong	Strong	Strong

Notes: Rows 1 and 2 are derived from table 6.2; row 3 is derived from table 6.1.

examines this relationship. Clearly, on the basis of an inverse relation-ship between export dependence and tariff rates, the model is accurate in the cases of Britain, Canada, Russia and the United States, though it is less reliable in the cases of Australia, Switzerland and Germany. These anomalies imply that there is an inverse relationship between trade dependence and tariff levels, but that it is looser than the model suggests. In short, therefore, trade dependence cannot provide a *sufficient* causal variable in explaining trade policy. Moreover, Amer-ican and Russian low trade dependence cannot in themselves explain why they became protectionist in the first place. Thus, while trade (and especially export) dependence has relevance, it is merely one variable among many that explain trade regimes.

The impact of an economy's degree of backwardness

Traditional social theory, borrowing from Gerschenkron's late devel-opment theory and Friedrich List's nationalist approach, assumes that Britain was free trading until 1913 because it was economically strong compared to the late European developers such as Germany and Russia (as well as Austria and Italy, the United States, Canada and Australia), whose backward economies and infant industries required tariff protection. This suggests an inverse relationship between national economic advancement and tariff rates. Thus, the more advanced the economy, the lower the tariff rate; the more backward the economy, the higher the tariff rate. An economy's overall level of development can best be measured through per capita national income. To appraise this argument, I begin by correlating tariff rates with per capita income levels measured as a proportion of Britain's level (where Britain = 100), laid out in table 6.3.

According to my estimates in table 6.3, the late development theory appears to be very weak in its ability to predict tariff rates. Only in the cases of Britain and Russia is there a strong correlation. However, it might be objected that this depiction fails to meet Gerschenkron's model head on. This is because his model is one of *industrialisation*, which requires a correlation of trade regimes with 'levels of industria-lisation' (i.e., per capita manufacturing output, as opposed to per capita income). I have, therefore, drawn up table 6.4 specifically to address this objection.

However, even under this set of calculations, the correlation between economic backwardness and trade regimes is weak, suggesting that

Table 6.3: *Per capita income levels and trade regimes*

Country	Economy in relation to Britain 1880	1913	Predicted level of protection 1880	1913	Actual level of protection 1880	1913	Model's predictive accuracy
Britain	100	100	FT	FT	FT	FT	Strong
Australia	—	173*	—	FT	—	MP	Weak
United States	116*	150*	FT	FT	HP	MP	Weak
Canada	90*	130*	LP	FT	MP	MP	Weak
Switzerland	73	76	MP	MP	LP	LP	Weak
Germany	61	74	M/HP	MP	LP	L/MP	Weak-moderate
Russia	26	31	HP	HP	HP	HP	Strong

Sources and notes: National income: detailed in appendix B. Population figures: United States: Department of Commerce (Bureau of the Census) (1970: 8); Canada: Urquhart and Buckley (1965: 14); Britain: Flora (1987: 80–9); Australia: Mitchell (1983: 14). Exchange rates: Bidwell (1970).

FT = free trade; LP = low protection; MP = moderate protection; HP = high protection; * approximation only.

These figures represent per capita national income, which is the best indicator of an economy's strength, and have been converted into index numbers so as to facilitate comparison. Data for European countries were derived from Crafts (1983: 389, 394). Crafts's figures were calculated using purchasing power parities, which is a much more accurate method of comparison than using exchange rates to convert into one currency. However, such calculations do not exist for the United States, Canada or Australia. I have, therefore, had to make the calculations by converting per capita product into sterling before comparing them with the British figures. The 1913 US data were taken from Bairoch (1982: 294) and checked against an exchange rate calculation. Note, however, that conversion with exchange rates is highly problematic; for details, see O'Brien and Keyder (1978: 34) and Crafts (1983: 388). Even so, this is the least unsatisfactory method available.

such a model cannot provide a sufficient explanation of trade regimes. Again, only in the cases of Britain and Russia is there a strong correlation. But even here, there are substantial problems with the late development model, not least because correlation does not necessarily equate with causality. I noted in chapter 3 that Russia ultimately sought (after much internal bureaucratic wrangling) a 'partial' rather than a 'full' industrialisation. This was because tsarist autocracy favoured despotism and military power, rather than the full development of the economy. It would, therefore, be wrong to assume that

Table 6.4: *Per capita industrialisation levels and trade regimes*

Country	Economy in relation to Britain		Predicted level of protection		Actual level of protection		Model's predictive accuracy
	1880	1913	1880	1913	1880	1913	
Britain	100	100	FT	FT	FT	FT	Strong
United States	44	110	M/HP	FT	HP	MP	Weak
Switzerland	45	76	M/HP	MP	LP	LP	Weak
Germany	29	74	HP	MP	LP	L/MP	Weak-moderate
Canada	11	40	HP	M/HP	MP	MP	Weak
Australia	—	17	—	HP	—	MP	Weak
Russia	11	17	HP	HP	MP	HP	Strong

Source and notes: These are index numbers (where Britain = 100), and were calculated from Bairoch (1982: 281, 286, 294). It is worth noting that there are various problems with this particular estimation of per capita industrialisation levels, not least its inability to include important factors such as productivity.

Russia underwent a 'forced industrialisation' as a response to 'economic backwardness', as late development theory argues. And the fact that the model cannot explain the case of tsarist Russia is problematic, if for no other reason than this was supposedly Gerschenkron's strongest case.

Moreover, although Britain's *relatively* strong economy was *a* factor in the Liberal government's decision to maintain free trade, economic 'forwardness' cannot provide a sufficient explanation, for two main reasons. Firstly, it cannot explain why the Conservatives – especially the free trading Conservatives – embraced protectionism after 1906 (which could have become actual state policy had the Conservatives returned to power in 1910). Secondly, and more importantly, Britain's trade policies were fundamentally entwined in fiscal politics. Fiscal politics actually took precedence over trade politics in Britain. How else could we explain the shift of even the staunchest Conservative free traders over to the 'devil' of protection? They were prepared to sacrifice the health of the economy (as they saw it) on the altar of regressive indirect taxes in pursuit of electoral power. Thus the condition of the economy provides only partial utility in explaining either Britain's maintenance of free trade, or Russia's shift to high protection.

The role of class analysis (Marxism)

Another common argument in the literature suggests that classes play a fundamental role in the determination of trade regimes. Thus, it is usually claimed that Britain was free trading because the bourgeoisie (especially the financiers in the City of London) were the strongest in the world and found free trade maximised their economic power. Russian industry (along with industry in Germany and the other countries discussed in this volume) was relatively weaker, and therefore favoured tariffs as a means to protect their domestic position from cheap and superior foreign imports (this echoes Friedrich List's (1841/1885) 'infant industry' argument). German grain tariffs were supposedly the result of lobbying by the Junker class, which, though economically in decline, still had access to considerable political power. While this argument reaches its apogee in Marxism, it is employed at a general level by a wide variety of perspectives and authors, particularly liberal/neoclassical (the latter being the subject of the next section).

Class analysis, while certainly having some relevance, is ultimately inadequate, and cannot provide a *sufficient* explanation for changes either in trade or tax regimes. To return to the German case, class analysis cannot adequately explain the 1879 grain tariff given that the Junker class, in whose trading interests the tariff was supposed to have been legislated, was in favour of free trade. Nor can it explain why grain tariffs came down in the 1890s, much to the annoyance of the Junkers who were clamouring for higher tariffs in the depth of agricultural recession (a point that is particularly problematic given neo-Marxism's tendency to define the Kaiserreich as a Junker/feudal state). Moreover, to a certain extent, the state took into account the whole agricultural producing community as opposed to the narrow interests of the Junkers. In the British case, the argument that free trade was maintained at the behest of the City of London is manifestly wrong. The City voted for Tory protectionism. But much more problematic for class analysis is the central argument of chapter 4: that the British state in 1909 maintained free trade by going directly against the long-run fiscal interests of the dominant classes in order to shore up its own political power. Class analysis probably struggles most in the case of tsarist Russia, where class interests had a negligible input into general government policy.

The most problematic Marxist assumption is that class interests and requirements are automatically translated into government policy. This is to assume that the state is in effect (despite considerable rhetoric and pleadings to the contrary) little more than a mirror of class forces. However, as shown in figure 6.3 (p. 191), class pressures are refracted when they enter the state into a variety of policy directions. There can be no one-to-one correspondence between class interests and government policy (as even many Marxists are forced to concede). However, this is no small concession, because this means that there must be something the state adds to government policy that is quintessentially unique to it and not reducible to class interests; that something is what I call state power. In chapter 7, we shall see why the Marxist notion of 'relative autonomy' cannot capture this lack of correspondence between class interests and government policy.

Nevertheless, despite these qualifications (to be treated more systematically in chapter 7), class politics and class requirements certainly helped shape trade policy, as the lower portion of figure 6.3 (p. 191) shows (class inputs will be integrated into my explanation at the end of this chapter).

Liberal/neoclassical theory of interest groups and trade regimes

Perhaps the best example of the liberal/neoclassical theory of trade regimes is found in the recent work by Ronald Rogowski (1989). Rogowski's analysis is impressive not least for the vast array of examples, produced through both time and space, used to support the theory. Invoking the Stolper–Samuelson model (in turn based on the Heckscher–Ohlin model), Rogowski argues that trade regimes can be predicted according to the weights or endowments of the various factors of production: land, labour and capital. Thus, in a period of rising trade (e.g., 1840–1914), where a particular factor of production is abundant, it will advocate free trade, whereas conversely 'scarcity' prompts a protectionist stance. While Rogowski has some success in predicting trade regime outcomes from this economistic 'interest group' model, there are sufficient anomalies to call the theory into question.

Firstly, the model predicts free trade in Britain and Switzerland (Rogowski 1989: 31, 34–7). While the model is accurate in the British case, its prediction of free trade in Switzerland is inaccurate; certainly the model is unable to explain Switzerland's low protectionist regime. Secondly, the model predicts that, after 1890, German industry moved rapidly towards free trade prompting the trade treaties of 1892–4. 'As Germany's accelerating economic growth raised it into the ranks of the capital-abundant countries after 1890, the protectionist "marriage of iron and rye" began to fray, exactly as the theory would predict' (Rogowski 1989: 40). The problem here is that the trade treaties of the 1890s were short-lived, iron and rye 'remarried' in 1902 and industrial and agricultural tariffs were raised again in 1906. Thirdly, though the model correctly predicts protectionism in Canada, the United States and Australia until 1900 (Rogowski 1989: 43–6, 47–9), the assumption that the North American countries had moved clearly towards free trade by 1913 is incorrect. In 1913, while US tariff rates had indeed come down (though from an extremely high base), the United States was still clearly protectionist, with average rates of 40 per cent on 'tariffed only' imports and 18 per cent on 'all' imports. Moreover, in Canada, not only did protectionism remain moderately high, but also, most importantly, it could not be differentiated in magnitude from the rates experienced from 1880 to 1912. Indeed, if Rogowski was correct, we would expect to see a definite decline in tariff rates from 1890 onwards; but no such trend is evident (see Dominion Bureau of Statistics 1925: 458). However, in the Canadian case, Rogowski admits that 'what the theory predicts simply does not come to pass' (1989: 49). Nevertheless, he offers an exception that supposedly proves the rule: namely that Canada remained protectionist only because of its over-riding fear of American imports. Thus, he argues that with all other countries – especially Britain and the countries of Continental Europe – Canadian tariffs supposedly came down (1989: 48). However, even this rejoinder is incorrect, since on all British imports as well as dutiable imports, the Canadian tariff rate in 1913 was higher than the average rate for the period 1869–1912 (Dominion Bureau of Statistics 1925: 458).

The neoclassical approach is often termed the 'rent-seeking perspective', derived from 'public choice' theory. This approach is essentially an 'interest group' theory. More specifically, it gives pride of place to 'producer' groups as opposed to 'consumer' groups. Following the classic analysis of Mancur Olson (1965, 1982), this approach sees 'producer' groups as more influential in shaping government trade policy because of their superior ability to organise effectively compared to the more heterogeneous and unwieldy consumer groups (Tullock 1967; Stigler 1971; Krueger 1974; Posner 1974; Caves 1976; Pincus 1977; Tollison 1982; Frey 1984). Effectively using what various public choice theorists call a 'capture' theory of government, the approach shares a basic similarity with Marxism, as Robert Tollison concedes (1982: 591). The only difference (found particularly in the analysis of Rogowski) is the notion that capital and labour often join together in pursuit of a particular trade policy. Despite this, the emphasis on producer groups in the determination of trade policy is very similar to Marxism's basic approach.

A further overlap with Marxism is the theory's assumption that government policy is always the outcome of the preferences of various factors of production. Again, I reiterate the point that there is no automatic translation of interest-group requirements into government policy because the state itself has certain interests (e.g., fiscal) which often cut across pure economic interests. In short, the neoclassical model cannot provide a sufficient basis for explaining or predicting national trade regimes in the late nineteenth century.

Tariff protectionism as an 'economically rational' strategy?

I have noted in the cases of Germany and Russia in chapters 2 and 3 that the tariff was not a principal economic concern of producers, either for importers or exporters. In fact, however, the tariff was merely one of a whole host of factors which affected the trade calculations of producer groups. In Russia, for example, high tariffs on foreign imports did not always offset or reduce imports, because foreign producers could provide a range of more important benefits that were missing within Russia. These ranged from superior quality goods, better marketing arrangements of foreign goods and quicker foreign delivery times, to name but a few. In addition, Russian producers sometimes found it cheaper to import from abroad rather than incur the high cost of Russian internal freight rates (Kirchner 1981; see also chapter 3 in this book). This single point has major ramifications for the theory of tariff protectionism found throughout the literature. From Marxist and liberal through to late development (statist) and nationalist theory, this would suggest that the 'economic' benefits of tariffs to domestic producers have been exaggerated, at least for the 1870–1913 period. The basic economistic assumption is that tariffs were a major factor which supported domestic producers.

The litmus test for the economic rationality of tariff protectionism is quite straightforward: if tariffs had a primarily *economic* rationale, foreign imports would have declined after 1880. But in all countries imports *increased* after 1880. The conventional account of nineteenth-century trade development argues that, between 1846 and 1873, Europe was in an economic up-phase, with free trade maximising the growth and development of international trade and, in turn, collective economic growth. This promoted interdependence, cooperation and ultimately peace. Conversely, the economic slow-down after 1873 to 1914 was accompanied by a return to mercantilism (often termed 'neomercantilism'). Supposedly high protectionist rates and low economic growth combined to stifle international trade, in turn reducing collective economic growth, promoting national hostility, autarchy and eventually war. This familiar account is, however, highly problematic.[2]

According to the calculations of Paul Bairoch (1976: 78), *real* European exports (i.e., exports measured as a proportion of total European income) stood at 9.4 per cent in 1860 and 10.9 per cent in 1870 (just before the 'crash'). The real level climbed to 12.5 per cent by 1880, levelling out to 12.6 per cent by 1890, and rising dramatically thereafter (particularly after 1900), to 14 per cent by 1913. Thus, in an age of so-called 'high protection' after 1890, the growth in trade was prolific (Bairoch 1988; Woytinsky and Woytinsky 1955: 40; Ashworth 1962: 183). Moreover, as Bairoch points out, it has 'not been sufficiently recognised that at the end of the [long] nineteenth century ... the relative importance of exports in relation to the gross national product reached a level in Europe that it has not equalled since' (1988: 1).

The fact is, therefore, that after supposedly thirty years of 'neomercantilism', exports had grown by a considerable 49 per cent in real terms over the 1860s 'free trade' level, and 28 per cent over the 1870 level (the latter date representing the peak of the free trade era). Of course, if it can be shown that the increase in exports went outside Europe, say to the third world (as many economistic theories of imperialism suggest), then it might feasibly be argued that tariff rates hindered intra-European or intra-first world trade (i.e., the United States and Europe). This, however, was not the case. In 1860, prior to the great colonial scramble, intra-first world exports accounted for 76.6 per cent of total European exports. In 1900, the figure was 77.8 per cent, dropping only very marginally to 75.4 per cent in 1910 (Bairoch 1976: 82; cf. Liepmann 1938: 412). In short, rising European trade after 1873 was absorbed *within first world* markets. European trade destined for third world markets remained stagnant. In 1860, 21 per cent of European exports went to third world markets, while in 1910 this stood at 22 per cent. As many others have pointed out, particularly with reference to Britain – most notably John A. Hobson (1902: 34) –

this single fact undermines those economistic theories which suggest that European imperialism occurred as a means of avoiding first world tariff barriers (see also Cameron 1993: 301; Cain 1979: 50; Crouzet 1975: 223). European tariff barriers posed no serious obstacle to intra-European trade – quite the reverse, with trade significantly increasing in real terms after 1880, and especially after 1890 (cf. Stein 1984: 372). In short, a marginal 1.6 per cent drop in intra-first world real trade between 1860 and 1910 cannot explain imperialism, nor can it support the notion that European protectionism had a fundamental economic core.

Moreover, we would expect the export strength of each economy to be high in the free trade era (c. 1850–70) and low in the subsequent down-phase (post-1873). However, in each country examined in this book, exports were higher in the 1880–1913 period than in the 1850–70 era, although the United States, Australia and Canada showed little change (Kuznets 1967: 96–120). As Bairoch also points out, 'the expansion of trade (and economic growth) was much faster in the countries which had adopted ... protectionism than in the United Kingdom which remained liberal' (1988: 89, see also 44).

In addition, it is worth noting that the growth of trade was not a simple function of economic growth. It is true that the growth in exports was enabled by the second industrial revolution and the development of industrialisation in various late developers, as well as the turn-of-the-century boom – in turn enabled by developing international cooperation engendered in part by states engaging in international conferences (Murphy 1994: especially ch. 4). But this cannot explain why the growth of foreign trade among the developed countries outstripped economic growth. Thus, between 1880 and 1913, total first world trade grew by 41 per cent, while total product grew by 32 per cent (Kuznets 1967: 16; Bairoch 1988). The liberal argument suggests that protectionism after 1879 stifled economic growth, while the earlier free trade period had promoted growth. But between 1890–2 and 1913, European product grew not only at very high levels, but at rates that outstripped those experienced at the height of European free trade (1858–60 and 1877–9).

Clearly, the label 'neomercantilism', used for the protectionist era after 1877, is exaggerated. Tariffs did not stifle intra-European trade, a fact which suggests that the conventional picture of tariffs, understood as simple economic weapons wielded at the behest of strong economic interest groups and classes, is something of a myth. Perhaps this is unsurprising, given that tariff rates were very rarely prohibitive (cf. Stein 1984). This is not to suggest that economic factors are irrelevant to an explanation of trade regime changes. It is to suggest, however, that economic factors are not as important as traditional analyses argue, and that certainly economic arguments cannot provide a sufficient explanation for the rise of protectionism after 1877.

This reinforces my claim that taxation was crucial in the rise of protectionism after 1877. Tariff levels were on the whole only moderate, and 'though often irritating, were not generally high enough to cause great difficulty' (Ashworth 1962: 216). And as Ashworth goes on to point out, 'governments could hardly afford to make them too high, since they wanted increased revenue from the duties' (1962: 143, 216). Thus, if economic rationality was not *central* to tariff protection, an alternative multidimensional geofiscal, fiscal, political and economic analysis is required.

The link between modes of taxation, fiscal accumulation and trade regimes

The central argument developed in this book is that changes in trade regimes can to an important extent be understood in terms of changes in taxation at the national level (itself a response to internal and external factors). This is because tariffs are indirect taxes. The linkage between taxation and tariff protectionism is relatively simple: where states moved towards indirect modes of taxation (Germany and Russia, the United States, Canada, Switzerland, Italy and Austria-Hungary), they shifted towards tariff protectionism. However, where the state moved away from indirect taxes towards a more progressive income-based mode of taxation, as in Britain, free trade could be maintained and protectionism avoided. To conceptualise this, I develop the concept of the *mode of taxation*.

As with Marx's famous 'mode of production', the mode of taxation comprises the *social relations of taxation* and the *forces of taxation*. The *relations of taxation* refers to where the burden of taxation lies – either on the lower or upper income orders – whereas the *forces of taxation* comprise the various means which support the relations of taxation. It is central to my argument that the relations of taxation are not determined simply by the social relations of production emanating within the 'national' sphere. Rather, the social relations of taxation (unlike Marx's relations of production) are determined by a complex set of international, national and sub-national factors: specifically geofiscal, political, fiscal, class and economic. In the rest of this chapter, I trace the 'forces of taxation' which comprised:

(1) international geofiscal pressures;
(2) national (unit-force) state power/state–society variables;
(3) international and domestic economic and fiscal variables.

These are laid out in schematic form in figure 6.3. Most importantly, the forces of taxation were different for each state, leading therefore to different trade policy outcomes. We shall take each in turn.

The limits of economism and neorealism: geofiscalism and trade regime changes, 1789–1913

Beginning with the top left-hand side of figure 6.3 (which deals with external/international inputs), we note that geofiscalism was a crucial factor which ultimately led to changes in trade regime. Thus, the increasing costs of war preparation associated with the second military revolution, as well as the rising tension internationally, prompted states to respond by raising taxes. In most cases (except Britain), this led to the rise of tariff protectionism. In order to assess and refine my theory, it is important, firstly, to compare it to its main rivals and, secondly, to place it in the context of trade regime changes in the long nineteenth century (1789–1913).

There are two main theories which emphasise the importance of 'international' causes of trade regime changes: long-wave Kondratieff cycle theory, and hegemonic stability/long-cycle political theory. The most common is the long-cycle economic theory based on Kondratieff's work. Essentially, Kondratieff claimed to have uncovered fifty-year economic cycles, subsequently dubbed 'Kondratieffs'. These Kondratieffs are treated as the independent variable, trade policies the dependent. The model predicts that an upturn in the cycle (i.e., the initial twenty-five years of prosperity) leads to an international free trade regime, while the subsequent downturn leads to an international protectionist regime. Measuring the long-wave fluctuations of prices from 1789 to 1913 reveals approximately two and a half cycles. According to Kondratieff (1935), the dates of these cycles are as follows: a first cycle going into an up-phase from 1789 to 1814,

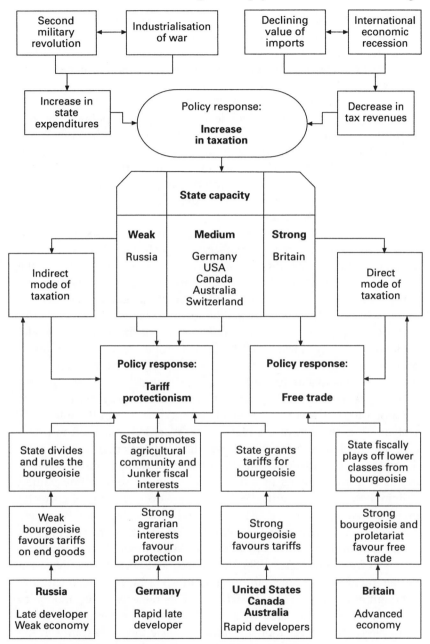

Figure 6.3: A multi-factor sociological theory of trade regime changes, 1870–1913

followed by a downturn from 1814 to 1849; a second phase going from 1849 to 1873, followed by a downturn from 1873 to 1896; and a third cycle beginning with an up-phase between 1896 and 1920. Most economistic theories – Marxist and liberal ones in particular – essentially assume that free trade accompanies an up-turn and a recession leads to protectionism. Indeed, the majority of works found in economic history, historical/political sociology and political science analyse the shift to protectionism on the basis of this long-cycle economistic model. Thus the shift to protection after 1873 is usually explained by the international economic downturn, with producers pressurising their states for protection. Implicitly (and sometimes explicitly), this explanation assumes that the 1849–73 up-phase explains the rise of free trade.

Although this argument has some merit (to be discussed shortly), it does have, however, some major anomalies. For, if this economistic long cycle theory has any explanatory foundation, it should, at the very least, be able to predict the shifts in trade regime after 1789. In the 1789–1814 up-phase, the model would predict movement towards free trade, while in the subsequent downturn (1814–49), Europe should revert back towards protectionism. However, at this point the model goes badly wrong. From 1789 to 1814, Europe increased its rates of protectionism (typified by Britain), while from 1814 to 1849, rates decreased (albeit slowly) rather than increased.[3] Moreover, in this period, it is worth pointing out that the economic price cycle was not autonomous, but was fundamentally affected by war in the inter-state system. Thus the end of the Napoleonic Wars led to a peak in prices (due to wartime shortages and war-debt repayments), which came down thereafter, also due in part to war-debt repayments, as well as technical improvements in efficiency also linked to wartime stimuli (Gilpin 1987: 106; Cameron 1993: 281). However, the model correctly predicts free trade for the 1849–73 period – or as Stein (1984) points out, *freer* trade (cf. Bairoch 1988: 42). The theory also correctly predicts protectionism from 1873 to 1896. But while the model would predict a return to freer trade after 1896, this subsequent period actually saw a deepening of protectionism throughout much of Europe. In conclusion, although this model is not without some relevance, its anomalies render it at best highly problematic as the basis of a general theory.[4]

An alternative international *political-economic* theory is found in the neorealist theory of hegemonic stability (HST from henceforth), first proposed by Edward Carr (1939), developed more fully by Charles

Kindleberger (1973, 1981) and more recently by various neorealists such as Robert Gilpin (1975, 1981, 1987), Stephen Krasner (1976, 1977a, 1977b, 1979) and David Lake (1988), as well as the 'long-cycle' perspective found in the works of George Modelski (1978) and Modelski and William Thompson (1988). It is also complemented by the economistic neo-Marxist variant, initiated by Immanuel Wallerstein (1984), and developed in particular by Robert Cox (1986, 1987), Christopher Chase-Dunn (1989), Joshua Goldstein (1988), Giovanni Arrighi (1990) and Stephen Gill (1990). Since the neo-Marxist variant explicitly links the Kondratieff cycles with both the hegemonic cycle and trade regime changes (the criticism of which is found above), we can focus here on the specific link between hegemony and trade regimes.

The standard correlations between 'hegemony and free trade' and 'declining hegemony and protectionism' appear on first sight plausible only for the post-1860 period. The theory argues that Britain was a hegemon after 1815, and would therefore predict free trade from that date onwards. Although tariff rates came down thereafter, they remained very high for several decades, especially in Britain (Weiss and Hobson 1995: 124–7). Moreover, although the corn laws were repealed in Britain in 1846, British free trade was not achieved until 1860 – the year that signalled a shift to 'freer trade' on the Continent. Given that British hegemony began in 1815 – or even earlier according to Modelski (1978) – and given also that HST predicts free trade under conditions of hegemony, why then did Europe have to wait at least half a century before such a shift transpired (cf. McKeown 1983: 76)? It might be retorted that, 'what's fifty years in some 500 years of capitalism?' But fifty years is a very long time when so-called 'British hegemony' was at its peak for only sixty.

My alternative model initially focuses on the impact of the international geofiscal cycle. Figure 6.4 correlates the rise and decline of central government expenditures with trade regime changes in the long nineteenth century.

My geofiscal model predicts that protectionism will be high from 1792 to 1815 (in line with the costly Napoleonic Wars). In the 1815–46 period, international politics was cooling off from the super-heated military activities of the 1792–1815 period, and states were embarking on a recovery phase, enabled by what has been termed the 'Thirty Years' Peace' (Martineau, cited in Joshua Goldstein 1988: 333). Nevertheless, although the inter-state system was moving into a relatively

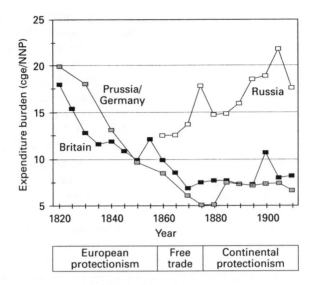

Source: Table B1, p. 289. For central government expenditures and national income data, see appendix B.

Figure 6.4: The international geofiscal cycle and trade regime changes, 1820–1913

peaceful phase, state budgets were still very high, owing largely to the extraordinarily high debt repayments incurred through wartime borrowing. The high demand for revenues led to reliance on indirect taxes, so that tariff rates remained high, diminishing only very slowly. In Britain, in particular, reliance on indirect taxes and tariffs diminished slowly, until finally, in 1846, with the income tax having been restored in 1842, Britain had the fiscal autonomy to shift to freer trade (Ralph Davis 1966; Brown 1958: 229; Hilton 1977: 257–68; Stein 1984: 363; Kindleberger 1987: 88–9; O'Brien and Pigman 1992: 97).

Nevertheless, even the shift to free trade had a fiscal rationale. The report of the Select Committee on Import Duties (published in 1840) noted that, of the 1,150 items subject to customs duty, a mere 9 produced some 90 per cent of total tariff revenue (Brown 1958: 144, 154–7). This meant that some considerable administrative energy was wasted in collecting the minuscule revenue from most items. Therefore, through the 1842, 1845 and 1846 budgets, Peel cut the vast majority of tariffs so as to cut down on administrative wastage (Brown 1958:

228–9; Fielden 1969: 82; Hilton 1977: 267; O'Brien and Pigman 1992: 96; Kindleberger 1987: 88). In the process, Britain moved rapidly towards free trade. Indeed:

> The repeal of the Corn Laws in 1846 cannot be regarded as a symbolic event signalling that Britain's political elite had already been 'converted' to free trade and intended to pursue a Cobdenite policy in relations with other states. Repeal was forced upon many politicians. They 'tidied up' tariffs for sound fiscal reasons.
>
> (O'Brien and Pigman 1992: 97)

On the Continent, the shift to free trade was even slower, occurring after 1860 with the Cobden–Chevalier Treaty of that year. The pressure to reduce indirect taxes was exacerbated on the Continent by the 1848 revolutions, where tax-payers revolted against oppressive and highly regressive indirect taxes.

As Karl Polanyi (1957) originally noted, in economic terms, there was nothing natural or inevitable in the shift to free trade in the middle of the nineteenth century. In fact, the rise of free trade is, in the context of trade regimes in the two centuries following 1700, undeniably unique. Free trade occupied no more than fifteen years out of some two hundred – and even then, it was hardly free. Indeed, given that protectionism had been the norm, the rise of free trade poses a particular theoretical challenge. I argue that the rise of free trade was to a large extent the outcome of a unique and contingent set of political circumstances that happened to come together by the middle of the century.

I have already pointed to the international geofiscal impact of relative peace in conjunction with a relatively successful balance of power diplomacy. But the geofiscal cycle was to an extent a function of the political 'cycle'. This revolved around various diplomatic manoeuvres which converged around the middle of the nineteenth century. Most importantly, Britain's and France's signing of the Cobden–Chevalier Treaty was premised on the diplomatic consideration of strengthening Anglo-French relations, so as to prevent a European war over Italy (Dunham 1930: 61–2; Fielden 1969: 89; Iliasu 1971; Ratcliffe 1975b: 146–8; Stein 1984: 364–5; O'Brien and Pigman 1992: 98–9). In particular, France's political isolation could be remedied through the signing of a free trade treaty. Moreover, Britain was anxious to sign a treaty with France because the government feared the build-up of French naval power (Iliasu 1971; McKeown 1983: 84–5; Krasner 1976).

Austria, traditionally a protectionist power, shifted to the 'most liberal tariff' in its history. 'The reduction of tariffs which began in 1851 did not result from the conversion of a protectionist dynasty to the principles of free trade, but was rather an economic expedient undertaken for a political end' (Eddie 1988: 826). Only by reducing duties could Austria hope to enter the Zollverein. Similarly Prussia kept the Zollverein's tariffs low mainly to prevent Austria from joining (Eddie 1988: 824–5; Fielden 1969: 88; McKeown 1983: 87). France was keen to sign a treaty with Prussia to prevent an anti-French coalition developing (Henderson 1968: 275). Italy's unification in 1861 coincided with a radical shift to free trade. In particular, Italy wished to cement its unification by forming alliances with Britain and France (Toniolo 1990: 54). Moreover, Italy wished to repay Britain and France for the political and military help they had provided during the recent unification process (Zamagni 1993: 110). In short, a series of contingent political events converged to substantially promote the possibility of European free trade, as states valued international cooperation over international conflict. These diplomatic manoeuvres simultaneously promoted the dip in the geofiscal cycle enabling free trade.

The relatively harmonious international relations of the middle of the century began to deteriorate by the 1870s. This was connected to a series of diplomatic developments as well as an upturn in the geofiscal cycle. Although Austria had perhaps artificially kept tariffs low in the 1850s and 1860s in an attempt to enter the Zollverein, when Prussia refused to modify or renew its treaty with Austria in 1877, Austria returned to its more traditional protectionist policy, instigating the 1878 tariff (Eddie 1988: 825). The 1878 Congress of Berlin humiliated Russia (although the empire tried to maintain good relations with Germany for several years thereafter). Nevertheless Russia was then brought back into European diplomacy as part of the international balance of power. In particular, the nationalist problems in the Balkans, as well as the growth of imperial rivalries and a growing precariousness of the balance of power (with the development of a bipolarity between the Triple Alliance and Triple Entente), led to increasing political tensions in the European state system.

These diplomatic manoeuvres were partially informed by changes in the distribution of power in the inter-state system. In particular, the rise of imperial Germany in 1871 and its subsequent post-1897 shift to *Weltpolitik* were undeniably important (Paul Kennedy 1988: 209–21). But at least as important was the impact of the second military revolution (Ashworth 1962: 149; McNeill 1982; Sen 1984; Stone 1984; Michael Mann 1993). This was partly premised on the ramifications of geopolitical power shifting away from sea to land power, as Halford Mackinder (1904) originally pointed out. This placed crucial military emphasis on the rise of the railway. In particular, what McNeill (1982) calls the 'industrialisation of war' ensured that the conduct of warfare was possible only with a strong industrial base. In short, industrialisation was stimulated in Russia and Germany (and elsewhere) partly as a means of strengthening their military base. The dual impact of the demise of the Concert of Europe and the second military revolution led to a general increase in government expenditures, as states pursued industrialisation mainly for military purposes. Crude calculations would show that *militarily induced* expenditures played a vital part in the growth of government expenditures in the last third of the nineteenth century (see especially table 3.3, p. 83). This is why figure 6.4 charts the growth of total central government expenditures rather than military expenditures.

If the lower expenditures of the 1846–73 period, associated with the relative peace and the low point in the international political cycle, enabled states to move away from indirect taxes and tariffs and towards freer trade, the subsequent upturn in the geofiscal cycle linked to the second military revolution promoted a shift to protectionism after 1877 (cf. Stone 1984: 62–6; O'Brien and Pigman 1992: 104; Stein 1984: 363; Kugler and Domke 1986: 47–8). The three different theories – long-wave Kondratieff theory, HST and my geofiscal model – are summarised and compared against the historical record in figure 6.5. I suggest that the predictive capacity of the geofiscal model is greater than either of the alternative 'international' theories.

Finally, to what extent were military expenditures the key to rising taxes and tariffs outside Europe: in the United States, Canada and Australia? American expenditures were predominantly military in nature throughout the 1789–1913 period. From 1789 to 1860, defence consumed 50 per cent of total gross expenditures, though if we add debt interest payments (which were military in origin), the figure rises to 60 per cent. From 1861 to 1913, defence consumed some 53 per cent (65 per cent with debt interest added on), while civil expenditures comprised only 34 per cent (calculated from Department of Commerce (Bureau of the Census) 1949: 299–301, 309–10 (Series P99–108, P165–9)). However, in the dominions of Canada and Australia, defence expenditures were insignificant because they were mainly paid for by Britain.

Figure 6.5: Three 'external' theories of trade regime changes in the long nineteenth century

	International economic cycle theory (Marxist/liberal)	Hegemonic stability theory (neorealist/Marxist)	International geofiscal theory
1789–1814	Up-phase	Hegemony challenged	Intense conflict (fiscal up-phase)
Trade regime prediction	Freer trade	High protection	High protection
Actual regime	High protection	High protection	High protection
1814–49	Down-phase	Rise of hegemony	Peace/diminishing but high expenditures (fiscal down-phase)
Trade regime prediction	Rising protection	Free trade	Diminishing protection
Actual regime	Diminishing protection	Diminishing protection	Diminishing protection
1849–73	Up-phase	Hegemony	Relative peace/low expenditures (bottom of down-phase)
Trade regime prediction	Freer trade	Free trade	Freer trade
Actual regime	Freer trade	Freer trade	Freer trade
1873–96	Down-phase	Declining hegemony	War-preparation (fiscal up-phase)
Trade regime prediction	Rising protection	Rising protection	Rising protection
Actual regime	Rising protection	Rising protection	Rising protection
1896–1913	Up-phase	Declining hegemony	War-preparation (fiscal up-phase)
Trade regime	Shift to freer trade	Deepening protection	Deepening protection
Actual regime	Deepening protection	Deepening protection	Deepening protection

In both cases, national civil construction and welfare were the sole sources of central government expenditures. Thus the specific geofiscal cycle could not be applied to Canada and Australia.

The limits of hegemonic stability theory: Britain as a 'wary titan'

It is important to point out that my model, based on the *international political/geofiscal cycle*, is very different to the neorealist hegemonic stability account of free trade and protectionism. Differentiating my geofiscal approach from HST's model enables further clarification of my position.

Firstly, my argument employs the term 'cycle' very loosely. For neorealism, a cycle is a predetermined phenomenon linked fundamentally to the distribution of power in the inter-state system, which as the term would imply, follows a specific trajectory. A hegemonic cycle begins with a phase of peace, cooperation and free trade enabled by the predominance of a hegemon (unipolarity); moves into a middle phase of increasing tension, declining hegemony and protectionism (increasing multipolarity); and ends in the outbreak of war and the eventual emergence of a new hegemon. The trajectory is inescapable, given that the 'costs of leadership' inevitably lead to hegemonic decline and changes in the distribution of power in the inter-state system. Thus the trade cycle follows this changing distribution of power, with free trade accompanying hegemonic unipolarity, and protectionism accompanying declining hegemony and multipolarity. I reject such a cycle, not least because it is my contention that Britain was not a hegemon in the nineteenth century (see below, pp. 200–3, and chapter 7). And even if we accept that the United States has been hegemonic in the twentieth century, a cyclical theory by definition cannot rest on one case alone (see also Russett 1985; Huntington 1988). Secondly, my international geofiscal 'cycle' refers only partially to the distribution of international political power. More importantly, I refer to the pressures of international military activity, measured by the *fiscal costs* of war and war preparation (i.e., the geofiscal cycle).

Thirdly, hegemonic stability theory's correlation between British hegemonic decline and the Continental shift to protectionism after 1877 is highly problematic. The theory assumes that British decline set in after 1873, following the data produced by W. Arthur Lewis (1978), which correlates closely with the return to protection after 1877. But there are a range of prominent estimates which challenge this. Various authors assume that decline set in during the 1890s (Aldcroft and Richardson 1969; Phelps-Brown and Handfield-Jones 1952; Wilson 1965), while others argue that decline occurred after 1900 (Pollard 1989; Saul 1985). These estimates would suggest that there is no correlation between the rise of protectionism and British economic decline. Moreover, according to a recent set of estimates, British decline set in after 1850 (Crafts, Leybourne and Mills 1991). In this scenario, there is a tight correlation between British decline and European free trade. Indeed, depending on which set of figures we select, we could postulate a variety of correlations including British decline and the rise of European free trade, or British hegemony and the rise of protectionism. Which one is correct is, of course, debatable, but it nevertheless poses a serious problem for HST.

Fourthly, considerations of collective European economic growth did not lie at the base of moves towards free trade after 1860 (even in the case of Britain's shift to free trade, as noted earlier). In fact, geofiscal developments within the inter-state system had a much more important impact. Indeed, even many of the more general 'liberal' domestic reforms that appeared economically inspired, such as the various Continental peasant emancipations, often had a fiscal-military origin. Emancipations often had such a core, as states sought to free up their peasantries from the grip of the nobilities in order to extract higher taxes (Weiss and Hobson 1995: 76–9, 101–2).

Fifthly and most importantly, HST has considerably overestimated the power of the British state in terms of its *ability to alter* the international politico-economic system (and, as we shall see in chapter 7, ignored the real source of the British state's international strength – namely its *adaptive capacity*). This is true not only for international trade but also international politics. As various writers have pointed out recently, Britain's role in the diffusion of free trade in Europe has been greatly exaggerated. Britain proved unable to impose or even persuade other states to adopt free trade after 1846 (McKeown 1983; Stein 1984: 364–6; Ratcliffe 1975b: 125–9; Keohane 1984: 36–7; O'Brien and Pigman 1992). Britain's *unilateral* free trade stance rendered the country impotent either to persuade or to coerce states to move towards free trade or, for that matter, to prevent them from turning to protectionism after 1877 (cf. Keohane 1984: 36–7). It was not until the Cobden–Chevalier Treaty was signed in 1860 that Europe began to liberalise. By this time, according to neorealism, Britain had been a 'hegemon' for no less than forty-five years! Moreover, it was France that did much to stimulate European free trade. And, contrary to the consensus, France's tariff regime was consistently lower than Britain's throughout the nineteenth century (Nye 1991); so, it might be added, was Prussia's for the first half of the century (McKeown 1983: 85–6).

While HST conjures up a mirror image of the 1846–73 and 1945–73 periods through a shared experience, not least of an international free trade regime, it is the differences rather than the similarities that are perhaps more salient. In terms of initiating, maintaining and securing free trade, the so-called 'British system' was far less effective than the 'American system'. The 1846–73 (or more accurately the 1860–79) 'free' trade regime was not based on an institutionalised multilateral structure as it was after 1945 under the GATT, where states met regularly for negotiations and consultations (Keohane 1984: 37). As Charles Lipson put it, in contrast to the GATT system, 'In a difficult environment, the liberal treaties of the 1860s offered little help in coordinating trade policies, limiting retaliation or tempering the growth of nationalist tariffs in Germany, France, Italy and elsewhere' (1983: 251).[5]

Just as the rise of free trade had little to do with British hegemony, so the return to protection after 1877 was unconnected to Britain's decline. According to the theory, a hegemon will resort to coercion (or at the very least, retaliatory protectionism) at its point of decline in order to maintain free trade. Neither at the diplomatic nor military or trading levels was any such British ambition evident. In time-honoured fashion, Britain simply watched from afar, maintaining its passive military and unilateral free trade stance (Lipson 1983: 241–2).

Equally as problematic is the theory's assumption that Britain was the global policeman. For the period 1870–1913, I have constructed a table (figure 6.6), which is based on the data produced in table 5.10. This shows that, of the world's Great Powers, Britain's real military burden (1870–1913), predicted to be the highest in the world by HST, was in fact one of the lowest, and remained so until 1913.[6] And this was equally true of the period 1815–70 in which Britain's so-called hegemony was at its peak (Rasler and Thompson 1989).

Moreover, Britain clearly did not aspire to such a role – at least not in Europe (Michael Mann 1993). Given that Britain had rejected a 'Continental commitment' in favour of a 'blue-water' strategy (Baugh 1988), it was clear that Britain was unable and, most importantly of all, *unwilling* to enforce peace in Europe. No British Continental

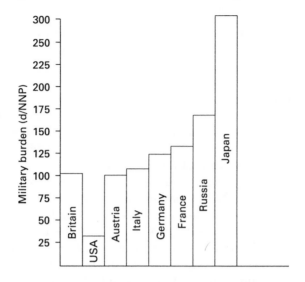

Figure 6.6: Britain's military burden in comparative perspective, 1870–1913

commitment meant that recalcitrant Continental behaviour would often go unchecked by Britain, as evidenced by the Franco-Austrian War (1859), the Austro-Prussian War (1866) and the Franco-Prussian War (1871) (Michael Mann 1993: 288). Most importantly, it was the multipolar balance of power, institutionalised in the 1815 Congress of Vienna, and *not* British hegemony, that 'policed' Europe through the long nineteenth century: 'Diplomacy was consciously geared to the very opposite of hegemonic stability theory: preserve peace and order, including reactionary class and market order, by *avoiding* hegemony' (Michael Mann 1993: 282, emphasis in the original).

Overall, Britain's hegemonic capacity was virtually non-existent (cf. McKeown 1983; Stein 1984; Keohane 1984: 37; Russett 1985; Huntington 1988; Michael Mann 1993: ch. 8). Therefore, I conclude that Britain in the late nineteenth century was not so much a 'weary titan' as Friedberg (1988) argues, but a *wary* titan, *unwilling rather than unable* to provide the costs of international leadership. But it was not just in the late nineteenth century that Britain's wariness was evident: it had been there all along, throughout the long nineteenth century.

In sum, most of the attributes of a hegemon that Robert Gilpin (1987: 72–80, 365–6) delineates simply do *not* describe Britain. Britain's commitment to economic liberalism was of a unilateral nature, with insufficient will to instigate or maintain an international free trade regime. Britain's military capacity throughout the long nineteenth century was inadequate in enabling the role of global policeman, premised on 'naval' rather than 'military' strength, as well as being based on an insufficient fiscal foundation. In short, Britain lacked a clear will for hegemony, preferring to hide in the wings rather than take a lead role on the centre stage of Europe.

Finally, does this mean that the British state was externally weak? Far from it. I argue in the next chapter that although the British state had insufficient hegemonic propensity to project its power outwards and alter the international system, nevertheless it had a strong ability to adapt to internal and external pressures (the major base of state strength). My theory of state power rests to an important extent on the strength of the relationship a state has with its own society. HST ironically tends to ignore states and state–society relations as conceptual variables in its explanatory model of trade regime changes. My model relies to a significant extent on the interplay of internal and external influences. Thus neither the international geofiscal cycle nor the change in the distribution of power in the inter-state system can fully explain trade regime changes. Rather, international changes need to be integrated with state–society variables. To borrow Nettl's (1968) phrase, states and their relations with society need to be treated as *independent conceptual variables* – independent in the sense that they are not simply passive receptors of external geopolitical forces (or internal economic forces). Paradoxically, despite the ostensible emphasis on states within neorealism and HST, in theoretical terms they are virtually ignored (a point which forms a central part of my critique of neorealism in chapter 7).

State capacity and the uneven development of state power accumulation in trade policies, 1870–1913

The influence of external (especially military) expenditure pressures, though important, was by no means solely responsible for the adoption of various trade and tax strategies. If they were, all states would have adopted identical trade and tax regimes. In actuality, of course, this did not happen. There are several reasons for this.

In particular, Germany's expenditure push came in the 1880s – too late for the 1879 tariff increase. Indeed Reich expenditures remained flat in the 1870s. Although military expenditure increases prompted tax and tariff changes after 1880, it was rather the need for a new independent source of government revenue that led Bismarck to raise tariffs in 1879 (this logic complementing the geofiscal in the 1885 and 1887 tariff acts). This means that in addition to the expenditure push, we need also to focus on the revenue-pull side of the equation occurring at the *national* level. In Russia, government expenditures increased rapidly after 1860, outstripping economic growth to 1909, and dropping off only marginally in the few remaining years of peace – although still remaining very high by world standards, and out-stripped probably only by Meiji Japan (John M. Hobson 1993: 487). Although the expenditure-push was very important, it was comple-mented by the revenue-pull factor: in this case, the ever-diminishing yield of (regressive) 'direct' taxes, and the state's weak capacity which led to the shift to indirect taxes and tariffs. In the British case, the expenditure push came after 1900. While this played an important part in the Tory Party embrace of tariff reform in Britain, once again it cannot provide the whole explanation. Equally as important is that Britain was undergoing a fiscal revolution, with the old indirect mode of taxation being replaced by a new direct tax regime after 1909. Indeed, this revenue-pull factor was probably more important than the expenditure-push. In sum, therefore, the rise and decline of govern-ment expenditures stimulated by military considerations provides a necessary though not sufficient explanation for the switch to protec-tionism after 1877.

Certainly, a major reason why the international realm did not invoke a uniform policy response is that states, as the units of the system, varied in their make-up and therefore refracted the incoming interna-tional geofiscal pressures in different policy directions. In short, states as institutions mediated external pressures, and provided autonomous unit-force inputs into trade and tax policies that varied in each country. Thus variations in state capacity had a partially autonomous input into tax and trade policies (see the upper middle part of figure 6.3). Before developing an analysis of the state as a conceptual variable in trade policy, it is worth noting that such a linkage has been discounted in the general literature. Thus Peter Gourevitch concludes in his study of nineteenth-century tariff policy in Britain, the United States, Germany and France that: 'the pattern of [trade] policy outcomes in those countries [Britain, the United States, Germany and France] was the same, suggesting that those aspects of the political system which were idiosyncratic to each country are not crucial in explaining the result' (1977: 307; see also 1986: 117). More specifically, a connection is some-times suggested between state regimes and trade regimes, along the lines that parliamentary states favour free trade and authoritarian states favour protectionism. However, such a possibility is usually discounted on the grounds that, 'the high-tariff nation [sic] in the nineteenth century was the United States' (Barkin 1987: 230). If we assume that states can be understood only by their 'form' or 'regime type', then such a connection must be discounted. But if we expand the definition of states and state power, we will find some clear linkages.

My central claim is that there is a linkage between states and tax regimes and, equally, a linkage between states and trade regimes. I therefore begin by posing the question that Weber asked: 'Will a certain type of ... political power structure determine the creation of characteristic forms of revenue and tax systems?' (Weber, cited in Braun 1975: 247). In answering this question, I suggest that such a linkage can be made if we recognise four basic attributes of state power:

(1) The degree of *concentration* (unitary/federal nature of the state, which ranges from high to low).
(2) The degree of state *penetrative* (infrastructural) power (strong/ weak).
(3) The form of state *autonomy* vis-à-vis society (embedded/iso-lated, also referred to as bounded/unbounded).
(4) The degree of *despotic* power (high/low).

It should be noted that the powers listed here are not exhaustive. They are merely the power endowments that are relevant in determining a state's fiscal capacity in the 1870–1913 period.

State *concentration* refers to the extent to which a state is fiscally centralised. This differentiates principally 'federal' from 'unitary' states: the former being only weakly centralised, having to compete with state provincial governments for revenue, and appropriating only a limited proportion of total revenues. Unitary states – in this case Britain and Russia – enjoyed much greater fiscal autonomy at the central level. Not only did they appropriate the majority of the

Figure 6.7:   The link between state 'concentration' and trade regimes

	Unitary (high concentration)	Federal/confederal (low concentration)
Free trade	Britain	
Protectionism	Italy Russia	Switzerland Germany Austria-Hungary Canada Australia United States

revenue, but more importantly, they also had a free hand as to the sources of taxation appropriated. In federal states, however, central governments in this period were to a significant extent limited to collecting indirect taxes, while the state governments tended to monopolise direct taxes. For the most part, the state governments (as opposed to the central federal state) tended to levy direct taxes and often bitterly attacked federal governments if they attempted to levy such taxes. In the federal regimes of the United States, Germany, Switzerland, Canada and Australia between 1870 and 1913, indirect taxes as a proportion of net tax revenues (NTR) at the central level ranged from 74 per cent in Germany to 98 per cent in Australia (1902–13), with Canada (83 per cent), Switzerland (84 per cent) and the United States (87 per cent for 1789–1913), lying between. Moreover, customs revenue as a proportion of NTR was 43 per cent in Germany, 59 per cent in the United States (1789–1913), 63 per cent in Canada, 80 per cent in Australia (1902–13) and 84 per cent in Switzerland. Clearly, tariffs on protectionist and revenue items were levied in order to meet the requirements of fiscal accumulation. We could add the case of Austria-Hungary to this list.[7] Thus central (federal) states relied overwhelmingly on indirect taxes (see figure 6.7), and were therefore protectionist.

The linkage between state and trade regime – specifically 'low concentration and protectionism', 'high concentration and free trade' – explains much. In particular, it links the American federal state with protectionism (a linkage that is usually overlooked). The high degree of concentration of the British state is also an important element in the maintenance of free trade. However, as is apparent from figure 6.7, this linkage does not explain why the Russian (unitary) state favoured protection (nor for that matter, why Italy was protectionist). Clearly, the 'concentration' state variable is inadequate on its own in explaining state and trade regime linkages.

In order to make sense of the tax/trade regimes of unitary Britain and Russia, we need to analyse the further endowments of state power (i.e., penetrative, autonomy, despotic). As figure 6.8 shows, after 1870, Britain increasingly moved towards a direct tax regime, while Russia moved to a non-tax and indirect tax regime, and hence tariff protectionism.

What accounts for the British shift to direct taxes and the converse Russian move towards indirect taxes? Firstly, the British state enjoyed high penetrative (infrastructural) power which enabled a relatively high degree of surveillance over its population. This is an essential prerequisite for the levying of a direct income tax (especially a personal income tax). Tsarism, however, for all its outward bravado, had only a moderate degree of penetrative power at its disposal. Thus, although it levied a *corporate* income tax after 1900, a personal income tax was simply not possible. Tsarism's inability to keep tight supervision over its populace had been a constant problem throughout its history. Indirect taxes were an easier option, and tariffs were simple to collect, skimmed off imports as they entered the country at specific and fixed locales (i.e., ports). States that have only low surveillance/infrastructural powers tend to rely on indirect taxes (especially tariffs), while those with high surveillance powers are able to rely more on income taxes (Tilly 1990: 88).

Secondly, and most importantly, Russia and Britain can be clearly differentiated in terms of state *autonomy* endowment. As will be discussed in more detail in chapter 7, 'autonomy' refers to a state's relations with civil society (state–society relations). All states can be situated along a continuum ranging from those polities that are 'embedded' within their societies at one end (Britain), to those which are 'isolated' from society at the other extreme (Russia). Tsarism, in pursuit of despotic power, sought to repress the population and seek autonomy *from* society. One aspect of this was the raising of high regressive taxes – that is, indirect taxes and tariffs which penalised the lower income orders. In contrast, because the British state was tightly and broadly embedded within society, it sought to cooperate with rather than despotically abrade with both the dominant and the subordinate classes. In particular, by the end of the nineteenth century,

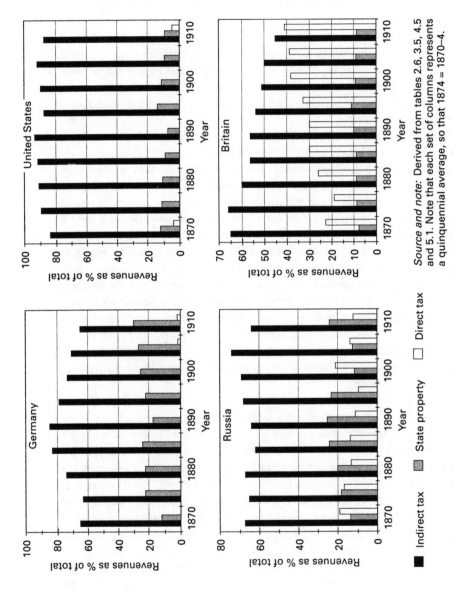

Figure 6.8: Proportions of the major categories of central tax revenues in Britain, Russia, Germany and the United States, 1870–1913

Source and note: Derived from tables 2.6, 3.5, 4.5 and 5.1. Note that each set of columns represents a quinquennial average, so that 1874 = 1870–4.

■ Indirect tax   ▨ State property   ☐ Direct tax

the Liberal Party was in the process of transition from an old Cobdenite ideology to a more radical and progressive 'new liberalism'. The party came to embrace progressive taxation and raised the income tax in 1909 in order to provide fiscal relief to the lower income groups, but in the process maintained free trade for much of the dominant class (as well as the working class).

Could it be argued, therefore, that autocratic states favoured protectionism and indirect taxes, while parliamentary states favoured direct taxes and the income tax? Such a formulation is to be rejected on several grounds. Firstly, had the Conservatives been in power in 1909, Britain might have moved back to protectionism. Secondly, the democratic United States remained protectionist throughout this period (as did Canada, Australia and even Switzerland), which suggests that the degree of a state's *concentration* is more important than its parliamentary nature. Thirdly, liberal France shifted to protectionism,[8] raising tariffs in 1882 and 1892, as did liberal Italy in 1878 and 1887.[9] However, we can assert that the rise of progressive new liberalism in Britain and its ability to be enforced through a parliamentary setting were important factors in Britain's maintenance of free trade and embrace of the income tax, while Russia's autocratic system ensured regressive and indirect taxes, hence protectionism.

But shifting to a progressive tax regime was not simply a function of 'embedded autonomy'. Rather, it required a particular configuration of state power variables based on institutional factors as well as state–society forces. In order to be able to effect a progressive redistribution of taxation, the British state required moderate-high 'concentration', high 'penetration', 'embedded autonomy' and no 'despotic power' (see figure 6.9, p. 219). All other states examined here had insufficient endowments of either penetrative power or concentration, or too much despotic power (or a combination of the above), and therefore relied mainly on indirect taxes (and hence protectionism). This links up with a state's relative political capacity (which I examine in detail in chapter 7). In short, strong states were able to employ free trade while weak states relied on protectionism. Britain had the highest degree of relative political capacity, based on the particular configuration of state power variables described above. Autocratic Russia had the lowest, with authoritarian Germany (and authoritarian Austria-Hungary) closer to Russia, and the liberal federal states – the United States, Canada, Switzerland and Australia – in the middle of the range, with moderate state political capacity.

Thus we can pose a linkage between trade and tax regimes, as well as a linkage between state regimes (defined in terms of multiple powers and capacities) and tax/trade regimes, based on the degree of state capacity. In sum, the 'uneven development of state power accumulation' is an important variable in understanding the different economic policy outcomes in each state (an argument that will be developed in chapter 7).

State power and trade regimes, 1870–c. 1990

To most theorists within the discipline of international relations, the rise and development of free trade after 1945 under the GATT appears as a simple function of American hegemony or Western economic might (especially in relation to the third world). The Listian argument appeals to both Marxian and realist perspectives: free trade is the policy of the strong. However, the ahistorical nature of this argument renders it problematic. This book has argued that nineteenth-century tariff protectionism was founded on a particular political and fiscal logic. Extrapolating my argument, we would predict that by the 1970s, most of the first world would be free trading, while much of the third world would be protectionist. This is only in part because economic strength has an affinity with free trade and economic backwardness with protectionism. More importantly, the upshot of the discussion so far can be summarised through a simple formula:

Strong states = income tax + free trade;

Weak states = indirect taxes + tariff protectionism.

After 1945, first world states were strong in terms of the endowments discussed above. They relied heavily on the income tax for revenues and, as a consequence, outgrew their dependence on extracting indirect tax revenues from protectionist tariffs. Conversely, third world states were weak and unable to rely on a strong income tax base, and should thereby become dependent on trade taxes – hence protectionism. Strong evidence has been marshalled to support this theory (Due 1971; Vanek 1971; Greenaway 1981; Stephen Lewis 1984).

Indeed, I have already noted in chapter 5 that the income tax relieved American governments of having to raise revenue from tariffs, though mainly after 1917. Although this did not lead to free trade immediately after 1917, it is clear that with such a solid fiscal base, the

Table 6.5:   *Share of revenue from trade taxes, c. 1980*

	Number of countries in sample	Trade taxes as % of total revenue (average)
Industrialised countries	18	4
Newly industrialising countries	14	15
Middle-income less-developed countries	33	28
Low-income less-developed countries	15	40

Source: Greenaway (1981).

state was able to move towards free trade after 1945. Thus, while the United States's economic strength in the aftermath of the Second World War was an important factor in such a shift, it cannot constitute a 'sufficient' factor.

Moreover, my perspective can shed light on a particular aspect of modern trade policy. While in the past, the tariff comprised the major (though not sole) trade weapon, today this is no longer the case. Trade tariffs have come down, particularly after the Kennedy and Tokyo rounds of the 1960s and 1970s, to an average rate of around 4 per cent for the advanced economies by the 1980s. However, the appearance of free trade masks the revival of the 'new protectionism' where non-tariff barriers (NTBs) have risen sharply. My fiscal model would predict that a return to first world protectionism would probably not take the form of tariffs. With the withering of their fiscal function, tariffs are no longer needed, thus potentially allowing the use of NTBs. In sum, the modern *form* of protection through NTBs (rather than tariffs) in the OECD can be explained partly through a long-run fiscal analysis, as can the rise and development of a freer trade regime after 1945. Of course, it might be argued that tariffs were avoided because of the constraints imposed by the international free trade regime set up by the GATT. But the key point to note is that the basis of the GATT was made possible only by the prior existence of the income tax. In this way, therefore, I return to Ruggie's concept of 'embedded liberalism', in which international free trade rested on a strong domestic interventionist social policy of income taxation.

Taxation and the role of political parties

To reinforce my fiscal analysis, it is worth briefly considering a common argument found in the literature: the role of political parties in the formation of trade policy. In most countries dealt with in this book, particularly for Germany, the United States, Canada and Britain, many authors have claimed that liberal (left) parties have favoured and indeed instigated free trade and income tax policies, while conservative (right) parties have favoured and instigated protectionist and indirect tax policies. To what extent can political parties be understood as a conceptual variable in explaining tariff and taxation policies?

It is clear that in each of these countries, left-of-centre parties leaned towards free trade/income tax policies, while right-of-centre parties leaned towards protectionist/indirect taxation policies. But political forces were constrained in federal states. Only in unitary Britain was the Liberal government able to maintain free trade through the income tax. In the federal state of Germany, and particularly in Canada, Australia and the United States, liberal parties were unable to instigate free trade policies, and reluctantly had to accept protectionism and indirect taxation as a fact of political life. It is worth citing again the quote by the American Democrat, Walker:

> No horizontal scale of duties is recommended because [this] ... would be a refusal to discriminate for revenue, and might sink that revenue below the wants of the government ... experience proves that as a general rule, a duty of 20 per cent ad valorem will yield the largest revenue. (cited in Young 1872: xciii)

In Canada, the Liberal government, in power from 1896 to 1911, accepted protectionism for fiscal reasons. As the Liberal finance minister Fielding put it in 1904, the 'tariff ... has on the whole proved most satisfactory', even though 'it has a considerable measure of *incidental protection*' (cited in Perry 1955: 102, Perry's emphasis). Similarly, the Australian Labor Party also presided over high tariffs after Australian federation. The National Liberals (under the right-wing faction) in Germany were unable to avoid the federal reliance on indirect taxes, and tacitly accepted protectionism as a necessary fiscal evil (as occurred also in Italy). In sum, political parties were not irrelevant to the formation of trade policy, but they were substantially constrained by the fiscal requirements of the state, which more often than not conflicted with pure party preferences.

The entwining of economic and fiscal variables

The role of the international economic cycle

I noted above that geofiscal/geopolitical pressures constituted important external or international sources in the development of the protectionist regime after 1870 (as well as informing trade regime developments through the long nineteenth century). But international economic variables were also important in the shape of the 'great depression' and the role played by imports in the late nineteenth century. I noted earlier that the key to the rise of protectionism involved not simply a geofiscal expenditure push after 1870, but also the importance of revenue-pull factors: in this case, the drying up of revenue sources as a result of the international recession (as shown in the top right-hand portion of figure 6.3, p. 191).

In many countries, the depression after 1873 was an important factor in the reduction in government revenues. The decline in the price of imports in the context of depression led to a reduction in tariff revenues, particularly in Germany, Canada, Austria-Hungary and Italy after 1873, and in Russia in 1876. This was an important factor in these states' decisions to raise tariffs in order to make good the revenue shortfall. The theoretical ramifications of this point suggest that the fiscal basis of tariff protectionism (i.e., the need to accumulate more revenues in the face of declining government income) can be understood only through integrating economic variables – in this case the effects of the great depression and the fall in import values.

In short, the international economic cycle must be integrated with the geofiscal cycle in order to make sense of changes in trade regimes after 1870 (cf. McKeown 1983: 89–91). However, as I noted above, the link between the international economic cycle and the trade cycle prior to 1870 (especially prior to 1850) is not as tight.

The importance of an economy's trade dependence

In addition to the international geofiscal and international economic cycles, we also need to include a further economic international variable: a country's trade dependence. As with the economic cycle, so an economy's trade dependence also affected the fiscal basis of tariff protection. But to make sense of the trade variable, we need to differentiate import from export dependence.

As discussed in chapter 5, the import dependence variable has particular relevance for an economy's level of tariff protectionism because of its fiscal implications. Thus those economies with low import dependence – especially the United States and Russia – but reliant on tariffs for some or much of their income had to levy high tariff rates on scarce imports in order to accumulate sufficient income. Those economies with high trade dependence – especially Switzerland – but reliant on tariff income levied low tariff rates on plentiful imports, and still derived sufficient income to meet government expenditures. This helps explain why Switzerland at one extreme had low tariff rates, and the United States and Russia at the other extreme had high tariffs. In addition, those countries in the middle of the 'trade dependence' spectrum – Australia, Canada, Germany, Italy and Austria-Hungary – could levy 'middling' tariff rates. This argument suggests that the fiscal and import trade dependence logics entwine. Thus a country's import dependence directly affects the level of tariff rates levied in order to derive sufficient central government income: where it is high, average tariff rates tend to be low; where it is low, average tariff rates tend to be high (for fiscal reasons).

Secondly, a country's level of export dependence has indirect ramifications for the degree of protection incurred, though for *economic* rather than fiscal reasons. This argument follows the economistic claim that if an economy relies on export income, it will levy low tariffs because it does not want to incur foreign retaliation which would only undermine its own economy (e.g., Switzerland and Britain). Conversely, if an economy is not particularly reliant on export income (e.g., the United States and Russia), it can afford to levy high tariffs given that it has little fear of foreign retaliation. While this export dependence argument is important, it should not be exaggerated, since some countries (e.g., Canada and Australia) were reliant on export income, and yet had quite high tariffs. Switzerland, on the other hand, had very high export dependence, but still levied moderately protectionist tariffs. Nevertheless, despite some limitations to this economistic argument, its role clearly has some relevance as one variable among many others.

In sum, a country's import dependence has vital *direct fiscal* ramifications for the level of tariffs raised, while a country's export dependence has *indirect economic* importance for tariff levels (though this linkage is strong). Thus, while trade policy is constrained or informed by fiscal policy, so fiscal policy is also informed to an extent by an economy's level of trade dependence.

The 'nature' of imports and fiscal analysis

The fiscal policies of various governments were informed by the specific nature of imports. In the late-developing states, especially Russia, raw materials and semi-manufactured imports flooded in as a consequence of Russian industrialisation requirements. Collected from these items, tariffs proved to be fiscally lucrative. In several states, the flood of grain imports provided a vital source of customs revenue, as in Germany, Italy, France and Austria-Hungary. In these countries, grain tariffs reached very high levels. In 1913, wheat tariffs stood at approximately 40 per cent in Germany, 35 per cent in France, 41 per cent in Italy and 36 per cent in Austria-Hungary (Liepmann 1938: 57, 65, 70, 80). It might be objected that such high tariffs would have served only to stifle imports as well as internal consumption, and therefore would have yielded limited customs revenue. However, because bread (the major grain product) was highly demand-inelastic (that is, it was an essential item and could not be avoided or substituted for by the consumer), substantial revenues could be safely collected without the prospect of diminished consumption.

This is borne out by three further points. Firstly, grain imports were clearly not stifled by these tariffs. Where such tariff rates were highest in this period (i.e., in Germany), grain imports continued to increase in real terms, rising steadily from 2.2 per cent of national income in 1880–2, to 2.5 per cent by 1910–12 (calculated from Hoffmann 1965: 507–9, 526). Secondly, wheat was a major import item. In Germany, Italy, France and Austria-Hungary, wheat imports comprised, on average, 38 per cent of total agricultural imports and 9 per cent of total imports (calculated from Liepmann 1938: 57, 65, 70, 80). This makes wheat one of the central import items in each of these countries. According to Mulhall, in 1893, thirteen times as much grain was shipped as in 1840, and that grain coupled with coal accounted for just under 50 per cent of total seaborne tonnage in 1893 (cited in Rogowski 1989: 23). Not surprisingly, the flood of wheat and grain imports into and within Europe was seized upon by many governments as a crucial source of government revenue. Thirdly, tariff levels were rarely prohibitive after 1877, mainly because they were required to provide governments with revenues (as noted in chapter 5). Nevertheless, on occasion, various individual goods received prohibitive tariffs, which clearly had no fiscal rationale, and can be explained only through economic analysis.

Integrating economic variables: 'class', 'late development' and state–society inputs

The impact of an economy's degree of backwardness

Moving to the bottom of figure 6.3 (p. 191), we note that a country's level or phase of development plays *a* role in determining trade policy. Traditional social theory, borrowing from Gerschenkron's late development theory and Friedrich List's 'nationalist' approach, assumes that Britain was free trading until 1913 because it was economically strong compared to the late European developers, such as Germany and Russia (as well as Austria, Italy, Canada and Australia), whose backward economies and infant industries required tariff protection.

This argument constitutes a part of the economic explanation developed here. In particular, in chapter 3, I argued that the economic requisite of late industrialisation was *one* factor in Russia's industrial and protectionist policies. Moreover, undoubtedly Britain's decision to remain free trading throughout this period was partly premised on the economy's relative strength (despite any problems of relative decline incurred after 1850). The issue of economic backwardness was undoubtedly important in the dominions – Australia and Canada. Moreover, until the 1870s in the United States, it was recognised that high tariffs were necessary to protect industry (though this rationale became less important after that point). Even so, as I was at pains to show in the first part of this chapter, this is merely one factor (and one of the least important) of the many which affected trade policy.

The role of class analysis (Marxism)

If we move up one level from the bottom of figure 6.3 (p. 191), we note that class requirements also play a part in trade policy. These, however, vary substantially from country to country. The weak Russian bourgeoisie contrasted with the politically strong German Junker class and the strong industrial classes in the United States, Canada, Australia and Britain. However, in Britain and Australia in particular, the working classes also affected trade policy. In general, class interests are important in my analysis, though clearly not to the extent that Marxists would have it. And as has been clarified throughout, class interests are mediated by the state through a bargaining process, as two partially

216

autonomous power actors engage in the process of taxation and trade policy. The state has various interests and forms of power which impact on 'incoming' class requests, and are in turn refracted in various policy directions.

State–society variables

Moving up to the third level from the bottom of figure 6.3 (p. 191), state–society variables are taken into account. State–society relations varied in each case studied here, not only because there were different classes in each country, but also because the nature and capacity of the state in each case varied, which in turn impacted on the strength and demands of the national classes concerned. In turn, state capacity varied also in part because of the nature of the national classes.

State–society relations were least embedded in Russia, where autocracy sought to accumulate despotic power over society (the pursuit of isolation), which in turn undermined the power of the industrial classes as well as the working classes. Moreover, although the Russian bourgeoisie favoured high tariffs on finished goods and lower tariffs on manufacturing inputs, such requests were largely ignored, since they clashed with the state's patrimonial desire to divide and rule the bourgeoisie. In addition, the need for government revenues outweighed the bourgeoisie's demand for a more economically rational tariff policy.

This contrasted with the British case, where the state was embedded within the dominant and subordinate classes. The state sought to maintain the free trading interests of the industrial bourgeoisie (though not the protectionist ambition of parts of the City of London). But in order to extend the income tax and thereby maintain free trade, the state played off the working class from the dominant class, appealing to the fiscal requirements of the former and the trading interests of much of the latter. The state was able to achieve this sophisticated balancing act because it was broadly 'embedded' in society (in clear contrast to the Russian state).

The German Reich, with its partially embedded autonomy, sought mainly to enhance the interests of the Junker class, both fiscally and economically (although in terms of specific tariff policies, the state also took into account the whole agricultural community). The federal governments in the United States, Canada, Germany, Austria-Hungary and Australia certainly took the economic interests of their manufacturing and agrarian classes into account when raising tariffs, which complemented their need for enhanced government revenues.

So, in sum, a mixture of economic and political inputs (depicted by the lower half of figure 6.3 (p. 191)) combined to produce the final trade policy undertaken in each country.

Conclusion: the state in the international political economy

My general theory of tariff protectionism seeks to integrate fiscal, political (state), economic, class and geofiscal/geopolitical variables, emanating from the international, national and sub-national dimensions. While I have emphasised fiscal factors in the rise of indirect taxes and protectionism, it is equally important to note that taxation as an independent causal variable cannot be treated as a *deus ex machina*. Taxation is not wholly autonomous, but is embedded within the international and national economy in much the same way as the national and international economic dimensions are to an extent embedded in the state's fiscal base. Thus I have pointed out that tax pressures were fundamentally entwined with the trade cycle as well as with the economy's trade dependence. Moreover, I have argued that class interests played a part in trade policy, as did the level of economic development achieved by each state.

However, it is also important to point out that economic variables cannot provide a sufficient explanation of trade regime changes. This means that the economistic consensus has exaggerated the importance of economic variables. Thus, economic factors must be downgraded as explanatory variables and integrated with non-economic variables, rather than eradicated altogether. This is inevitable if we seek to develop a genuinely multi-causal analysis which emphasises not only state power, but also inter-state and international economic pressures, as well as domestic economic and state–society variables.

I have shown in this chapter how the *forces of taxation* – state, fiscal, military/geofiscal, economic and class – varied in each state, and therefore gave rise to different tax and trade regimes. These are represented diagrammatically in figure 6.9.

In Russia, in the face of high government expenditures, economic recession and declining revenues, the forces of taxation comprised: low state capacity, the autocratic patrimonial desire to repress the lower

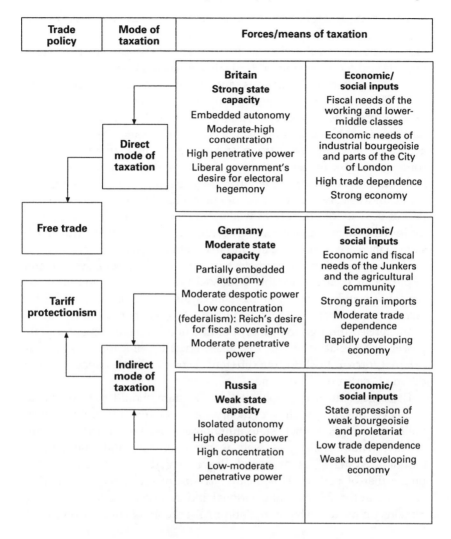

Trade policy	Mode of taxation	Forces/means of taxation	
		Britain **Strong state capacity** Embedded autonomy Moderate-high concentration High penetrative power Liberal government's desire for electoral hegemony	**Economic/ social inputs** Fiscal needs of the working and lower-middle classes Economic needs of industrial bourgeoisie and parts of the City of London High trade dependence Strong economy
Free trade	**Direct mode of taxation**	**Germany** **Moderate state capacity** Partially embedded autonomy Moderate despotic power Low concentration (federalism): Reich's desire for fiscal sovereignty Moderate penetrative power	**Economic/ social inputs** Economic and fiscal needs of the Junkers and the agricultural community Strong grain imports Moderate trade dependence Rapidly developing economy
Tariff protectionism	**Indirect mode of taxation**	**Russia** **Weak state capacity** Isolated autonomy High despotic power High concentration Low-moderate penetrative power	**Economic/ social inputs** State repression of weak bourgeoisie and proletariat Low trade dependence Weak but developing economy

Figure 6.9:   Modes of taxation and trade policies, 1870–1913

orders, moderate infrastructural/penetrative state power, a weak
economy and weak bourgeoisie, and low import trade dependence.
These all combined to produce a regressive and indirect tax regime
and a highly protectionist tariff regime. In Germany, initially, in the
face of economic recession and declining government revenues, the
forces of taxation comprised: a moderately weak state capacity in a

federal context, a political struggle between Reich and *Länder* over taxation, moderate state penetrative power, the economic needs of agriculture and fiscal and agricultural needs of the Junkers, high grain imports and moderate import trade dependence. These all combined to prompt a shift to indirect taxes, and therefore tariff protectionism in 1879. Thereafter, in the face of economic recession and higher Reich expenditures, the state deepened its commitment to indirect taxes and tariff protectionism. In Britain, the forces of taxation were different again. These comprised strong state capacity in a unitary political context, the specific electoral requirements of the Liberal government, high state penetrative power, the fiscal needs of the working and lower-middle classes and the economic needs of much of industry and part of the City of London (as well as much of the working class), high trade dependence and a strong economy; together they pushed the state to increase the income tax and maintain free trade.

This suggests that the character of the units of the state system, and in particular their relationship with society, is at least as important as the impact and demands of the state system itself in accounting for taxation and foreign economic policy. A large part of this can be characterised through the concept of the 'uneven development of state power accumulation' (which is determined by unit-force as well as external forces). In short, the different degrees of state capacity led to different trade policy outcomes.

The argument of this book is that the state should not occupy an exclusive position within a theory of economic (or political and military) change. Rather, state autonomy must be grounded or embedded within society, as well as the inter-state and international economic systems, as described above. My theory of state power, unlike that of realism, is *mutually inclusive* of economic and political variables at the sub-national, national and international 'levels'. It now remains for me to flesh out my 'non-realist theory of state power'.

7 State capacity in the international/ national vortex: a non-realist theory of state power and international politics

This chapter seeks to achieve several objectives. I begin by examining the shortcomings of traditional theories of the state and economic change – namely Marxism, liberalism, statism, neorealism in general and HST in particular. I then go on to develop a non-realist theory of state power/capacity, which examines the domestic and international sources of state power. This is an important component of my comparative explanation of trade policies undertaken by the various states examined. From this, ten theses on state capacity and a refined Weberian definition of the modern state are derived. The latter part of the chapter applies this theory to an examination of the First World War and its revolutionary aftermath. This demonstrates how a socio-logical non-realist theory of state power can enrich the study of international relations (IR) and sociology. Indeed, a major task here is to produce both a sociology of IR and an IR of sociology. Finally, a possible research agenda for what Jan Aart Scholte (1993b) has called 'world-historical-sociology' studies is proposed.

The limits of reductionist state theory: what's the matter with Marxism and liberalism?

The main faultline in the Marxist theory of social change and IR is its economically reductionist theory of the state. The famous quote from the *Communist Manifesto* is unequivocal: 'The executive of the modern state is but a committee for managing the common affairs of the whole bourgeoisie' (Marx 1848/1977: 35). Of course this claim is not new, and is one that most neo-Weberians have made (e.g., Skocpol 1979; Giddens 1981, 1985; Michael Mann 1986, 1993; John A. Hall 1986; and most eloquently by Frank Parkin 1979). But of course few neo-Marxists accept this charge of reductionism. It is, however, my central contention that a non-reductionist Marxism is a non-sequitur. It is therefore vital to examine critically these so-called 'non-reductionist' Marxist analyses.

Many strategies have been employed by Marxists in an attempt to avoid the reductionist charge. The most common strategy involves the 'concept' of the 'relative autonomy' of the state, first developed by the French structuralists, Louis Althusser and Etienne Balibar (1970), as well as Nicos Poulantzas (1973: 44–56, 187–9, 255–321), but has since entered and spread throughout the general neo-Marxist literature (e.g., Miliband 1973; O'Connor 1973; Stuart Hall 1984; Offe 1984; Simon Clarke 1988). But this strategy fails to provide a solution. In fact, it merely reinforces the problem. For, in this formulation, the state does not act in the 'short-term' interests of the bourgeoisie (viz. the *Communist Manifesto* position). Rather, the state merely acts in their 'long-term' interests. In effect, all that has happened is that the phrase 'long-term' has been substituted for 'short-term'. But the state still unequivocally acts in the interests of the bourgeoisie. Echoing Poulantzas, Claus Offe (1984) argues that the state can best be understood as an 'ideal collective capitalist'; rather than representing a specific fraction of capital, the state is able to stand back and maintain the long-term unity of the dominant class in its fight against the subordinate classes. Again, the state is defined only in terms of its capitalist base. Moreover, Marxists are unequivocal that the state is determined in the first instance by the mode of production. And there is no real notion that the state has any power *in and for itself* (other than to inaugurate or reinforce 'bourgeois rule').

The 'concept' is effectively meaningless, because for something to have autonomy – albeit 'relative' – it must exist and have power that is in some way unique to it (cf. Miliband 1973: 88). In other words, the notion of the relative autonomy of the state can have meaning only if the state is assumed to have some degree of power that is not reducible to class interests (Parkin 1979). But the infusion of 'statist' or Weberian premises into Marxism ultimately undermines the Marxist project through 'bourgeois contamination'. Thus, quite understandably, neo-Marxists have strenuously resisted the 'statist' paradigm. Failing to attribute to the state any real 'autonomy' renders the 'concept' of 'relative autonomy' effectively meaningless and reductionist.

It is worth noting that the economic reductionism of the 'relative autonomy' approach is entirely congruent with Marx's classic statement espoused in his *Eighteenth Brumaire of Louis Bonaparte* (1852/ 1977). Although the essay has been mistakenly understood by most revisionist Marxists as an acceptance of state autonomy (albeit 'relative'), Marx's intention was to show precisely the opposite: that although Bonaparte's regime *appeared* to be autonomous, in fact, he argued, it was not. Time and again, Marx proudly reiterated his reductionist thesis: 'state power is not suspended in mid-air ... Bonaparte feels it to be his mission to safeguard bourgeois order ... by protecting its [the bourgeoisie's] material power, he generates its political power anew' (1852/1977: 317, 322). Such pride in a revolutionary reductionism – the very essence of Marxism – has strangely become a source of embarrassment and even shame for modern academic Marxists.

A further strategy employed by Marxists is to deny the importance of the 'base–superstructure model' outlined not by Althusser, but by Marx in his *Preface to a Contribution to the Critique of Political Economy* (1859/1976). The denial of the base–superstructure model involves collapsing the distinction between politics and economics. Thus Perry Anderson argues that all

> previous [i.e., pre-capitalist] modes of exploitation operate through extra-economic sanction – kin, customary, religious, legal or political. It is therefore, in principle, always impossible to read them off from economic relations as such. The superstructure of kinship, religion, law or the state necessarily enters in to the constitutive structure of the mode of production in pre-capitalist social formations.
> (Anderson 1974: 403; cf. Althusser and Balibar 1970: 13)

Or as Terrell Carver put it, 'how can a legal and political superstructure be distinguished from the economic structure when the latter has a "quasi-legal" character?' (1982: 27). This line of argument has been pursued by many neo-Marxists (e.g., Wood 1981; Jessop 1990), and most recently by Justin Rosenberg (1994) in his structural Marxist theory of IR. This, in effect, simply returns us to the basic position adopted by Poulantzas (1973), who argues that the mode of production is not simply an economic category but is also affected (albeit 'relatively') by the political and ideological 'levels'. This is complemented by the growing interest within IR in the Italian Marxist, Antonio Gramsci, who argued against economic determinism, claiming that there was no simple correspondence between the political 'superstructure' and the economic 'base' (Cox 1983, 1986; Gill 1990; Murphy 1994; Rupert 1995).

However, this strategy raises more problems than it solves. If non-economic and economic categories cannot be separated, thereby merging to form a totality, then the problem of causality becomes acute. What determines what? Such a position tends towards a Parsonian functionalism in which all variables interact to reproduce the mode of production. Here, Marxism's key explanatory variable – the mode of production – has turned 'into nothing more than a synonym for the social structure itself, occasionally masquerading as one of its principal parts' (Parkin 1979: 8).

But we need to remind ourselves that downgrading the mode of production is supposed to be an exclusively 'bourgeois' rather than Marxist trait. Indeed, the key to Marxism is not simply that the economic (the mode of production) *can* be separated from the non-economic, but above all, that the mode of production *must* be accorded primacy. In fact, as we shall see shortly, failure to separate economic from non-economic variables is exactly the methodological trap that non-Marxists 'fall into' (according to Marx, at least). Logically, there-fore, this 'strategy' of effective denial of the base–superstructure model gives rise to what might be termed 'bourgeois Marxism'. This becomes apparent when we revisit *Capital*, to which we now turn. *To summarise my position: a non-reductionist Marxism is a non-sequitur.* Why then must the Marxist method be economically reductionist?

Marx claimed in the preface to *Capital* to have uncovered the 'laws of motion' of modern capitalism (1867/1954: 20). His approach was supposedly 'scientific'. Marx's 'science' was based on a *dialectical* approach in which the everyday appearance of things must be pene-trated for their underlying essential base. This base comprises contra-dictory social relations of production. Failure to uncover the underlying base of contradictory social relations is to fall into the bourgeois trap of 'fetishism' (Marx 1857/1973: 267, 297, 308, 528–9, 585, 684, 700–2, 745, 758–9, 822; 1867/1954: 366, 483, 567–70; 1867/1959: 45–8, 168, 392–9, 827, 829–31; 1863/1972: 454–523). This was precisely the trap that the 'bourgeois' liberal political economists such as Adam Smith, David Ricardo, James Mill and Nassau Senior 'fell into' (Marx 1867/1954: 14–16, 66, 94–6, 155–60, 412–21; 1867/1959: 168, 392–3, 817–18, 827). In the case of commodities, fetishism occurs when the observer assumes that the commodity appears to have a value (or power) independent of the social relations that produced it. As Marx put it, thus 'a definite social relation between men ... assumes in their eyes the fantastic form of a relation between things' (Marx 1867/1954: 77, 54–88; Marx 1867/1959: 172, 826–7; Marx 1859/1976: 31, 51–2). Thus the commodity has no power in itself: its power or value is derived exclusively from the exploitation of labour within the mode of production.

Most significantly, this dialectical approach was applied to all economic and political phenomena. As Marx put it, 'All science would be superfluous if the outward appearance and the essence of things did not coincide' (1867/1959: 817). Thus in strict accordance with the dialectical approach, Marx argued that the state could not be understood as something which has its own power independent of the social relations that produced it. The political world, especially that of 'citizenship' and the 'nation-state', is one of distortion. Thus in his *Introduction to a Critique of Hegel's Philosophy of Right*, he asserted that individuals may be equal in the 'heaven' of their political world, but they are certainly not equal in the earthly existence of society (Marx 1843/1977). Only by uncovering or 'reducing' the political sphere to underlying class relations can Marxism make sense of the political. Thus remaining true to his dialectical approach, Marx saw Louis Bonaparte's state as having no power in itself. Bonaparte unequivocally represented bourgeois class interests.

In short, Marxist 'science' denies the notion of state power or autonomy. States, like all other phenomena, must be reduced to their underlying class base. Clearly, therefore, the approach is reductionist, giving unequivocal primacy to class relations. This is why Marxists who attempt to avoid the charge of reductionism are considered to occupy the internally contradictory position of '*bourgeois* Marxism'. Thus, in *Capital*, there is no sign or evidence of an 'epistemological break' that Althusser (1969) accused Marx of, ironically in the guise of a 'defence' of Marx. True to his revolutionary politics, Marx remained unashamedly reductionist right to the end and never undertook any such epistemological break from his early works.

Even at this stage, there will no doubt be Marxists who choose to ignore this critique. They will still claim that a non-reductionist Marxism is possible. The response to this follows on from the argument already made. What are the specifically *political* ramifications of producing a 'non-reductionist' theory for Marxism? If states have power and autonomy and cannot be simply reduced to the mode of production, then logically class power cannot be the essence of state power. In turn,

225

classes can no longer constitute the central actors in politics or history. To undermine the centrality of class struggle effectively undermines the notion of revolution and thereby 'eternalises capitalism' – something which Marx warned expressly against – the very basis of his vitriolic attack on 'bourgeois' liberal political economy (Marx 1867/ 1954: 23–4, 85, 483, 504, 528). Thus for Marx, granting states (or any other non-class actor) power can lead only into a 'bourgeois' cul-de-sac.

In short, a revolutionary Marxist theory must by definition be economically reductionist. Conversely, a non-reductionist 'Marxism' must lead by definition to a revisionist (*bourgeois*) reading of history. It is however, entirely possible to create a non-reductionist radical theory that includes class analysis. But it could not be described as Marxist: 'critical' maybe, but 'Marxist' – definitely not. In short, if a theory is not class-reductionist, then it's not Marxist. And if it is class reductionist, it's flawed. Most fundamentally, then, this means that it is simply not possible to create the sort of 'flexible' Marxism outlined by Robert Cox (1986). This is because Marxist epistemology employs strict parsimony, and any attempt to go beyond such parsimony can lead only to a theoretical 'embourgeoisement' of Marxism.

Despite the various attempts by neo-Marxists to avoid the charge of economic reductionism – not to mention the masses of rhetoric to the contrary – Marxism has failed to provide a non-reductionist theory of the state. The litmus test in this situation is to suggest that the state has power and autonomy. The Marxist reply will always follow along the lines of: 'but states are not suspended in mid-air ... they are grounded in determinant socio-economic class relations.' Thus when the crunch comes, Marxists always resort to economic determinism, as indeed they should if they are to remain true to their favoured revolutionary-dialectical approach. The structuralist strategy failed to abolish economism from Marxism. As Paul Hirst put it, 'The result of the failure of [the relative autonomy of the state] has been to return us to the status quo ante [i.e., economism], but with the recognition that the status quo ante is untenable' (Hirst 1977: 129). Such a conclusion clearly applies not just to structural Marxism, but to all strands of neo-Marxism which try to exorcise the reductionist spirit of Karl Marx.

Marxism ultimately shares with liberalism an epistemological denial of the concept of autonomous state power. Less time will be given here to liberalism, mainly because the reductionist charge is not contentious. The liberal theory, perhaps best represented by pluralism, is usually explained by proponents through the metaphor of the state as 'cash-register' (Latham 1953). Through a simple input–output characterisation, the state effectively adds up all incoming requests from various interest groups, and produces a policy which satisfies the most powerful influence at any given time. According to this view, the state is simply a pawn, beholden to the most powerful interests. It is clear that in liberalism there is no real notion that states have power and autonomy to pursue their own interests (Michael Mann 1993: 47). Of course, some have claimed that pluralism, unlike Marxism, portrays the state as a neutral actor which supposedly implies some degree of autonomy. But this is really just a semantic point; nowhere in any pluralist text is there an analysis of the state as an autonomous actor, which acts according to its own set of defined interests which are non-reducible to societal groupings.

The general problem with Marxism and liberalism is that neither accepts that the state has any autonomous power to effect social or political change. The unavoidable fact to note is that, with the possible exception of a few authors – notably Fred Block (1987), Ellen Trimberger (1978) and Colin Mooers (1991) – state power/autonomy has not featured meaningfully in Marxist or liberal works. However, although Block, Trimberger and Mooers go considerably beyond crude economic reductionism and undoubtedly succeed in producing important and interesting work, in the last instance they all fall short of attributing the state with any real autonomy. Thus Block insists that states are structurally constrained by the need to maintain business confidence. Mooers discusses the considerable tensions between the state and the nobility in Europe, but concludes that ultimately the absolutist state sought merely to shore up the power of the nobility. And Trimberger argues that the state has autonomy only to the extent that class power has been initially weakened, which is the essential formula of the Bonapartist relative autonomy approach.

In the next section I broaden my discussion of state theory to a critique of statism and neorealism, while laying down the foundations of my alternative approach.

An introductory critique of Marxist, statist and realist theories of the state: grounding the state

It is undoubtedly the case that the notion of state autonomy conjures up for many an image of the state as a supreme sovereign 'leviathan', standing over or apart from society and transcending all social actors. The state is wholly separate and autonomous from society, domestic or foreign policy is initiated and determined by the state, and autonomy supposedly reaches its apogee in those instances where the state goes against the interests of the dominant class. The commonly held assumption is that the 'autonomy' of the state implies the irrelevance of social forces (in turn implying a trade-off between state autonomy and societal autonomy). This image, though pervasive, is obfuscatory. I label this conception of the state 'vulgar statism' (elitism). Indeed, given this common perception, it is hardly surprising that so many in the social sciences have reacted in such a hostile way to 'statism' and realism.

The term 'state autonomy' sounds suspiciously like Hans Morgenthau's famous 'sixth principle of political realism', which claims that 'the political realist maintains the autonomy of the political sphere, as the economist, the lawyer, the moralist maintain theirs' (1964: 11). Herein lies the nub of the claim that the neo-Weberian historical sociology school (which insists on according the state 'autonomy') is simply a revised realism, or rather a 'realist wolf dressed up in sociological sheep's clothing'. Such a claim is unfounded, because the definition of state autonomy laid out in this volume is radically different to realism's.

Morgenthau's notion of state autonomy implies a structural *separation* of the state from society and the economy. Here, the autonomy of the state is *absolute. However, the crux of my sociological definition is that it seeks to ground the state in societal and economic relations.* All states and their capacity are to a greater or lesser extent grounded in their relations with society. Those states that are 'embedded' in society tend to be strong, while those that seek 'isolation' from society are invariably weak. In essence, state capacity is considerably enhanced through social power. Accordingly the term 'autonomy' is ambiguous, unless it is prefixed with various adjectives. At a specific level, state autonomy can be 'embedded' within society, or, at the other extreme, it can be 'isolated'. At a general level, state autonomy is 'partial'. States have never been 'absolutely' autonomous, nor 'potentially' autonomous, nor 'relatively' autonomous, but have always been *partially* autonomous because they interact with other partially autonomous actors both inside and outside society. In other words, we reject the view that state autonomy implies the irrelevance of social forces; rather, state autonomy implies the very existence of such forces.

228

Indeed, *pace* statism and neorealism, states are not primary, bounded and unitary actors which always act in perfectly rational and coherent ways. States do not determine everything either inside or outside their borders. Perhaps the central problem with neorealism is its claim that states can be understood simply through the concept of 'sovereignty'. But 'sovereignty' tells us very little about states and their various power attributes. Indeed in Kenneth Waltz's (1979) depiction, theories that actually differentiate states are labelled 'reductionist'. States are sovereign 'like-units', all sharing similar functions as a result of the homogenising impact of the inter-state system, and are all free of outside influences to rule unilaterally over their populations. However, not only does the concept of sovereignty (unashamedly) tell us little about states and nothing about their power attributes, but it also makes erroneous assumptions about the domestic/international relationship. By equating sovereignty with states, whose primary (and only important) relationship is with other states, neorealism makes the mistake of parcelling the international off from the domestic. States have never existed in autonomous 'political' spheres (not even in seventeenth-century Europe), discrete from social actors and the economy; nor has the international sphere been neatly separated from the domestic. States vary in their power attributes precisely because of their different relations with society (Migdal 1988). Indeed, state power does not hang in mid-air. Rather, it is ultimately grounded in state–society relations.

To help differentiate my sociological theory of the state from the statist/elitist and neorealist alternatives, it is useful to follow the lead taken by Michael Mann (1993: ch. 3), who points out that there are in fact two 'statist' approaches, which he terms 'true elitism' (which we label vulgar statist/realist), and 'institutional statism' (although we eschew the term 'statism' because of its association with elitism and realism). The elitist or vulgar statist approach has much in common with the 'leviathan' image conveyed above, which finds its greatest expression in realist theory with its exclusive emphasis on 'sovereignty'. The institutional approach is quite different. It moves away from grandiose notions of power elites imbued with supreme sovereign power wielded absolutely against and autonomous of societal groups, towards a more subtle *logic of political institutions and their connections with social power within society*.

In the general perception of statist theory, the litmus test for 'state autonomy' is usually the degree to which the state acts against the interests of the dominant class, or even society in general. Thus, if the state fails to act against the interests of society and/or the dominant class, then it cannot be said to be autonomous. This of course informs all Marxist critiques of 'statism', which essentially reject statism on the grounds that states always respect (at least in the long term) the economic requirements of the dominant class and capitalist mode of production. But this critique disposes only of the vulgar statist approach. The institutional-statist approach is quite congruent with the notion that states support the dominant class, through what Peter Evans (1995) has called 'embedded autonomy' (see also Weiss and Hobson 1995; cf. Zhao and Hall 1994). Marxism, as Eric Nordlinger (1981: 23–34) points out, is quite unable to recognise those situations in which the state follows its own interests but in the process shores up the power of the dominant class. Given that, more often than not, precisely this occurs, it becomes only natural to assume mistakenly that states act in (and for) the interests of the dominant class.

Ultimately the problem with Marxism is its assumption that there is a zero-sum game of power between different actors – more specifically, that there is a trade-off between state power and class power. Given the unequivocal existence of class power, it is axiomatic for Marxists to assume that state power cannot exist. Realists also argue that state power is maximised through zero-sum power, where the state abrades against other states (or even society). But if we accept that power can occur in 'collective' settings, then it becomes straightforward to argue that states can demonstrate power or autonomy even where they help the dominant class. Moreover, we go further and argue that it is only when the state acts collectively that state capacity can be maximised. Most fundamentally, much of the critical literature assumes that state autonomy is equivalent to despotic power. In my formulation, however, despotic power is differentiated from state capacity and autonomy. Moreover, there is an inverse relationship between despotic power and state capacity. In short, strong states seek to enhance their power or capacity *through societal or dominant class power, since collective power is more effective than distributive* (Nordlinger 1981; Michael Mann 1986, 1993; John A. Hall 1986; Ikenberry 1986). Thus, state strength is achieved through negotiation with society rather than abrasion against it. Therefore, 'bringing the state back in' must not involve kicking society back out. Paradoxically, my central claim is that the state can be brought back in only by bringing society back in.

230

I can therefore reject the usual Marxist critique of 'statism', sum-marised by Andrew Cooper as follows:

> there is a danger in state-centred analysis of slippage into a kind of state determinism, where the state appears for itself as an unfettered political actor, instead of a set of institutions embedded in a domestic (and of course, international) context. (Cooper 1994: 544)

Although applicable to vulgar statism, this critique fails to confront the institutional statist approach. Indeed, the whole point of my socio-logical approach is to achieve precisely what Cooper himself advo-cates: namely an analysis where states are recognised as variously embedded within the domestic societal, and international economic and political realms (as indeed classes are embedded within the domestic and international political dimensions). Likewise, Richard Ashley's (1986) critique of statism might well apply to realism and elitism, but not my position. Thus his argument (1986: 268–70) – that a statist perspective assumes that the state has 'unproblematic unity: [it is] an entity whose existence, boundaries ... interests and capacities to make self-regarding decisions can be treated as given, independent of ... class ... and undisputed' – does not apply to my theory. My approach generally rejects treating states as wholly independent of class as much as it fundamentally rejects treating states as simple unified and hermetically bounded territorial monoliths.

Similar criticisms have been made by leading Marxist sociologists, which are equally misplaced. Speaking for most Marxists, in a particularly passionate critique, Paul Cammack suggests that statism seeks to separate 'state' from 'society' (as part of some alleged 'right-wing backlash'), apparently so as to deny that class interests could affect government policy (Cammack 1989; see also Jessop 1990: 287–8). And non-Marxists have made similar criticisms. Thus Peter Goure-vitch argues that 'the [statist] argument has a problem ... in its criticism of the "reductionist" elements of societal arguments; it discounts those elements, leaving the group elements theoretically unexamined and undeveloped' (1986: 117). But my argument is precisely that state and society are mutually interdependent and, indeed, that class interests do affect government policy. I simply deny that class or group interests are the sole foundation of government policy.

Moreover, the alternative theory proposed by the likes of Ashley (1986) and Cox (1986) can be criticised in ways reminiscent of their critique of neorealism. Focusing on 'class' in an unproblematic way, as though classes are pure unified entities independent of the political (state) framework within which they are embedded, is highly problematic. Neither classes nor states are *absolutely* autonomous; they are mutually constitutive of and embedded in each other as partially autonomous power actors. Indeed, paraphrasing Cooper, we can issue a word of warning to the response of various Critical[1] and Marxist theorists, that

> there is a danger in class-centred analysis of slippage into a kind of class determinism where class appears for itself as an unfettered economic actor, instead of a partially autonomous agency embedded in a political (i.e., state and inter-state) context.

Of course, my claim that state and society are interdependent is ironically similar to the argument made by Marxists and Critical theorists in their critique of 'statism' and neorealism. However, the ramifications of this position are extremely awkward not just for statists and neorealists, but above all for Marxists and various Critical theorists. Returning to a point made earlier (concerning the 'relative autonomy' of the state), if state and society are truly interdependent, then we must assume that both exist in their own right, since if one does not have power, then there is nothing with which the other can be interdependent. In short, arguing for the interdependence of state and society logically implies that states as well as society/classes have power in and of themselves. But in characteristic Marxian fashion, Bob Jessop, who argues forcefully for such interdependence, really gives the game away with his final thesis in his (thirteen-point) 'non-reductionist' theory of the state, in which he claims that 'State power can only be assessed relationally. The state as such has no power – it is merely an institutional ensemble' (1990: 269–70). To claim that the state has no power is to logically deny that state and society are interdependent, and implicitly to fall back on a crude societal/class reductionism (despite the not inconsiderable rhetoric to the contrary).

In short, if Marxists and liberals want to argue for the interdependence of state and society (as they constantly assert), then logically they must also accept that the state (and not just classes/societal interests) has power and autonomy (albeit partial). Failure to accept that the state has power and partial autonomy renders Marxist and liberal arguments for the interdependence of state and society as simply disingenuous.

The multiple 'specific' domestic sources of state capacity

The central claim here is that states can be understood only by differentiating the notions of *state power, sovereignty* and *state capacity*. In fact, sovereignty is unimportant in my analysis; the basis of my theory rests on state power and state capacity. State capacity is derived from a particular configuration of state powers, which in turn are derived from state–society relations (social power), as well as specifically politico-institutional factors. Before examining these, we need to define state capacity briefly.

In an important article, Jacek Kugler and William Domke (1986) argue that external state capacity (or 'relative political capacity' – RPC from henceforth) refers to a state's ability to wage war effectively, and that this is based on a state's domestic power base – in particular, the ability of the state to penetrate society from which it extracts sufficient fiscal revenues (this resonates with Michael Mann's notion of infrastructural state power). While this provides my point of entry, four refinements to the 'basic-force' Kugler and Domke model need to be made.

Firstly, a state's RPC within the international state system is not based solely on its ability to maintain its position within the system from external attack, but also, as Lewis Snider (1987; cf. Migdal 1988) points out, its ability to avoid attack from within – social revolution (or what Buzan, Jones and Little (1993) refer to as the 'double-security dilemma'). War capacity and revolution are linked, as Skocpol (1979) has shown. They are, however, linked primarily by a state's RPC. When this is low, a state might well lose a war and, in its aftermath, be overthrown from within. When it is high, a state may be victorious in war, and maintain or even enhance its power domestically. Only by examining a state's ability to wage war and maintain consent domestically can we adequately 'compare the strength of states'.

Secondly, in my analysis, RPC is founded on a variety of state powers. *Pace* Kugler and Domke, infrastructural/penetrative power is merely one among several forms of state power – and not the most important. I emphasise the importance of a state's 'embedded autonomy' relations with society as fundamental to a state's RPC. This particular state–society relationship is completely ignored in the Kugler–Domke model.

The third adjustment to be made to the basic-force Kugler and Domke model is to note that, while state–society relations provide the key to a state's RPC, we can in turn understand this relationship only by noting that the domestic arena is to an important extent shaped by the international realm. The state–society relationship, though very important, is not absolutely autonomous. States enhance and (sometimes) undermine their own power internally through manoeuvring in the international system. Thus an inside-out (as well as outside-in) approach is facile, since the internal and external realms are not self-constituting but are fundamentally overlapping and mutually constitutive of each other (dual reflexivity).

Finally, Organski and Kugler (1980), in a similar analysis to that of Kugler and Domke, argue that state expenditures should provide the basis of an index of state power. However, an index of state capacity needs to be based on taxation, rather than expenditures (Snider 1987). Snider argues that strong states are those that can extract high amounts of taxation as opposed to non-tax revenues (e.g., state property revenues). In addition, he also argues that a state's ability to collect direct taxes (especially the income tax) as opposed to indirect taxes is a crucial component of state capacity, primarily because indirect taxes are highly vulnerable to external shocks – especially war (1987: 324) – though we would add that the income tax is in general potentially far more productive than indirect taxation. This is particularly important because we argue that the ability to raise progressive income taxation as opposed to regressive indirect taxes was the key to enhancing state capacity during the First World War.

It remains now to examine the various state powers that give rise to state capacity. These are laid out in schematic form in figure 7.1.

State autonomy and the social basis of state power

The first and most important state power variable is that of *autonomy*, which refers to the state's relations with society. The term is problematic because it implies separation from society (as in the realist or elitist formulation). However, my central claim is that state capacity can be maximised through cooperation with society (i.e., close or embedded relations with society). I refer here to what Peter Evans (1995) calls 'embedded autonomy', or what Zhao and Hall (1994) call 'bounded autonomy'. In such a situation, state power and class power advance together, *collectively*. Conversely, weak states are characterised more by antagonistic (i.e., isolated/unbounded) relations with society. This raises the 'paradox of embedded autonomy', well summarised by

234

State capacity	State powers				
Relative political capacity	State autonomy (state–society)	Despotic power	State penetrative power	State concen-tration	State–dominant class relations
Britain	**Strong (embedded)**	Embedded/ bounded	None	High	Moderate-high (unitary)	Competitive-cooperation
Germany	**Medium (partially embedded)**	Partially embedded	Moderate	Moderate	Low (federal)	Competitive-cooperation
Russia	**Weak (isolated)**	Isolated/ unbounded	High	Low-moderate	High (unitary)	Competition

Figure 7.1: State capacity and the uneven accumulation of state power

Zhao and Hall: 'some degree of autonomy from societal pressures is necessary in order to organise and rationalise a society' (1994: 213). And yet, simultaneously, 'states need to be constrained by their societies' (1994: 211). In short:

> *State strength = autonomy/insulation from private interests + social constraint and embeddedness in society.*

Each of the three main states dealt with here (i.e., Germany, Russia and Britain) enjoyed some degree of autonomy from society – that is, autonomy in the sense of *bureaucratic insulation* from the everyday private interests of individuals. According to Max Weber (1922/1978), this is the essence of the modern state as opposed to the traditional/ feudal or patrimonial state. In the latter, administrators owned and controlled their office so as to advance their own private interests, while in the former, modern bureaucrats are separated from the own-ership and control of the means of administration and there is a clear *institutional separation* of public and private functions. Thus, unlike traditional states, modern states are insulated to the extent that they are *institutionally differentiated* from society (Weiss and Hobson 1995: ch. 2; Giddens 1985: 67–8, 134–7, 159; Evans 1995). Specifically, modern states are institutionally separated from the private economy, unlike traditional states, where the institutions of government and economy fundamentally overlap.

But the paradox here is that insulated states are well placed to become *interactively embedded* within the national economy (Weiss and Hobson 1995; Evans 1995). Moreover, in order to maximise the state's RPC, states negotiate closely and indeed cooperate with key groups in society. This twofold manoeuvre – insulation from, and simultaneous cooperation with, society – forms the basis of 'embedded autonomy'. It is both the taproot of a state's RPC and the basis of the irony of state strength: that state strength is based on distance from, and yet close proximity to, society. To reiterate therefore: state autonomy – or more specifically 'embedded autonomy' – rests on a bounded and interactive relationship between state and society. In short, state capacity is crucially founded on a high degree of social power. This is what fundamentally differentiates my position from the realist or elitist, which seeks to separate the state from society.

The British state's autonomy was *embedded* within society, looking towards the dominant as well as lower classes, bounded by the parameters of a range of social groups in society. However, this, we argue, was central to Britain's high RPC, because it enabled the state to maximise revenue-extraction in wartime, while maintaining consent. It also enabled the state to play off the dominant classes with the lower-middle and working classes. Thus, while maintaining free trade, which was favoured by much of industry and the working classes (and, though to a lesser extent, in the City of London), the state was able to push through reforms (the extension of the income tax) against the long-term fiscal interests of the dominant classes in favour of the lower-middle and working classes (and of course the state). This stood it in excellent stead when the First World War finally erupted. Thus, while maintaining consensus, the state was able to increase its RPC considerably.

Germany, however, was only 'partially' embedded or bounded within society. The Reich had a close relationship with the agrarian Junker class, while its domestic linkages with the working class were more isolated. This gave the state less freedom of manoeuvre to push through reforms against the Junkers. Although it managed to manipulate the Junkers at various times (e.g., the introduction of the 1879 tariff and the 1890s trade treaties), its ability to introduce an income tax at the central level was much more limited. This stood it in poor stead when the First World War broke out.

236

Tsarist Russia suffered from high or 'isolated' autonomy, in strict contrast to Britain. Conversely, state weakness is based on *isolation* from society. Tsarism – unlike Britain – was isolated from society, with no social base. It was truly suspended in a void (Weber, cited in Beetham 1985: 183; McDaniel 1988), cut loose from its societal moorings and left to drift aimlessly into self-destruction. Ironically, because the state had no social base, tsarism's RPC was very limited. In other words, highly autonomous states tend to be very weak, while embedded states tend to be strong. This gives rise to my first sociological non-realist principle of state capacity:

> *State capacity is positively related to the degree of a state's interactive embeddedness within society; the broader and deeper the social embeddedness, the stronger the state's capacity.*

This first thesis can be expressed differently. As Michael Mann defined it, 'despotic' state power refers to the 'ability of a state to function without routine negotiation with groups in society' (1988: 5; 1993: 59). Thus, the British state's strong embedded autonomy negated the possibility of despotic power. The German Reich, though embedded in the Junker class, was clearly despotic in its relations with the working class, while tsarist Russia despotically repressed all social groups – dominant and subordinate alike. This returns us to the inverse relationship between despotic power and state capacity noted earlier. For it was Russia that was most vulnerable in the First World War; Britain was considerably less so. This gives rise to my second sociological non-realist principle of state capacity:

> *State capacity is inversely related to the level of despotic power accumulated.*

This position, of course, inverts the standard assumption that strong states are those imbued with high despotic power, weak states with low despotic power. The notion that strong states are those which can intervene against the interests of various groups pervades the literature. This finds expression in Stephen Krasner's (1977a, 1977b, 1978) statist analysis, in which he presents a threefold typology ranging from weak to strong states. Weak states are unable to resist private pressure, to change private behaviour in intended ways or to change the social structure. Conversely, strong states are able to resist private behaviour and, most importantly, change private behaviour as well as the social structure (Krasner 1978: 56–7). However, I would argue that all three states – imperial Russia, imperial Germany and parliamentary Britain –

could resist private pressure, change private behaviour and change the social structure, as I have noted in earlier chapters (for a fuller historical discussion, see Weiss and Hobson 1995: 15–131).

However, the main point to note here is that the wielding of despotic power over society is *not* the litmus test for strong state capacity (as Krasner assumes). Above all, strength can be achieved only through *effective* politics; and this ultimately requires a strong dose of cooperation as opposed to abrasion with society (Weiss and Hobson 1995; Evans 1995; Nordlinger 1981; Michael Mann 1986, 1993; John A. Hall 1986; Hall and Ikenberry 1989: 12–13, 95–7, 105; Zhao and Hall 1994; Gourevitch 1986: 238). To put it differently, being able to consistently resist civil pressures is the sign of weakness, not strength. This is what Ikenberry refers to as the 'irony of state strength' (1986: 106, 134–7; 1988a: 219–21; 1988b: 160–3, 175–7; see also Weiss and Hobson 1995: 8, 46, 48, 57, 89, 129, 244–5).[2] I can therefore generalise McNeill's observation that state power increases as compulsion diminishes (1992: 121). The upshot here is that autonomy from society is not sufficient to guarantee state capacity; it must be accompanied with embeddedness (Weiss and Hobson 1995; Evans 1995).

Competitive-cooperation and embedded autonomy

One of the major problems with current state theory is that the notion of state strength and weakness is plagued with simple dichotomies: autonomous versus dependent, centralised versus decentralised, coercive versus cooperative. This tends to reinforce the 'binary', 'either–or' approach to state autonomy (cf. Zhao and Hall 1994: 212). But we cannot get very far unless we recognise that state power can be competitive and cooperative simultaneously. That is, it would be wrong to argue that pure cooperation with society is the sole source of a state's strength. Thus standing Krasner on his head might advance state theory, but it will not be sufficient. At this point, we return to the paradox of embedded autonomy.

Often states compete with the dominant class in order to further their interests. Thus Bismarck managed to invoke a shift to protectionism in 1879 even though the dominant Junker class favoured free trade. Tariff rates were reduced in the 1890s when the Junkers were calling for higher tariffs. In Britain, the state went fundamentally against the long-run fiscal interests of the capitalist classes in 1909 by raising the income tax. But these two moves were effective only because both states simultaneously gained the consent of their dominant classes (see below, and pp. 244–6). The tsarist state, however, was clearly the most competitive in relation to the capitalist class (and every other class for that matter).

To capture this complex aspect of state–dominant class relations, we refer to the notion of 'competitive-cooperation' (a term which is adapted from Richard Boyd's (1987) concept of 'competitive-collaboration'). This concept relates closely to what Samuel Huntington has called 'complementary conflict', in which two entities (in this case states and dominant classes) can get along because the nature of their conflict is not zero-sum, but rather collectively beneficial (1991: 226). Despite occasional conflict, each entity has an interest in ensuring the survival of the other. This applies to the British and German cases. However, *duplicative conflict* occurs where two entities conflict to the extent that each calls into question the existence of the other. A good example of this type of conflict occurred in tsarist Russia, where the state sought despotic power over the noble, capitalist, working and peasant classes. Strong despotic power could not sit alongside strong class power.

Perhaps the principal arena in which states compete and cooperate with dominant classes is the sphere of taxation. More specifically, states often bargain with societal actors, especially over taxation (Levi 1988). As Margaret Levi points out, the key to this approach is to note that the relative bargaining power of rulers is determined by the extent to which others control resources on which rulers depend, and the extent to which rulers control resources on which others depend (Levi 1988: 17). In other words, where the capitalist class provides states with much-needed resources, it enhances its bargaining power vis-à-vis the state, and can demand something in return. From a historical point of view, by granting the capitalist class property rights, the state gained tax revenues in return. More specifically, the British state in 1909 maintained free trade which was in the trading interests of much of industry and various factions in the City. In the process, the state gained sufficient bargaining power to attack the fiscal privileges of the dominant classes through a higher income tax.

In following the argument of Levi (1988), rulers can enhance their bargaining power vis-à-vis the ruled by maximising cooperation. The political economy of tariff protectionism and free trade provides such an example. Thus the state granted key social groups trade benefits in return for revenues (as happened most clearly in Britain). Or, as in Germany in 1879, Bismarck promised the Junkers tax cuts (as well as a more right-wing government) in return for their support for tariff reform. Hence cooperation with society minimises transaction and bargaining costs, thereby enhancing state capacity. It is precisely this bargaining process between states and social actors that constitutes the *competitive* as well as cooperative nature of state–society relations. This gives rise to the third principle of my sociological non-realist theory of state capacity:

> *In order to maximise their capacity, states need to gain insulation from private demands (institutional autonomy) and simultaneously engage in competitive-cooperation with key social actors (interactive embeddedness).*

So far, we have dealt with the *social* basis of state capacity. We now turn to an examination of its *institutional* bases. This involves an analysis of power that is derived solely from the institutional make-up of the state, and is in no way linked to social power emanating from society.

State 'concentration' and relative political capacity (RPC)

The concept of 'concentration' refers to the degree of fiscal centralisation of the central state. The principal differentiation here is between federal states and unitary states. Federal states have low fiscal concentration because of the three-tier governmental structure, with many political functions undertaken by the provincial state and local governments (as opposed to the central federal government). Central governments in unitary states, however, have control over a wider set of political functions. Most importantly, they control far greater fiscal resources than federal central governments. Moreover, until 1913, unitary central governments had greater scope in their choice of raising taxes, which could be either direct or indirect in nature. Federal central governments, however, had to rely on state property and, above all, indirect taxes. A state's *concentration* – high in nineteenth-century Russia, moderately high in Britain, and low in federal states (e.g., the United States, Canada, Australia, Switzerland and Germany) – is a vital state power variable which has direct implications for fiscal and trade policy. Low concentration promoted indirect taxes and hence protectionism in the federal states, while high concentration (i.e., unitary states) enabled income taxation and free trade.

For the period examined here, the degree of concentration is a further important variable in shaping RPC. Both Britain and Russia were unitary states, and were therefore not constrained by other

240

political bodies to adopt one form of taxation at the expense of another. Britain was able to rely on a high-yielding direct income tax which greatly enhanced its RPC, as demonstrated in the First World War. Conversely, the various federal governments relied overwhelmingly on low-yielding indirect taxes which undermined their RPC during the First World War. Thus unitarism conveys a distinct advantage over federalism in the period examined here, although, as the case of Russia reminds us, it is by no means a sufficient guarantor of fiscal strength. This gives rise to the fourth principle of my sociological non-realist theory of state capacity:

> *State (fiscal) capacity is potentially enhanced in unitary states and limited in federal states.*

State 'penetrative' power and RPC

Penetrative power is what Michael Mann (1988, 1993) calls 'infrastructural' power. This mode of state power forms the principal component of Mann's definition of state strength, and refers to the ability of a state logistically to reach into society – a fundamental prerequisite for a state's extractive capacity. And as noted above, this forms the foundation of the basic-force Kugler and Domke model.

What set Britain apart from Germany and Russia was not only its embeddedness, but also its superior ability to penetrate society. A personal income tax requires not only high amounts of consensus (what Levi calls 'quasi-voluntary compliance'), but also high surveillance or penetrative ability to actually collect the tax (Ardant 1975; Finer 1975; Snider 1987; Levi 1988; Tilly 1990; Michael Mann 1993). Conversely, indirect taxes, especially tariffs, could be collected even with only a moderate penetrative base because of their low administrative cost/yield ratio and limited number of collection points – i.e., ports (Greenaway 1981: 137; Stephen Lewis 1984).

One of the major reasons why tsarism failed to come to rely on a strong progressive income tax base was because it had only a moderate level of penetrative power. This became obvious during the First World War after Russia had instigated the income tax in 1916. The reasons for its impoverished yield stemmed partly from the population's poverty, but mostly from the state's inability to penetrate society and collect the tax. As Norman Stone points out, most Russians kept their own accounting books and so could not be properly reviewed for direct tax purposes. This, he argues, 'would need a vast and expensive bureaucratic machinery' (1975: 289). The irony here was that for all its legendary 'totalitarian' powers, autocracy had far less effective surveillance powers to watch, and extract taxation from, its population than liberal Britain. Germany was constrained in its ability to levy an income tax mainly because of its low concentration and the considerable fiscal sovereignty held by the *Länder*, as well as its restricted embeddedness in the upper classes.

Thus penetrative power was an important factor in the strong degree of state capacity in Britain, compared to the weaker forms in Germany and especially Russia. Nevertheless, penetrative power could not constitute a sufficient factor in accounting for the differing fiscal strategies chosen by each state. This gives rise to the fifth principle of my sociological non-realist theory of state capacity:

> *State capacity requires a high degree of penetrative/infrastructural power.*

I now move from the *specific* to the *general* domestic sources of state power.

The multiple 'general' domestic sources of state capacity

State power and territorial centralisation

The first point here returns us to an earlier discussion concerning the state's institutional differentiation from society. The state in feudal times was extremely weak; everyday government was in practice undertaken by private actors, the nobility. The modern state as a territorially centralised institution with monopolies of rule-making, tax collection and violence is a vital background source of institutional state power in both the internal and the external arenas.

Secondly, following Max Weber and following on from the first point, Michael Mann (1988: ch. 1) argues that autonomy is conferred from the unique socio-spatial location of the modern state. A state's centralised spatial position is not occupied by any other social actor. Because the modern state is involved in a multiplicity of roles – not least, defence, tax collection, public order, income redistribution, welfare, economic regulation – its interests are by definition greater or broader than the specific interests of the dominant class, which are *institutionally* restricted to profit-making. Because of this, 'states cannot be the simple instruments of classes, for they have a different territorial (socio-spatial) scope' (Michael Mann 1988: 16). By and large, if the state can bring its multiple needs into harmony with the dominant class's narrow economic requirements, it will. But this is by no means a certainty, and is not always achieved, as we have seen in the cases of Britain, Germany and Russia (see pp. 31–9, 51–8, 101–4, 107–14, 138–47). Moreover, the state's spatial position and functional roles bring it into relationships with multiple internal (and external) groupings.

Given their institutional and functional differentiation, by definition, state–society interests cannot always coincide. In particular, the state will be able to manoeuvre and play off various groups to enhance its power. The Kaiserreich, for example, played the bourgeoisie off against the Junkers in the 1890s in order to reduce tariff levels, which was important for Chancellor Caprivi's political programme. However, the British state was perhaps the most accomplished, playing off the lower classes against the industrial and financial capitalist classes in 1909 in order to increase income taxation. Ironically, Britain seems to have most ably managed to play various classes off to enhance its own capacity, and perhaps best conforms to the supposedly Continental ability to perform the 'Bonapartist' balancing act. And as Michael Mann puts it, speaking of the Bonapartist balancing act: 'This manoeuvring space is the birthplace of state power' (1988: 15). This gives rise to my sixth sociological non-realist thesis of state capacity:

> *National/domestic territorial centralisation provides the state with a funda-mental basis of power in the internal and external arenas.*

State power and the 'polymorphous' nature of state and dominant classes

A vital source of a state's capacity derives from its multiplicity of interests, as noted above. Michael Mann (1993) captures this point conceptually through the notion of the 'polymorphous' state. This array of activities and interests enables the state to play off classes in order to enhance their domestic and international power, reaching its apogee in Britain, as noted above. Paradoxically, therefore, down-grading realism's monolithic notion of a homogeneous and geopoliti-cally rational state, in favour of a more complex and 'polymorphous' conception, allows us to reinstate the state as a power variable.

But classes, just like states, are polymorphous. They are not simple

243

monoliths, as Marxism suggests, but are divided in a variety of ways (both between different 'fractions' and even within single 'fractions'). Neo-Marxism has not gone far enough in recognising this point. Thus Poulantzas (1973) classically argued that the bourgeoisie was internally fractionated, comprising various competing factions. But we have seen that the dominant class is fractionated in a much more fundamental way. Classes are often 'cross-pressurised', as Peter Gourevitch (1986: 114) labelled it; that is, they might face a variety of pressures, the resolution of one of which might prevent or exacerbate problems faced in other areas. For example, the Prussian Junkers in 1879 were internally divided between their fiscal, trading and political interests. For agricultural purposes, they favoured free trade. Fiscally, however, they favoured indirect taxes and hence tariffs, while politically they favoured a right-wing government coalition, which could be advanced only by raising tariffs. Similarly in Britain in 1909, the industrial bourgeoisie and parts of the City of London favoured free trade for their business concerns, but unequivocally favoured indirect taxes and tariffs for their personal tax concerns. This point has major ramifications for social theory.

This means that classes are often internally contradictory, and cannot therefore be understood in conventional Marxist terms. More importantly, the fractionated composition of the dominant class enables the state to enhance its domestic position. The Reich government played off the various contradictory interests of the Junker class in order to push through tariff reform in 1879. The British state did the same by playing off the contradictory trading and fiscal interests of the bourgeoisie in 1909, in order to raise the income tax. This gives rise to my seventh sociological non-realist thesis of state capacity:

> *State capacity and autonomy can be enhanced through the polymorphous nature of both the state and the dominant classes.*

A further paradox results: that the polymorphous nature of states can enhance state capacity, just as the polymorphous nature of classes can enhance state capacity.

Embedded autonomy and relative political capacity differentials

To summarise this section, we can apply my findings to redefine 'state intervention' in the three case studies, Britain, Germany and Russia, in the late nineteenth and early twentieth centuries. For this period, state strength in the general literature is predicated on the degree of intervention in the economy; high intervention implying state strength, minimalist intervention implying state weakness. Thus, the consensus argues that Britain was probably the best example of a minimalist 'night-watchman' state, while its authoritarian counterparts, especially autocratic Russia and imperial Germany, were the best examples of strong interventionist states (e.g., Gerschenkron 1962; Katzenstein 1977a, 1977b; Jessop 1978). This chapter refutes this conceptualisation. Rather, it was Britain that was the strongest, Russia and Germany lying towards the weaker end of the continuum of state power.

On what basis is this revisionist claim made? The literature has generally assumed that social, economic, political and military policies can be compartmentalised, such that while Britain may have been relatively interventionist socially, it was only minimalist in the economic sphere. But such compartmentalisation is highly problematic. The reason for this is quite simple. Trade and economic policies were fundamentally entwined with taxation issues. Britain's so-called economic minimalism, evidenced primarily through its free trade policy, was premised on a highly interventionist and radical fiscal policy of income tax extraction. Had the income tax not been possible to implement on the scale that it was, Britain might well have returned to protectionism (as chapter 4 argues). The level of income taxation extracted was premised on the state's ability to go against the long-term fiscal interests of the dominant classes.

The best comparison here is between Britain and Germany. The fact is that the authoritarian Reich government never seriously challenged the dominant classes in the fiscal arena through the introduction of a progressive income tax. While the Reich did not always harmonise with the Junkers, and did indeed play off the various dominant class factions, nevertheless it maintained regressive indirect taxation. The British Liberal government, however, struck at the fiscal nerve centre of all fractions of the dominant class. In chapter 4, following Ruggie (1983), we referred to this as 'the compromise of embedded liberalism'. The 1909 'red budget' was a type of social revolution from above. Paradoxically, such a revolution was achieved by maintaining the grudging consent of the dominant class. This, for a variety of reasons (discussed above, pp. 236–40), was not possible in Germany or Russia.

One major reason why the British state was able to go against the long-term interests of the dominant class was that it enjoyed a wide sense of embeddedness within society. While Germany was embedded within the dominant class, its relationship with the lower classes was much more distant. This strongly contrasted with the British case, where the state was far more embedded within the lower-middle and working classes. As a result, the British state was able to play off the dominant and the subordinate classes so as to maximise its fiscal capacity. The implications of this for the First World War were profound, and are analysed in detail towards the end of this chapter (pp. 254–68). In short, behind Britain's external minimalism of free trade policy was a strong fiscal policy, wielded by a strong state. Ironically, Continental protectionism was reflective of weak states, particularly in relation to Britain's strength and interventionism.

But the most significant conclusion to be derived from this analysis is a rejection of understanding states as either 'interventionist' or 'minimalist'. As Colin White has argued, 'Such a distinction is misleading ... Government and market are inextricably enmeshed' (1987: 130). In short, conceptualising states as embedded, albeit to different degrees, is a more accurate way of understanding the relationship between states and economies.

The multiple international sources of state capacity

Central to my sociological approach is its assumption that the state derives much of its transformative capacity (i.e., its ability to affect and initiate social and economic change) by virtue of its spatial location, since it straddles the international and sub-national dimensions with its feet fixed firmly in both. Thus states are (spatially) *janus-faced*, looking both inwards and outwards (Hintze 1975: 183; Skocpol 1979: 32; Michael Mann 1988: 3; Ikenberry 1988c: 35–40; 1991: 161; Katzenstein 1977a: 899; Linklater 1991; Halliday 1994: 84–6, 140). Or as Nettl classically put it, 'the state is the gatekeeper between intrasocietal and extrasocietal flows of action' (1968: 564; cf. Katzenstein's 'doorman' metaphor).

However, it is important not to exaggerate the state's intervening role. The 'gatekeeper' or 'doorman' metaphor should be qualified because it implies that nation-states are hermetically sealed, with external forces entering only through a narrow state-regulated corridor (implicitly reinforcing realism's sovereignty premise). However, plenty of external pressures penetrate and enter societal space, with or without the overseeing regulation of the state (Burton 1972). While it is vital not to reify states, this should not, however, lead us to underestimate their importance in the international system.

A key issue is at stake here. For while it is an important aspect of the perspective adumbrated here that the *international* or *transnational* can often structure the *national*, it is important to resist the spatial determinism of the world systems school, which argues that societies are created by the exogenous impact of the world economy. Rather, states often *mediate* the impact of changes in the inter-state system or the world economy upon the domestic environment. States are not mirrors of external processes, nor are they merely filter mechanisms. Rather, states actively process and channel international influences to bolster their domestic power position, although they do not always manage this successfully (Skocpol 1979: 31; Trimberger 1978; Block 1987: 66–7, 87–9; Randall Collins 1986; Michael Mann 1988: ch. 1).

There are two main international sources of state power: the inter-state military system and the international economy.

State capacity and international trade

Each of the states dealt with here had recourse to international trade to enhance its power base within domestic society. However, each did so to enhance a different aspect of state power. Paradoxically, using the international system might bolster some aspects of state power, but it can also lead to the undermining of state capacity (as the German and Russian cases demonstrate).

The German Reich (as well as Australian and Canadian federal governments) resorted to taxing international trade primarily to enhance its *concentration* power vis-à-vis the provincial state governments, thereby shifting the political terms of rule in its favour. Thus Bismarck increased taxes on international trade, the proceeds of which went to enhancing the revenues of the central state (Reich). These revenues funded the *Länder*, making them dependent on the Reich, thereby shifting the political terms of rule in favour of the latter. However, Bismarck was only moderately successful in this venture.

Much more successful were the federal governments in Australia and Canada, which provided the state governments with a large proportion of their funds. Between 1874 and 1913, the Canadian dominion government provided, through the tariff, between 29 per cent and 58 per cent of all state government revenues, while the Australian commonwealth government passed on approximately 75 per cent of all tariff revenues to the states. Most federal states used taxes (tariffs) on international trade to shift the terms of rule away from the state governments towards the centre. In addition, the authoritarian states in which parliaments existed (e.g., Germany and Austria-Hungary) also resorted to taxing international trade in order to enhance their executive autonomy in relation to parliament. This was especially important in Germany.

Britain used international trade to enhance its RPC, and to instigate fiscal reform that went against the fiscal interests of the various fractions of the dominant classes. This was what we referred to as the 'compromise of embedded liberalism'. The dominant classes, which to a large, though by no means exclusive, extent favoured free trade, accepted that progressive income taxes would be raised. The pay-off for free trade was domestic social-fiscal reform. To use the terminology of Margaret Levi (1988), the British state enhanced its relative bargaining power vis-à-vis the dominant classes by maintaining free trade. Thus free trade enabled the state sufficient autonomy to increase the income tax and thereby enhance the state's relative political capacity.

Russia, on the other hand, like Britain, was a unitary state, enjoying one of the highest levels of concentration of any European state. It used taxes on international trade to accumulate revenues as well as to enhance its despotic power against the bourgeois, noble, working and peasant classes. Furthermore, maintaining high tariff rates on industrial inputs (raw materials and semi-manufactured goods) was a crucial weapon in dividing and ruling the capitalist class. Paradoxically, the reliance on regressive indirect taxes and the lack of an income tax may have enhanced despotic power, but they fundamentally undermined tsarist RPC in the international and domestic arenas (as we shall see shortly).

State capacity and the international system of states

These states also used the inter-state military system to shore up their domestic power bases. Britain was able to push through the income tax against the fiscal interests of the dominant classes, partly because the funds would increase the country's military base through dreadnought construction (although in large part these revenues would fund

working-class pensions). Shoring up the country's military base increased the state's bargaining power vis-à-vis the dominant classes,
which, coupled with the maintenance of free trade, enabled the state to
introduce higher income tax rates, as well as funding working-class
pensions. This considerably enhanced the state's RPC.

Russia used the requirements of geopolitics to increase indirect
taxes, a logic that initially smoothed the switch to such taxes. The
defeat in the Crimean War enabled the state to enhance its despotic
power over both the lower and the upper orders, enabling some
radical domestic social reforms (e.g., the emancipation of the serfs in
1861). Moreover, defence requirements were a crucial component in
the state's patrimonial 'divide and rule' strategy vis-à-vis the capitalist
class. It purposefully nurtured a public and a private defence industry
in order to prevent the latter from becoming too powerful.

I can, therefore, assert my eighth and ninth sociological non-realist
propositions on state capacity:

> *Inter-state territorial decentralisation can provide the state with a potentially
> enhanced base of power within the domestic and international realms.*

> *Transnational and international economic relations can provide the state
> with a potentially enhanced base of power within the domestic and interna-
> tional realms.*

It is important to note that I use the term 'potentially' because we
need to keep in mind that states have a choice in pursuing their
various political strategies. They can use the international or national
arenas to enhance different powers (which may or may not enhance
the state's RPC). Thus the British state used the international economic
system to enhance its fiscal and hence political capacity through
negotiating with societal actors. However, in the case of tsarist Russia,
the international economy was used to enhance the state's despotic
power, which ultimately undermined the state through defeat in war
and revolution. And, in Germany, the international economy was used
to enhance the Reich's degree of concentration, also leading to state
incapacity in the First World War.

In general, we can understand the various powers of the state in the
internal and external arenas only by noting how states enhance their
position or bargaining power vis-à-vis society through recourse not
just to their domestically centralised socio-spatial location, but also
through their position within the decentralised international political
and economic systems.[3] It should be noted that thesis 8 (see below,

p. 252) is not a reiteration of the realist argument about sovereignty. Rather, it suggests that the state's role in warfare and inter-state military relations enhances the power of the state to push through domestic reforms. (It is not the lack of a world government that enhances the state's domestic power, but international and transnational military pressures that enable this.)

My claim (thesis 9, p. 252) that international and transnational trade and capital flows can bolster state power stands in strong contrast to the popular argument that such flows have undermined the basis of the modern state (see especially Camilleri and Falk 1991; Burton 1972; Barnett and Müller 1974). There are several problems here. Firstly, the argument concedes far too much to the realist claim that states are best defined as 'sovereign' entities. The assumption usually made is that the state, which was 'sovereign' once (usually in the post-1648 period), is now no longer so. The problem here is in equating states or state power with sovereignty. States, however, are much more than 'sovereign' monoliths. Rather than analyse how the demise of sovereignty has led to the demise of the state and state power, we need to begin by disaggregating a state's multiple powers, and then examine the impact of transnational forces on each. Moreover, we have seen already how states have used such transnational forces to bolster various state powers. This, in turn, has had a differential impact on a state's RPC, enhancing it in Britain's case and weakening it in Germany's and Russia's. Moreover, the failings of Germany and Russia in 1918 and 1917 respectively occurred because the state elites sought to bolster the wrong state powers. In other words, they had a choice in how they responded to international forces and pressures. States are not simple victims (*Träger*) of external forces, but are able to mediate such forces, although they do this to varying degrees.

A further problem with the popular argument is that it tends to paint a picture of freely floating transnational forces (typified by multinational corporations, MNCs, in the late twentieth-century context) which, through their superior mobility, are able to pick off 'territorially fixed' states at will (again ironically conceding too much to realism). States are portrayed as slow lumbering monoliths trapped within a national-territorial iron cage, gradually sapped of their strength (read sovereignty) by the surreptitious attack of transnational forces. But my main point is that states are also socially mobile, enjoying a dual spatial anchorage in the internal and external arenas. Indeed, national states are able – like MNCs – to utilise what Hirschman (1978) called

250

the 'exit strategy' by using the international system to shore up their domestic position.

Thirdly, as Huntington (1991: 222–7) has argued, such a thesis assumes a zero-sum game of power between the capitalist class and the state. In the modern state, with the exception of autocracy, states enter into *duplicative conflict* where, in general, the interests of the state and the capitalist class coincide (cf. Bull 1977: 272). Indeed, this returns us to my main argument: that state power can best be achieved through cooperation rather than conflict.

Fourthly, this view is undermined by the single fact that states actually formed as a result of the impact of international and transnational forces. The premise that transnationalism/international capitalism and state power are mutually exclusive is unfounded. Put simply, transnationalism and state power have grown together from roughly AD 500 until 2000. Thus states made the inter-state system and the world economy, and the inter-state system and world economy made states (Weiss and Hobson 1995: 15–131).

Ten theses on state capacity

I am now in a position to realise two central objectives: to provide a definition of the state and a non-realist framework for analysing state power and capacity. The key to my approach is in noting that state capacity comprises various forms of state power. Differing configurations of state powers (which are based on state–society relations and politico-institutional powers) give rise to differing degrees of capacity, where capacity refers to a state's ability to extract sufficient revenues to maintain itself in the inter-state system, while simultaneously maintaining domestic consensus. Drawing on the discussion so far, we can forward ten theses on state capacity:

(1) State capacity is positively related to the degree of a state's interactive embeddedness within society; the broader and deeper the social embeddedness, the stronger the state's capacity.

(2) State capacity is inversely related to the level of despotic power accumulated.

(3) In order to maximise their capacity, states need to gain insulation from private demands and simultaneously engage in competitive-cooperation with key social actors (the

paradox of embedded/bounded autonomy and competitive-cooperation).

(4)   State (fiscal) capacity is potentially enhanced in unitary states and limited in federal states.

(5)   State capacity requires a high degree of penetrative/infrastructural power.

(6)   National/domestic territorial centralisation provides the state with a fundamental basis of power in the internal and external arenas.

(7)   State capacity and autonomy can be enhanced through the polymorphous nature of both the state and the dominant classes.

(8)   Inter-state territorial decentralisation can provide the state with a potentially enhanced base of power within the domestic and international realms.

(9)   Transnational and international economic relations can provide the state with a potentially enhanced base of power within the domestic and international realms.

(10)   State strength in the domestic arena is a vital prerequisite for strength in the international system.

Refining the Weberian definition of the modern state

I am now able to define the modern state through refining the famous Weberian definition. Although neo-Weberian analyses have led the way in developing the concept of 'state autonomy', this is not reflected in the formal Weberian definition of the state. In particular, I add a social dimension to the common 'institutional' definition. Adapting and developing the Weberian definition produced by Michael Mann (1988: 4) and Norbert Elias (1939/1994), we can see that the modern state contains the following five endogenous elements:

(1)   A differentiated set of political institutions comprising public/vocational personnel (i.e., bureaucrats),

(2)   embodying centrality in the sense that political relations radiate outwards (i.e., penetrative/infrastructural power) to cover

(3)   a territorially consolidated (unified) area over which it exercises

(4)   a legitimate monopoly of rule-making through a legitimate

monopoly of the means of taxation backed up by a legitimate monopoly of the means of violence,

(5) and which enters in to varying degrees and mixes of competitive-cooperative relations with key social actors (i.e., state–society relations) from which it generates power internally and externally.

Moreover, while Weberian analyses have been very much at the forefront of exploring the reciprocal relations between the internal and external dimensions, this is not reflected in the formal Weberian definition of the state. This then is the second main shortcoming in the Weberian definition: its failure to take into account states' international presence and how it relates to their domestic position, as well as how their domestic position affects their international position. The modern state, therefore, comprises the following four components, derived from the external arena:

(6) A set of political institutions differentiated from other states, global institutions and capitalist actors, comprising public and national personnel,

(7) whose international reach radiates outwards across

(8) territorially decentralised political and economic systems,

(9) and which generates bargaining power and strength in relation to its own domestic society and the international economic and political systems by playing off the internal and external realms against each other.

Points 1–4 cover the state's formal institutional position within society, while points 6–8 emphasise a state's formal institutional position in the international system. Points 5 and 9 refer to the basis of state capacity in the internal and external arenas. The common criticism of the Weberian definition, usually made by Marxists, is that it fails to take into account the relationship between state and society. I resolve this deficit through points 5 and 9.

Ultimately, the importance of my analysis rests on the dual (spatial) anchorage theme of the state, where the janus-faced state looks both inward and outward, and in the process derives considerable power and autonomy, often by playing each spatial dimension off against the other. In short, states are not passive victims (*Träger*) caught between the Scylla of global capitalism/inter-state system and the Charybdis of society/societal forces. Rather, states actively shape both arenas by drawing on one to enhance their position in the other. This then is the ultimate Bonapartist balancing act, where states balance the international with the national in order to shift the social balance of power or 'terms of rule' inside and outside society in their favour. In turn, a state's particular relations with society have major ramifications for its relative political capacity, internally and externally. In sum, the state plays an important role within what I call here the *dual reflexivity* of the internal and external realms: that is, where both realms shape and promote change in the other under the *partial* intervening role of the state.

The 'wealth of states' and state capacity in the international politics of war and revolution

My tenth thesis on state capacity suggests that a state's power in the international system is largely derived from its particular state–society relationship (in conjunction with various internal institutional powers). This means that IR could be enhanced by engaging with a Weberian sociological analysis of the state–society nexus. This section develops this claim through examining the First World War and its turbulent aftermath, developing the fiscal-sociological analyses of chapters 2 through 5.

Synthesising sociological and international relations theories of the state

I noted earlier that a state's relative political capacity (RPC) rests on its ability not only successfully to wage war externally, but also to maintain consensus and avert revolution internally. I noted that war and revolution are linked, principally through a state's RPC. My approach overlaps with that of James Rosenau (1981; cf. Ikenberry 1988c: 206–8), who points out that a state's capacity to survive is based on its ability to adapt and respond to pressures emanating from inside and outside itself. For the period under review here I note two major pressures, both linked through taxation. The key internal challenge comprised the rise of the working class and the desire for more progressive tax regimes. The key external challenge comprised the need to raise taxes, especially a broad-based progressive income tax (as well as develop a military-industrial base) in order to shore up the state's military power. The higher the degree of adaptation and ability

Figure 7.2: The uneven relative political capacity and the 'adaptability' of states in the early twentieth century

	Russia (promotive)	Germany (acquiescent)	Britain (preservative)
Internal RPC (adaptability)	Weak	Weak-moderate	Strong
External RPC (adaptability)	Weak	Weak-moderate	Strong

to respond and accommodate these various pressures, the greater the state's RPC. With these two categories in mind I can draw up a typology for the three main states dealt with here.

On the continuum, Russia is the least adaptive, failing to respond to working-class citizenship demands, particularly the social push for progressive taxation. Instead, tsarist autocracy sought to repress the lower orders (as well as the dominant capitalist class) through regressive indirect taxes. And although tsarism took international military pressures rather more seriously, it still did not do nearly enough. In particular, failing to adapt to internal pressures for an income tax fundamentally undermined the state's external military capacity. In Rosenau's terminology, this makes tsarism a 'promotive state', wherein 'those who act for the state treat both the internal and external challenges as minimal' (1981: 38). This was the ultimate source of tsarism's structural weakness: its *maladaptability* or inflexibility to respond to and meet these internal and external challenges. This illustrates the paradox of state power: the more despotic the state, the weaker it becomes.

Germany was rather more adaptive, granting basic social citizenship rights, although these were only limited and crucially did not extend to 'progressive taxation'. Moreover, the central government was unable to raise sufficient progressive taxation largely because of the federal and partially embedded nature of the state (as discussed in chapter 2), which fundamentally affected its war effort, as well as leading to the alienation of the working classes. Nevertheless, its ability to adjust to the military pressures of the inter-state system was greater than Russia's because of its ability to foster a strong military-industrial base. This means that the state leaned towards what Rosenau calls 'acquiescence', where those who act on behalf of the state give higher priority to external than domestic pressures. Nevertheless, the failure to meet the internal social/fiscal challenge led to a vulnerability externally. In short, it is not possible to remain adaptive (and hence strong) externally without achieving high levels of adaptability internally (as tsarist Russia and imperial Germany found out at the end of the First World War, and as the Soviet Union and the Warsaw Pact countries would similarly learn in the late 1980s).

Finally, Britain responded favourably to working- and lower-middle-class demands for a progressive income tax. Simultaneously this helped it to survive the First World War, making it in Rosenau's terminology a 'preservative' state, where state rulers give high priority to meeting internal and external challenges. Of the three states examined here, Britain's relative fiscal capacity, and hence RPC, was the most effective and adaptive.

The litmus test for this argument is to see, firstly, how well these states prepared for the First World War, and, secondly, how well these states weathered the war and its turbulent aftermath. This is the subject of the next two sections. Such a discussion is important because it allows us to develop an empirical set of case studies which not only illustrate the relevance of my sociological approach to international politics (as opposed to IPE), but also allow us to critique neorealism further on its own specific terrain – namely, the study of war. Neorealism focuses on what Waltz (1959) termed the 'third image' (which refers to the inter-state system as the independent variable), and ignores the importance of the 'second image' (the state and state–society complex). In what follows, I argue that an analysis which focuses on the second image is crucial for understanding war. To cite the title of a recent book, the following sections trace the 'domestic bases of Grand Strategy' (Rosecrance and Stein 1993). If there is any saliency in the analysis discussed above, we would expect to see Germany and especially Russia come unstuck externally as a result of military pressures associated with the First World War and, internally, as a result of social pressures emanating from society (both of which were linked by taxation strategies), while Britain would have been better able to survive such pressures before, during and after the war.

Relative political (state) capacity differentials: the domestic foundations of war preparation, 1900–1914

In the next section I argue that the differentials in relative political capacity were a crucial factor in the outcome and aftermath of the First

World War. However, the effects of these state capacity differentials can be traced back to the pre-1914 period. The argument made here is that Germany's moderate state capacity put it in a disadvantageous position relative to Britain even prior to the beginning of the war (which was exacerbated once fighting had begun). Here, I follow the lead taken recently by D'Lugo and Rogowski (1993), who argue that Germany lost the naval race before 1914 and, as a result, went into the First World War severely disadvantaged vis-à-vis Britain. They argue that this was a result of the differential in 'constitutional fitness' (or what I refer to as RPC) between a moderately weak German state and a strong British state. While I endorse much of their analysis, I seek to refine and qualify it in a number of ways.

Germany's moderate state capacity constituted a major obstacle to the development of its military power. In particular, Germany lost the naval race with Britain in part because of fiscal weakness (D'Lugo and Rogowski 1993: 70, 82). Indeed, by 1914, Britain had twenty-four dreadnoughts and a total of sixty capital ships compared to Germany's sixteen dreadnoughts and thirty-eight capital ships. The problem was (as was made clear by all serious naval strategists at the time) that Germany required a *superiority* of naval forces over Britain for it to actually win the war (D'Lugo and Rogowski 1993: 82–3), which in turn required a much larger extraction of fiscal resources. Germany entered the war suffering a 'naval gap' with Britain because of the Reich's inability to extract the necessary taxation to boost naval spending. In short, there developed a fundamental gap between Reich military 'will' and fiscal-political capacity (Niall Ferguson 1994; Paul Kennedy 1987: 326).

After 1900, the Reich once again faced fiscal crisis (Craig 1987: 279; Percy Ashley 1909), as it had done in the 1870s. This was not a result of higher expenditures, nor even the post-1897 turn to *Weltpolitik* (as many German historians have argued), because the Reich military burden and total burden peaked in the 1886–90 period, and actually declined thereafter until 1913 (see table 2.8). The problem lay on the tax side: in particular, the inability of the Reich to levy a high-yielding income tax which could expand the tax base, and a consequent dependency on indirect taxes. This weakness was clearly reflected in the resort to higher loans (Paul Kennedy 1987: 325; Witt 1970, 1987a, 1987b; Holtfrerich 1986; Sumida 1989: 196; Niall Ferguson 1994: 160), as well as the difficulty in selling such loans (Paul Kennedy 1987: 325–6; 1989: 190; Niall Ferguson 1994: 160; Kitchen 1978: 262).[4]

Why was the Reich so heavily dependent on indirect taxation? As discussed in chapter 2, an important reason lay with the *federal* nature of the state. A compromise similar to the one between the *Länder* (state governments) and the Reich (central government) occurred in all federal states in the nineteenth century (see chapter 5). This compromise, between two competing levels of government, ensured that there was a strict fiscal demarcation, such that the state governments would enjoy a virtual monopoly of direct taxation, and the central government would have a virtual monopoly of indirect taxation. Federalism also constrained the Reich, because most of the tax burden was incurred at the *Länder* and *Gemeinde* levels. This simply crowded out the Reich's room for manoeuvre: the central government managed to extract at most only 30 per cent of total revenues in Germany in 1913 (Schremmer 1988: 482).[5] This might have been alleviated by a Reich income tax, but this was not forthcoming, firstly, because of resistance put up by the state governments and, secondly, because of the intransigence of the Prussian Conservatives.

The Reich government was not sufficiently embedded in society as a whole, unlike the British state which was firmly embedded in society and paradoxically was able to play off the working class with the dominant classes. Britain had greater room for manoeuvre than the Reich both institutionally and socially – and was therefore able to instigate radical taxation policies which went against the long-term fiscal interests of the dominant classes. The Reich's partial embeddedness (i.e., embedded only within the upper classes) precluded such an option. In addition (as noted in chapter 2), the Reich suffered the *sovereignty paradox*: in concentrating on achieving fiscal autonomy from the *Länder* through increasing indirect taxes and hence tariffs, the empire ended up with a weak fiscal capacity.

Britain, on the other hand, enjoyed a firmer fiscal foundation for military spending. As D'Lugo and Rogowski (1993) argue, this was based on Britain's (direct) income tax base, which was radically extended in the 1909 budget (as was explained in detail in chapter 4). At this point, however, I need to qualify the argument made by D'Lugo and Rogowski. They mistakenly argue that, prior to 1914, Britain was able to allocate far greater sums to military spending, thus enabling victory in the naval race. There are several problems with this claim.

First and foremost, D'Lugo and Rogowski base their argument on absolute spending figures expressed in sterling. This leads them to claim that in 1911 the British state imposed a *total* burden some 30 per cent higher than in Germany (1993: 72). However, as economic historians and defence economists point out, fiscal burdens *can be measured only* by expressing absolute spending *as a proportion of national income* – referred to in earlier chapters as the cge/NNP or d/NNP ratio (Gavin Kennedy 1983: 36). This is because absolute figures tell us nothing about a taxpayer's actual ability to pay. If the British taxpayers paid more (expressed in sterling), this was because they could afford to do so, given that average incomes as well as per capita national income were higher than in Germany. Secondly, the argument here requires a comparison of 'military' rather than 'total' expenditures. Thirdly, even when expressed in absolute terms (i.e., in sterling), the data fail to fully support D'Lugo and Rogowski's argument. Table 7.1 incorporates these points.

This table (col. 4) shows that Germany spent more on defence preparation *overall* in real terms than Britain in the all important 1908–13 years (Britain spending more in the earlier period merely because of the Boer War). And even using the various data sets produced by Gerloff (1913), the *Statistisches Jahrbücher für das Deutsche Reich*, and the data provided in Andic and Veverka (1964), Germany's overall real burden is still higher in the 1908–13 period (cf. John M. Hobson 1993: 478–9; Niall Ferguson 1994). Surprisingly, from 1908 onwards, even when expressed in sterling (col. 1), Germany spent more overall. However, in line with D'Lugo and Rogowski's central argument, Britain clearly spent more on naval building (cols. 2 and 5) – exactly twice as much as Germany in the 1900–13 period in real terms.

Certainly, British military spending was more easily borne prior to 1914, as it would be once fighting had begun. As D'Lugo and Rogowski (1993) point out, the British government was able to run surpluses after 1902 and retire debt precisely at a time when the German national debt was skyrocketing (see also John M. Hobson 1993: 496; Sumida 1989: 196; Witt 1970: 386; Paul Kennedy 1987: ch. 17). The confidence that this engendered led to much lower interest rates charged on treasury bonds in Britain than in Germany. The problem lay not so much in higher spending in Britain, but rather with insufficient Reich fiscal capacity to win the naval race. To win, Germany had to boost taxes. But unlike in Britain, the financial revolution required to achieve this (i.e., the development of a strong and permanent income tax base) failed to occur. Germany remained dependent on indirect taxes with their modest yield compared to the

Table 7.1: *Absolute and real military spending in Britain and Germany, 1901–1913*

Period	(1) Total defence (£m)	(2) Navy (£m)	(3) Army (£m)	(4) Total defence (d/NNP)	(5) Navy (d/NNP)	(6) Army (d/NNP)
Germany						
1901–7	54	12	34	3.4	0.7	2.1
1908–13	78	21	47	3.7	1.0	2.2
1901–13	65	16	40	3.5	0.9	2.2
Britain						
1901–7	86	33	54	4.8	1.8	3.0
1908–13	66	38	27	3.2	1.8	1.3
1901–13	77	35	42	4.0	1.8	2.2

Sources and notes: Germany: Military expenditures: Witt (1970: 380–1). Total military expenditures: based on the Witt data but several adjustments have been made, partly to ease comparison with the British figures, as well as to effect the right direction of bias for my argument. This requires using a low military burden (d/NNP) figure, which in the case of Germany means using a low military expenditure set. To this end, I have made two deductions from the Witt data. Firstly, I have subtracted interest payments on loans, taken from Andic and Veverka (1964). Secondly, I have deducted the amounts paid out on purely strategic railways, assuming these to be an average RM 30m per annum (an approximate figure given to me by Professor Witt in a private conversation). The other additions that Witt made to the *Statistisches Jahrbuch* data seem reasonable to include. In sum, the final estimates used here seem reasonable to compare with the less controversial British data. Army and naval data: perhaps most importantly, I have not included various capital expenditures connected to the military (which would have added some 10 per cent to the navy and army expenditures). In this way, I have ensured that these estimates have not been exaggerated, thus again enabling a fair comparison with the British data. National income: Hoffmann (1965: 506–9).

Britain: Military expenditures: Mitchell and Deane (1962: 398). National income: Feinstein (1972: table 1, T4–T7). To effect the right direction of bias for the purposes of my argument, I need to maximise the British military burden (d/NNP) data, which can be done by using the lowest national income data. The Feinstein data is one of the lowest sets available (see appendix B for further discussion).

strong British income tax base, and accordingly failed to win the naval race.

However, while the foundations for German military weakness vis-à-vis Britain were clearly laid prior to 1914, their ramifications were not really evident until *after* the war broke out (the point at which D'Lugo and Rogowski end their analysis). In sum, D'Lugo and Rogowski are correct to point to what they call the British state's superior *constitutional fitness* (i.e., relative political capacity) compared to Germany's, but they exaggerate the implications of this in understanding the war preparation of both states *prior to 1914* (cf. Friedberg 1988).[6] Rather, the importance of Britain's stronger relative political capacity before 1914 lay mainly in the fact that the 1909 'financial revolution', which led to a strong income tax base, stood the country in excellent stead for the coming war compared to the much weaker position of Germany, with its reliance on loans and indirect taxes. (Note that tsarist Russia suffered a similar problem to Germany.) The differences in RPC became clear once fighting began, and it is to this that we now turn.

Relative political (state) capacity differentials: the domestic foundations of war outcomes and revolution, 1914–1919

The relative political capacities of Britain, Germany and Russia were, however, really tested only during the First World War. Christopher Chase-Dunn (1989) points out that a good test of state strength involves examining the amount of revenues a state can extract (measured as a proportion of national income) *during a period in which state power is challenged* (1989: 113, 114–16, 174, 181). As we would anticipate, British war finance, relying on an expandable income tax base, was considerably superior to the fiscal armoury available to both Germany and Russia.

In Germany, the prewar weakness of the fiscal and federal system of government, which had led to an inability to increase taxation (with revenues dropping in the first three years of the war), continued after 1914, forcing the Reich to rely almost wholly on loans for war finance. As a result, the ordinary budget was burdened with paying the interest on the loans – some 86 per cent of total ordinary expenditures (Gerloff 1929: 67; cf. Roesler 1967: 197). Because of the Allied blockade, indirect taxes (especially customs) had only a very limited yield. However, the government only belatedly brought in direct taxes, and this to little avail. With a narrow tax base, the state relied on a combination of loans and printing paper money. Two principal problems stemmed from this.

Firstly, printing paper money led to inflation. War finance provided the initial impetus of the hyper-inflation of the early 1920s in Germany (Holtfrerich 1986: 102–80, 192–3, 331; Witt 1987a, 1987b; Karl Hardach 1976: 10, 16; Paul Kennedy 1988: 270; Berghahn 1973: 48–9). This considerably destabilised the regime. Secondly, and even more problematically, is the fact that reliance on regressive indirect rather than direct taxes to fund the albeit limited ordinary budget led to widespread social discontent and, in particular, undermined morale (Paul Kennedy 1988: 270), as indeed it had done prior to the war. This was clearly a factor in the ensuing November 1918 revolution when the Kaiserreich was finally overthrown. The inability of the Reich to adapt to the internal (especially fiscal) demands of the working classes rebounded in its face, precipitating its final demise. Indeed in the months following the revolution, Matthias Erzberger sought to base the Reich on the income tax, which became one of the major political issues of the Weimar period (Epstein 1959; Holtfrerich 1986, 1987). Holtfrerich points to the linkage between Reich fiscal policy, defeat in war and revolution:

> Defeat ... was the event in the international political arena which determined the subsequent course of the inflation; the revolution of November 1918 was the corresponding domestic political event because of its budgetary implications: parties came to power that were concerned to promote social reforms and a more equitable distribution of income and wealth. (1986: 192–3)

However, the ramifications of Germany's weak RPC go well beyond the revolution of 1918. The hyper-inflation that exploded in 1923 – the result of the state's inability and unwillingness to extract sufficient revenues (due to the poor progressive tax yield) to pay the required reparations – brought the Weimar state to its knees. Tragically, this had particular ramifications for the future of the international state system itself. As David Thomson put it, speaking of the Weimar hyper-inflation:

> The unknown and incalculable result was the mood of black fear and hysteria fostered among the dispossessed middle classes, who alone might have given the new regime stability and permanence. Hitler's failure in 1923 would turn into success ten years later. (1977: 607)

The state's relative political incapacity was a major factor not only in the military defeat and the subsequent revolution, but also in the hyper-inflation, the demise of Weimar and the future rise of the Third Reich.

This provides a strong contrast with the British case, where the state resorted increasingly to the income tax. Through the war, the standard rate of income tax rose from 6.25 per cent to 30 per cent, rising from 14d in the final years before the war to 60d in 1917/18, and then remaining at 72d in the pound from 1918 to 1923 (Mitchell and Deane 1962: 429). Together with the super-tax, higher incomes were subjected to a rate of about 50 per cent (Gerd Hardach 1977: 164). Thus, within the space of five years (1914–18), the already relatively high rate of income tax in Britain had more than quadrupled. As Holtfrerich points out,

> In Great Britain it proved possible to meet a considerable part of war expenditure out of current [ordinary] taxation. The centrally and efficiently organised English system already possessed powers of direct taxation – income tax in particular.
>
> (1986: 111; see also Gerd Hardach 1977: 157)

The use of direct taxation in Britain was crucial in enabling the state to finance between 20 and 30 per cent of total war costs by taxes (Holtfrerich 1987: 129), which was at least twice as high as the proportion achieved by Germany (Gerd Hardach 1977: 155; Karl Hardach 1976: 10), or over three times higher according to alternative estimates (Knauss, cited in Balderston 1989: 224). The importance of direct taxation in Britain is not a contentious issue. As Balderston puts it: 'There can thus be no doubt that the income tax with its wartime extension, the excess profit duty, was the foundation of British war taxation' (1989: 231). In particular contrast to Germany, Britain in the years after the war raised taxes in order to keep inflation at bay and pay off foreign debt. From 1919 to 1923, no less than 24.4 per cent of national income was appropriated in taxation. Accordingly, there was no revolution in Britain, in part because the working classes had not been alienated by unfair regressive taxation before and during the war.

Russia provides a dramatic contrast. Although tsarism did bring in an income tax in 1916, its yield was so minute as to make it almost undetectable. As Stone puts it, its total tax yield of Rb 130 million in the war (out of a total of tens of billions of roubles collected) was 'less than enough to pay for a week-end of the war' (1975: 290). Russia, like

Germany, increased indirect taxes (Bogolepoff 1918: 346), though their yield similarly proved to be highly inadequate. Not surprisingly, tsarism came to rely on the old method of printing paper money to finance the war. As with Germany, this was to a large extent responsible for the chronic wartime inflation (Stone 1984: 368–9), where the overall price index rose over ten times in the space of three years. As Stone points out:

> The need for printed money became such, in summer 1917, that the quality of the paper was considerably lowered; and there was not even time to put numbers on it: clients had to be told to ink in the numbers on the notes themselves.   (1984: 369)

Inflation hit all groups hard, but the lower orders – the working classes and peasantry – came off particularly badly (Stone 1975: 291–301). The price of bread, for example, went up over thirty times in the space of just twelve months after January 1917, since grain production was effectively crippled by the inflation (Stone 1975: 291–301; 1984: 370).

When this was coupled with the unpopularity of the regime, which had effectively treated its population as cannon fodder throughout the war (and political fodder before and during the war), it would only be a short period of time before the state would be properly held to account. And so it was that

> the garrisons of the cities ... including the crucial Petrograd garrison, were swollen with recent recruits apprehensive about going to the front and directly familiar with the circumstances of the civilian workers suffering from skyrocketing prices and shortages of basic necessities ... Once the initial rebellion was underway, it spread irrepressibly from military unit to military unit, from factory workers to railway men, from the capital of Petrograd to Moscow and to the provincial cities.
> (Skocpol 1979: 98; see also Stone 1975; 1984: 370–1; McDaniel 1988)

Russia's low political capacity was directly responsible not only for its defeat in war, but also for its internal downfall in 1917, beaten externally by the Axis powers, and internally by the peasants and workers in collusion with the army. Paul Kennedy put it aptly:

> the [tsarist] regime helped dig its own grave by recklessly unbalanced fiscal policies; having abolished the trade in spirits (which produced one-third of its revenue), losing heavily on the railways (its other great peacetime source of income), and – unlike Lloyd George – declining to raise the income tax upon the better-off classes, the state resorted to floating ever more loans and printing ever more paper

money in order to pay for the war. The price index spiralled from a nominal 100 in June 1914 to 398 in December 1916, to 702 in June 1917, by which time an awful combination of inadequate food supplies and excessive inflation triggered off strike after strike.

(1988: 264; cf. Skocpol 1979; Stone 1984)

Britain, on the other hand, though clearly war-weary and exhausted carried on, 'business as usual'.[7]

The immediate implications for IR of this analysis of the RPCs of these states are as follows: firstly, it helps explain the outcome of the First World War by introducing unit-force variables – relative political capacity differentials; secondly, this analysis helps explain the revolutions in Germany and Russia and the subsequent rise and demise of the Weimar Republic in the former (along with the rise of the Nazis) and the rise of the Bolsheviks in the latter, by taking into account external and internal factors, both of which were fundamentally mediated by a state's RPC. This is important because it helps provide an explanation of the Second World War. The theoretical ramifications principally revolve around the claim that the state and state–society relations (i.e., the 'second image' or level of analysis) are crucial for understanding not only warfare in the inter-state system, but also revolutions and how they in turn go on to affect the inter-state system. It is to a discussion of this that we now turn.

A sociology of international relations and an international relations of sociology

It is, however, the theoretical implications of the analysis of the First World War and its revolutionary aftermath that primarily concern us. This analysis returns us to the discussion in chapter 1 of Fred Halliday's (1987, 1994) work, where I discussed what I termed the 'spatial trinity'. This involves a chain of reactions beginning in the international arena, progressing to the national arena and then reacting back on the international system, thus completing the circle. Halliday's example (illustrated in figure 7.3) is that of revolutions, where defeat in war (external) leads to social revolutions (internal), which lead on to war in the inter-state system (external). There is, then, a continuous 'feedback loop': *international–national–international*. Here I develop two interrelated spatial trinities: the first applies to the study of trade regimes and IPE (figure 7.4); the second, the study of war and state behaviour in IP (figure 7.5). Figure 7.4 shows that international

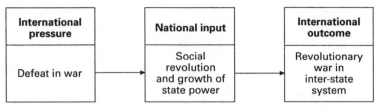

Figure 7.3: Halliday's 'spatial trinity': revolution and war in international politics

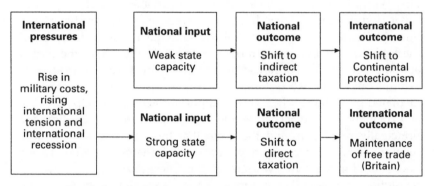

Figure 7.4: A fiscal-sociological 'spatial trinity' (IPE): taxation and state capacity in trade regime changes

(military and economic) imperatives pushed states to raise taxes at the national level; weak states turned to indirect taxes, which in turn led to tariff protectionism and a shift in the international trade regime (as in Germany, Russia and indeed much of the European continent). However, strong state capacity led to the income tax, which led to the maintenance of free trade externally, as in Britain. I also argue that a sociological approach can re-orient the traditional study of international political conflict/war. Taxation and state power lie at the heart of a state's RPC, which has ramifications for the state's role and performance in the system of states. In figure 7.5, I synthesise these findings with the basic-force Halliday model (figure 7.3).

Following Skocpol, Halliday begins with the assumption that states are weakened through external defeat in war, and are then toppled through revolution internally. But this does not explain why those states were defeated in war in the first place. Nor does it *fully* explain why those states were overthrown, since it ignores crucial internal revolutionary pressures. Refining the basic-force Halliday model, my

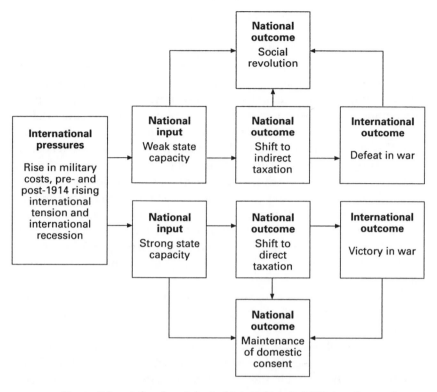

Figure 7.5: A fiscal-sociological 'spatial trinity' (IP): taxation and state capacity in war and social revolution

argument suggests that defeat in war and the subsequent revolutions can be explained by an analysis of the relative political capacity differentials of the states concerned.

As figure 7.5 demonstrates, Britain enjoyed a high RPC enabling it to extend the *progressive* income tax, which increased the state's military ability in the First World War, as well as maintaining internal legitimacy before, during and after the war. Germany, and especially Russia, however, had moderate/low RPC, relying on *regressive* indirect taxes and loans which undermined their ability to wage war and also alienated the working classes and the peasantry in the process. It was the low RPC of Germany and Russia which prompted their defeat in war and the subsequent revolutions. Thus a crucial part of my argument involves the domestic repression of the peasantry and working classes, which was undertaken by the state partly through taxation and, in turn, prompted the revolutions after these states had succumbed in war.[8]

I have, therefore, identified a significant 'spatial trinity' or 'feedback loop' for the study of international politics. Thus, increasing military costs, generated partially from the international system, prompted fiscal changes at the national level. These, however, were significantly determined by state–society relations, which in turn led to either defeat or victory in war, depending on the particular nature of these relations. But this spatial trinity leads to the development of a second feedback loop. Thus, in the defeated powers, the states were overthrown through revolution, which in turn led to the rise of Bolshevism, and later Nazism in Germany. These states were highly militaristic and, in turn, eventually sought to rearrange the international system through warfare, as Halliday (1994) has argued. In short, the sociological study of tariff protection and taxation has ramifications not just for the study of IPE, but also for the study of war and international politics. What lies at base of all these arguments, however, is taxation and relative political capacity. Thus I suggest that a sociological model can provide an important methodological organising principle for traditional IR as well as IPE.

Equally, it should be clear that these 'spatial trinities' are also important to the sociological study of society. Indeed, the study of fiscal and tariff politics in the nineteenth century has traditionally been a favourite of historical sociologists, as it provides a powerful case study in societal processes. Through the study of taxation, we learn much not only about trade regime changes, but also about state–society relations. Moreover, we have also seen how domestic state–society relations – traditionally analysed through endogenous theory in sociology – can be fully understood only through the impact of international forces. States as well as societies are not simple byproducts of endogenous forces, but are partly shaped by external pressures and opportunities (Elias 1970/1978: 168–72; Skocpol 1979; Michael Mann 1986; Giddens 1985; Randall Collins 1986; Runciman 1989). However, to complete the picture, we need to inquire more fully into the causes and determinants of these international forces that helped shape societies in the first place. My sociological approach has sought to achieve precisely this.

The upshot of this analysis is that sociology would be enriched through drawing on IR and its terrain of inquiry quite as much as IR would be enriched by applying insights from sociology. Since neither the international nor the national/societal dimension is separate and self-constituting, the disciplines of IR and sociology should enter into a close dialogue, from which both would certainly benefit.

A non-realist theory of state power: a critique of hegemonic stability theory

I can conclude by fully differentiating my approach from that of neorealism in general and HST in particular. It differs not just with respect to the definition of state power and capacity adopted here, but, above all, in locating the state within complex spatial and multi-power nexuses. Neorealist HST views 'strong' states as *hegemonic* actors, able to project their power outwards and alter the international system. Weak states are typically 'free riders' unable to change the international system. The ramification of my analysis so far is that external strength needs to be entirely redefined. In doing so, we come across yet another crucial paradox.

Unravelling the paradox of Britain's high external 'relative political capacity' and 'hegemonic incapacity'

Neorealist HST argues that a 'hegemon' is the strongest state in the international system, on the basis that it has a preponderance of economic and military power enabling it to persuade or coerce other states to comply with its wishes (whether these are 'benign' or 'predatory'). The theory ascribes this 'power' to Britain in the nineteenth century and the United States after 1945. However, I suggest two main paradoxes that emerge from my analysis. Firstly, while Britain's ability to *change* the international system in the nineteenth century was low, nevertheless the state had a high external RPC. Secondly, hegemonic strength is not synonymous with strong external capacity, but might instead be a product of internal weakness. A striking irony of my analysis is the claim that Britain enjoyed a high degree of RPC but was unable, in a hegemonic sense, to impose changes on the international system. This claim can be made only if we disaggregate external strength, breaking it down into hegemonic capacity on the one hand and adaptability or relative political capacity on the other.

Stephen Krasner (1977b) has argued that Britain in the nineteenth century and the United States after 1945 were able to change the international system through external hegemonic strength, but were internally very weak in relation to society, and that this internal weakness constrained and eventually helped undermine both hegemons' international strength (see also Krasner 1976). The analysis made in this chapter and chapter 6 suggests a different picture. In terms of domestic strength, I have argued that the British state was internally strong, able to push through fiscal policies and able to maintain a high level of consensus, but had only a negligible hegemonic capacity. Paradoxically, however, its strong internal political base conferred upon it a strong external political capacity, as noted above.

The difference between RPC and hegemonic strength lies in the difference between the ability to adapt and respond to external changes in the former case, and the ability actually to impose changes in the international system in the latter. Krasner defines a state's international (hegemonic) power according to the latter definition as 'the ability of central decision makers to change the behaviour of other international actors and to provide collective goods for the international system' (1977b: 637). Where this is high, a state is hegemonic. In Ikenberry's terminology (1988c: 14–19), Krasner assumes that Britain had a high capacity to initiate major *international offensive* adjustment strategies (where the state creates and maintains a new international order). But as I noted in chapter 6, Britain lacked the will and indeed ability to initiate changes in international trade regimes throughout the long nineteenth century. Nor did Britain act as a global policeman, preferring a 'blue-water' strategy rather than a serious 'Continental commitment', and enjoying one of the lowest fiscal-military burdens of all the great powers.

My definition of international power rests on the ability of a state effectively to adapt and respond to external pressures by undertaking what G. John Ikenberry (1988c) termed major *domestic offensive* adjustment strategies (where the state reforms the domestic structure in order to be able to maintain state power and meet external challenges). In this respect, Britain demonstrated high political *adaptability* or flexibility to external (and internal) challenges, even if it had a low or non-existent hegemonic capacity to change the behaviour of other states. While Krasner argues that Britain's internal weakness constrained its ability to maintain its hegemonic capacity, I argue that the state's internal strength was the source of its external strength (and perhaps its hegemonic incapacity).

It is problematic to define a state's strength in terms of its ability to change the external structure in order to maintain its interests. I can illustrate this by considering the case of the hegemonic United States after 1945. Undeniably the United States's ability to initiate change in the international system after 1945 has been profound (as well as clearly being far greater than Britain's in the nineteenth century). But changing the behaviour of other states means that the hegemon is able to put off reforming its own domestic structures. Why bother to respond to external challenges if they can be minimised, blocked or avoided in the first place? Transforming international regimes, there-fore, allows the hegemon – in this case the United States – to postpone undertaking crucial domestic adjustment strategies. As a result, the 'protected' domestic structure ossifies. Perhaps the United States's hegemonic role has all along constituted a highly sophisticated form of domestic protectionism.[9] If this is the case, then American free trade policy and hegemonic strategies after 1945 have simply been a con-tinuation of its traditional protectionist stance: *of protectionism by other means.*[10]

Indeed, there are clear signs that this ossification is happening in the United States today. The United States is clearly unable to deal effectively with the economic challenge of Japan and East Asia (Weiss and Hobson 1995: ch. 7). It is instructive to note that the United States has responded to the East Asian challenge in classic hegemonic fashion: namely by attempting to reinforce the liberal international regime and by forcing liberalisation upon Japan in particular. Even so, despite Japan's considerable concessions, the United States still endures a massive trade deficit (even in the era of the high or soaring yen – *endaka*). The problem is less 'others' (i.e., so-called free riders) – in this case Japan – and more the United States's inability to look inward and make the necessary domestic adjustments required to compete with Japanese economic power.[11] In this way, Japan has typically become a scapegoat for the United States's deep economic problems. And in general, the United States has grown weak, spoilt by the excessive luxury of forcing change on everyone else rather than under-going the tough domestic fiscal and economic reforms required to improve its declining position. Blaming others is simply a manifesta-tion of this fundamental weakness.

External strength is maximised when a state relies on making the necessary domestic adjustments to external challenges, rather than reforming the international system itself (see also Ikenberry 1988c:

206–8). Hegemonic capacity, therefore, may well be a sign of state weakness rather than strength. Conversely, therefore, hegemonic incapacity might be *a* precondition for strong RPC (as was the case for Britain in the nineteenth century).

A critique of neorealism: 'wanted – the dynamic duo'

Finally, I return to the structural neorealist theory of the state and IP found in the work of Kenneth Waltz (1979). My major criticism of Waltz is that his analysis is reductionist – placing analytical primacy on the system of states – to the detriment of the state and state–society complex. Despite the common objection that neorealism reifies the state, my criticism is that this considerably underestimates the state's transformative potential. To deny that the state is a conceptual variable – as Waltz unequivocally argues – is to fall back on a theory of the state that is no more sophisticated than the Marxist argument. Only when we recognise that states have power, and that they are both national and international actors, can we advance 'beyond realism and Marxism' (to quote the title of Andrew Linklater's book (1991)).

In general terms, the state is to a certain extent a perpetrator and agency that creates the interdependence of international and domestic space. This is an important point, not least because it stands neorealism on its head. As Anthony Jarvis has put it, 'the state [in IR] has so far been an analytical obstacle to what we now require the discipline to produce, a fit between societies, states and geopolitics' (1989: 291; see also Halliday 1987: 221). Neorealism's excessive emphasis on sovereignty indeed prevents an analysis of the interpenetration of the different spatial dimensions (Camilleri and Falk 1991: ch. 9; Justin Rosenberg 1990b: 299–300). But such a criticism is usually used to support analysis that moves away from the state in order to focus solely on non-state actors (e.g., Lipschutz 1993). Conceptually doing away with sovereignty should not, however, involve kicking the state back out. Rather it should involve reinstating the state as an important conceptual variable in both the national and international arenas.

Therefore, I argue that the concept of sovereignty should be abandoned as a central organising principle of both IP and state behaviour, precisely because it underplays the importance of the latter in the former. In analysing the state, we need to move away from the static image conveyed by 'sovereignty' as *an aprioristic* given towards the view that the state is an active and transformative agency that interacts with an array of power actors at the domestic and international 'levels' (Nettl 1968: 562; Halliday 1987: 226). As Nettl puts it,

> The difficulty of relating state and sovereignty as a primary identification is not so much that the relationship is, in socio-economic terms, inapplicable, as that it is insufficient, both in the sense that it is too narrow by leaving out spatial and social dimensions and that it is too broad in that it fails to 'prepare' the concept for the right level at which it relates to other relevant concepts.   (Nettl 1968: 562)

In particular, what is required is an analytical separation of the two concepts – state power and sovereignty – and, in turn, state power and relative political capacity. The substantial differentiation of the two concepts of state power and state sovereignty is reflected most acutely in the fact that while state sovereignty has in some respects declined through the twentieth century, paradoxically state power has considerably strengthened for most first world states in the same period.

Rejecting 'sovereignty' as a central organising principle has one further ramification – namely, bringing into question the analytical importance of 'international anarchy'. Waltz's argument is that international anarchy is the central structuring principle to which all states must inevitably conform. But the problem here lies with the neorealist assumption that states are merely passive receptors of external constraints. Ironically, such an argument mirrors the Marxist claim that states are merely passive receptors of the mode of production. Indeed, the common Marxist argument suggests that states are wholly constrained by capitalism because of the need to maintain business confidence upon which the state's fiscal requirements are based (O'Connor 1973; Jessop 1978: 18; Stuart Hall 1984: 23; Block 1987: 85; Chase-Dunn 1989: 117).

States are not *Träger* (passive receptors of internal or external forces), but active power agencies (although this does not imply an internally coherent state organisation, imbued with perfect rationality – as chapter 3 amply testifies). Not only do they enter into a complex array of relations – geopolitical, economic, class, social, fiscal and so on – but they are also able to fundamentally affect external political relations as well as internal societal relations. As Hendrik Spruyt has recently argued (1994), paraphrasing Wendt's famous phrase, 'anarchy is made by states.' And in response to Marxism, states are not simply constrained by global capitalism; rather capitalism from its inception has been significantly determined by states (Weiss and Hobson 1995). Perhaps, though, this is to impute rather too much agency to states at the cost of recognising the partial constraints of the external and internal arenas. To paraphrase Marx, states make their own history, but they do not make it just as they please.

Indeed, states have had constant recourse to the international system, which has been a vital base upon which they have bolstered their domestic bargaining position, as I have argued throughout this chapter. *Pace* Waltz, the international system cannot be understood simply as a structure which 'socialises' and constrains states to behave in specific ways. Tsarist Russia, for example, perished in 1917 not simply because the state had failed to adapt to the exigencies of modern warfare but, above all, because of the state's inability to adapt to internal demands emanating from civil society (which in turn undermined its external military capacity as well as internal legitimacy).

I therefore reject the static duality of 'international anarchy' and 'state sovereignty' in favour of a dynamic duo. And as Halliday points out, one major consequence of Waltzian neorealism is that it 'paradoxically downplays the force of the international' (1994: 140). If we downgrade the analytical importance of international anarchy and sovereignty, we can paradoxically reintegrate the international and national dimensions as mutually reflexive, and bring the state and state–society complex as partially autonomous power forces back in to the study of IR.

This returns us to the paradox that I pointed to in chapter 1. For, on the one hand, neorealism reifies the state's domestic position in that it becomes a supreme actor wholly autonomous within society, and on the other, it denigrates the state as a conceptual variable externally, reducing it to the primacy of the logic of international anarchy. The upshot of my argument suggests that by downgrading the state as the supreme actor domestically, in favour of an embedded state–society relationship, we can reinstate the state as a conceptual variable externally; and the state becomes non-reducible to the exigencies of the inter-state system (as well as the mode of production). *Indeed this is the central paradox of my argument: downgrading 'sovereignty' (and the mode of production) enables the state to be brought back in to domestic as well as international politics.* In sum, we need to reject the static dualism of sovereignty and anarchy, and replace them with a dynamic duo of state capacity/state–society relations on the one hand, and international political and economic systems on the other.

Conclusion: out of the impasse

As Halliday (1994) points out, IR currently finds itself in an impasse. Anxious to abandon its traditional realist paradigm, the discipline is unsure of the way forward. Marxism's reductionist alternative suffers many of the deficiencies found in realism, and cannot therefore provide a way forward. The current disciplinary confusion is only exacerbated by the nihilism of postmodernism. Fortunately, we do not have to give up on explaining the world, but can advance out of the impasse. To conclude, therefore, it is worth briefly summarising my sociological approach as a way forward, differentiating it from its main rivals, Marxism and neorealism. In contrast to Marxism, the key assumptions developed here are that:

(1) States have power and autonomy both domestically and internationally.
(2) Capitalism can enhance state power.
(3) States compete and cooperate with the dominant class: strong states tend to cooperate, weak states conflict.
(4) An exclusively internalist approach based on class struggle can explain neither domestic nor foreign government policy nor the process of economic change.

While there are some similarities with my sociological approach and neorealism, these, I would argue, are only superficial; indeed the differences are more important. Thus, in contrast to neorealism, the key assumptions developed here are that:

(1) States are conceptual variables that have power and can autonomously affect international politics.
(2) The inter-state system can enhance state power at the national level.
(3) State power is largely, though by no means exclusively, determined by strong connections with social power in society; in particular, strong states are those that can adapt to internal and external pressures, especially through cooperating rather than abrading with society.
(4) An exclusively externalist approach, based on conflictual state

relations, can sufficiently explain neither government foreign policy nor the process of economic change. Internal factors – in particular, states and state–society relations – provide vital inputs into foreign economic and military policies.

In short, the state needs to be 'brought back in' not only to historical sociology and economic history, but above all into IR. Paradoxically, neorealism – the theory that supposedly focuses on the notion of state autonomy – is inadequate precisely because it underestimates the state as a conceptual variable.

Many theorists within IR assume that Marxism poses an alternative (viable or otherwise) to realism. This of course is particularly argued by those who are in some way sympathetic to Marxism. But from my perspective, the similarities rather than the differences between Marxism and realism are particularly striking and pertinent. These can be summarised as follows. Firstly, both theories exaggerate the role of conflict in social and political change. There can be no cooperation between states (realism) or classes (Marxism). Their respective key actors are conceptualised as irreconcilable opposites. Secondly, ontologically both exaggerate their key actors, in the process creating anthropomorphic states (realism) and anthropomorphic classes (Marxism). Thirdly, both assume that international politics has a single essence (the state system in neorealism, the mode of production in Marxism). I noted earlier that the Marxist dialectical approach digs down deep beneath the 'superficial mystificatory' appearances of phenomena to uncover the real essential base of society – contradictory class relations. Kenneth Waltz applies exactly the same methodology, though he does not call it 'dialectical', and he reduces phenomena to contradictory state relations rather than class relations. Other than in substituting the term 'state' for 'class', how is this approach in any way different to Marxist dialectical materialism? Indeed, both Marx and Waltz emphasise the importance of the 'scientific method'. Both argue that social science should be concerned with uncovering the 'laws of motion' of the mode of production (Marx 1867/1959: 20) or the inter-state system (Waltz 1979: 10, 40–60, 116). And any attempts to bring in other variables are similarly dismissed as either 'bourgeois' (Marx) or 'reductionist' (Waltz). Finally, both argue that the state is a passive bearer of structures (class in Marxism, or the inter-state system in Waltzian neorealism). Thus the state is substantially constrained by the inter-state system for Waltz in the same way that it is constrained by capitalism for Marxism. It is for these reasons that Marxism cannot provide an alternative to neorealism, since there is such a closely shared epistemological base.

A major ramification of my analysis is that realism's 'state' and Marxism's 'class' must be downgraded. Power actors – classes and states – are not monolithic and entirely homogeneous and rational: they are inherently *promiscuous* (Michael Mann 1986: ch. 1), or *systactic* (Runciman 1989). That is, not only are they complex with multiple interests, but they are also structured by a multiplicity of power forces. States are partially shaped by class interests (as well as military, fiscal, political and economic factors) just as classes are partially determined by states and their actions. Neither is as pure as traditional Marxist and realist theory have assumed. I need, therefore, to note that power actors are not homogeneous and cannot be conceived of as monolithic, self-constituting 'billiard balls'. Rather, power actors and power forces *entwine* (Michael Mann 1993), or *interweave* (Elias 1970/1978: 79–99, 154). Only by recognising this can we move away from the static and reified analyses produced by Marxism and neorealism. The same argument applies to the mode of production and the inter-state system. Neither is purely constituted, but comprises important elements of each (dual reflexivity). Because of this we have to analyse the mutual interactions of states and classes, inter-state systems and state–society relations. Above all, we have to recognise that state, class, society, world economy and inter-state system have not absolute but *partial interactive* autonomy.

Accepting this leads us to conclude that the debate over the 'state' within sociology and, most especially within IR, has essentially missed the point. This debate on the importance or relevance of the state has revolved around the specific theme of 'absolute state power' (viz. realism, elitism) versus 'no state power'. Thus if it can be demonstrated that the state does not in fact have absolute power (a task which is not especially difficult), then it is usually concluded that the actual concept of the state should be dispensed with altogether (e.g., Yale Ferguson and Mansbach 1989). But why is the test of the relevance of the state based on the presence or absence of 'absolute' autonomy? Such a test is never applied to other power actors, most notably the dominant economic class. This is highly convenient for critics of realism and statism because, of course, no power actor has ever been absolutely autonomous – neither classes nor states. If we accept that the state has *partial* autonomy (just like classes), then the false debate between 'absolute state power versus no power' as the test of the relevance of the state misses the point, which in turn means that the state should not be jettisoned as a conceptual variable.

Finally, it is worth reminding ourselves in this so-called postmodern age that no conceivable amount of wishful thinking can possibly imagine the state out of existence. Far better to accept, whether we like it or not, that the state unequivocally exists and does in fact have power and autonomy to affect the world in a myriad of fundamental ways, and accordingly develop a theory that can account for all of this. Only then can we develop an adequate theory of global and domestic social, economic and political change, and thereby propel social science out of the impasse that it now finds itself in. To give up on understanding the world is surely to abdicate responsibility for ourselves and to leave us exposed as little more than *Träger* – that is, passive victims of the (sometimes sadly) very real forces that undeniably exist in the world. Producing better theory offers us not only a way out of nihilism but, more importantly, as Karl Marx argued, the chance perhaps to change the world for the better.

Kenneth Waltz argued, as did Karl Marx, that a theory of IP should above all be elegant and scientific; by which he meant that it should be general and parsimonious in its explanatory framework. But this is the greatest trap. Parsimonious theories have given rise to the most extreme and violent political movements, which have offered various panaceas for the world on the basis of simplistic left- and right-wing theories. Movement away from parsimony and elegance is not only essential for better theory; it also safeguards against the extreme political movements that the twentieth century has suffered from all too often. My alternative sociological theory may not be particularly elegant compared to realism, but perhaps it is more 'realistic'.

A general research agenda for social science (especially IR, sociology and economic history)

All of this begs the question of a future research agenda for IR, sociology and economic history.[12] The common denominator of these three disciplines is an appreciation of history, although IR is perhaps overly concerned with the present. By overly focusing on the present to the detriment of tracing the historical origins of international politics, IR sees much of what goes on as natural. A serious commitment to a historical and sociological approach can help overcome this problem and provide a more complete explanation of IP and IPE. This book is merely part of a much larger agenda (which I have already started in *States and Economic Development*). In this vein I propose the following research agenda for what Jan Aart Scholte (1993b) has called 'world-historical-sociological' studies, which is fundamentally concerned with the development of global history:

(1) An analysis of the rise and development of the state, inter-state system and international economy in the global context from AD 500–2000 (following the demise of the Roman Empire).

(2) An analysis of the interrelationship between the three dimensions of space – sub-national, national and international – whose configurations have constantly changed through time.

(3) An analysis that takes the state seriously, as an adaptive and transformative power actor that not only straddles the international and national 'spheres', but actively shapes and is shaped by multiple power actors/forces within the sub-national and international spheres from AD 500 to the present.[13]

Finally, it is important to note that I am *not* suggesting that IR should transmutate into pure international history or sociology. There will always be room for traditional core IR topics. What I am suggesting, however, is that the discipline could be enriched and complemented through engaging in a dialogue with historical sociology, as much as historical sociology could undoubtedly benefit through engaging with IR. Moreover, at a more general level, this book calls for a broadening and convergence of the social science disciplines, on the basis that there is an 'elective affinity' between the 'multi-disciplinary ethic and the spirit of the social sciences'. Perhaps my central task is not simply to demonstrate the relevance of sociology for IR (and indeed vice versa), but rather to point out that no discipline is entirely self-constituting. This is the underlying theme of this book, and its success should perhaps be measured in terms of this objective, rather than as to whether the reader is entirely convinced of the specific arguments proposed.

Appendices

Appendix A
Additional German data

Table A1: *The fiscal balance of payments between Prussia and the Reich, 1871–1913 (in RM m)*

Year	MCs	Revenues from the Reich	Diff-erence	Balance as % of Prussian income	Year	MCs	Revenues from the Reich	Diff-erence	Balance as % of Prussian income
1871	55		−55	−14	1893	226	206	−20	−2
1872	52		−52	−10	1894	234	232	−2	0
1873	33		−33	−5	1895	233	242	+9	1
1874	33		−33	−5	1896	244	253	+9	1
1875	32		−32	−5	1897	256	264	+8	1
1876	32		−32	−6	1898	278	285	+7	1
1877	37		−37	−6	1899	298	291	−7	−1
1878	42		−42	−8	1900	321	310	−11	−1
1879	44		−44	−8	1901	350	340	−10	−1
1880	39	23	−16	−2	1902	356	340	−16	−1
1881	53	41	−12	−2	1903	347	332	−15	−1
1882	52	51	−1	0	1904	135	120	−15	−1
1883	45	52	+7	1	1905	131	116	−15	−1
1884	40	63	+23	4	1906	142	127	−15	−1
1885	62	70	+8	1	1907	141	121	−20	−1
1886	71	83	+12	2	1908	137	120	−17	−1
1887	101	107	+6	1	1909	105	74	−31	−2
1888	127	168	+41	6	1910	142	111	−31	−2
1889	134	215	+81	9	1911	132	98	−34	−2
1890	183	229	+46	5	1912	154	117	−37	−2
1891	191	232	+41	5	1913	160	122	−38	−1
1892	192	218	+26	3					

Sources and notes: Matricular contributions (MCs), 1871–1910: Gerloff (1913: 526); also Prochnow (1977: 40); revenues from the Reich, 1871–1910: Gerloff (1913: 526); 1911–13: calculated from the totals presented in Gerloff (1913: 522) and the *Statistisches Jahrbücher für das Deutsche Reich*, cited in Newcomer (1937: 23), on the basis that Prussian figures were 60 per cent of the total. Prussian income is calculated from Prochnow (1977). Note that Prussian income is *net* (i.e., SP expenditures have been deducted).

Appendix B
Calculating tax/government burdens: national income and government expenditure data

It should be noted that the government expenditure burden is best calculated by measuring spending as a proportion of national income (i.e., cge/NNP, or d/NNP). All national income data are based on *net national product at factor cost*. Where the data sets used were constructed according to a different definition of national income (e.g., GNP, GDP), I have made the necessary calculations to derive NNP at factor cost (the results of which can be found in table B1).

Before discussing its derivation, it should also be noted that measuring the government burden through national income is not without its problems. For example, the construction of national income data is made problematic by the index number problem (see Gregory 1982; Morgenstern 1963: 242–82). Additional problems are incurred when making comparisons. It is worth noting that in a recent discussion, Crafts (1983) has separated the existing national income data of the various European economies into two categories: 'countries with relatively good data' and those with 'relatively poor data'. The income estimates of the countries dealt with here which are included in those having 'relatively good data' comprise Britain, France, Germany, Italy and Russia (the latter for the 1885–1913 period only). I would add the United States, Australia and probably Canada to this list. This leaves only Russia (1860–84) and Switzerland. Nevertheless, the national income data for these countries would not be so inaccurate as to make a significant difference to the conclusions drawn in the text. And although all national income data are to some degree problematic prior to 1914, nevertheless measuring government expenditures against NNP 'is the least unsatisfactory measure' of a country's spending burden (Gavin Kennedy 1983: 36).

AUSTRALIA: *Net national product*: Butlin (1962: 6). *Central government income*: Commonwealth Bureau of Census and Statistics. Nos. 2 (1909: 800); 3 (1910: 789); 8 (1915: 692). *Central government expenditure*: Barnard (1986: 18).

AUSTRIA: *GDP*: Kausel (1979: 692–3, 718). *Central government expenditure*: Statistische Zentralkommission (1894: 271; 1904: 387; 1914: 418). Note that while the figures given for 1894–1913 are in krona, before 1894 they are reported as gulden. These were converted into krona on the basis that 1 gulden = 2 krona. Note that Austria is the only country where I have not used NNP data (and have used GDP instead). I did not subtract capital depreciation (nor deduct income from abroad), mainly because the military expenditure figure includes the amount spent by Bosnia-Herzegovina (which is therefore partly absorbed by the GDP data). Note also that I have collected data for the Austrian *Reichshalf* only. Hungary has not been included because there are no adequate Hungarian national income data. The only Hungarian data available have been produced under the defunct Marxian concept of 'net material product' (which omits income from services). Given that services are indeed productive of income, this omission renders the concept implausible. In any case, all other data sets have included services. *Military expenditures*: von Kesslitz (1912: 181–4, 387–8).

BRITAIN: *Net national product*: For 1800–12, derived from the commodity output (CO) data in Mathias and O'Brien (1976: table 4, p. 609). These were adjusted up to NNP on the basis that CO was some 55 per cent of national output in this period; for 1813–29, derived from the CO data in O'Brien and Keyder (1978: 31, 58), and revised up as described above; for 1830–54, derived from the GNP data in Deane (1968: table A, p. 104) and revised down to NNP using the various figures supplied in Deane; for 1855–1913, taken from Feinstein (1972: table 1, T4–T7). *Central government expenditure*: 1800–1913: Mitchell and Deane (1962: 397–8).

CANADA: *Net national product*: Firestone (1958: 74–5). Note that Firestone produced only decadal figures for 1870, 1890, 1900 and 1910. While the reliability of these figures is regarded as reasonable, I have produced annual figures by extrapolating forwards from 1870 using the growth rate data provided in Firestone. *Central government income and central government expenditure*: Dominion Bureau of Statistics (1925: 739–42).

FRANCE: *Net national product*: For 1870–1913, based on the GDP data supplied in J.-C. Toutain (1987: 146–54), and converted into NNP by adding net foreign income and deducting capital consumption (figures supplied in Lévy-Leboyer and Bourguignon 1990: 312–16). *Central government expenditure*: Mitchell (1992: 796–9). *Military expenditures*: Fontvielle (1976: 2116–24).

ITALY: *Net national product*: Fuà (1965: 61–2). These figures are presented in 1938 prices. They have been deflated using the price index in Ercolani (1978: 437–8). *Central government expenditure*: Ercolani (1978: 445–6). *Military expenditures*: Stato Maggiore Dell'Esercito (1980: 508–9).

JAPAN: *Net national product*: These are not available at factor cost. I have, therefore, made the necessary adjustments. NNP at market prices was taken from Ohkawa and Shinohara (1979: 266–7). To derive NNP at factor cost, I subtracted indirect taxes and government enterprise surplus, but added government subsidies. These were taken from Emi and Shionoya (1966: 172–5). *Central government expenditure and military expenditures*: Emi and Shionoya (1966: 186–7, 212–13).

PRUSSIA/GERMANY: *Net national product*: For 1820–60, Leineweber (1988: table 1, p. 311); for 1870–1913, Hoffmann (1965: 506–9). *Central government expenditure*: For 1820–60, Leineweber (1988: 311); for 1870–1913, Gerloff (1929: 18). Also used: *Statistisches Jahrbuch für das Deutsche Reich* (1882: 154–7; 1892: 170–3; 1896: 157–9; 1900: 178–9; 1904: 218–19; 1908: 276–7; 1912: 339–41); Witt (1970: 380–1). Prussian data prior to 1870 are not presented on a yearly basis (which exist only in the *Preußische Jahrbuch*). Therefore, I have not used quinquennial averages in the pre-1870 period, thus unavoidably sacrificing some accuracy. The actual years used were 1821, 1829, 1840, 1852 and 1862. Nevertheless, the pre-1870 data are significant for figure 6.4 only in so far as they reveal a declining burden trend after the Napoleonic Wars. I was able to use quinquennial averages in the post-1870 period.

RUSSIA: *Net national product*: (1860–85) Russian figures unfortunately go back only to 1885. Although yearly NNP data do not exist prior to 1885, nevertheless there are the Goldsmith (1961) national income growth rates from 1860 onwards, thus making it possible to calculate the necessary figures. However, Paul Gregory, in his highly authoritative study, has pointed out that Goldsmith's growth rate figures are too low (1982: 72–6). Gregory himself did not produce annual data going back from 1885 to 1860, on the grounds that the figures would be extremely crude. However, for my purposes it is useful (for figure 6.4) to attempt such a calculation.

Goldsmith assumed a 2.25 per cent annual growth rate for 1860–85, while I have assumed an approximate 2.5 per cent growth rate. While the NNP figures are extremely crude, they do provide a base with which to calculate the government expenditure burden. For this reason, I have put the 1860–84 figures in parentheses to denote their crudeness in table B1 below.

The main problem with the existing data (produced by Paul Gregory) in the 1885–1913 period is that for my purposes I require NNP *at factor cost* (whereas Gregory produces NNP *at market prices*). I have, therefore, made the necessary calculations, which were done on the following basis. To reduce Gregory's figures from market prices to factor cost I have deducted indirect taxes and government enterprise surplus (taken from Khromov 1950). I then added on 'subsidies' to the private sector. Unable to find these, I have made a best guesstimate, on the basis that the annual figure was approximately Rb 50m (from 1885–1900) and Rb 100m (1901–13). I then checked these against similar data produced in Gregory for intermittent years (see 1982, appendix F, chart F1, p. 252), with the figures broadly concurring. Gregory made a similar calculation of NNP at factor cost, but for 1913 only. His figure was Rb 18,701m, compared to my estimate of 18,746m (or a marginal 0.2 per cent differential). *Central government expenditure*: Khromov (1950: 514–29).

SWITZERLAND: *Net national product*: Zwingli and Ducret (1964: 356, 367). The figures provided by Zwingli and Ducret were presented at five-yearly intervals. I have derived yearly data for my calculations by extrapolating the data on the basis of the growth rate figure produced by Zwingli and Ducret (1964: 362). The data, however, are not highly reliable, partly because of the approximate growth rate figure provided, and partly because of the nature of the data used (as mentioned above). *Central government income and central government expenditure*: Statistisches Bureau des Eidgenossenschaft (1891: 250–1; 1894: 310–13, 346–7; 1904: 302–5, 311; 1913: 288–91; 1914: 206–9).

UNITED STATES: *Net national product*: Department of Commerce (Bureau of the Census) (1960: 143; cf. Kuznets 1952; 1946: 86). Note that these data were compiled by Simon Kuznets, who did not include military expenditures as a component of NNP (on the basis that these are not productive). However, since all other data sets include this item, I have added them. *Central government expenditure*: Department of Commerce (Bureau of the Census) (1949: 299–301, 309–10 (Series P99–108, P165–9)), and similar data produced in the later volume: Department of Commerce (Bureau of the Census) (1975).

I have used these data sets to compile the various estimates of defence and central government expenditure burdens. In particular, in chapter 5, I compared the various government expenditure and defence burdens (tables 5.9 and 5.10), and in chapter 6, I compared the trends of the government burdens of various powers (figure 6.4).

Comparison of data derived from national income is, of course, a highly problematic exercise. It might be objected that if there are large errors in the NNP data sets, then the government burdens derived will be at best highly spurious and, at worst, incorrect. Two replies can be made. Firstly, as regards the comparison with Switzerland made in chapter 5, it is important that all countries' burdens err on the low side, in order to effect bias in the right direction. This means that I need to select national income data which err (if anything) on the high side for all countries. In most cases, I have used not only the most authoritative data sets, but of all those available for each country, the highest data (or thereabouts), especially in the cases of Russia, France and the United States. The only notable exception to this is Britain, where the Feinstein data are lower than most rival sets, notably those of Jeffreys and Walters (1955: 1–40), Alan Prest (1948: 31–62) and Deane and Cole (1962: 330) (also see below). As a sensitivity test, I calculate that to equal the Swiss government burden, the national income of all countries dealt with here would have to have been overestimated by a minimum of 51 per cent (Canada) ranging to 329 per cent (France), 529 per cent (Russia) and 811 per cent (Japan). Such margins of error are unrealistic and therefore support the conclusions made in chapter 5.

It is also important to note here that the government and military burdens have also been constructed so as to maximise the British and minimise all other states' burdens. This is vital to my claim in chapter 6 that Britain's military burden was lower than all other great powers bar the United States. (This single fact provides an important part of my argument that Britain was not in fact a 'hegemon'.) As noted, I have used one of the lowest data sets produced (i.e., Feinstein 1972). This means that I have effected bias in the right direction, providing a strong foundation for my claim that Britain was not a hegemon weighed down with a high military burden.

Secondly, even if the national income data used here are not especially accurate, this should not affect figure 6.4, based on the data in table B1. This is because here I am interested only in the individual trends for each country. Even if each country's burden is inaccurate, the trend should not be affected.

Table B1: *Central government burdens (cge/NNP) of the Great Powers, 1820–1913*

Period	Britain	Prussia/Germany	Russia
1820–4	18.0	19.9	
1825–9	15.4		
1830–4	12.8	18.0	
1835–9	11.6		
1840–4	11.9	13.1	
1845–9	10.9		
1850–4	9.9	9.7	
1855–9	12.1		
1860–4	9.9	8.5	(12.5)
1865–9	8.6		(12.5)
1870–4	6.9	6.1	(13.7)
1875–9	7.5	5.1	(17.8)
1880–4	7.7	5.1	(14.7)
1885–9	7.7	7.5	14.8
1890–4	7.3	7.3	15.9
1895–9	7.3	7.2	18.5
1900–4	10.7	7.3	18.8
1905–9	8.0	7.4	21.7
1910–13	8.2	6.6	17.5

Notes: For the most part, annual figures were used for each of the quinquennial periods. However, this was not possible for Prussia, as described on p. 286. If extrapolated backwards in time, Britain's burden is as follows: 1800–4: 22.6; 1805–9: 25.0; 1810–14: 30.5; 1815–19: 25.3. For Prussia the burden for 1800–4 was 23.0. In other words, the declining expenditure burden trend, observed from 1820 until 1860–70 (see figure 6.4), actually began at a higher point back in the Napoleonic War period.

Table B2: *Reworked national income (NNP at factor cost) of various countries, 1870–1913*

Year	Italy (Li m)	Russia (Rb m)	Japan (¥ m)	France (Fr m)	Austria (Kr m)	United States ($ m)
1870	8,308			23,385	2,989	6,264
1871	8,347			23,148	3,376	6,264
1872	9,404			24,389	3,438	6,264
1873	10,753			23,643	3,292	6,986
1874	10,468			25,346	3,571	6,986
1875	9,003			25,558	3,569	6,986
1876	9,161			23,855	3,713	6,986
1877	10,121			24,971	3,970	8,533
1878	9,405			24,298	4,256	8,533
1879	9,323			22,237	4,093	8,533
1880	9,775			24,675	4,247	8,533
1881	8,865			25,736	4,525	8,533
1882	9,406			27,051	4,545	10,357
1883	8,859			26,413	4,845	10,357
1884	8,839			25,182	5,130	10,357
1885	9,127	5,927	735	24,230	5,113	10,357
1886	9,531	5,528	721	24,345	5,431	10,357
1887	9,037	6,798	714	24,264	5,740	11,063
1888	8,835	7,076	701	24,817	5,755	11,063
1889	9,581	6,277	769	26,541	5,951	11,063
1890	10,165	6,360	1,066	28,004	6,643	11,063
1891	10,288	6,083	920	28,425	7,002	11,063
1892	9,354	7,040	973	27,753	7,264	11,880
1893	9,602	7,431	991	27,180	7,193	11,880
1894	9,388	7,800	1,192	27,410	8,024	11,880
1895	9,983	7,131	1,309	26,149	8,417	11,880
1896	9,834	7,887	1,351	27,752	8,700	11,880
1897	9,592	8,532	1,653	29,416	8,830	15,185
1898	10,814	9,527	2,119	30,912	9,831	15,185
1899	10,736	10,570	1,846	31,566	10,142	15,185
1900	11,591	10,442	2,112	31,821	10,114	15,185
1901	11,810	10,862	2,125	29,954	10,720	15,185
1902	11,381	12,139	2,044	30,912	11,011	21,428
1903	12,530	11,278	2,391	32,939	11,127	21,428
1904	12,123	12,635	2,431	32,127	11,508	21,428
1905	12,938	11,839	2,419	32,318	13,090	21,428
1906	13,900	11,814	2,827	34,779	14,172	21,428
1907	15,105	12,642	3,172	37,959	15,581	27,496
1908	14,849	14,268	3,218	36,556	15,710	27,496
1909	16,130	15,243	3,144	39,299	15,977	27,496
1910	16,383	16,061	3,124	40,167	16,377	27,496
1911	17,752	15,629	3,741	44,349	17,216	27,496
1912	18,648	18,244	4,135	48,594	18,907	34,600
1913	19,752	18,746	4,299	48,838	18,746	34,600

Note: Methodology explained in appendix B.

Notes

1 A sociology of international relations and an international relations of sociology

1 Michael Mann talks about the 'promiscuity' of the two realms (1986, 1993; cf. Elias 1970/1978: 168–72), while Giddens uses the term 'inter-societal systems' (1981, 1985; cf. Runciman 1989).

2 All subsequent data in this section are derived from Bairoch (1988).

3 In particular, what we have come to see as the quintessential basis of the American way of life – free trade and economic liberalism – is only a very recent development. It escapes notice that the United States was the most protectionist economy – bar Russia – in the 'first world' throughout the nineteenth century.

2 Protectionism in imperial Germany: moderate state capacity and indirect taxation

1 In fact, the vast bulk of wheat imports came from Russia, Austria-Hungary and the United States, while rye imports came overwhelmingly from Russia, followed by France and Austria-Hungary (Tirrell 1968: 21).

2 For data, see Farnsworth (1934: 294–6, 347); Lambi (1963: 132–3); Hoffmann (1965: 552–4); Karl Hardach (1967: 74–5); Tirrell (1968: 21, 25).

3 And although Max Weber did not undertake a full analysis of the causes of German protectionism, in the various cursory statements that he made, he greatly exaggerated the influence of the Junkers (1919/1970: 373, 382).

4 This is documented in some detail in German archives. See *Bundesarchiv der Bundesrepublik Deutschlands*, Abt Potsdam, Reichskanzlei Nr. 1108, 'Promemoria des deutschen Landwirtschaftsrat' (25 December 1893). I am grateful to Professor Witt for this reference.

5 See Hardach (1967: 80–123).

6 See Hardach (1967: 73–7).

7 I am grateful to Professor Witt for pointing this out to me.

8 Again, I am grateful to Professor Witt for pointing this out.

9 The Junker was a landlord ennobled at the lowest grade (the German *von*).

This group tended to own no more than two or perhaps three *Güter* (properties), which comprised at most 1,000 hectares (ha). However, the large landholders owned a minimum of between 1,000 and 2,000 ha (although a few exceeded this). See especially pp. 60–1 for further discussion.

10 However, some excises were collected at the *Länder* level.

11 For a fuller version of this quote, see Dawson (1904: 51).

12 Similar statements were made intermittently in the years to 1879. See John M. Hobson (1991: 44–7); Dawson (1904: 50–6); Henderson (1975: 219); Lambi (1963: 169).

13 However, it should be noted that the 1878/9 budget deficit was partly induced by Bismarck, who as Prussian prime minister manipulated the budget in order to exert pressure on the Reichstag to grant his various proposed fiscal reforms – especially the government monopolies (Pflanze 1990a: 446).

14 Considerable defaulting occurred in the cities (see Pflanze 1990a: 448).

15 Even as late as 1913, only 11 per cent of the population earned over RM 3,500 (calculated from Popitz, 'Einkommensteuer', in *Handwörterbuch der Staatswissenschaften*, 4th edn, vol. III (Jena, 1926), pp. 400–91).

16 Named after its founder, Freiherr Georg von Franckenstein, of the Centre Party.

17 Tariff rates can be set in one of two ways: an ad valorem rate where the tariff is set as a proportion of the value of the product; and, secondly, a specific tariff, which is set according to the weight of the product.

18 Although it should be noted that rye was still the most important bread grain (see Tirrell 1968: 24; Farnsworth 1934: 303).

19 Calculated from Hoffmann (1965: 292).

20 Of the most important eastern estates, in the decade after 1885, more than 24,000 were sold as a result of mortgage indebtedness. By 1900, more than 50 per cent of these old knightly estates were owned by commoners (Tipton 1976: 117).

21 Bismarck originally proposed a tariff of RM 60 per ton on wheat and rye. But this was deemed to be too high by the Centre Party and National Liberals, and a final compromise settled on RM 50 (Tirrell 1968: 75).

22 The Lex Huene had been passed in the Prussian Landtag on 14 May 1885. Introduced by the Centre Party member, Huene, this law permitted the Prussian Treasury to retain only RM 15m of the surplus revenues received from the Reich after payment of the matricular contributions; the rest was to be distributed to the city and county governments. Note that the Centre Party, though it had only limited sympathy with parliamentarism, was nevertheless very keen to maintain the federal nature of Germany. Indeed, this was the same rationale that had prompted the Franckenstein clause in 1879.

23 For the 'economistic' argument about the 1902 tariff, see Kehr (1977: 38–49); Berghahn (1973: 29–42); Wehler (1985: 94–9); Fischer (1975: 14–16); Calleo (1978).

24 See especially the scathing comments of Max Weber as regards the lowliness of the Junkers in the late nineteenth century (1919/1970: ch. 15).

25 See also Dumke's Ph.D dissertation, 'The Political Economy of German Economic Unification' (Wisconsin, 1976).

26 Tables 2.5 and 2.6 also show the increasing importance of state property revenues. These played an increasingly important role in financing Reich expenditures. They were favoured mainly because they did not require approval by the Reichstag (Pflanze 1990a: 329–30; Michael Mann 1993: 388). Their anti-democratic nature was particularly attractive given the problems incurred in instigating progressive taxation at the Reich level.

27 In 1912, the SPD secured 34.8 per cent of the vote and 27.2 per cent (Berghahn 1987: 34–6) of Reichstag seats, compared to the 10.8 per cent of seats and 9.2 per cent of the vote secured by the Conservatives.

3 Protectionism and industrialisation in tsarist Russia: weak state capacity and indirect taxation

1 Despite the very considerable similarities in the analyses of Gerschenkron and von Laue, they differ on this key point. Von Laue (1963) argued that despite the considerable achievements of Sergei Witte, tsarism did not in fact take off into sustained development after 1907. Von Laue also gave more weighting to geopolitics than Gerschenkron. Nevertheless, geopolitics was not systematically integrated into the theoretical framework of either author (see also n. 2).

2 Gerschenkron recognised that defence requirements influenced state policies (as mentioned in n. 1). As he put it, 'It is quite possible, however, to attempt a primarily political approach to the industrial history of the period and to see the stress on producers' goods as essentially determined by the immediate military needs of the government ... [This] would be capable of considerable elaboration.' However, he goes on to argue that, 'this writer at least has felt that his general approach ... offers a fuller and more plausible explanation of ... [Russian] development' (1962: 360–1).

3 Even so, Japanese industrialisation was propelled forward by a mixture of intended and unintended consequences of militarism.

4 The 'first military revolution' occurred in Europe between 1550 and 1660 (see Weiss and Hobson 1995 for a fuller discussion).

5 Indeed, this method of calculating tsarist military expenditures is broadly the same as that employed for Germany by Peter-Christian Witt (1970), whose figures I used in chapter 2. However, in the Russian case, I have not uncovered the hidden conscription expenses (see Gatrell 1994: 139–40).

6 In this period, only Japan spent more in real terms, reaching an average of over 10 per cent of national income – if we include military debt interest payments (see John M. Hobson 1993).

7 Various historians have argued that by 1913, the average Russian had 50 per cent more of his income appropriated by the state for current defence than did the average British citizen, even though the Russian's income was only 27 per cent that of his British contemporary (Rogger 1983: 77; Paul Kennedy 1988: 236; Miller 1926: 137).

8 The nobles, not surprisingly, were bitterly hostile to the state as it set about emancipating the peasantry. The MVD initially tried to negotiate and cooperate with the nobility. When this met with non-compliance on the part of the nobles, the state simply forced the nobility's hand. As Yaney put it, with the appointment of the Editing Commission in March 1859, 'the Tsar and his hatchet men [MVD] would issue a command, and the gentry would have to obey' (1973: 185–6).

9 For a brief historical discussion of the rise of the MVD, see John M. Hobson (1991: 154–9). For fuller histories, see the excellent discussions in Orlovsky (1981) and Yaney (1973).

10 He also constantly called for a reduction in military expenditures.

11 There was, firstly, the lure of hard profits on government contracts, especially for railway equipment, at inflated prices; secondly, high tariffs mainly for heavy industries; thirdly, the high level of Russian interest rates; and finally, the favourable publicity abroad intensified by the formation of the political alliance with France prior to any such conversion (Falkus 1972: 61, 72; Kahan 1967: 71–3; Crisp 1991).

12 *Kustary* were small industrial producers who utilised for the most part hand tools rather than machinery. There were approximately 5 million such producers (although estimates vary considerably owing to definitional problems). For a fuller discussion, see Crisp (1976: 48–52); Gatrell (1986: 154–7).

13 36 lb.

14 It is worth speculating (on reading his various works), however, that Paul Gregory would not altogether disagree with some of these points.

4 Free trade versus protectionism in liberal Britain: strong state capacity and the conflict over taxation

1 Whole Hoggers were those Tories who supported tariff protection (mainly as a means to reverse Britain's economic decline).

2 After 1880, two major protectionist movements emerged: the National Fair Trade League and the Imperial Federation League (an offshoot of which was the United Empire Trade League). The National Fair Trade League, created in 1881, explicitly blamed the distressed conditions in British industry on the revived protectionism of various Continental countries, coupled with the British government's reluctance to fight for reciprocal trade opportunities via retaliatory duties (see Zebel 1940: 161–8). The Imperial Federation League was founded in 1884, although internal wranglings and conflict with the National Fair Trade League brought its early demise (see Tyler 1938: 107–15, 176–209).

3 For a fuller discussion of Chamberlain's imperial preference scheme and its multiple objectives, see Friedberg (1988: 30–3).

4 This was expanded into popular form in the *National Review* by the pro-tariff *Observer* editor, J. L. Garvin, in his September 1907 article, 'Free Trade as a Socialist Policy' (reprinted in Garvin 1910: 105–12).

5 As is made explicitly clear in Weiss and Hobson (1995).

5 Tariff protectionism and indirect taxation in federal states: the United States, Canada, Australia and Switzerland

1 Mark Hansen (1990) has also argued that revenue requirements played a major role in the determination of tariff policy. However, I go on to qualify the second part of his argument which emphasises the importance of party political preferences.

2 See especially Finance Minister Tilley's March 1879 budget speech, part of which is cited in Perry (1955: 67).

3 Named after Sir Edward Braddon at the Federal Convention in 1897.

4 A 'fair and reasonable wage' would be defined as one that could support a worker with a wife and three children.

5 In fact, and to the considerable frustration of this author, Switzerland rarely features at all in the discussion of either tariff policy or general economic history. Perhaps economic history shares with realist international relations an unacceptable bias towards the great powers. But this is particularly ironic given that Switzerland has been and still is the richest country in the world (in per capita terms)!

6 A sociological theory of international economic change: the transition to tariff protectionism, 1870–1913

1 For a good discussion of this and other problems in measuring tariff levels, see Woytinsky and Woytinsky (1955: 272–4) and Liepmann (1938: ch. 2).

2 In particular, it is interesting to note that it was in the period of protectionism that the interdependence of the world economy escalated (Murphy 1994). By 1910, there had developed a whole series of international agreements. While only 45 such agreements had been reached in the free trade period (1852–80), in the subsequent period (1881–1910), some 129 had been concluded (Pollard 1981: 271).

3 For further details of the movement of tariff rates in this period, see Bairoch (1988: 14–23).

4 Interestingly one of the major economistic 'long-cycle' theorists, Joshua Goldstein, alludes to the problem raised here. In a footnote he writes: 'But I wonder if this relationship [between long cycles and trade regime changes] is specific to the nineteenth century. Mercantilist measures were used as a source of revenue ... more than to protect domestic industries' (1988: 330). While such a statement lends credence to my argument, it poses a major problem for long-cycle theorists. For if their model can not even explain simple changes in trade regimes (something which such a theory should be able to explain relatively easily), then it is tempting to suggest that using such a model to explain great power wars might be a case of trying to make the theory run before it can even walk.

5 We could carry this point about differences between the 1846–73 and 1945–73 periods much further. American hegemony had a relatively consensual base, not least because the Western world was militarily dependent upon it, which was in turn an important factor in promoting international economic

cooperation. But Britain was a military and economic *competitor* of all states in Europe in the nineteenth century; this was a crucial factor in undermining any international consensus for British hegemony, in turn diminishing Britain's ability to affect the international economy. Moreover, Britain in the nineteenth century had neither the economic nor the military muscle, let alone the will, required of a hegemon, unlike the United States after 1945 (Russett 1985; John A. Hall 1990).

6 It is worth noting that stability theorists as well as a host of historians have argued that Britain declined before 1913 through 'imperial overstretch' (Gilpin 1981; Paul Kennedy 1988; Lance Davis and Huttenback 1988; O'Brien 1990). But given Britain's low fiscal-military burden, it must be the case that any pre-1913 decline could not have been the result of 'imperial overstretch' (see John M. Hobson 1993).

7 Austria-Hungary was a confederal system, in which tariff revenues were specifically linked to meet the common defence of the Dual Monarchy (Eddie 1988: 815; Niall Ferguson 1994: 161). Austria-Hungary's shift back to protectionism began with the mild 1878 tariff, which was essentially a revenue tariff. And, as in Russia, customs duties were paid in gold to enhance government revenues (Eddie 1988: 825).

8 Even here, a fiscal analysis is possible. Tariffs were reintroduced in France in 1872, solely to meet the fiscal crisis that emerged as a result of the defeat in the Franco-Prussian War (Percy Ashley 1920: 307–12). Grain tariffs were increased in 1885, and jumped in 1887 with the duty on wheat increasing from Fr 12 to 50 per ton (22 per cent of the price on the home market). Finally, following particular pressure from agricultural and manufacturing interests, the new Méline tariff of January 1892 was enacted. The customs administrators calculated that had the new minimum tariff been imposed in 1889, revenues would have increased by 32 per cent. On the general tariff, an extra Fr 212m would have been derived – or an increase of 60 per cent (Bairoch 1988: 65–6). Like most Continental states, France in this period shifted to indirect taxes, which comprised as much as 50 per cent of total tax revenues in 1913 (Schremmer 1988: 390–9).

9 Italy also had difficulty in meeting its expenditure requirements in the early 1870s, with as much as 37 per cent of the budget going to meet interest payments on the national debt between 1872 and 1876 (Coppa 1970). With a deficit of some 23m lire in 1877, the case for new taxes was compelling. Wide support for the reversion to protectionism in 1878 was elicited by means of the fiscal argument (Coppa 1970: 745; Clough 1964: 115). Agostino Depretis had often argued that only the financial argument would make him accept protectionism (Coppa 1970: 745). The 1878 tariff was fiscally lucrative, initially meeting the requisites of fiscal accumulation. However, by the early to mid-1880s, the problem of deficits returned; it reached some 386m lire by 1887, mainly because the expenditure burden had increased dramatically. To meet this problem, the government raised tariffs in that year, coming into effect on 1 January 1888 (Coppa 1970: 748–9; Zamagni 1993: 110; Bairoch 1988: 62–3;

Clough 1964: 116). The tariff was tolerated, as it was in Canada, the United States and Australia, because of its fiscal productivity. And as Coppa points out, 'Few were surprised, therefore, when the committee reporting on the tariff indicated that its main aim was to increase receipts' (Coppa 1970: 749).

The influx of American grain came later in Italy, accelerating between 1884 and 1887, with grain imports tripling. In February 1888, the government hiked the duties on wheat from 30 to 50 lire per ton (i.e., about 22 per cent of its value) (Bairoch 1988: 64; Percy Ashley 1920: 312). As in Germany, the government was keen to levy tariffs on grain since this was the major import and fiscally lucrative – so much so that Giolitti fought a lowering of the grain duties in 1901, 1903–5, 1907 and 1909 on the grounds that the higher bread prices were worth keeping, so as to maintain the urgently needed revenue (Coppa 1970: 765).

7 State capacity in the international/national vortex: a non-realist theory of state power and international politics

1 The 'Critical theory' perspective within IR is a diverse perspective (more so than the sociological Critical theory perspective). For example, Robert Cox (1986, 1987) adopts a Gramscian Marxist perspective, while Andrew Linklater (1991) eschews a specifically Marxist foundation for a Critical perspective.

2 My definition of power overlaps considerably with that found in the emerging feminist literature; see especially Tickner (1988).

3 In a related point, Jackson and Rosberg (1982) argue that even weak states in the modern era can maintain themselves because of their sovereign position within the inter-state system.

4 In 1890, for example, a Reich bond issued at RM 100 at 4 per cent sold at RM 106. However, by 1913, the same bond sold at only RM 98.6 (a figure given to me in a private conversation with Professor Peter-Christian Witt). Moreover, the Reich's fiscal problems were revealed in the media when the price of 4 per cent bonds fell below that of 3.5 per cent Italian bonds (Kroboth, cited in Niall Ferguson 1994: 160).

5 Gerloff provides an even lower figure (1929: 21–2).

6 It has not escaped this author's notice that there is a certain incongruence between Rogowski's work on free trade and protectionism (1989) and his more recent work (with D'Lugo, 1993) on the relationship between states and war. The earlier work was unequivocally economistic, as particularly revealed in his attempt to explain many political movements such as Nazism and populism through economic categories. The recent work clearly rejects economism and is in fact a particularly sophisticated analysis which effectively accords a certain autonomy to political/state factors.

7 A further qualification to the basic-force Kugler and Domke model needs to be made. Although they point out that Britain's RPC in the war years was considerably superior to Russia's (as well as to those of Italy, the United States and Japan), nevertheless their figures suggest that Germany's RPC was higher than Britain's (1986: 51). My argument clearly differs because it disaggregates

the sums raised by the respective governments. The vast majority of the German figure comprises loans – a much higher amount than the British figure. This deficit financing led to inflation, and served to undermine the war effort. Thus if Kugler and Domke's coefficient is recalculated to measure relative *tax* (as opposed to overall *expenditure*) capacity, then the German figure would certainly be lower than the British. Additionally, we need to differentiate tax revenues, because reliance on regressive indirect taxes alienated the German and Russian proletariats (and peasantries), in strong contrast to the British situation.

8 For a discussion of how state repression (as opposed to capitalist exploitation) can create revolutionary consciousness, see Lipset (1985); Michael Mann (1988, 1993: ch. 18); John A. Hall (1988); McDaniel (1988); Katznelson (1985).

9 Note that this argument is quite different to the more common claim that hegemony has provided the US state with substantial 'private' as opposed to 'public' goods. Nor does it equate with Gilpin's claim that the exercise of hegemony through the provision of public goods has undermined the United States. It is not the United States's 'sacrifices' for the greater good of the world system (and the associated 'free rider problem') that have undermined it, but rather its own *inability* to adapt to the development of rival national economies.

10 This is, of course, reminiscent of the liberal critique of protectionism, which argues that states only undermine their economic base by pursuing protectionism. This is because the domestic economy is protected from external competition, and therefore becomes lazy and inert.

11 Exactly the same argument can be applied to the late twentieth-century US tax regime. Despite the complaints of American taxpayers, the fact is that they are not overburdened; they are not so much weary as *wary* taxpayers, unwilling rather than unable to pay taxes. The United States enjoys one of the lowest tax burdens in the OECD. Accordingly, therefore, the United States's massive budget deficit is less the result of high military expenditures, and more fundamentally linked to low rates of US taxation. So-called 'hegemonic military expenditures' have become a convenient scapegoat for the wary American taxpayer (see Calleo 1987: ch. 7; 1990; Friedberg 1989: 388–92; Huntington 1988: 79).

12 This would also include history, anthropology, political science and political geography.

13 I have already begun this project, the findings of which will be presented in a forthcoming book, *The Adaptive State in Long Run International Change*.

Bibliography

Primary documents

Australia

Commonwealth Bureau of Census and Statistics 1908, 1909, 1910, 1915, 1916: *Official Year Book of the Commonwealth of Australia.* Melbourne. Nos. 1 (1908); 2 (1909); 3 (1910); 8 (1915); 9 (1916).

Austria

Statistische Zentralkommission 1894, 1904, 1914: *Österreichisches Statistisches Handbuch.* Vienna.

Britain

Public Funded Debt of Great Britain and Ireland, from 1694 to 1858/9. *British Parliamentary Papers* [*BPP*], Vol. XXXIII (1857–8); *BPP*, Vol. XXXV (1868–9); *BPP*, Vol. LII (1898); *BPP*, Vol. CXII (1914–16).
Reports from his Majesty's Representatives Abroad Respecting Graduated Income Taxes in Foreign States. *BPP*, No. 2, Cd 2587, Vol. LXXXV (1905).

Canada

Dominion Bureau of Statistics 1925: *The Canada Year Book, 1924.* Ottawa.

France

Annuaire Statistique de la France 1913, 1914 (Vols. XXXIII and XXXIV), Résumé rétrospectif.

Germany

Handwörterbuch der Staatswissenschaften 1926. 4th edn, Vol. III. Jena.
Statistisches Jahrbuch für das Deutsche Reich 1882, 1886, 1892, 1896, 1900, 1904, 1908, 1912. Berlin: Verlag von Puttkamer und Mühlbrecht. Buchhandlung für Staats- und Rechtswissenschaft. Vols. III (1882); VII (1886); XIII (1892); XVII (1896); XXI (1900); XXV (1904); XXIX (1908); XXXIII (1912).

Bibliography

Italy

Stato Maggiore Dell'Esercito 1980: *L'Esercito Italiano Dall'Unità Alla Grande Guerra 1861–1918*. Rome: Ufficio Storico.

Switzerland

Statistisches Bureau des Eidgenossenschaft, Departments des Innern 1891, 1894, 1904, 1913, 1914. *Statistisches Jahrbuch der Schweiz* (Bureau de Statistique du Département Suisse des Finances, *Annuaire Statistique de la Suisse*). Finance data.

United States

Department of Commerce (Bureau of the Census) 1949: *A Statistical Abstract Supplement to the Historical Statistics of the United States, 1789–1945*. Washington, DC: Government Printing Office.

   1960: *Historical Statistics of the United States: Colonial Times to 1957*. Washington, DC: Government Printing Office.

   1975: *Historical Statistics of the United States: Colonial Times to 1970*. Washington, DC: Government Printing Office.

Non-governmental sources:

League of Nations 1929: *Tariff Level Indices*. Compiled by Alan Loveday. Geneva: International Economic Conference.

Tariff Reform League 1907: *Speakers' Handbook*. London (4th edn).

   1910: *A Handbook for Speakers*. London (6th edn).

Secondary sources: books and articles

Aitken, Hugh G. (ed.) 1959: *The State and Economic Growth*. New York: Social Science Research Council.

Aldcroft, Derek H. 1968: *The Development of British Industry and Foreign Competition, 1875–1914*. London: Allen and Unwin.

Aldcroft, Derek and Richardson, Harry W. 1969: *The British Economy, 1870–1939*. London: Macmillan.

Alexander, Fred 1973: *Australia Since Federation*. Melbourne: Thomas Nelson.

Almond, Gabriel 1989: 'The International–National Connection', *British Journal of Political Science* 19 (2): 237–59.

Althusser, Louis 1969: *For Marx*. London: Allen Lane.

Althusser, Louis and Balibar, Etienne 1970: *Reading Capital*. London: NLB.

Amery, Julian 1969: *Joseph Chamberlain and the Tariff Reform Campaign, Vol. VI*. London: Macmillan.

Anan'ich, Boris V. 1982: 'The Economic Policy of the Tsarist Government', in Guroff and Carstensen (eds.), pp. 125–39.

Anderson, Perry 1964: 'Origins of the Present Crisis', *New Left Review* 23: 26–53.

   1974: *Lineages of the Absolutist State*. London: Verso.

Andic, Suphan and Veverka, Jindrich 1964: 'The Growth of Government

Expenditure in Germany Since the Unification', *Finanz Archiv* 23 (2): 169–278.

Ardant, Gabriel 1975: 'Financial Policy and Economic Infrastructure of Modern States and Nations', in Tilly (ed.), pp. 164–242.

Arrighi, Giovanni 1990: 'The Three Hegemonies of Historical Capitalism', *Review* 13: 365–408.

Ashley, Percy 1909: 'The Financial Position of the German Empire'. Papers and Memoranda, British Board of Trade.

1920: *Modern Tariff History*. London: John Murray.

Ashley, Richard K. 1986: 'The Poverty of Neorealism', in Keohane (ed.), pp. 255–300.

Ashworth, William 1962: *A Short History of the International Economy Since 1850*. London: Longman.

Bairoch, Paul 1976: *Commerce extérieur et développement économique de l'Europe au XIXe siècle*. Paris: Mouton.

1982: 'International Industrialisation Levels from 1750 to 1980', *Journal of European Economic History* 11 (2): 269–333.

1988: 'European Trade Policy, 1815–1914', in Mathias and Pollard (eds.), pp. 1–160.

Balderston, Theo 1989: 'War Finance and Inflation in Britain and Germany, 1914–1918', *Economic History Review* 42 (2): 222–44.

Banks, Michael and Shaw, Martin (eds.) 1991: *State and Society in International Relations*. London: Harvester.

Barkin, Kenneth 1987: '1878–1879: The Second Founding of the Reich. A Perspective', *German Studies Review* 10: 219–35.

Barnard, Alan 1986: *Commonwealth Government Finances, 1901–1982*. Canberra: Australian National University (Source Papers in Economic History).

Barnett, Richard J. and Müller, Ronald E. 1974: *Global Reach*. New York: Simon and Schuster.

Bates, Robert H. and Da-Hsiang, Donald Lien 1985: 'A Note on Taxation, Development and Representative Government', *Politics and Society* 14 (1): 53–70.

Baugh, Daniel 1988: 'Great Britain's "Blue Water" Policy, 1689–1815', *International History Review* 10: 33–58.

Baykov, Alexander 1954: 'The Economic Development of Russia', *Economic History Review* 7 (2): 137–49.

Beetham, David 1984: 'The Future of the Nation-State', in McClennan, Held and Hall (eds.), pp. 208–22.

1985: *Max Weber and the Theory of Modern Politics*. Cambridge: Polity Press.

Bendix, Reinhard 1978: *Kings or People*. Berkeley: University of California Press.

Berghahn, Volker R. 1973: *Germany and the Approach of War in 1914*. London: St Martin's Press.

1987: *Modern Germany*. Cambridge: Cambridge University Press.

Bickel, Wilhelm 1964: 'Die öffentlichen Finanzen', *Schweizerische Zeitschrift für Volkswirtschaft und Statistik* 100 (2): 273–302.

Bidwell, R. L. 1970: *Currency Conversion Tables*. London: Rex Collings.

Blewett, Neal 1968: 'Free Fooders, Balfourites, Whole Hoggers: Factionalism Within the Unionist Party, 1906–1910', *Historical Journal* 11 (1): 95–124.

Block, Fred 1987: *Revising State Theory*. Philadelphia: Temple University Press.

Blum, Jerome 1968: *Lord and Peasant in Russia from the Ninth to the Nineteenth Century*. New York: Atheneum.

Bogolepoff, M. 1918: 'Public Finance', in Raffalovich (ed.), pp. 329–51.

Böhme, Helmut 1967: 'Big Business Pressure Groups and Bismarck's Turn to Protectionism, 1873–1879', *Historical Journal* 10 (2): 218–36.

Bosshardt, Alfred and Nyedegger, Alfred 1964: 'Die schweizerische Aussen-wirtschaft im Wandel der Zeiten', *Schweizerische Zeitschrift für Volks-wirtschaft und Statistik* 100 (2): 302–28.

Boyd, Richard 1987: 'Government–Industry Relations in Japan: Access, Com-munication and Competitive-Collaboration', in S. Wilks and M. Wright (eds.), *Comparative Government–Industry Relations*, pp. 61–90. Oxford: Clarendon Press.

Braun, Rudolf 1975: 'Taxation, Socio-Political Structure and State Building: Britain and Brandenburg Prussia', in Tilly (ed.), pp. 243–327.

Brebner, John B. 1948/1962: 'Laissez-Faire and State Intervention in Nineteenth-Century Britain', in E. M. Carus-Wilson (ed.), *Essays in Eco-nomic History, Vol. III*, pp. 252–62. London: Edward Arnold.

Broomhall, George J. 1904: *The Corn Trade Year Book*. London: St Mary's Chamber.

Brown, Lucy 1958: *The Board of Trade and the Free Trade Movement, 1830–1842*. Oxford: Clarendon Press.

Bull, Hedley 1977: *The Anarchical Society*. London: Macmillan. Rev. edn, 1995. London: Macmillan.

Bürgin, Alfred 1959: 'The Growth of the Swiss National Economy', in Aitken (ed.), pp. 213–36.

Burton, John W. 1972: *World Society*. Cambridge: Cambridge University Press.

Butlin, Noël G. 1959: 'Colonial Socialism in Australia, 1860–1900', in Aitken (ed.), pp. 26–78.

   1962: *Australian Domestic Product, Investment and Foreign Borrowing, 1861–1938/9*. Cambridge: Cambridge University Press.

Buzan, Barry 1983: *People, States and Fear*. Brighton: Harvester Wheatsheaf.

Buzan, Barry, Jones, Charles and Little, Richard 1993: *The Logic of Anarchy*. New York: Columbia University Press.

Cain, Peter J. 1979: 'Political Economy in Edwardian England: The Tariff Reform Controversy', in Alan O'Day (ed.), *The Edwardian Age*, pp. 34–59. London: Macmillan.

Cain, Peter J. and Hopkins, Anthony G. 1986: 'Gentlemanly Capitalism and British Expansion Overseas I. The Old Colonial System, 1688–1850', *Economic History Review* 39 (4): 501–25.

Calleo, David P. 1978: *The German Problem Reconsidered*. Cambridge: Cambridge University Press.

1987: *Beyond American Hegemony*. New York: Basic Books.

1990: 'The US in the 1960s: Hegemon in Decline?', in M. Mann (ed.), *The Rise and Decline of the Nation State*, pp. 146–71. Oxford: Basil Blackwell.

Cameron, Rondo 1993: *A Concise Economic History of the World*. Oxford: Oxford University Press.

Camilleri, Joseph and Falk, Jim 1991: *The End of Sovereignty*. Aldershot: Edward Elgar.

Cammack, Paul 1989: 'Review Article: Bringing the State Back in?', *British Journal of Political Science* 19 (2): 269–90.

Carr, Edward H. 1939: *The Twenty Years' Crisis, 1919–1939*. London: Macmillan.

Carver, Terrell 1982: *Marx's Social Theory*. Oxford: Oxford University Press.

Caves, Richard E. 1976: 'Economic Models of Political Choice: Canada's Tariff Structure', *Canadian Journal of Economics* 9: 279–300.

Chase-Dunn, Christopher 1989: *Global Formation*. Oxford: Basil Blackwell.

Clarke, Peter F. 1969: 'British Politics and Blackburn Politics, 1900–1910', *Historical Journal* 12 (2): 302–27.

1971: *Lancashire and the New Liberalism*. London: Cambridge University Press.

Clarke, Simon 1988: *Keynesianism, Monetarism and the Crisis of the State*. Aldershot: Edward Elgar.

Clough, Shepard B. 1964: *The Economic History of Modern Italy*. New York: Columbia University Press.

Cohn, Samuel 1972: *Die Finanzen des Deutschen Reiches seit seiner Begründung*. Glashütten im Taunus: Verlag Detlev Auverman KG.

Collins, David N. 1973: 'The Franco-Russian Alliance and the Russian Railways', *Historical Journal* 16 (4): 777–89.

Collins, Randall 1986: *Weberian Sociological Theory*. New York: Cambridge University Press.

Cooper, Andrew 1994: 'State Power and Patterns of Late Development: A Comment on Zhao and Hall', *Sociology* 28 (2): 539–46.

Copland, Douglas B. 1980: 'Some Problems of Taxation in Australia', in Wilfred Prest and Mathews (eds.), pp. 35–46.

Coppa, Frank 1970: 'The Italian Tariff and the Conflict Between Agriculture and Industry', *Journal of Economic History* 30 (4): 742–69.

Cox, Robert W. 1983: 'Gramsci, Hegemony and International Relations', *Millennium* 12: 162–75.

1986: 'Social Forces, States and World Orders: Beyond International Relations Theory', in Keohane (ed.), pp. 204–54.

1987: *Production, Power and World Order*. New York: Columbia University Press.

Cox, Robert W. with Timothy J. Sinclair 1996: *Approaches to World Order*. Cambridge: Cambridge University Press.

Crafts, Nicholas F. R. 1983: 'Gross National Product in Europe, 1870–1910: Some New Estimates', *Explorations in Economic History* 20: 387–401.

Crafts, Nicholas, Leybourne, S. J. and Mills, T. C. 1991: 'Britain', in Sylla and Toniolo (eds.), pp. 109–54.

Craig, Gordon 1964: *The Politics of the Prussian Army, 1640–1945.* Oxford: Oxford University Press.

1987: *Germany.* Oxford: Oxford University Press.

Crisp, Olga 1953: 'Russian Financial Policy and the Gold Standard at the End of the Nineteenth Century', *Economic History Review* 6 (2): 156–72.

1976: *Studies in the Russian Economy Before 1914.* London: Macmillan.

1989: 'Peasant Land Tenure and Civil Rights Implications Before 1906', in Crisp and Edmondson (eds.), pp. 33–64.

1991: 'Russia', in Sylla and Toniolo (eds.), pp. 248–68.

Crisp, Olga and Edmondson, Linda (eds.) 1989: *Civil Rights in Imperial Russia.* Oxford: Clarendon Press.

Cross, Colin 1966: *The Liberals in Power, 1905–1914.* London: Barrie and Rockliffe.

Crouzet, François 1975: 'Trade and Empire: The British Experience from the Establishment of Free Trade Until the First World War', in Ratcliffe (ed.) 1975a, pp. 209–36.

1982: *The Victorian Economy.* London: Methuen.

Curtiss, John S. 1979: *Russia's Crimean War.* Durham, NC: Duke University Press.

Davis, Lance and Huttenback, Robert A. 1988: *Mammon and the Pursuit of Empire.* Cambridge: Cambridge University Press.

Davis, Ralph 1966: 'The Rise of Protection in England, 1689–1786', *Economic History Review* 19 (2): 306–17.

Dawson, William H. 1904: *Protection in Germany.* London: King and Son.

Deakin, Alfred 1980: 'The Chariot Wheels of the Central Government', in Wilfred Prest and Mathews (eds.), pp. 13–18.

Deane, Phyllis 1965: *The First Industrial Revolution.* Cambridge: Cambridge University Press.

1968: 'New Estimates of Gross National Product for the United Kingdom, 1830–1914', *Review of Income and Wealth* 14 (2): 95–112.

Deane, Phyllis and Cole, W. A. 1969: *British Economic Growth, 1688–1959.* Cambridge: Cambridge University Press.

Dewey, Davis R. 1968: *Financial History of the United States.* New York: Capricorn Books.

D'Lugo, David and Rogowski, Ronald 1993: 'The Anglo-German Naval Race and Comparative Constitutional "Fitness"', in Rosecrance and Stein (eds.), pp. 65–95.

Downing, Brian M. 1991: *The Military Revolution and Political Change.* Princeton, NJ: Princeton University Press.

Drummond, Ian M. 1976: 'The Russian Gold Standard, 1897–1914', *Journal of Economic History* 36 (3): 663–89.

Due, John F. 1971: *Indirect Taxation in Developing Countries.* Baltimore: Johns Hopkins University Press.

Dumke, Rolf H. 1976: 'The Political Economy of German Economic Unification', Ph.D thesis, University of Wisconsin, Madison.

1991: 'Tariffs and Market Structure: The German Zollverein as a Model for Economic Integration', in W. R. Lee (ed.), *German Industry and German Industrialisation*, pp. 77–115. London: Routledge.

Dunham, Arthur L. 1930: *The Anglo-French Treaty of Commerce of 1860 and the Progress of the Industrial Revolution in France.* Ann Arbor: University of Michigan Press.

Easterbrook, W. T. and Aitken, Hugh G. 1958: *Canadian Economic History.* Toronto: Macmillan.

Eddie, Scott M. 1988: 'Economic Policy and Economic Development in Austria-Hungary, 1867–1913', in Mathias and Pollard (eds.), pp. 814–86.

Eichengreen, Barry 1990: 'Phases in the Development of the International Monetary System'. Paper presented to the ESRC Conference, 'Structural Change in the West', Emmanuel College, Cambridge (5–7 September).

Eley, Geoffrey 1986: *From Unification to Nazism.* London: Allen and Unwin.

Elias, Norbert 1939/1994: *The Civilizing Process, Vol. II.* Oxford: Basil Blackwell.

1969/1983: *The Court Society.* Oxford: Basil Blackwell.

1970/1978: *What Is Sociology?* London: Hutchinson.

Ellison, Herbert J. 1965: 'Economic Modernisation in Imperial Russia: Purposes and Achievements', *Journal of Economic History* 25 (4): 523–40.

Emi, Koichi and Shionoya, Yuichi 1966: *Estimates of Long-Term Economic Statistics of Japan Since 1868.* Tokyo: Keizai Shimposha.

Emmons, Terence 1968: *The Russian Landed Gentry and the Peasant Emancipation of 1861.* Cambridge: Cambridge University Press.

Emy, Hugh V. 1972: 'The Impact of Financial Policy on English Party Politics Before 1914', *Historical Journal* 15 (1): 103–31.

Epstein, Klauss 1959: *Matthias Erzberger and the Dilemma of German Democracy.* Princeton, NJ: Princeton University Press.

Ercolani, Paulo 1978: 'Documentazione statistica di base', in Fuà.

Evans, Peter B. 1985: 'Transnational Linkages and the Economic Role of the State', in Evans, Rueschemeyer and Skocpol (eds.), pp. 192–226.

1995: *Embedded Autonomy.* Princeton, NJ: Princeton University Press.

Evans, Peter B., Rueschemeyer, Dietrich and Skocpol, Theda (eds.) 1985: *Bringing the State Back in.* Cambridge: Cambridge University Press.

Eyck, Erich 1968: *Bismarck and the German Empire.* London: Allen and Unwin.

Falkus, Malcolm 1968: 'Russia's National Income, 1913: A Revaluation', *Economica* 35 (137): 52–73.

1972: *The Industrialisation of Russia, 1700–1914.* London: Macmillan.

Farnsworth, Helen C. 1934: 'Decline and Recovery of Wheat Prices in the Nineties', *Wheat Studies of the Food Research Institute* 10: 289–352.

Feinstein, Charles H. 1972: *National Income, Expenditure and Output of the United Kingdom, 1855–1913.* Cambridge: Cambridge University Press.

Feis, Herbert 1930: *Europe, the World's Banker.* New Haven, CT: Yale University Press.

Ferguson, Niall 1994: 'Public Finance and National Security: The Domestic Origins of the First World War Revisited', *Past and Present* 142: 141–68.

Bibliography

Ferguson, Yale H. and Mansbach, Richard W. 1989: *The State, Conceptual Chaos and the Future of International Relations Theory*. Boulder, CO: Lynne Rienner.

Field, Daniel 1976: *The End of Serfdom*. Cambridge, MA: Harvard University Press.

Fielden, Kenneth 1969: 'The Rise and Fall of Free Trade', in C. J. Bartlett (ed.), *Britain Pre-Eminent*, pp. 76–100. London: Macmillan.

Finer, Samuel E. 1975: 'State and Nation-Building in Europe: The Role of the Military', in Tilly (ed.), pp. 84–163.

Finlay, John L. and Sprague, Douglas N. 1979: *The Structure of Canadian History*. Scarborough, Ontario: Prentice-Hall.

Firestone, O. J. 1958: *Canada's Economic Development, 1867–1953*. Review of Income and Wealth Series VII. London: Bowes and Bowes.

Fischer, Fritz 1975: *War of Illusion*. London: Chatto and Windus.

Flora, Peter 1987: *State, Economy and Society in Western Europe, 1815–1975, Vol. I*. London: Macmillan.

Fontvielle, Louis 1976: *Evolution et croissance de l'Etat Français: 1815–1969*. Paris: Economies et Sociétés (Cahiers de l'ISMEA Série AF, XIII).

Fraser, Peter 1966: *Joseph Chamberlain*. London: Cassell.

Fremdling, Rainer 1977: 'Railroads and German Economic Growth: A Leading Sector Analysis', *Journal of Economic History* 37: 583–601.

Frey, Bruno S. 1984: *International Political Economics*. Oxford: Basil Blackwell.

Friedberg, Aaron L. 1988: *The Weary Titan*. Princeton, NJ: Princeton University Press.

1989: 'The Political Economy of American Strategy', *World Politics* 41 (3): 381–406.

Frieden, Jeffry A. and Lake, David A. (eds.) 1987: *International Political Economy*. New York: St Martin's Press.

Frisch, M. J. (ed.) 1985: *Selected Writings and Speeches of Alexander Hamilton*. Washington, DC: American Enterprise Institute for Public Policy Research.

Fuà, Giorgio 1965: *Notes on Italian Economic Growth, 1861–1914*. Milan: n.p.

1978: *Lo Sviluppo economico in Italia*. Milan: Franco Angeli.

Fuller, William C. 1985: *Civil Military Conflicts in Imperial Russia, 1881–1914*. Princeton, NJ: Princeton University Press.

Gall, Lothar 1986: *Bismarck*. London: Allen and Unwin.

Gallarotti, Giulio M. 1985: 'Toward a Business-Cycle Model of Tariffs', *International Organization* 39 (1): 155–87.

Garvin, James L. 1910: *Tariff or Budget*. London: n.p.

Gatrell, Peter W. 1982: 'Industrial Expansion in Tsarist Russia, 1908–1914', *Economic History Review* 35 (1): 99–110.

1986: *The Tsarist Economy, 1850–1917*. London: Batsford.

1994: *Government, Industry and Rearmament in Russia, 1900–1914*. Cambridge: Cambridge University Press.

Gerloff, Wilhelm 1908: 'Verbrauch und Verbrauchsbelastung kleiner und mittlerer Einkommen in Deutschland um die Wende des 19. Jahrhunderts', *Jahrbuch für Nationalökonomie und Statistik III*, vol. 35.

1913: *Die Finanz- und Zollpolitik des Deutschen Reiches.* Jena: Gustav Fischer.

1929: 'Der Staatshaushalt und das Finanzsystem Deutschlands', in Gerloff and Meisel (eds.), pp. 1–69.

Gerloff, Wilhelm and Meisel, Franz (eds.) 1929: *Handbuch der Finanzwissenschaft, Vol. III.* Tübingen: J. C. B. Mohr.

Gerschenkron, Alexander 1943: *Bread and Democracy in Germany.* London: Cambridge University Press.

1962: *Economic Backwardness in Historical Perspective.* Cambridge, MA: Harvard University Press.

1965: 'Russia: Agrarian Policies and Industrialisation, 1861–1917', in M. M. Postan and H. J. Habbakuk (eds.), *Cambridge Economic History of Europe,* Vol. VI (2), pp. 706–800. Cambridge: Cambridge University Press.

1968: *Continuity in History and Other Essays.* Cambridge, MA: Belknap Press.

1970: *Europe in the Russian Mirror.* Cambridge: Cambridge University Press.

Giblin, Lyndhurst F. 1980: 'Federation and Finance', in Wilfred Prest and Mathews (eds.), pp. 47–62.

Giddens, Anthony 1981: *A Contemporary Critique of Historical Materialism, Vol. I.* London: Macmillan.

1985: *The Nation State and Violence.* Cambridge: Polity Press.

Giffen, Robert 1971: *Economic Inquiries and Studies.* Shannon: Irish University Press.

Gill, Stephen 1990: *American Hegemony and the Trilateral Commission.* New York: Cambridge University Press.

Gilpin, Robert 1975: *US Power and the Multinational Corporation.* New York: Basic Books.

1981: *War and Change in World Politics.* New York: Cambridge University Press.

1987: *The Political Economy of International Relations.* Princeton, NJ: Princeton University Press.

Glyn, Andrew and Sutcliffe, Bob 1972: *British Capitalism, Workers and the Profit Squeeze.* Harmondsworth: Penguin.

Goldscheid, Rudolf 1958: 'A Sociological Approach to the Problem of Public Finance', in Richard A. Musgrave and Alan T. Peacock (eds.), *Classics in the Theory of Public Finance,* pp. 202–14. London: Macmillan.

Goldsmith, Ray W. 1961: 'The Economic Development of Tsarist Russia, 1860–1914', *Economic Development and Cultural Change* 9 (3): 441–75.

Goldstein, Edward R. 1980: 'Vickers Limited and the Tsarist Regime', *Slavonic and Eastern European Review* 58 (4): 561–71.

Goldstein, Joshua S. 1988: *Long Cycles.* London: Yale University Press.

Goldstein, Judith 1988: 'Ideas, Institutions and American Trade Policy', *International Organization* 42 (1): 179–217.

Goldstone, Jack A. 1991: *Revolution and Rebellion in the Early Modern World.* Berkeley: University of California Press.

Gorlin, Robert H. 1977: 'Problems of Tax Reform in Imperial Russia', *Journal of Modern History* 49: 246–65.

Gourevitch, Peter A. 1977: 'International Trade, Domestic Coalitions and Liberty: Comparative Responses to the Crisis of 1873–1896', *Journal of Interdisciplinary History* 8 (2): 281–313.

1978: 'The Second Image Reversed: The International Sources of Domestic Politics', *International Organization* 32 (4): 881–911.

1986: *Politics in Hard Times.* Ithaca: Cornell University Press.

Green, E. H. H. 1985: 'Radical Conservatism: The Electoral Genesis of Tariff Reform', *Historical Journal* 28 (3): 667–92.

Greenaway, David 1981: 'Taxes on International Transactions and Economic Development', in Alan T. Peacock and Francesco Forte (eds.), *The Political Economy of Taxation*, pp. 131–47. New York: St Martin's Press.

Gregory, Paul R. 1972: 'Economic Growth and Structural Change in Tsarist Russia: A Case of Modern Economic Growth?' *Soviet Studies* 23 (3): 418–34.

1974: 'Some Empirical Comments on the Theory of Relative Backwardness: The Russian Case', *Economic Development and Cultural Change* 22 (4): 654–66.

1982: *Russian National Income, 1885–1913.* Cambridge: Cambridge University Press.

1991: 'The Role of the State in Promoting Economic Development: The Russian Case and Its General Implications', in Sylla and Toniolo (eds.), pp. 64–79.

Groenewegen, Peter 1983: 'The Political Economy of Federalism, 1901–1981', in B. Head (ed.), *State and Economy in Australia*, pp. 169–98. Melbourne: Oxford University Press.

Guroff, Gregory and Carstensen, Fred V. (eds.) 1982: *Entrepreneurship in Imperial Russia and the Soviet Union.* Princeton, NJ: Princeton University Press.

Gwynne, H. A. 1903/1982: 'The City and Mr Chamberlain's Fiscal Proposals. Memorandum for Joseph Chamberlain', in W. W. Mock (ed.), *Imperiale Herrschaft und nationales Interesse*, pp. 393–7. London: Klett-Cotta.

Halévy, Elie 1952: *A History of the English People in the Nineteenth Century.* London: Ernest Benn.

Hall, John A. 1986: *Powers and Liberties.* Harmondsworth: Penguin.

1988: *Liberalism.* London: Palladin.

1990: 'Will the United States Decline as Did Britain?', in M. Mann (ed.), *The Rise and Decline of the Nation State*, pp. 114–45. Oxford: Basil Blackwell.

Hall, John A. and Ikenberry, G. John 1989: *The State.* Milton Keynes: Open University Press.

Hall, Stuart 1984: 'The State in Question', in McClennan, Held and Hall (eds.), pp. 1–28.

Halliday, Fred 1987: 'State and Society in International Relations: A Second Agenda', *Millennium* 16 (2): 215–29.

1994: *Rethinking International Relations.* London: Macmillan.

Hamilton, Alexander 1782/1985: 'The Continental Papers, No. 5', in Frisch (ed.), pp. 55–60.

1791/1985: 'Report on Manufactures', in Frisch (ed.), pp. 278–317.

Hansen, John Mark. 1990: 'Taxation and the Political Economy of the Tariff', *International Organization* 44 (4): 527–51.

Hardach, Gerd 1977: *The First World War, 1914–1918*. Berkeley: University of California Press.

Hardach, Karl W. 1967: *Die Bedeutung wirtschaftlicher Factoren bei der Wieder-einführung der Eisen- und Getreidezölle in Deutschland, 1879*. Berlin: Duncker und Humblot.

　1976: *The Political Economy of Germany in the Twentieth Century*. London: University of California Press.

Harris, José 1972: *Unemployment and Politics*. Oxford: Clarendon Press.

Heckscher, Eli F. 1935: *Mercantilism*, 2 vols. London: Allen and Unwin.

Held, David 1995: *Democracy and the Global Order*. Cambridge: Polity Press.

Henderson, Walther O. 1967: *The Industrial Revolution on the Continent*. London: Frank Cass.

　1968: *The Zollverein*. London: Frank Cass.

　1975: *The Rise of German Industrial Power, 1834–1914*. London: Temple Smith.

Hentschel, Volker 1978: *Wirtschaft und Wirtschaftspolitik im wilhelminischen Deutschland*. Stuttgart: Klett-Cotta.

　1988: 'German Economic and Social Policy, 1815–1939', in Mathias and Pollard (eds.), pp. 752–813.

Herz, John 1957: 'Rise and Demise of the Territorial State', *World Politics* 9 (4): 473–93.

Heß, Klauss 1990: *Junker und bürgerliche Großgrundbesitzer im Kaiserreich*. Stuttgart: Franz Steiner.

Hilton, Boyd 1977: *Corn, Cash, Commerce*. Oxford: Oxford University Press.

Hintze, Otto 1975: *The Historical Essays of Otto Hintze*, edited by Felix Gilbert. Oxford: Oxford University Press.

Hirschman, Albert O. 1978: 'Exit, Voice and the State', *World Politics* 31 (1): 90–107.

Hirst, Paul Q. 1977: 'Economic Classes and Politics', in A. Hunt (ed.), *Class and Class Structure*, pp. 125–54. London: Lawrence and Wishart.

Hobsbawm, Eric J. 1967: *Industry and Empire*. Harmondsworth: Penguin.

Hobson, John A. 1902: *Imperialism*. London: Nisbet & Co.

Hobson, John M. 1991: 'The Tax-Seeking State: Taxation, Protectionism and State Structures in Germany, Russia, Britain and America, 1870–1913', Ph.D thesis, London School of Economics.

　1993: 'The Military-Extraction Gap and the Wary Titan: The Fiscal-Sociology of British Defence Policy, 1870–1913', *Journal of European Economic History* 22 (3): 461–507.

Hoffding, H. 1912: 'Recent Financial and Trade Policy of Russia', *Russian Review* 1.

Hoffmann, Walther G. 1965: *Das Wachstum der deutschen Wirtschaft seit der Mitte des 19. Jahrhunderts*. Berlin: Springer-Verlag.

Hoffmann, Walther G. and Müller, J. H. 1959: *Das deutsche Volkseinkommen, 1851–1957*. Tübingen: J. C. B. Mohr.

Holland, Bernard 1980: *The Fall of Protection, 1840–1850*. Philadelphia: Porcupine Press.

Holtfrerich, Carl-Ludwig 1986: *The German Inflation, 1914–1923*. Berlin: Walter de Gruyter.

1987: 'The Modernisation of the Tax System in the First World War and the Great Inflation, 1914–1923', in Witt (ed.) 1987c, pp. 125–36.

Holton, Robert J. 1985: *The Transition from Feudalism to Capitalism*. London: Macmillan.

Hoselitz, Bert F. 1959: 'Economic Policy and Economic Development', in Aitken (ed.), pp. 325–52.

Howard, Michael 1976: *War in European History*. Oxford: Oxford University Press.

1985: *The Causes of War*. London: Unwin.

Howe, Anthony C. 1992: 'Free Trade and the City of London, c. 1820–1870', *History* 77 (251): 391–410.

1994: 'Free Trade in the British Empire: The Rise and Fall of the Anglo-Australian Ideal, 1846–1908', unpublished paper, London School of Economics, Department of International History.

Hunt, James C. 1974: 'Peasants, Tariffs and Meat Quotas: Imperial German Protectionism Reexamined', *Central European History* 7: 311–31.

Huntington, Samuel P. 1988: 'The United States – Decline or Renewal?', *Foreign Affairs* 67 (2): 76–96.

1991: 'Transnational Organisations in World Politics', in R. Little and M. Smith (eds.), *Perspectives on World Politics*, pp. 212–28. London: Routledge.

Iggers, George (ed.) 1985: *The Social History of Politics*. Leamington Spa: Berg Publishers.

Ikenberry, G. John 1986: 'The Irony of State Strength: Comparative Responses to the Oil Shocks in the 1970s', *International Organization* 40 (1): 105–37.

1988a: 'An Institutional Approach to American Foreign Economic Policy', *International Organization* 42 (1): 219–43.

1988b: 'Market Solutions for State Problems: The International and Domestic Politics of American Oil Decontrol', *International Organization* 42 (1): 151–77.

1988c: *Reasons of State*. Ithaca: Cornell University Press.

1991: 'The State and Strategies of International Adjustment', in R. Little and M. Smith (eds.), *Perspectives on World Politics*, pp. 157–68. London: Routledge.

Iliasu, A. A. 1971: 'The Cobden–Chevalier Commercial Treaty of 1860', *Historical Journal* 14 (1): 67–98.

Imlah, Albert 1958: *Economic Elements in the Pax Britannica*. Cambridge, MA: Harvard University Press.

Ingham, Geoffrey 1984: *Capitalism Divided?* London: Macmillan.

Jackson, Robert H. and Rosberg, Carl G. 1982: 'Why Africa's Weak States Persist: The Empirical and the Juridical in Statehood', *World Politics* 35: 1–24.

Jarausch, Konrad H. 1973: *The Enigmatic Chancellor*. London: Yale University Press.

Jarvis, Anthony P. 1989: 'Societies, States and Geopolitics: Challenges from Historical Sociology', *Review of International Studies* 15: 281–93.

1993: 'Remaking the State: Towards an Integrated Explanation of World Politics', DPhil thesis, University of Oxford.

Jasny, Naum 1936: 'Wheat Problems and Policies in Germany', *Wheat Studies of the Food Research Institute* 13 (3): 65–140.

Jeffreys, J. B. and Walters, D. 1955: 'National Income and Expenditure of the United Kingdom, 1870–1952', *Review of Income and Wealth* Series V. Cambridge: Bowes and Bowes.

Jessop, Bob 1978: 'Capitalism and Democracy: The Best Political Shell?', in G. Littlejohn (ed.), *Power and the State*, pp. 10–51. London: Croom Helm.

1990: *State Theory*. Cambridge: Polity Press.

Jones, Eric L. 1981: *The European Miracle*. Cambridge: Cambridge University Press.

Kahan, Arcadius 1967: 'Government Policies and the Industrialisation of Russia', *Journal of Economic History* 27: 460–77.

Kaiser, David E. 1983: 'Germany and the Origins of the First World War', *Journal of Modern History* 55 (3): 442–74.

Kalberg, Stephen 1994: *Max Weber's Comparative-Historical Sociology*. Cambridge: Polity Press.

Katzenstein, Peter J. 1977a: 'Conclusion: Domestic Structures and Strategies of Foreign Economic Policy', *International Organization* 31 (4): 879–920.

1977b: 'Introduction: Domestic and International Forces and Strategies of Foreign Economic Policy', *International Organization* 31 (4): 587–606.

Katznelson, Ira 1985: 'Working-Class Formation and the State: Nineteenth-Century England in American Perspective', in Evans, Rueschemeyer and Skocpol (eds.), pp. 257–84.

Kausel, Anton 1979: 'Österreichs Volkseinkommen 1830 bis 1913', in *Geschichte und Ergebnisse der zentralen amtlichen Statistik in Österreich, 1829–1979*, pp. 689–720. Vienna: Austrian Central Statistics Office.

Kehr, Eckhart 1977: *Economic Interest, Militarism and Foreign Policy*. London: University of California Press.

Kennan, K. K. 1910: *Income Taxation*. Milwaukee: Burdick and Allen.

Kennedy, Gavin 1983: *Defence Economics*. London: Duckworth.

Kennedy, Paul M. 1987: *The Rise of the Anglo-German Antagonism, 1860–1914*. London: Ashfield Press.

1988: *The Rise and Fall of the Great Powers*. London: Unwin Hyman.

1989: 'Debate: The Costs and Benefits of British Imperialism', *Past and Present* 125: 186–92.

Keohane, Robert O. 1984: *After Hegemony*. Princeton, NJ: Princeton University Press.

(ed.) 1986: *Neorealism and Its Critics*. New York: Columbia University Press.

Kesslitz, Rainer von 1912: 'Die Lasten der militärischen Rüstungen Österreich-

Ungarn im Neusten Zeit, 1868–1912'. *Kriegsarchiv*, Vienna MS. Allg. Nr. 54 II. 45. 163.

Khromov, Pavel A. 1950: *Ekonomicheskoe razvitie Rosii v XIX–XX vekakh, 1800–1917*. Moscow: Gospolitizdat.

Kindleberger, Charles P. 1973: *The World in Depression, 1929–1939*. Berkeley: University of California Press.

1978a: *Economic Response*. Cambridge, MA: Harvard University Press.

1978b: 'Government and International Trade'. Essays in International Finance, No. 129, International Finance Section, Department of Economics. Princeton, NJ: Princeton University.

1981: 'Dominance and Leadership in the International Economy', *International Studies Quarterly* 25 (2): 242–54.

1987: 'The Rise of Free Trade in Western Europe', in Frieden and Lake (eds.), pp. 85–103.

Kipp, Jacob W. 1975: 'M. Kh. Reutern on the Russian State and Economy', *Journal of Modern History* 47 (3): 437–59.

Kirby, M. W. 1981: *The Decline of British Economic Power Since 1870*. London: Allen and Unwin.

Kirchner, Walther 1981: 'Russian Tariffs and Foreign Industries Before 1914: The German Entrepreneur's Perspective', *Journal of Economic History* 41 (2): 361–78.

Kiser, Edgar 1986/7: 'The Formation of State Policy in Western Europe Absolutisms: A Comparison of England and France', *Politics and Society* 15 (3): 259–96.

Kitchen, Martin 1978: *The Political Economy of Germany, 1815–1914*. London: Croom Helm.

Kochan, Lionel 1966: *Russia in Revolution, 1890–1918*. London: Weidenfeld and Nicolson.

Kondratieff, Nikolai 1935: 'The Long Waves in Economic Life', *Review of Economic Statistics* 17 (6): 105–15.

Krasner, Stephen D. 1976: 'State Power and the Structure of International Trade', *World Politics* 28 (3): 317–47.

1977a: 'Domestic Constraints on International Economic Leverage', in K. Knorr and F. N. Trager (eds.), *Economic Issues and National Security*, pp. 160–82. Lawrence, KS: Allen Press.

1977b: 'US Commercial and Monetary Policy: Unravelling the Paradox of External Strength and Internal Weakness', *International Organization* 31 (4): 635–71.

1978: *Defending the National Interest*. Princeton, NJ: Princeton University Press.

1979: 'The Tokyo Round: Particularistic Interests and Prospects for Stability in the Global Trading System', *International Studies Quarterly* 23 (4): 491–531.

(ed.) 1983: *International Regimes*. Ithaca: Cornell University Press.

Kreudener, Jürgen von 1987: 'The Franckenstein Paradox in the Intergovernmental Fiscal Relations of Imperial Germany', in Witt (ed.) 1987c, pp. 111–24.

Krueger, Anne O. 1974: 'The Political Economy of the Rent-Seeking Society', *American Economic Review* 64: 291–303.

Kugler, Jacek and Domke, William 1986: 'Comparing the Strength of Nations', *Comparative Political Studies* 19 (1): 36–69.

Kuznets, Simon 1946: *National Product Since 1869*. New York: NBER.

1952: 'Long-Term Changes in the National Income of the United States', *Income and Wealth of the United States: Trends and Structures* Series II. Cambridge: Bowes and Bowes.

1967: 'Quantitative Aspects of the Economic Growth of Nations: X. Level and Structure of Foreign Trade: Long-Term Trends', *Economic Development and Cultural Change* 15 (2): 1–140.

Lake, David A. 1988: *Power, Protection and Free Trade*. Ithaca: Cornell University Press.

Lambi, Ivo N. 1963: *Free Trade and Protectionism in Germany, 1868–1879*. Wiesbaden: Franz Steiner Verlag GMBH.

Latham, E. 1953: *The Group Basis of Politics*. Ithaca: Cornell University Press.

Laue, Theodore H. von 1963: *Sergei Witte and the Industrialisation of Russia*. New York: Columbia University Press.

Leineweber, Norbert 1988: *Das säkulare Wachstum der Staatsausgaben*. Göttingen: Vandenhoeck and Ruprecht.

Levi, Margaret 1988: *Of Rule and Revenue*. London: University of California Press.

Lévy-Leboyer, Maurice and Bourguignon, François 1990: *The French Economy in the Nineteenth Century*. Cambridge: Cambridge University Press.

Lewis, Stephen R. 1984: *Taxation for Development*. New York: Oxford University Press.

Lewis, W. Arthur 1978: *Growth and Fluctuations, 1870–1913*. London: George Allen and Unwin.

Liepmann, Heinrich 1938: *Tariff Levels and Economic Unity of Europe*. New York: Macmillan.

Linklater, Andrew 1991: *Beyond Realism and Marxism*. London: Macmillan.

Lipschutz, Ronnie D. 1993: 'Reconstructing World Politics: The Emergence of Global Civil Society', *Millennium* 21 (3): 389–420.

Lipset, Seymour M. 1985: *Consensus and Conflict*. New Brunswick, NJ: Transaction Books.

Lipson, Charles 1983: 'The Transformation of Trade: The Sources and Effects of Regime Change', in Krasner (ed.), pp. 233–72.

List, Friedrich 1841/1885: *The National System of Political Economy*. London: Longmans, Green & Co.

Litvinov-Falinsky, V. P. 1908: *Nashe ekonomicheskoe polozhenie i zadachi budushchego*. St Petersburg: n.p.

Longstreth, Frank H. 1979: 'The City, Industry and the State', in C. Crouch (ed.), *State and Economy in Contemporary Capitalism*, pp. 157–90. New York: St Martin's Press.

Lotz, Walther 1931: *Finanzwissenschaft*. Tübingen: J. C. B. Mohr.

Lyashchenko, Peter A. 1970: *The History of the National Economy of Russia to 1917*. New York: Octagon.
McClennan, Gregor, Held, David and Hall, Stuart (eds.) 1984: *The Idea of the Modern State*. Milton Keynes: Open University Press.
McCord, Norman 1970: *Free Trade*. Newton Abbot: David & Charles.
McDaniel, Tim 1988: *Autocracy, Capitalism and Revolution in Russia*. Berkeley: University of California Press.
McInnis, Edgar 1960: *Canada*. New York: Holt, Rinehart and Winston.
McKeown, Timothy J. 1983: 'Hegemonic Stability Theory and Nineteenth-Century Tariff Levels in Europe', *International Organization* 37 (1): 73–91.
Mackinder, Halford J. 1904: 'The Geographical Pivot of History', *Geographical Journal* 23: 421–37.
McLennan, David 1977: *Karl Marx*. Oxford: Oxford University Press.
McNaught, Kenneth 1975: *The Pelican History of Canada*. Harmondsworth: Penguin.
McNeill, William H. 1982: *The Pursuit of Power*. Oxford: Basil Blackwell.
1992: *The Global Condition*. Princeton, NJ: Princeton University Press.
Mallet, Bernard 1913: *British Budgets, 1887–1913*. London: Macmillan.
Mann, Fritz K. 1943: 'The Sociology of Taxation', *Review of Politics* 5 (2): 225–35.
Mann, Michael 1986: *The Sources of Social Power, Vol. I*. Cambridge: Cambridge University Press.
1988: *States, War and Capitalism*. Oxford: Basil Blackwell.
1993: *The Sources of Social Power, Vol. II*. Cambridge: Cambridge University Press.
Manning, Roberta T. 1982: *The Crisis of the Old Order in Russia*. Princeton, NJ: Princeton University Press.
Marrison, A. J. 1977: 'The Development of a Tariff Reform Policy During Joseph Chamberlain's First Campaign, May 1903–February 1904', in W. Chaloner and B. M. Ratcliffe (eds.), *Trade and Transport*, pp. 214–41. Manchester: Manchester University Press.
Marx, Karl 1843/1977: *Introduction to a Critique of Hegel's Philosophy of Right*, in McLennan (ed.), pp. 63–74.
1848/1977: *The Communist Manifesto*. Harmondsworth: Penguin.
1852/1977: *The Eighteenth Brumaire of Louis Bonaparte*, in McLennan (ed.), pp. 300–25.
1857/1973: *Grundrisse*. London: Random House.
1859/1976: *Preface and Introduction to A Contribution to the Critique of Political Economy*. Beijing: Foreign Languages Publishing House.
1863/1972: *Theories of Surplus-Value, Vol. III*. London: Lawrence and Wishart.
1867/1954: *Capital, Vol. I*. London: Lawrence and Wishart.
1867/1959: *Capital, Vol. III*. London: Lawrence and Wishart.
1875/1977: *A Critique of the Gotha Programme*, in McLennan (ed.), pp. 564–70.
Mathias, Peter and O'Brien, Patrick K. 1976: 'Taxation in Britain and France, 1715–1810: A Comparison of the Social and Economic Incidence of Taxes

Collected for the Central Governments', *Journal of European Economic History* 5 (3): 601–50.

Mathias, Peter and Pollard, Sidney (eds.) 1988: *The Cambridge Economic History of Europe*, vol. VIII, *The Industrial Economies*. Cambridge: Cambridge University Press.

Migdal, Joel S. 1988: *Strong Societies and Weak States*. Princeton, NJ: Princeton University Press.

Miliband, Ralph 1973: *The State in Capitalist Society*. London: Quartet Books.

Miller, Margaret S. 1926: *The Economic Development of Russia, 1905–1914*. London: King and Son.

Mills, Richard C. 1980: 'The Financial Relations of the Commonwealth and the States', in Wilfred Prest and Mathews (eds.), pp. 63–76.

Milward, Alan S. and Saul, S. B. 1977: *The Development of the Economies of Continental Europe, 1850–1914*. London: Allen and Unwin.

Mitchell, Brian R. 1975: *European Historical Statistics, 1750–1970*. Basingstoke: Macmillan.

1983: *International Historical Statistics: The Americas and Australasia*. London: Macmillan.

1992: *International Historical Statistics: Europe, 1750–1988*. Basingstoke: Macmillan.

Mitchell, Brian R. and Deane, Phyllis 1962: *Abstract of British Historical Statistics*. Cambridge: Cambridge University Press.

Modelski, George 1978: 'The Long Cycle of Global Politics and the Nation-State', *Comparative Studies in Society and History* 20: 214–35.

Modelski, George and Thompson, William R. 1988: *Seapower in Global Politics, 1494–1993*. Seattle: University of Washington Press.

Moeller, Robert G. 1981: 'Peasants and Tariffs in the Kaiserreich: How Backward Were the Bauern?', *Agricultural History* 55 (4): 370–85.

(ed.) 1986: *Peasants and Lords in Modern Germany*. London: Allen and Unwin.

Mooers, Colin 1991: *The Making of Bourgeois Europe*. London: Verso.

Morgenstern, Oskar 1963: *On the Accuracy of Economic Observations*. Princeton, NJ: Princeton University Press.

Morgenthau, Hans J. 1964: *Politics Among Nations*. New York: Alfred Knopf.

Mousnier, Roland 1971: *Peasant Uprisings in Seventeenth-Century France, Russia and China*. London: Allen and Unwin.

Murphy, Craig N. 1994: *International Organization and Industrial Change*. Cambridge: Polity Press.

Murray, Bruce K. 1973: 'The Politics of the "People's Budget"', *Historical Journal* 16 (3): 555–70.

1980: *The People's Budget, 1909–1910*. Oxford: Clarendon Press.

Nettl, John P. 1968: 'The State as a Conceptual Variable', *World Politics* 20: 559–92.

Newcomer, Mabel 1937: *Central and Local Finance in Germany and England*. New York: Columbia University Press.

Nichols, John A. 1958: *Germany After Bismarck*. Cambridge, MA: Harvard University Press.

Nordlinger, Eric A. 1981: *On the Autonomy of the Democratic State*. Cambridge, MA: Harvard University Press.

Nye, John V. 1991: 'The Myth of Free-Trade Britain and Fortress France: Tariffs and Trade in the Nineteenth Century', *Journal of Economic History* 51 (1): 23–46.

O'Brien, Patrick K. 1988: 'The Political Economy of British Taxation, 1660–1815', *Economic History Review* 41 (1): 1–32.

 1990: 'The Imperial Component in the Decline of the British Economy Before 1914', in M. Mann (ed.), *The Rise and Decline of the Nation State*, pp. 12–46. Oxford: Basil Blackwell.

O'Brien, Patrick K. and Keyder, Caglar 1978: *Economic Growth in Britain and France, 1780–1914*. London: Allen and Unwin.

O'Brien, Patrick K. and Pigman, Geoffrey 1992: 'Free Trade, British Hegemony and the International Economic Order in the Nineteenth Century', *Review of International Studies* 18: 89–113.

O'Connor, James 1973: *The Fiscal Crisis of the State*. New York: St Martin's Press.

Offe, Claus 1984: *Contradictions of the Welfare State*. London: Hutchinson.

Ohkawa, Kazushi and Shinohara, Miyohei 1979: *Patterns of Japanese Economic Development*. London: Yale University Press.

Olson, Mancur 1965: *The Logic of Collective Action*. Cambridge, MA: Harvard University Press.

 1982: *The Rise and Decline of Nations*. London: Yale University Press.

 1993: 'Dictatorship, Democracy, and Development', *American Political Science Review* 87 (3): 567–76.

Organski, A. F. K. and Kugler, Jacek 1980: *The War Ledger*. Chicago: University of Chicago Press.

Orlovsky, Daniel 1981: *The Limits of Reform*. Cambridge, MA: Harvard University Press.

Owen, Thomas C. 1982: 'Entrepreneurship and the Structure of Enterprise in Russia, 1800–1880', in Guroff and Carstensen (eds.), pp. 59–83.

Parker, Geoffrey and Smith, Lesley (eds.) 1978a: *The General Crisis of the Seventeenth Century*. London: Routledge and Kegan Paul.

 1978b: 'Introduction', in Parker and Smith (eds.) 1978a, pp. 1–25.

Parkin, Frank 1979: *Marxism and Class Theory*. London: Tavistock.

Peacock, Alan T. and Wiseman, Jack 1961: *The Growth of Public Expenditure in the United Kingdom*. Princeton, NJ: Princeton University Press.

Perry, J. Harvey 1955: *Taxes, Tariffs and Subsidies*. Toronto: University of Toronto Press.

Pflanze, Otto 1990a: *Bismarck and the Development of Germany, Vol. II*. Oxford: Princeton University Press.

 1990b: *Bismarck and the Development of Germany, Vol. III*. Oxford: Princeton University Press.

Phelps-Brown, Ernest H. and Handfield-Jones, S. J. 1952: 'The Climacteric of the 1890s: A Study of the Expanding Economy', *Oxford Economic Papers* 4 (3): 266–307.

Pincus, Jonathan J. 1977: *Pressure Groups and Politics in Antebellum Tariffs*. New York: Columbia University Press.

Pintner, Walter M. 1959: 'Inflation in Russia During the Crimean War Period', *American Slavic and East European Review* 18 (1): 81–7.

1967: *Russian Economic Policy Under Nicholas I*. Ithaca: Cornell University Press.

1984: 'The Burden of Defence in Imperial Russia, 1725–1914', *Russian Review* 43: 231–59.

Pipes, Richard 1974: *Russia Under the Old Regime*. Harmondsworth: Penguin.

Poggi, Gianfranco 1978: *The Development of the Modern State*. London: Hutchinson.

Polanyi, Karl 1957: *The Great Transformation*. New York: Octagon Press.

Pollard, Sidney 1981: *Peaceful Conquest*. Oxford: Oxford University Press.

1989: *Britain's Prime, Britain's Decline*. London: Edward Arnold.

Posner, Richard A. 1974: 'Theories of Economic Regulation', *Bell Journal of Economics and Management Science* 5: 335–58.

Poulantzas, Nicos 1973: *Political Power and Social Classes*. London: NLB.

Powelson, John P. 1994: *Centuries of Economic Endeavour*. Ann Arbor: University of Michigan Press.

Prest, Alan R. 1948: 'National Income of the United Kingdom, 1870–1946', *Economic Journal* 58 (229): 31–62.

Prest, Wilfred and Mathews, Russell L. (eds.) 1980: *The Development of Australian Fiscal Federalism*. Canberra: Australian National University Press.

Prochnow, Peter-Michael 1977: 'Staat im Wachstum: Versuch einer finanzwirtschaftlichen Analyse preußischen Haushaltsrechnungen, 1871–1913', Ph.D thesis, University of Münster.

Puhle, Hans-Jürgen. 1986: 'Lords and Peasants in the Kaiserreich', in Moeller (ed.), pp. 81–110.

Raeff, Marc 1957: 'The Russian Autocracy and Its Officials', in H. McLean (ed.), *Russian Thought and Politics*, pp. 77–92. Cambridge: Harvard Slavic Studies.

1966: *Origins of the Russian Intelligentsia*. New York: Harcourt, Brace and World.

Raffalovich, Arthur (ed.) 1918: *Russia*. London: King and Son.

Rasler, Karen A. and Thompson, William R. 1989: *War and State-Making*. Sydney: Allen and Unwin.

Ratcliffe, Barrie M. (ed.) 1975a: *Britain and Her World, 1750–1914*. Manchester: Manchester University Press.

1975b: 'The Origins of the Anglo-French Commercial Treaty of 1860: A Reassessment', in Ratcliffe (ed.) 1975a, pp. 125–52.

Ratner, Sidney 1967: *Taxation and Democracy in America*. New York: John Wiley.

Rempel, Richard A. 1972: *Unionists Divided*. Newton Abbot: David and Charles.

Ricardo, David 1817/1971: *On the Principles of Political Economy and Taxation.* Harmondsworth: Penguin.

Rieber, Alfred J. 1966: *The Politics of Autocracy.* Paris: Mouton.

1982: *Merchants and Entrepreneurs in Imperial Russia.* Chapel Hill: University of North Carolina Press.

Robinson, Geroid T. 1973: *Rural Russia Under the Old Regime.* New York: Macmillan.

Roesler, Konrad 1967: *Die Finanzpolitik des Deutschen Reiches im ersten Weltkrieg.* Berlin: Duncker and Humblot.

Rogger, Hans 1983: *Russia in the Age of Modernisation and Revolution, 1881–1917.* London: Longman.

Rogowski, Ronald 1989: *Commerce and Coalitions.* Princeton, NJ: Princeton University Press.

Röhl, John C. G. 1967: *Germany Without Bismarck.* London: Batsford.

Rosecrance, Richard and Stein, Arthur A. (eds.) 1993: *The Domestic Bases of Grand Strategy.* Ithaca: Cornell University Press.

Rosenau, James N. 1981: 'The State in an Era of Cascading Politics: Wavering Concept, Widening Competence, Withering Colossus or Weathering Change?', in J. A. Caporaso (ed.), *The Elusive State*, pp. 17–48. London: Sage.

Rosenberg, Hans 1943: 'The Political and Social Consequences of the Depression of 1873–1896 in Central Europe', *Economic History Review* 13 (1): 58–73.

Rosenberg, Justin 1990a: 'A Non-Realist Theory of Sovereignty? Giddens' *The Nation State and Violence*', *Millennium* 19 (2): 249–59.

1990b: 'What's the Matter with Realism?', *Review of International Studies* 16: 285–303.

1994: *The Empire of Civil Society.* London: Verso.

Rostow, Walter W. 1971: *Politics and the Stages of Growth.* London: Cambridge University Press.

1978: *The World Economy.* London: University of Texas Press.

Rowland, Peter 1968: *The Last Liberal Governments.* London: Barrie and Rockliffe.

Rubinstein, William D. 1977: 'Wealth, Elites and the Class Structure of Modern Britain', *Past and Present* 76: 99–126.

Rueschemeyer, Dietrich and Evans, Peter B. 1985: 'The State and Economic Transformation: Toward an Analysis of the Conditions Underlying Effective Intervention', in Evans, Rueschemeyer and Skocpol (eds.), pp. 44–77.

Ruggie, John G. 1983: 'International Regimes, Transactions and Change: Embedded Liberalism in the Postwar Economic Order', in Krasner (ed.), pp. 195–232.

Runciman, W. Gary 1989: *A Treatise on Social Theory, Vol. II.* Cambridge: Cambridge University Press.

Rupert, Mark 1995: *Producing Hegemony.* Cambridge: Cambridge University Press.

Russett, Bruce M. 1985: 'The Mysterious Case of Vanishing Hegemony: Or, Is Mark Twain Really Dead?', *International Organization* 39 (2): 207–23.

Saul, S. B. 1960: *Studies in British Overseas Trade, 1870–1914.* Liverpool: Liverpool University Press.

1985: *The Myth of the Great Depression, 1873–1896.* London: Macmillan.

Savin, N. N. 1918: 'The Machine Industry', in Raffalovich (ed.), pp. 200–16.

Schlote, Werner 1952: *British Overseas Trade from 1700 to the 1930s.* Westport, CT: Greenwood Press.

Scholte, Jan Aart 1993a: 'From Power Politics to Social Change: An Alternative Focus for International Studies', *Review of International Studies* 19: 3–21.

1993b: *International Relations of Social Change.* Milton Keynes: Open University Press.

Schremmer, David E. 1988: 'Taxation and Public Finance: Britain, France and Germany', in Mathias and Pollard (eds.), pp. 315–494.

Schumpeter, Joseph A. 1918/1954: 'The Crisis of the Tax State', in A. T. Peacock and R. Turvey (eds.), *International Economic Papers*, pp. 5–38. New York: Macmillan.

Seligman, Edwin R. A. 1908: *Progressive Taxation in Theory and Practice.* Princeton, NJ: Princeton University Press.

Semmel, Bernard 1960: *Imperialism and Social Reform.* London: George Allen and Unwin.

Sen, Gautam 1984: *The Military Origins of Industrialisation and International Trade Rivalry.* London: Frances Pinter.

Senghaas, Dieter 1985: *The European Experience.* Leamington Spa: Berg Publishers.

Seton-Watson, Hugh 1952: *The Decline of Imperial Russia, 1855–1914.* London: Methuen.

1988: *The Russian Empire, 1801–1917.* Oxford: Oxford University Press.

Shann, Edward 1948: *An Economic History of Australia.* Cambridge: Cambridge University Press.

Shaw, Martin 1991: 'State Theory in the Post-Cold War World', in Banks and Shaw (eds.), pp. 1–18.

1993: *Global Civil Society and International Relations.* Cambridge: Polity Press.

Sheehan, James J. 1978: *German Liberalism in the Nineteenth Century.* London: Methuen.

Shißler, Hanna. 1986: 'The Junkers: Notes on the Social and Historical Significance of the Agrarian Elite in Prussia', in Moeller (ed.), pp. 24–51.

Simms, James 1977: 'The Crisis in Russian Agriculture and the End of the Nineteenth Century: A Differentiation', *Slavic Review* 36: 377–98.

Skelton, Oscar D. 1914: 'General Economic History, 1867–1912', in A. Short and A. G. Doughty (eds.), *Canada and Its Provinces, Vol. IX*, pp. 95–276. Toronto: Glasgow, Brook and Co.

Skocpol, Theda 1979: *States and Social Revolutions.* Cambridge: Cambridge University Press.

1985: 'Bringing the State Back in: Strategies of Analysis in Current Research', in Evans, Rueschemeyer and Skocpol (eds.), pp. 3–42.

Smith, Adam 1776/1961: *The Wealth of Nations*. London: Methuen.

Smith, Michael J. 1986: *Realist Thought from Weber to Kissinger*. London: Louisiana State University Press.

Snider, Lewis 1987: 'Identifying the Elements of State Power: Where Do We Begin?', *Comparative Political Studies* 20 (3): 314–56.

Snyder, Jack 1991: *Myths of Empire*. Ithaca: Cornell University Press.

Sobolev, M. N. 1918: 'The Foreign Trade of Russia', in Raffalovich (ed.), pp. 298–328.

Sombart, Werner 1913: *Krieg und Kapitalismus*. Leipzig: Duncker and Humblot.

Spruyt, Hendrik 1994: *The Sovereign State and Its Competitors*. Princeton, NJ: Princeton University Press.

Stein, Arthur A. 1984: 'The Hegemon's Dilemma: Great Britain, the United States and the International Economic Order', *International Organization* 38 (2): 354–86.

Stigler, George J. 1971: 'The Theory of Economic Regulation', *Bell Journal of Economics and Management Science* 2: 3–21.

Stone, Norman 1975: *The Eastern Front, 1914–1917*. London: Hodder and Stoughton.

1984: *Europe Transformed, 1878–1919*. Cambridge, MA: Harvard University Press.

Studenski, Paul and Kroos, Herman E. 1952: *Financial History of the United States*. New York: McGraw Hill.

Sumida, Jon T. 1989: *In Defence of Naval Supremacy*. London: Unwin Hyman.

Sweezy, Paul M. 1970: *The Theory of Capitalist Development*. New York: Monthly Review Press.

Sykes, Alan 1979: *Tariff Reform in British Politics, 1903–1913*. Oxford: Clarendon Press.

Sylla, Richard and Toniolo, Gianni (eds.) 1991: *Patterns of European Industrialisation*. London: Routledge.

Szamuely, Tibor 1988: *The Russian Tradition*. London: Fontana.

Tarbell, Ida M. 1911: *The Tariff in Our Times*. New York: Macmillan.

Taussig, Frank W. 1964: *The Tariff History of the United States*. New York: Capricorn Books.

Taylor, Arthur J. P. 1955: *Bismarck*. London: Hamish Hamilton.

Terrill, Tom E. 1973: *The Tariff, Politics and American Foreign Policy, 1874–1901*. Westport, CT: Greenwood Press.

Teuteberg, Hans-Jürgen and Wiegelmann, Günter 1972: *Der Wandel der Nahrüngsgewohnheiten unter dem Einfluß der Industrialisierung*. Göttingen: Vandenhoeck and Ruprecht.

Thomson, David 1977: *Europe Since Napoleon*. Harmondsworth: Penguin.

Tickner, J. Ann 1988: 'Hans Morgenthau's Principles of Political Realism: A Feminist Reformulation', *Millennium* 17 (3): 429–40.

Tilly, Charles (ed.) 1975: *The Formation of National States in Western Europe*. Princeton, NJ: Princeton University Press.

1981: *As Sociology Meets History*. London: Academic Press.

1990: *Coercion, Capital and European States, AD 990–1990*. Oxford: Basil Blackwell.

Timoshenko, Vladimir P. 1928: *Wheat Prices and the World Market*. Ithaca: Cornell University Press.

Tipton, F. Ben 1974: 'Farm Labour and Power Politics: Germany, 1850–1914', *Journal of Economic History* 34 (4): 951–80.

1976: *Regional Variations in the Economic Development of Germany During the Nineteenth Century*. Middletown, CT: Wesleyan University Press.

Tirrell, Sarah R. 1968: *German Agrarian Politics After Bismarck's Fall*. New York: AMS Press.

Tollison, Robert 1982: 'Rent-Seeking: A Survey', *Kyklos* 35 (4): 575–603.

Toniolo, Gianni 1990: *An Economic History of Liberal Italy, 1850–1918*. London: Routledge.

Toutain, Jean-Claude 1987: *Le Produit intérieur brut de la France de 1789 à 1982*. Paris: Economies et Sociétés (Cahiers de l'ISMEA: Série Histoire quantitative de l'Économie française, XV).

Trebilcock, Clive 1981: *The Industrialisation of the Continental Powers, 1780–1914*. London: Longman.

Tribe, Keith 1989: 'Prussian Agriculture – German Politics: Max Weber, 1892–1897', in Tribe (ed.), *Reading Weber*, pp. 85–130. London: Routledge.

Trimberger, Ellen K. 1978: *Revolution from Above*. New Brunswick, NJ: Transaction Books.

Tullock, Gordon 1967: 'The Welfare Costs of Tariffs, Monopolies and Theft', *Western Economic Journal* 5: 224–32.

Tyler, James E. 1938: *The Struggle for Imperial Unity, 1868–1895*. London: Longmans Green.

Urquhart, Malcolm C. and Buckley, Kenneth A. H. 1965: *Historical Statistics of Canada*. Cambridge: Cambridge University Press.

Vanek, Jaroslav 1971: 'Tariffs, Economic Welfare and Development Potential', *Economic Journal* 81: 904–13.

Varzar, V. 1918: 'Factories and Workshops', in Raffalovich (ed.), pp. 105–64.

Vogler, Carolyn M. 1985: *The Nation-State*. Aldershot: Gower Press.

Volin, Lazar 1970: *A Century of Russian Agriculture*. Cambridge, MA: Harvard University Press.

Wallerstein, Immanuel 1974: *The Modern World System, Vol. I*. London: Academic Press.

1984: *The Politics of the World-Economy*. Cambridge: Cambridge University Press.

1989: *The Modern World System, Vol. III*. London: Academic Press.

Waltz, Kenneth N. 1959: *Man, the State and War*. New York: Columbia University Press.

1979: *Theory of International Politics*. New York: McGraw Hill.

Webb, Stephen B. 1980: 'Tariffs, Cartels, Technology and Growth in the German Steel Industry, 1879–1914', *Journal of Economic History* 40 (2): 309–31.

1982: 'Agricultural Protection in Wilhelminian Germany: Forging an Empire with Pork and Rye', *Journal of Economic History* 42 (2): 309–26.

Webber, Carolyn and Wildavsky, Aaron 1986: *A History of Taxation and Expenditures in the Western World*. New York: Simon and Schuster.

Weber, Max 1919/1970: *From Max Weber*. Edited by H. H. Gerth and C. Wright Mills. London: Routledge and Kegan Paul.

1922/1978: *Economy and Society*, 2 vols. Berkeley: University of California Press.

1923/1981. *General Economic History*. London: Transaction Books.

Wehler, Hans-Ulrich 1985: *The German Empire, 1871–1918*. Leamington Spa: Berg Publishers.

Weiss, Linda 1993: 'War, the State and the Origins of the Japanese Employment System', *Politics and Society* 21 (3): 325–54.

Weiss, Linda and Hobson, John M. 1995: *States and Economic Development*. Cambridge: Polity Press.

White, Colin M. 1987: *Russia and America*. London: Croom Helm.

White, Daniel S. 1976: *The Splintered Party*. London: Harvard University Press.

Wilson, Charles H. 1965: 'Economy and Society in Late Victorian Britain', *Economic History Review* 18 (1): 183–98.

Witt, Peter-Christian 1970: *Die Finanzpolitik des Deutschen Reiches von 1903 bis 1913*. Lübeck and Hamburg: Mathiesen Verlag.

1985: 'The Prussian Landrat as Tax Official, 1891–1918: Observations on the Political and Social Function of the German Civil Service', in Iggers (ed.), pp. 137–54.

1986: ' "Patriotische Gabe" und "Brotwucher". Finanzverfassung und politische System im deutsches Kaiserreich', in Uwe Schultz (ed.), *Mit dem Zehnten fing es an: Eine Kulturgeschichte der Steuer*, pp. 189–200. Munich: C. H. Beck.

1987a: 'The History and Sociology of Public Finance: Problems and Topics', in Witt (ed.) 1987c, pp. 1–18.

1987b: 'Tax Policies, Tax Assessment and Inflation: Towards a Sociology of Public Finances in the German Inflation, 1914–1923', in Witt (ed.) 1987c, pp. 137–60.

(ed.) 1987c: *Wealth and Taxation in Central Europe*. Leamington Spa: Berg Publishers.

Witte, Sergei 1921: *The Memoirs of Count Witte*. London: n.p.

Wood, Ellen M. 1981: 'The Separation of the Economic and the Political in Capitalism', *New Left Review* 127: 66–95.

Woytinsky, Wladimir S. and Woytinsky, Emma S. 1955: *World Commerce and Governments*. Baltimore: Baltimore Press.

Yalvaç, Faruk 1991: 'The Sociology of the State and the Sociology of International Relations', in Banks and Shaw (eds.), pp. 93–114.

Yaney, George 1973: *The Systematisation of Russian Government*. London: University of Illinois Press.

Young, Edward 1872: 'Special Report on the Customs-Tariff Legislation of the United States'. 42nd Congress, 2nd Session, House of Representatives (Ex. Doc. No. 109). Washington, DC: Government Printing Office.

Zamagni, Vera 1993: *The Economic History of Italy, 1860–1990*. Oxford: Clarendon Press.

Zebel, Sydney H. 1940: 'Fair Trade: An English Reaction to the Breakdown of the Cobden System', *Journal of Modern History* 12 (2): 161–85.

1967: 'Joseph Chamberlain and the Genesis of Tariff Reform', *Journal of British Studies* 7 (1): 131–58.

Zhao, Ding-xin and Hall, John A. 1994: 'State Power and Patterns of Late Development: Resolving the Crisis of the Sociology of Development', *Sociology* 28 (1): 211–29.

Zwingli, Ulrich and Ducret, Edgar 1964: 'Das Sozialprodukt als Wertmesser des langfristen Wirtschaftswachstums', *Schweizerische Zeitschrift für Volkswirtschaft und Statistik* 100 (2): 328–68.

Index

CAMBRIDGE STUDIES IN INTERNATIONAL RELATIONS